Figure 3.

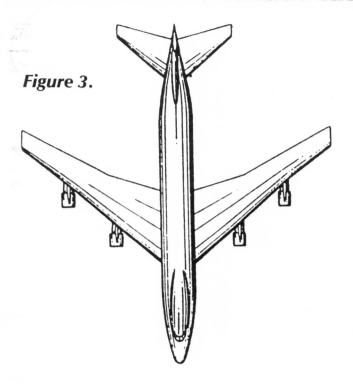

Figure 4.

Reference Cited
UNITED STATES PATENTS

D.202,749   11/1965   Holtby et al. -------------------------------------- D71—1

OTHER REFERENCES
Interavia, October 1965, p. 1607, Boeing 727 at left middle of page;
Interavia, August 1965, p. 1172, BAC-VC-10 at right middle of page;
Interavia, June 1965, p. 961, Douglas C-SA at bottom of page;
Interavia, January 1965, p. 99, Boeing CXHLS at bottom of page.

WALLACE R. BURKE, *Primary Examiner.*

ALAN P. DOUGLAS, *Assistant Examiner.*

WIDE-BODY

THE TRIUMPH OF THE 747

■

Clive Irving

WILLIAM MORROW AND COMPANY, INC.
New York

Library of Congress Cataloging-in-Publication Data

Irving, Clive.
    Wide-body : the triumph of the 747 / Clive Irving.
      p. cm.
    Includes bibliographical references and index.
    ISBN 0-688-09902-5
    1. Boeing 747 (Jet transports)—History. I. Title.
  TL686.B65I78   1993
  629.133′340423—dc20   92–18665
                                      CIP

Printed in the United States of America

First Edition

1 2 3 4 5 6 7 8 9 10

BOOK DESIGN BY LISA STOKES

■ Acknowledgments

Many engineers have patiently led me through the intricacies of their craft. I have tried to make their story accessible without oversimplifying it, and I hope they will forgive the generalizations that may make light science of their achievements. It is because of the arcane nature of what they do that the limelight usually falls, with unfair stress, elsewhere. Nevertheless, without the brilliance of men like these, there would have been no machines to test the Right Stuff.

I am particularly indebted to Joe Sutter, who not only fielded a lot of dumb questions but directed me to many other invaluable sources. I would also like to thank Mrs. Mef Allen, Jon Bedinger, Robert Blake, John Borger, Tex Boullioun, Al Ghery, Art Golofon, W. T. Hamilton, Ed Hartz, Milt Heinemann, Ken Holtby, Tex Johnston, Robert Jones, Maynard Pennell, Ken Plewis, George Schairer, Malcolm Stamper, Jack Steiner, Everette Webb, T. Wilson, and Bob Withington.

Marilyn Phipps at the Boeing archive supplied crucial historical background. David Jimenez, John Wheeler, and Elizabeth Reese of Boeing's public affairs department were very helpful.

Two people, George C. Larson, the editor of *Air & Space*,

the Smithsonian, and Richard P. Hallion of the National Air and Space Museum, the Smithsonian Institution, Washington D.C., led me to the historical framework in which the swept wing was developed. Al Misenko, of the history office at Wright-Patterson Air Force Base, Dayton, Ohio, also found essential documentation for me. Every step of my research was made easier by the counsel and guidance of Pete Bush, who is second to none in reading the entrails of the Boeing Company. Through him I was able to gain the confidence of the generation of engineers whose story this largely is.

The idea of this book grew out of an article for *Condé Nast Traveler*. I thank my colleagues there for their encouragement.

Clive Irving
Sag Harbor, New York

Contents

Genesis

The turning point was not very scientific. It involved a piece of hemp rope, a quarter of an inch thick and thirty-five feet long. Milt Heinemann bought the rope at a hardware store in Seattle. He tied two knots in it, one at twenty feet and the other at twenty-nine feet. He stuffed the rope in his briefcase along with a wad of documents, not knowing quite how he was going to use it. Then he took a flight to New York.

Nobody else flying on the Boeing 707 that day early in 1966—virtually nobody else in the world—had a more intimate knowledge of the 707's cabin. Heinemann shared a patent for the design of the doors of the 707. It was such an ingenious door that even Boeing's competitors had had to adopt it—the jet age was made safer by Heinemann's door. People had told him it wouldn't work, to which his characteristic answer had been *"Baloney!"* He had worked over many details of the 707's cabin with a similar obduracy.

The next morning, Heinemann was meeting Juan Terry Trippe in the boardroom of Pan Am on the fifty-second floor of the fifty-nine-story Pan Am Building in New York. Heinemann had been sent to New York to get Trippe to change his mind. Trippe was the creator of Pan Am, its master, and an imperial presence. Heinemann was, despite his achievements, a modestly ranked engineer at the Boeing Airplane Company. Trippe would know the face, but need reminding of the name.

When Boeing men made a pitch for a new airplane to an airline, Heinemann was always the last to speak. He came after a succession of engineers who had their own concerns: the airframe, the engines, the controls. It was Heinemann's ploy to remind his audience that he was responsible for the only part of the airplane that would generate a profit: the payload. "Everybody else here is a liability," he would joke, and then he would talk his own science, packing in the people and cargo. And people always listened to Heinemann carefully. He had a reputation as a man who knew how to use every inch of space in an airplane cabin. Once he had Boeing add six inches to the length of a fuselage because he worked out that with that difference he would be able to get in another row of seats.

He spoke confidently, with a meticulous, almost pedantic attention to details. But the confidence had been hard-won. Heinemann had become a payload man by pure chance, selected almost on a whim. At the dawn of the jet age, airlines regarded Boeing as a company with its heart in military airplanes, a company that was too casual with its airline customers and inattentive to details like passenger comfort. Its technical brilliance was not in itself enough. It had to start taking airlines more seriously. Heinemann was the company's first experiment in listening more carefully to what the airlines wanted. Back in 1952 he had been plucked from a military program and told that from that day forward he was responsible for the cabin of Boeing's first jetliner.

Thinking ahead to his meeting with Trippe, Heinemann could reflect that it was nothing like as daunting as his first day on his new assignment. He had been really frightened then, and had very nearly given up. He had never been part of the company's elite corps of engineers, men with backgrounds at MIT, Boeing's own *wunderkind*. He had been recruited in 1940 from the University of Washington, part of a local intake as the company geared up its production of bombers for an inevitable war. But now here he was, fourteen years after his sudden reassignment, at the age of fifty, unquestionably the carrier of Boeing's philosophy on cabin design and payload. And now he had to carry his belief in an idea more persuasively than ever before. It was a big idea. Without exaggeration and quite literally, the biggest idea in the airline business. Nothing written on paper quite did justice to the idea. Heinemann always tried to think three-dimensionally, and that was why he had gone out and bought the rope.

Heinemann deliberately arrived early at the Pan Am Building, and got a secretary to let him into the boardroom. The table ran the length of the room, and at the end, on the room's short dimension, there were floor-to-ceiling windows. Heinemann rolled back the blinds. You could look straight down the center of Park Avenue, feeling for a second as if you owned the city. (The building had desecrated the old New York skyline since 1963, by being imposed like a vast tombstone atop Grand Central Station.) He pulled out the rope from his briefcase.

Stretching it wall-to-wall across the windows, Heinemann noted that the boardroom was only barely wider than the twenty feet marked by one of the knots on the rope. He hadn't dared to hope that he would be that close. He pulled out a chair from the table and stood on it (he was short and stocky), stretching to the ceiling with the rope. The room was a tad higher than the nine-foot measure. Heinemann couldn't believe his luck; this was the scenario he had dreamed of. He stuffed the rope back in his case, pulled out his papers, and sat down.

A little later, Trippe came in with a small retinue. After the formalities, Trippe and the others sat down across the table from Heinemann, waiting.

The subject of the day was a new airplane. Just about the only fixed thing about this airplane was its Boeing model number: 747. For months there had been uncertainty about the size, shape, and ambition of the 747. In the jargon of the engineers, the design simply would not "close." Boeing was reworking it day and night. Configuration drawings were being discarded by the hundreds. Trippe and his engineers were pressing for coalescence. Something, however, was not right in the Boeing project. They were still hedging. Heinemann was the bearer of the latest notions from Seattle, and Trippe was visibly impatient to have them.

"Gentlemen," said Heinemann, "this airplane is two and a half times the size of the 707. We could be talking of carrying five hundred people. That's the basis for the economics of the airplane. We're extrapolating from the technology we have on the 707, and we're confident that we can manage it."

Heinemann knew what they were thinking: he had heard worries from various Pan Am officials on the lines of "My God, we lose an airplane, we lose five hundred people." But Heinemann was responsible for working out how you evacuated that many people from a cabin, and he knew it depended on the design of the cabin.

He stood up and walked to the windows. "For all practical purposes, you are sitting in the middle of your airplane now. The walls are almost vertical, because the cabin is so wide— twenty feet wide. Nine feet high. For the first time, you'll be in a room, not a tube."

Trippe's response to this *coup de théâtre* was no warmer than a flicker of surprise. The problem was that Heinemann was beginning to describe an airplane that Trippe did not recognize as the one for which he had already signed up. All along, Trippe had relished the prospect of selling a catchy new concept for the big jet, the "double-decker." Every drawing Pan Am had seen for the 747, until now, had shown a two-deck cabin. One version had six seats a row on the top deck and five below; another had seven on the top and eight below. Now Heinemann was describing a cabin wide enough for ten tourist-class seats on *one* deck.

In fact, although nobody at Pan Am knew it, there had been stubborn doctrinal disputes among the Boeing engineers about the choice between a double-deck and single-deck airplane. There was a strong conventional wisdom that airports were running out of space and that it would be a lot easier to turn around an airplane that was twice as high rather than twice as long. However, the single-decker as now just conceived was not significantly longer than the double-decker. It was just a lot *wider*—wider than anyone at Pan Am had ever imagined. Something novel was being proposed: the volume of the 747's fuselage, and hence its capacity for people and cargo, was a factor of width, not just height and length.

It was Heinemann's ability to convey this simple picture of *volume* that first brought home to Trippe and his engineers that a fundamental change in the accustomed layout of airplanes was being proposed. Instead of one aisle between the seat rows, there would be two aisles—a virtue, as Heinemann pointed out, when it came to evacuating the large number of passengers in an emergency. In the event, Heinemann's rope trick would prove to mark the beginning of the end for the double-decker. At this point no airplane had been designed around the single-deck fuselage; it existed almost only as a chimera, a vast beast independent of other essential limbs, like wings and a tail. Trippe would not actually commit himself to the single-decker without seeing it as an actual-size wooden mock-up. But eventually the promotional lure of the double-decker would fade in the light of the new hyphenated soubriquet that fell from someone's lips and was adopted for the 747: wide-body.

Part One

*General Crocco Draws
on a Napkin*

■

1 ■ The First Shall Be Last

William M. Allen, president of the Boeing Airplane Company, and Juan Trippe had a history of talking each other into hair-raising deals without leaving any trace—for example, during a golf game or a fishing expedition. This was Trippe's preferred style, not Allen's, and to introduce an element of record to the transactions Allen got into the habit of taping follow-up phone calls to Trippe. It didn't always produce a very precise or coherent kind of record. Trippe tended to deliver extended monologues, in the manner of a man unused to challenge. He would pour out ideas in a jumbled, telescoped stream. He was driven by visions, not details. Details you delegated.

Sometimes Allen had trouble getting Trippe to listen, to grasp a point. It was like that during a call on September 27, 1965, when Allen was hoping that Trippe would be present when a team of engineers Allen was sending to Pan Am the following Friday would reveal the latest thinking about their next generation of airliner, the 747.

At the time, Trippe's consuming vision was for a supersonic transport, the development of which would be largely subsidized by the U.S. government. Trippe had lobbied Washington for the SST with a relentless, personal zeal, making it an issue of national self-esteem. Unlike the Anglo-French Concorde, he contended, an American SST would not be for elitist junkets, but for the common man.

Trippe acknowledged that before this dream could be achieved, he would need, as a stopgap, a subsonic jet larger than the Boeing 707s and Douglas DC-8s that he now operated. Once it was superseded by the SST, he wanted this stopgap airplane to end its life carrying cargo, the flying equivalent of a lumbering cargo ship. And, as far as he was concerned, this was the role of the 747. He wasn't interested enough to be in New York when the Boeing men called. He would, he told Allen, be away at a golf tournament.

"Well," said Allen, knowing his man, "you can't miss those."

Later in the conversation, Trippe casually dropped a name that rang alarms for Allen. Referring to the concept represented by the 747, he said, "This is a cup of tea that the Douglas fellows are interested in—they've dropped everything else out there."

The Douglas Aircraft Company had a place deep in the psyche of Boeing, and of Bill Allen. Although Boeing had established a worldwide reputation with its first jet transport, the 707, Douglas was still a formidable contender and Trippe had not carelessly invoked its name: Pan Am could only gain from playing off Boeing and Douglas against each other, as it had always done.

Boeing had never faced an enterprise of the magnitude of the 747. It would be entirely financed by private money; in the past similar ventures had always been cushioned financially by military programs. There was no hope of a military derivative of the 747 to lessen the risk. Not for the first time, Allen would be betting the company on one unproven airplane. This time he had only the vaguest notion of what it might cost. The 747 would have millions of separately listed parts. Building airplanes was a process of converting money, dollar by dollar, into metal, plastic, fiberglass, rubber, glass, fabric. It was an exacting and unforgiving process making a machine as large as the 747 to the tolerances of a Swiss watchmaker. Yet there was no equally precise way of accounting the cost. Allen was in a business in which money seemed to lose all normal value.

In a life of gambles, each one greater than the last, this was the mother of all gambles. All Boeing's gambles had had numbers attached to them, and a lot of sevens seemed to be involved: 247, B-47, 707, 727, 737.

247—that was a bad number to remember. It reminded Allen of Donald Douglas, and of how easy it was in this business to believe that you had found the holy grail, only to see it turn to dust in your hands. Trippe had needled him with the hint that Douglas was squaring off for another fight, coming after Boeing again, this time with the big jet. Nobody outside of Boeing and Douglas remembered the 247. Every Boeing engineer worth his salt never forgot it.

PASADENA, JANUARY 1932

Theodor von Karman, a leonine Hungarian in his early fifties, had been waiting for such a moment. A wooden model of a new airplane was being set up for tests in the wind tunnel at the California Institute of Technology, Caltech. Nobody, anywhere, had seen an airplane quite like this. It was a twin-engine transport that, on sight, rendered every existing airliner obsolete. The airplanes then being flown by the cluster of fledgling American airlines were trimotors: boxy, ungainly, and noisy, at their best able to cruise at only around 120 mph. The airplane in the Caltech tunnel was no box: its shape had been purged of all gracelessness; it was manifestly the first product of a new design regime called streamlining.

Von Karman had been in America barely two years, and in that time had played himself into the role of the venerable European protogenius. He had been brought from Germany to Caltech to design the wind tunnel. No one in the world was believed to know more about how to advance the science of aerodynamics through the application of a steady blast of air through the test section of a tunnel. He had been a prize student of the man acknowledged to be the father of aerodynamics, Ludwig Prandtl of Göttingen University. Von Karman emanated the European conceit that when it came to the aviation sciences America was a wayward student, lacking both rigorous thought and intuitive courage.

The model in his wind tunnel had been shipped from the Boeing company in Seattle. Von Karman barely knew where Seattle was, and the idea that an airplane as radical as this one had come virtually from the backwoods was disconcerting but instantly stimulating.

Everybody who knew of the Boeing model was equally excited. There was a degree of security around the tunnel, because the Boeing engineers who had come with the model impressed on everyone that it represented the sum of their company's best brains. It aspired to such a quantum leap in speed, the ability to cruise at nearly 200 mph, that the Caltech tunnel was the only facility on the West Coast modern enough to test its behavior. Von Karman tended to see the same argument in reverse: the Boeing design was the only airplane sophisticated enough to test his tunnel to its limits.

Yet the security at Caltech was questionable. Three significant airplane builders were based in southern California: Consolidated at San Diego, Lockheed at Burbank, and Douglas at Santa Monica. Von Karman's tunnel was indispensable to their future. Douglas had, from the beginning, cultivated its own inside track at Caltech. Arthur Raymond, a key engineer at Douglas, moonlighted at Caltech lecturing on airplane design. He used the opportunity to function as a talent scout for Douglas, and one of the students he picked out early on, Bailey Oswald, happened to be a performance analyst on the Boeing tests.

In fact, Boeing was exposing its best thinking right under the nose of Douglas, a company with a corps of engineers as gifted as any in the business. At this moment, though, it seemed that Douglas was making too much steady money from building clunky military airplanes to be interested in competing in the commercial transport business, which was notoriously volatile and chancy.

Boeing had numbered its new model the 247. None of the principles it embraced was in itself new. The all-metal single-wing airplane had been pioneered in Europe. American designers had been doubtful about the structural integrity of this form, and had clung to the idea of bracing wings with external struts, even on the trimotors that had large single wings. Boeing, however, had done its own pioneering work with all-metal airplanes and realized that this was, inevitably, the form of the future. Boeing worked to perfect what was called a cantilever wing: an all-metal wing with its strength in the carefully calculated load-bearing structure under the wing's skin, and with the skin actually taking some of the load itself. But Boeing's chief engineer,

Charles Monteith, had written a classic textbook on aeronautical engineering, and was wary of monoplanes. He had seen them destroyed by a strange phenomenon called flutter, in which an airplane would suddenly shake itself to bits. Monteith, instinctively conservative, proceeded slowly.

Boeing first used the metal cantilever wing on a revolutionary single-engine mail carrier with an open cockpit, the Monomail, and then used it again on a twin-engine bomber, the B-9. These two aircraft were, in fact, incremental rehearsals for a visionary airliner. Skeptics of the cantilever wing were disarmed, but the argument then moved to whether two engines were enough to ensure the safety of an airliner.

Trimotors—the Fokker, the Ford, and the Boeing 80— might be ponderous, but they were perceived as less risky than twin-engine airplanes. The third engine gave better margins of safety. Monteith and Boeing's vice president and general manager, Claire Egtvedt, set, and met, what seemed at the time an almost unattainable goal: a twin-engine airplane so aerodynamically "clean" that it would be able to climb with a full load under the power of one engine.

Preliminary design on the 247 began in September 1931. But from the beginning, a deep philosophical schism developed over the size of the airliner. Monteith stressed that it should be small and fast—the premium, he argued, was on speed, not comfort, and he advocated carrying only eight passengers, fewer than half the number a trimotor carried, for the sake of a significant gain in speed. An opposing faction argued, unsuccessfully, for a much larger airplane with the stress on passenger comfort. The provision of a lavatory became definitive of the schism: Monteith, the spartan, discounted its value; the advocates of comfort thought it essential.

Before these disputes were resolved, and before any metal could be cut to begin building the 247, the first outline design had to be tested as a wooden model in a wind tunnel. The 247 was, in a sense, a thesis: it would have to "fly" first as a fixed object with air blasted at it at speeds of 200 mph or more under controlled conditions. Only in this way could its aerodynamic soundness be proved and the design cleansed of "drag," the irregularities of airflow that could produce costly penalties in performance.

By February 1932, the first results from Pasadena were

encouraging enough for Boeing to begin the detailed design of the 247, although all the data from the tunnel would not be available in Seattle until the summer. The final size was a compromise, but one inclined to Monteith's view. The number of passengers went up to ten, and a lavatory was added. Egtvedt and Monteith were confident that Boeing now exclusively possessed the airliner of the future. But a disaster in the skies over Kansas suddenly introduced an aggressive competitor.

On the morning of March 31, a farmer working in a field near Bazaar, Kansas, heard an airplane in the thick clouds overhead. He gave it scant attention until the engine note changed to a strangled coughing and then died. The airplane, missing one wing, came spinning to earth. The impact was so great that one engine was buried two feet in mud. The severed wing followed, floating to a soft landing. It was a Fokker trimotor of Transcontinental & Western Air, TWA.

Six passengers and the two pilots were killed instantly. It was a serious enough accident to call for a detailed investigation, but the identity of one of the passengers made this the death knell of the Fokkers and of the trimotor age. There was virtually a state of national mourning for Knute Rockne, the legendary coach of the Notre Dame football team. The bad publicity put a blight on TWA, although the crash was traced to rot in the wooden main spar of the Fokker's wing.

Jack Frye, vice president in charge of operations at TWA, urgently needed to replace his trimotors. By that summer the revolutionary intent of the Boeing 247 was known to the airlines, and Frye told Boeing he was keen to buy 247s as soon as they became available. But Boeing turned him away. United Airlines, tied to Boeing under an elaborate conglomerate of aviation interests, had ordered the first sixty 247s, and there was no prospect of TWA's getting 247s for years.

Frye was furious. At twenty-nine, a former Hollywood stunt pilot, he was the youngest vice president in the airline business, and not the kind of character ready to wait in line behind United. He called together the best of his own engineers and asked them to set down the criteria for the optimum airplane for TWA's route structure. Oddly enough, when Frye looked at their ideas, they wanted another trimotor, not a twin like the Boeing 247.

Airlines were in their infancy. Flying was an immensely expensive way to travel and was regarded as needing strong nerves. It was hard to wean airline men away from the safety margin of a third engine. TWA wanted an airplane able to suffer the loss of one engine on takeoff and still safely get airborne with a full load of twelve passengers, two pilots, and cargo. On top of this, Frye specified a range of one thousand miles and a top speed of 185 mph. (A year earlier, without the example of the 247, these targets would have seemed fanciful.)

A short letter from Frye, giving his bare criteria, went to several airplane manufacturers, but it was Douglas that rose most confidently to the challenge.

Donald Douglas, who had a Scottish father, seemed to epitomize the virtues and caution of those Scottish engineers whose work, from Budapest to Buenos Aires, gave nations their bridges, railroads, and steamships. He was one of the earliest graduates in aeronautical engineering from MIT, and after flirtations with various aspirant airplane companies, he founded his own from the back room of a barbershop on Pico Boulevard, Santa Monica. There was nothing revolutionary in any of the airplanes he built: he was careful and pedestrian as an engineer and calculating as a proprietor. As the Depression wiped out many more imaginative airplane builders, Douglas lived well enough from military contracts to pay out $1.15 million in dividends between 1930 and 1932. Douglas allowed himself one piece of ostentation reflecting his wealth—a yacht named after one of his first successful airplanes, *Cloudster*. By the summer of 1932, when Frye's letter tempted Douglas to leave the security of military contracts, the yacht served as a love nest for Douglas and the woman who would become his permanent mistress, Peggy Tucker. Douglas was forty years old. This arrangement, compensating for an unhappy marriage, cloaked in the hypocrisies of the time, would eventually influence the way Douglas ran his company. But in 1932, it may well have been just sufficient to lighten his mood enough to take an uncharacteristic gamble.

Boeing was also Depression-proof, thanks in part to the conglomerate that had grown around it, which included Boeing Air Transport, United Air Lines, Pratt & Whitney aero engines, and Hamilton Standard propellers. All this had started in 1916 with a floatplane launched from a converted boathouse on Lake

Union in Seattle. The Boeing Airplane Company, so christened in 1917, was fashioned by Bill Boeing, a well-heeled and patrician young figure who could easily have been taken for a dallying dilettante.

Bill Boeing had little in common with Donald Douglas. He had family wealth, from lumber and mineral interests, cosmopolitan blood and taste (German father, Viennese mother), an incomplete Ivy League education (he quit an engineering course at Yale a year before graduation), and the physique for vigorous outdoor sports. Expeditions to Alaska had drawn him west, and he had settled in Seattle as a place where sailing and outdoor sports mingled nicely with practical business.

It was not Bill Boeing's style to function from the airplane plant, on the fringes of an industrial sprawl developing to the south of the city's main dockyards. He used an office in downtown Seattle. After knitting the conglomerate together, he announced his intention to retire in 1932, when he would be fifty. The company had been built by engineers, and its founder was happy to leave men like Egtvedt in day-to-day charge, while he thought of the bigger picture.

In 1930, a young lawyer from Montana who had discreetly supervised the arrangements of the succession of mergers was put on the board of Boeing Air Transport, and a year later of the Boeing Airplane Company. His name was Bill Allen. Bill Boeing took to Allen for his sagacity and independence of mind. Carrying out his work for Boeing, Allen had become a veteran of flying in primitive airliners over the hazardous mountain routes of the Pacific Northwest and the Rockies. Although the Boeing assignment was lucrative and came to take all Allen's attention, he remained on the payroll of his Seattle law firm, Donworth, Todd & Higgins.

Meanwhile, Donald Douglas had reasons other than the libidinal to increase his confidence that he could take on Boeing. One was a new alliance with a maverick aviation genius named Jack Northrop, who had briefly been involved in the Boeing conglomerate. Douglas had gathered other clever men around him, but it was Northrop who talked the future most convincingly, because he had some pet theories he wanted to put into metal. Douglas was also encouraged by what seemed to him obvious shortcomings in the Boeing 247, particularly its small size.

On the face of it, the 247 represented epochal gains for the airlines: with a cruising speed of nearly 190 mph, the 247 was at least 50 mph faster than the airliners it replaced. It introduced wing and tail de-icing and supercharged engines to fly far higher, to 25,000 feet, and it had a range of 840 miles. There was a galley as well as the toilet at the rear of the cabin, and a stewardess. The ten seats, five on each side, had a generous forty-inch pitch between them (the average pitch of the tourist-class seats in a 747 is thirty-three inches). Yet the more the Douglas designers looked at the 247, the more they thought Boeing was selling its own concept short. The cabin was narrow, and passengers had to clamber over a huge hump on the floor, over the wing spar.

In 1932, Charles Lindbergh was technical adviser to TWA; his transatlantic coup of 1927 had given his name great commercial value, simply by association, and TWA came to call itself "the Lindbergh line." Donald Douglas sent his assistant chief engineer, Arthur Raymond, to see Lindbergh in New York. Raymond and his engineering boss, J. H. "Dutch" Kindelberger, had ruled out a trimotor for their proposed airliner.

Raymond had to convince Lindbergh that a twin could be just as safe. He said the airplane Douglas would deliver would be able to take off and climb out on only one engine. Lindbergh was receptive, but blunt: "If you can do it, we'll buy the airplane. If not, we'll go elsewhere."

Raymond hated flying, and rarely did. He steeled himself to take a TWA trimotor back as far as Kansas City to get a personal sense of the flying environment they were setting out to consign to oblivion. He was appalled by the experience. Back in Santa Monica, Kindelberger put Raymond in charge of the project. Raymond had a large cutaway drawing of the 247 put up on a wall of the engineering department, carrying the warning: "Don't copy it! Do it better!"

And Jack Northrop knew how to do it better—a lot better. He took the cantilever wing and changed its whole structure. Instead of being built around transverse beams, in the Boeing manner, Northrop's wing was formed of multicellular parts. This saved a lot of weight, and proved under load-bearing tests to be much stronger. Northrop was also adept at the design of what was called the monocoque fuselage, simply a hollow metal shell held together by a sophisticated combination of its skeletal structure and skin—essentially, the hollow tube we know today as the cabin of every modern airliner.

The airframe taking shape in Santa Monica was, like the Boeing 247, first tested as a model in the Caltech tunnel. By then, the suspicion at Boeing was that Douglas had actually received Caltech's 247 wind tunnel data *before* Boeing had. If so, this ranks as one of the first and most significant acts of high-tech industrial espionage. But Caltech itself had cause to trumpet its work on the 247, the first proof positive that von Karman's tunnel was working as well as he had said it would. Hiring out the tunnel to airplane manufacturers helped pay for Caltech's pure research, and where Boeing and Douglas came, others would follow.

The Douglas prototype was called the DC-1. The first model put into the ten-foot tunnel, made at the odd scale of one-eleventh actual size, revealed terrible characteristics. Indeed, it would have been virtually unflyable. At higher speeds it was subject to violent buffeting, and the center of its balance was in the wrong place. Northrop had seen similar buffeting on an earlier design of his own, and knew the cause: the junction of the wing with the fuselage was too abrupt and caused dangerous turbulence. The solution was to remove the sharp corners by molding an extra cosmetic layer of metal around the junction. Caltech christened these moldings "fillets," and it was von Karman himself who climbed into the tunnel with a can of putty and, like a potter fixing up a distorted work, crafted the curves until the airflow became benign. This change alone produced a gain of 17 mph in the airplane's top speed.

The problem of balance was solved by raking back the leading edge of the wing sharply, a characteristic that lived on through the DC-3 and gave the Douglas airliners a racy look that—for all most people knew—was a felicity of design rather than the improvised remedy of an error.

There was a significant difference between Boeing's use of Caltech's resources and the Douglas team's diagnostic approach to the DC-1. Boeing worked tightly within the engineering network of its own conglomerate; Douglas, instead of depending solely on its own rich talent, cast its net more widely and involved many of the nation's best aviation minds. The wing's airfoil section was fine-tuned at the laboratories of the National

Advisory Committee for Aeronautics, NACA, at Langley in
Virginia. NACA also helped to streamline the engine installa-
tions. And because Douglas, unlike Boeing, was not tied to one
engine manufacturer, it fomented competition between designers that led to an increasingly powerful series of engines from
Wright, the Cyclones, which, from the start, gave the Douglas
airplanes an edge in size.

To this extent, Boeing's remoteness left its own dogmas
unchallenged. One critical example was a device that Monteith
obstinately spurned for the 247, wing flaps. Von Karman's runs
in the tunnel showed that the DC-1's wing flaps improved the
airplane's lift on takeoff by 35 percent and brought even greater
gains in lowering landing speed. Other detailing added another
27 mph to the top speed. Raymond's young protégé, Bailey
Oswald, devised a formula to demonstrate that the DC-1 could
safely meet Lindbergh's stringent standards for single-engine
performance. In short order, Oswald left Caltech for the Douglas
payroll.

The Boeing 247 made its maiden flight on February 8, 1933.
The DC-1 followed on July 1, only 332 days after Frye's letter
arrived on Donald Douglas's desk. However, although the
DC-1's superiority over the 247 was clear, the Douglas victory
was not immediate. The 247 went into service with United without significant further changes, and pilots and passengers found
it a revelation in comfort and speed. The DC-1, on the other
hand, was really a flying laboratory. Frye wanted changes,
mostly adding seats and therefore increasing size, which led to
the DC-2. TWA ordered twenty DC-2s, and it was the making
of the airline. Frye, a punchy, Cagneyesque figure in snappy
suits and a fedora, on familiar terms with Hollywood stars, became a great booster for his new fleet.

But it was another young risen power of the airline industry
who pushed Douglas to create its masterwork. Peppery Cyrus
R. Smith had made his name as one of the most rigorous op-
erational managers in the country, at a regional airline called
Texas Air Transport. After the merger that created American
Airlines, he rose irresistibly to the top. In the summer of 1935,
Smith spent more than $300 on a two-hour long-distance call to
Donald Douglas.

Had that call never been made, there might well never have

been a Douglas DC-3. What Smith wanted, and what Douglas reluctantly agreed to, was a revamp of the DC-2 to produce a bigger airplane with a fuselage fat enough to take overnight sleeping berths. Strange are the accidents and whims that beget serendipity. Smith's nocturnal fantasy ended up being 90 percent a new airplane and, fatally for Boeing, clearly the best the world would see for some time.

The DC-3 could carry more than twice as many passengers as the 247 in far greater comfort. After the DC-3, the commercial profitability of the airlines was secure; the industry had come of age. By 1937, United Airlines bowed to the inevitable and reequipped with DC-3s. Within a year, the Douglas airliner was carrying 95 percent of all airline passengers in the United States and 90 percent of all overseas passengers.

The DC-3 was a truly beautiful thing. Its form had been classically ordained by function, the need to pass through air as cleanly as possible. In the lines of the Boeing 247 and then the Douglas airliners, a new machine-age aesthetic was created. The fashion of streamlining moved swiftly to railroads and cars and even to stationary objects like refrigerators and lamps. There is a nice irony in all of this—a form arrived at by strict scientific method, with hardly a nod toward aesthetics, appropriated by the aesthetes of the salon, the bathroom, and the kitchen.

It was an elaborate joke that a solid engineer might get pleasure from. However, inside the sleek skin of the new airliner, anachronism prevailed. The theme and the hierarchy were nautical. You entered a *cabin* where if not *stewards* awaited there were *stewardesses*, and sometimes even a *purser*. The pilot was a *captain* with naval braid on his sleeves and cap. In later airplanes there would be *aft* and *lower* cabins. With this borrowed nomenclature began the manners and the furnishings of the airliner as we know it.

As Bill Allen would ruefully reflect toward the end of his career, the Boeing 247 forced the Douglas company into the commercial airplane business, where it remained at the top for a generation, a generation in which it eclipsed the best that Boeing could pit against it. Today, the Boeing 247 is a virtually forgotten airplane.

Who was culpable? In part, Boeing was penalized by the

self-serving and incestuous dialogues of the conglomerate: a captive engine maker and a captive airline excluded the oxygen of open debate. What resulted was an unhappy compromise involving both sweeping vision and fatal myopia. It seems like an act of lunacy to have conceded to United's demand for a monopoly of the first sixty airplanes. While Boeing's constricted plant was filling that order, the rest of the airline industry turned to California. Boeing did not display the same nerve as Douglas in committing to volume production.

However, it was not his defeat at the hands of Douglas that brought Bill Boeing's romance with aviation to an end. A more lethal threat surfaced with the election of Franklin D. Roosevelt to the White House.

The Boeing conglomerate had profited mightily from the patronage of the U.S. Post Office Department, which had allocated the airmail routes. Walter Folger Brown, put in charge of the post office after Herbert Hoover's election in 1928, had single-mindedly reconstructed the American airline business to serve his vision of the airmail routes. Later, Brown's regime was vilified as a dictatorship carried out according to the simple principle that big business was better business. Yet what stands out in retrospect about Brown is not how *political* his policy was, but how *corporatist.*

Brown was ruthless and unsentimental in a very modern way. He set out to consolidate an industry that was notoriously fragmented. He showed no mercy toward the hundreds of small, independent carriers who had struggled with minimal resources and poor equipment to fly unviable routes. He saw, with undeniable logic, that a national airline business needed a critical mass of capital resources and superior equipment. To achieve this, he forced a series of mergers in which only the fittest or most politically adept survived.

These mergers, enacted simultaneously with those conceived by Bill Boeing, have had a remarkably enduring influence. The nucleus of the modern American airline industry is discernible as having been born then. Airmail routes were allocated to the companies that eventually became American, TWA, United, Northwestern, and Eastern. By means of this sudden transformation of scale, an industrial base was formed that for the first time put American aviation on an equal footing with

European. One proponent of the airmail system, comparing the infrastructures of Europe and the United States, said the airmail routes were "the only great thing" America had that they did not. He pointed out that although in Europe the mail could get almost anywhere overnight by train, once the vast and perilous skies of America were made safe for a dependable airmail service, the nation would have gained an airline system of unparalleled reach.

Brown's policy was music to the ears of men like Boeing and Frederick B. Rentschler, the creator of Pratt & Whitney. They were able to see the doctrine from another perspective. Brown was, in fact, a little ahead of his time. His industrial logic could not be faulted, but the scientific support for it was not quite in place. That came, fortuitously, with the research and development that led to the Boeing 247 and the Douglas airliners, able to give wing to the grand design.

Many interests were bruised by Brown. Some of the beneficiaries of the mergers were so busy feuding among themselves that he had to bang their heads together. The series of meetings he held in his office to complete these deals became known as the "spoils conferences," implying that they were underhanded. In fact, they were announced in daily press releases and negligently reported at the time. In a period of widespread cynicism and frequent malfeasance, an odor of conspiracy clung to so large a dispensation of valuable franchises, carried out without congressional oversight. Inevitably, Brown's actions brought ideological reprisals with Roosevelt's New Deal.

The man Roosevelt chose to pursue Brown was a senator from Alabama with a deadly forensic reputation who happened also to be a self-admitted former member of the Ku Klux Klan, Hugo Black. Black was deceptively mild in manner and cultivated a silky drawl that worked like the slow but precise movements of a knife through soft flesh.

Black headed a committee of three Democrats and two Republicans charged ostensibly with getting at the truth of how the airmail contracts had been handed out. But more was involved than that: it became a trust-busting crusade with the objective of unraveling both the airline mergers and the manufacturing conglomerates. There were many consequences of the Black Committee, but the most unexpected and needless was that Bill Boeing and the Boeing Airplane Company parted ways.

Late in 1933, Boeing and Rentschler were called to Washington. A few months earlier, Boeing had kept his vow of early retirement and, at the age of fifty-one, pulled out of all executive roles and sold off some of his stock. In Washington, it soon became clear that Boeing was temperamentally unsuited to the political cockpit. The adversaries each sustained the other's prejudices. To Black, Boeing could be impugned with Teddy Roosevelt's phrase as a "malefactor of great wealth." To Boeing, an unrepentant capitalist, FDR was the next thing to a Bolshevik.

Black targeted Boeing's first airmail contract, ignoring the fact that at the time nobody except Boeing had thought it possible to make money on such a low bid. Boeing did not handle himself well. He failed to point out that he had risked $750,000 of his own money (a vast sum at the time) to set up Boeing Air Transport with no certainty that it could make a profit. Black charged that with success, the value of Boeing's own stock had grown inordinately. It was the pit of the Depression and it was easy for Black to make rich men seem wholly unsympathetic.

Rentschler was more vulnerable to this line of attack than Boeing. He had made a paper profit of $21 million on an investment of $253; before the Wall Street crash his profit would have been $35 million. During the same period, Rentschler earned more than $1.5 million in salary and bonuses, and Black had little trouble in making both the new fortune and the paychecks look obscene. Rentschler, however, unlike Bill Boeing, was combative and unbending. The money, he pointed out, had not been stolen from the taxpayer. Who in America was virtuous enough to apologize for being too successful? What the country needed was a lot more companies like his, if it was to be competitive.

They were an odd pair for the pillory. In a Washington beset by the calamity of the Depression, they seemed out of another world, part of an industry that, far from going belly-up, was indecently resilient. They were not, nor did they resemble, robber barons. They were not extractors of ore, pumpers of oil, or dealers in bonds. They were not, in fact, recognized for what they really were: the harbingers of a new corporatism that called for a higher order of technical brilliance (with concomitant risks) than any enterprise before it.

Rentschler had the pertinacity and certitude often found in a mechanical genius (the Wrights had it, too). His early fortune had been made by making a better machine. Bill Boeing had created a company that followed the same credo. It seemed an affront to him that his efforts should be cause for moral rebuke. At that moment something snapped in Boeing. He returned to Seattle and, without waiting for the outcome of the Black hearings, washed his hands of the business that bore his name. He disposed of the rest of his stock and ended all connection with the company.

In the beginning, Boeing had taken up aviation as something of a sport. But he had quickly grasped its possibilities and given the business his own stamp. A peculiar brand of creative conservatism had taken root in the Boeing Airplane Company. It became doctrinal to future generations of engineers who never knew him. In his own words, the rubric he bequeathed to the company was: "Our job is to keep everlastingly at research and experiment, to adapt our laboratories to production as soon as practicable, to let no new improvement in flying and flying equipment pass us by." At the time of his petulant exit, he little realized that he had founded a business in which his own name would transcend the corporation and become generic, a noun in virtually every language in the world.

2 ■ The Young Bloods

Allen was sixty-six years old when he committed Boeing to the 747 program. His style was that of a benign authoritarian. He ran the company through a small number of trusted advisers. And when it came to trusting people, he seemed to have a marked preference for two professions: lawyers and engineers. Among both he looked for technical fluency and an underlying bedrock of probity. (Allen disliked dealing with bankers, a group he regarded as overpaid and underworked.)

Beyond this Boeing fraternity, Allen had cultivated friendships with a variety of the willful figures who had built up the American aviation industry, some of them public names from the professional hall of fame, like Lindbergh and Rickenbacker, others who were less well known but whose business was vital to Boeing, like C. R. Smith of American Airlines. Juan Trippe didn't encourage intimacy, and for all their sporting diversions together Allen and Trippe were essentially business associates rather than country club companions.

The ethic of Boeing had the inimitable tincture of locale. One look at the corporate headquarters, for example, exposed both the company's solidity and its poverty of style. Allen operated from the third floor of the executive building on East

Marginal Way in south Seattle, a wide, busy strip with a rusting railroad track running down one side. The executive building stood out as the only pleasing detail: it had the soaring, bold Deco touches of the best old airline terminals. It was of that period, the late 1930s. The rest of the Boeing complex had no more flair than its signs indicated—Plant 1, Plant 2, and so on.

There were no executive limousines. Managers used either their own cars or a station wagon from the company pool. There were no executive jets. It was Allen's reasonable decree that if you built airliners you ought to fly in them like other people, the better to know your product. The furnishings in the executive offices were no grander than in a small-town bank. Engineers who crafted machines of surpassing elegance had on their office walls art that looked bulk-bought from a mall. This insensitivity to refinement, the failure to suggest through corporate patronage that your taste is higher than it actually is, was part of a secure self-esteem.

Allen himself did have a singular preference when it came to paintings. As a child he had been taken to the cabin in Glacier Lake Park where the Western naturalist painter Charles Russell lived. The simple, unmolested majesty of the Western landscape was in Allen's Montana blood, the reality a little enhanced by Russell's Arcadian vision, Russell "the Cowboy Artist," who reinforced Allen's love of place and his plain, rock-solid values. C. R. Smith had discovered Allen's adoration of Russell. Smith's Park Avenue apartment was stuffed with Russells, and he gave one, over protests, to Allen. The two of them had probably not paused to reflect that they were in a line of business that would do a good deal to destroy the isolation of Charlie Russell's West. (Russell was a frontier atavist whose favorite bar in Montana had a clock that ran backward—you had to look in a mirror to see what time it was.)

In 1965, Allen had been running Boeing for twenty years. There was speculation about how much longer he would remain in charge. He showed no sign of physical or mental debility or even of fatigue. He was large and forceful. His face had thinned and sharpened with age. For the most part it was an equable face. Warning of a shift in temper came when his eyes turned a darker brown, typically when there had been some breach of propriety. It was clear that unlike Trippe, whose regime discouraged visible successors, Allen was, in an unhurried way, carefully weighing the Boeing succession, considering the kind of company it had become and what that required of a new generation.

If, in fact, Allen chose a generational change he would have to disappoint a man who, under an impassive mask of modesty, had long coveted the top job. Next to Allen, Edward Curtis Wells was, in the eyes of many of his peers, the quintessence of the Boeing ethic and the keeper of its engineering conscience. Wells was indispensable to Allen; no fundamental decision on an airplane was taken without seeking Wells's assent. Wells had risen with extraordinary speed after joining Boeing in 1931, at the age of twenty, from Stanford University's engineering school.

By the age of twenty-three, Wells was leading the team designing a bomber that became the legendary B-17 Flying Fortress. Taking into account Wells's workaholic habits, it was calculated that he had made less than fifty cents an hour while ensuring that Boeing won what was in its day the most lucrative military contract on offer. Wells was a laconic, private man, immovable when it came to engineering principles. Technically, he was a generalist with an intuitive grasp of how an airplane should come together as a whole. Boeing discouraged the idea of the individual as a star, and Wells abhorred egoism, but he had become a revered figure among his own and a succeeding generation of engineers and, though never acting the part, their leader.

When Allen decided that the time had come to move the 747 from a paper concept to the stage known as preliminary design—in essence, the task of defining its performance and characteristics—it was left to Wells to select the chief engineer for the program. Many of the company's best minds were working the supersonic transport problem. Others were wrestling with a small, relatively unambitious design, the 737, that was proving to be a nightmare. And there was a newly orphaned design group who had developed Boeing's unsuccessful contender for a new large military transport, the C5a.

Any one of a half-dozen or so of the senior engineers had the right background to tackle the 747. The only real technical challenge was in the airplane's size, which work on the C5a had

done a lot to rehearse. Wells saw no case for getting too innovative: the 747 could, more or less, grow out of the body of
experience gained with the 707. Compared with the SST, a voyage into the unknown, the design of the 747 lay well within
thoroughly tested principles. And yet, as the case of the 737
showed, if you got overconfident with an airplane it could turn
into a mess.

There was also the numbing responsibility involved in designing an airplane that carried four hundred or more passengers. The 747 called for someone of an independent will who
would put safety above the many competing compromises that
any designer faced. Unless you had designed an airliner you
couldn't really know what it felt like to carry that responsibility.
Wells had made his name with bombers, where the criteria were
rather different. But he did have one airliner to his name, the
only one that was wholly of his own devising, and it had not
started well.

SEATTLE, MARCH 20, 1939

It was a crystal day in a city more known for its mists. Boeing
test pilot Julius Barr could not have wished for a better omen.
The company was introducing an important customer, KLM
Royal Dutch Airlines, to its new model, the Boeing 307 Stratoliner, a hybrid concocted by Ed Wells that combined the wings
and tail of the B-17 bomber with a new, corpulent fuselage. The
307 was going to be the first big airliner with a fully pressurized
cabin, able to fly above much of the bad weather.

The airplane Barr was demonstrating, the first 307, was
not pressurized. It had so far made eighteen test flights. KLM
had sent one of its senior pilots, Albert von Baumhauer, to try
out the airplane. Von Baumhauer had never flown a four-engine
airliner. Very few airline pilots had. With KLM, Boeing faced
a company already predisposed toward Douglas. KLM had been
the first European customer for the DC-3; it had bought twenty-
four. Von Baumhauer arrived at Boeing with explicit concerns.
The Stratoliner's weight and power made it a hotter ship than
the DC-3, and he wanted particularly to measure the forces
brought to bear on the Stratoliner's controls in the marginal

conditions near stalling speed, which pilots might inadvertently encounter in turbulence.

Other airlines had had similar concerns with the Stratoliner. On the previous flight, TWA's chief pilot deliberately stalled the Boeing. He had recovered easily, but he had noticed in mild form the troubling phenomenon of flutter on the elevator when the Stratoliner hit 240 mph—only 18 mph faster than its recommended cruising speed and well within the speeds that the airliner should easily have coped with. Flutter, which could be lethal, had been identified as a problem by NACA in 1928, and pilots looked out for it in a new airplane with the kind of sixth sense a deer might reserve for a wolf.

On the ground, the Stratoliner was distinctive and futuristic. The cockpit was molded like a lofty gallery into the unbroken curves of a wide, rounded nose. The impression of corpulence was created by a fuselage with a perfectly circular cross section, chosen by Wells because it was the safest way to handle pressurization. The fuselage had to be pressure-sealed just as the hull of a submarine had to be to withstand the pressure differences, inside and out, at great depths, except that in the sky the pressures were reversed—the higher the airplane flew, the lower the pressure outside became; the air inside remained constant at the equivalent of flying at eight thousand feet instead of, say, twenty thousand feet. In a submarine the water outside wanted to crush the hull; in an airplane the air inside wanted to explode outward. This fat fuselage could generously seat thirty-three passengers and a crew of five.

For the KLM test flight, von Baumhauer insisted on taking the copilot's seat, even though Earl Ferguson, a Boeing test pilot with experience of four-engine flying, would normally have backed up Barr. Ferguson climbed aboard anyway, with two of Boeing's key designers, chief engineer Jack Kylstra and chief aerodynamicist Ralph Cram. The TWA pilot who had stalled the Stratoliner on its previous flight, Harland Hull, joined them. All eight men on the flight wore parachutes.

Barr filed a flight plan that would take them southeast toward the 14,410-foot summit of Mount Rainier, which that morning was sharply white against the blue horizon. Mount Rainier presides over Seattle like an evanescent deity; on those days when visibility is clear, the mountain, some fifty miles to the south, appears to reduce the scale of everything around it. Over the years, Boeing appropriated the peak as its regional brand image—new Boeing airplanes are, to this day, invariably photographed flying over it as though in some ritual blessing. On this Saturday morning, Barr was not attempting to fly over the summit of Rainier. Once they reached eleven thousand feet, over the foothills, he planned to level off and give von Baumhauer the chance to try a stall.

Just before 1:30 P.M., several people in the small town of Alder, on a lake southwest of Rainier, heard the airliner overhead. It sounded as though the engines were laboring, and because it was high, the airplane seemed almost to be standing still, like a droplet of mercury caught in the sun. Suddenly it began to fall, almost serenely at first, in a series of flat spins, the engines becoming louder. Then pieces fell off. An engine broke away and fell, still roaring. What survived in one piece fell behind a hill, leaving a smell of high-octane gasoline in the air.

The Stratoliner's last moments were reconstructed by the Civil Aeronautics Administration. In those days there were no voice recorders in the cockpit, and no black box. Cram, the aerodynamicist, had made notes up to the point that the pilots had lost control. One of the pilots, probably von Baumhauer, had stalled the plane, just as TWA's Hull had done. But, inexperienced with a plane of this size, the Dutchman had almost certainly overcorrected coming out of the stall and put the Stratoliner into a series of flat spins.

Once in the spin—though from the ground it would have seemed unstressed—the airplane exceeded the gravitational forces—G-forces—it was designed for. The control surfaces broke up first, followed by part of the wings. For the wings to have failed meant that the loads had reached nearly 5 G, five times the force of gravity. The investigators concluded that the disintegration of the Stratoliner had begun with flutter in an elevator. Among the CAA's recommendations in its crash report was a continued study of the causes of flutter. The CAA's report was less critical of the Stratoliner itself than of the test procedures, and recommended only minor structural changes to increase its stability.

The airplane that crashed had been destined for Pan Am,

and although Pan Am and TWA did take delivery of a few Stratoliners, its commercial future was curtailed by the looming world war. Howard Hughes, who had built up a holding of 30 percent in TWA, developed a passion for the Stratoliner and often flew one himself; Jack Frye, who was now running the airline, was also a Stratoliner fan. But Boeing's failure to persuade influential international carriers like KLM to buy the first pressurized four-engine airliner left the feeling that for most airlines, Boeing was not a match for Douglas. The Stratoliner, as the pioneer of pressurization, ended up like the 247, a tiny, glinting crystal in the bedrock of aviation history.

Had it been successful, the Stratoliner might have preempted Donald Douglas's first four-engine airliner, the DC-4, forerunner of the most successful series of four-engine airliners of the propeller age. But the DC-4 exposed an unscrupulous side of Douglas. In 1939, a prototype DC-4, partly assembled, was shipped to Japan, ostensibly for trials with Greater Japan Airlines. In fact, the Japanese stripped it down and used its technology as a guide to designing a four-engine bomber. Douglas had sold DC-3s to the Japanese and licensed them to build the airplane themselves. Boeing, on the other hand, as early as 1932, had acceded to an Air Corps request not to sell 247s to Japan because its structure incorporated ideas used on bombers which they did not want to see copied. Later, and with transparent evasion, Douglas claimed that his deals were done "before things started hotting up."

Anticipating that Hugo Black's inquisition would lead to antitrust action, the Boeing conglomerate had dismantled itself, and the weakest surviving fragment of the octopus was the Boeing Airplane Company itself: financially drained, technically overextended, seemingly marooned in the far Northwest. And now the loss of the Stratoliner seriously depleted the company's technical and intellectual resources. The deaths of Kylstra and Cram decapitated the design staff. Monteith had already gone, through ill health, and Kylstra had replaced him. Only two accomplished designers remained: Wells, who was increasingly preoccupied with the development of the Flying Fortress, and Wellwood Beall, a very different and more problematical asset. Beall was a jocular salesman who worked the airlines very hard, and he was also a designer inclined to the monumental. He designed and sold to Pan Am the concept of the great Boeing 314 Clipper flying boats which were used to launch the first scheduled transatlantic service. Neither Boeing nor Pan Am made any money with the Clippers, but they were decisive in proving that the Atlantic was bridgeable.

As valuable as Wells and Beall were, Boeing had no one with a background at the cutting edge of the aviation sciences. Wells himself, though the signal talent left in the company, would have admitted this himself. Three places produced minds of the quality Boeing sorely needed: MIT, NACA, and Caltech. Bill Cook, a Texan with a master's degree from MIT, had just joined Boeing, but the company needed someone with a combination of scientific distinction and more experience in the daily grind of an airplane plant.

Boeing's weakness in test-flying procedures, pointed out by the CAA, had already effectively been ended by the arrival of a new chief test pilot, Eddie Allen. No test pilot in America had more illustrious credentials, although Allen never fulfilled anyone's expectation of what a test pilot should look like. He was small and dressed like a fussy, pedantic clerk. The heroic, daredevil breed of American pilots who barnstormed their way around state fairs appalled him. To Eddie Allen, flying an airplane was no stunt, it was a quest for the mastery of great works of engineering.

There was hardly an airplane company in America that had not, at one time or another, sent for Allen to help cure some intractable prototype—including Douglas, where Allen had been the first to prove that the DC-1 could take off on one engine, earning the praise that he was "an engineer's dream."

By 1939, Allen was the world's expert on flying multiengine airplanes. He had test-flown the Stratoliner before turning it over to Barr, and the way it had broken up in the air—although probably not in Barr's hands—deeply affected his thinking. He realized that Boeing's multiengine leviathans could carry much more sophisticated test equipment, that it was now possible to plan systematic testing from the wind tunnel all the way through the test flights—that they could move the laboratory into the airplane.

Allen initiated a systemic change at Boeing, a research unit that would be independent of the design process and, instead, work alongside the test pilots. Until then, the aerodynamicists (and there were few enough of them) had been confined to the design teams, responding to what pilots reported but not regarded as part of the flight test regime.

It was Eddie Allen, rather than Wells, who went looking for the scientific stars that Boeing needed. He recalled receiving a letter from a young engineer at the Consolidated Company in San Diego. It was crisp and to the point: the vertical tail surfaces on the prototype 314 Clipper flying boat were too small. This was obvious, said the letter, just from a photograph of the Clipper on the cover of an aviation magazine. The warning was prophetic. When Allen gunned the Clipper across Puget Sound for its first takeoff it snaked and wallowed so badly that Allen had to fight to regain control of it. The tail was enlarged.

In the summer of 1939, as Allen was beginning to build up his staff, he had a call from the engineer in San Diego, asking if there was a job at Boeing. Allen told him to come right away. Thus appeared George Schairer. Although Schairer had been born and educated in America, he had the look of a European intellectual, with a high-domed skull, wide, searching eyes with a hint of the basilisk behind wire-framed glasses, and a supercilious curl to his lip which he did nothing to restrain. Charm was not immediately one of Schairer's qualities, and people very soon learned that his bite was every bit as bad as his bark—or rather, his hiss.

Schairer had graduated at the trough of the Depression with a master's degree from the aeronautical department of MIT, where he was weaned on the wind tunnel and became its ardent apostle. When he moved to Consolidated he coordinated its tunnel testing, which was carried out at Caltech, and there he fell naturally within the force field of von Karman.

In Seattle, Schairer found that Eddie Allen, then forty-seven, was the graybeard. Beall, who had taken Kylstra's place as chief engineer, was thirty-two; Wells, now assistant chief engineer, was twenty-nine; Schairer was twenty-six. Even then, Schairer felt that the company needed more new blood with a stronger scientific training. Boeing was proof of something Schairer had already taken to heart about the airplane business: you could never have as many people as you had problems.

Some people were muttering that the trouble with Boeing was that it was in Seattle. There was an average of only forty-five sunny days in a year. The climate curtailed test flying and made people perceptibly moody. Why weren't they in California, where their competitors enjoyed a far more salubrious climate? Schairer, fresh from California, would have none of it. He liked Seattle. He liked it better than California. He liked water and sailboats and he particularly liked the treachery of water. Working on the problem of flying-boat hulls, he found water a devious adversary and worthy of his time. Furthermore, he liked Eddie Allen. And he liked Wells.

This was interesting chemistry. With only three years between them, Wells and Schairer were contemporaries of a very different mettle. Indeed, they might have proved fatally combustible on contact. But, with profound consequences for Boeing, they did not. Schairer immediately saw and conceded Wells's formidable gifts, manifest in the Flying Fortress and the improvements being made to it. Wells had a manner older than his years—a kind of monkish calm that others found reassuring. Wells said little, but when he did speak it all came out as if it had been edited of anything extraneous. Schairer responded to the civility and forbearance in Wells, possibly recognizing that they were virtues that he would never himself exhibit.

Schairer very quickly became a kind of one-man technology transfer. His style, a peculiar combination of intuition, scientific deduction, and critical asperity, had been honed in the laboratories of MIT at Cambridge. He had fallen under the influence there of Charles Stark "Doc" Draper, a pioneer of flight instrumentation and mentor of several generations of aeronautical engineers. There were cogent Draper aphorisms—"I can walk into any one of these labs and say, 'It won't work,' and ninety percent of the time I'll be right"—and lurid Draper anecdotes about barnstorming and the flying circuses. Draper's credo, that it was as important to solve problems in the air as in the laboratory, was the perfect text for Eddie Allen's new regime at Boeing.

When Schairer began building the intellectual seedstock of Boeing, he was predisposed to turn to Cambridge. Although he told recruits that he was looking for people "to shut me out of office," he was actually in search of men who could give him combat. None of his recruits would ever be free of his goading. Gradually, over the decade after his arrival at Boeing, Schairer established a cadre of young engineers who would take the company through some of its riskiest ventures. Eventually, under his eye, they would find the equivalent in aerodynamics of a genetic code, discoveries that simultaneously unlocked and exploited fundamental mysteries of flight. And this work would give Boeing a proprietary formula with which it would dominate the world's commercial aviation industry.

When Schairer spotted an embryonic talent he was not easily deflected. Jack Steiner is a case in point; Steiner would become one of the world's most accomplished airplane designers, but Schairer had almost to play the role of surrogate father to get him. Steiner came from Seattle. He had first shown up at Boeing, as Wells had done, by taking a summer job, in his case to help pay his way through the University of Washington. Times were hard for many people, but Steiner's father could easily have helped him. The problem was that his father ran a successful law firm and was of the kind, quite common then, who thought a career in aviation was low-caste, smacking too much of workshops and overalls. The real career was in the law firm. Resisting this, Steiner took his father to Boeing Field to explain the wonders of aviation. Unfortunately, as they watched, a Boeing pursuit plane on test looped and crashed, right in front of them.

From that moment Jack Steiner was cut off from any more family funding for an education in aeronautics. Even so, he graduated at the top of his class at Washington and, at Schairer's urging, won a place at MIT. To get to Cambridge he borrowed money, some of it surreptitiously provided by his mother. But before he could complete his course for a master's degree he went broke, and appealed to Schairer for help.

It happened that Schairer was plagued by problems with the hull of an experimental seaplane Boeing was designing for the Navy. He made a deal with Steiner: if Steiner would write his master's thesis on hydrodynamics, and obligingly address the problems of the seaplane's hull, Boeing would get Steiner through the rest of his time at Cambridge. Steiner successfully tackled the problem of the hull—it was prone to a form of instability called porpoising—and won his master's, as well as a job in Eddie Allen's flight test unit.

Schairer was acutely aware of the burden to Boeing of having to take its research to tunnels all over the country. Since the days of the 247's journey to Caltech, the small aeronautics department at the University of Washington in Seattle had acquired a low-speed tunnel, which Boeing used, but the advanced work still had to go wandering to either Caltech, MIT, or NACA at Langley. These tunnels were also urgently needed by other manufacturers, and booking time involved waiting in line. Furthermore, Schairer felt that none of these tunnels was good enough for the kind of work he foresaw. So he proposed that Boeing build its own.

On the face of it, the idea was preposterous. Here was a company barely able to meet either its financial or its production obligations being asked to make an investment in research facilities that could not cost less than $1 million. Also, Schairer wanted it to meet targets not matched by the tunnels at any of the country's pure research institutions. However, Schairer had on his side a raw nerve. Old hands remembered how porous Boeing's 247 secrets had been in the Caltech tunnel. Schairer advanced a proposition that Boeing's management had to concede was irrefutable: no other research tool would in the future be as decisive to success as the wind tunnel, and by having its own, Boeing would keep its trade secrets far more secure.

The company had a deficit of $3.4 million. With the help of some Seattle bankers, it had raised a loan of $5.5 million from the government-sponsored Reconstruction Finance Corporation. The stockholders had agreed to a new issue of 450,000 shares to help raise more capital. The first commitment to a wind tunnel would be to spend only the $25,000 required to build a working model, yet some people remember this as the most disputed expenditure in the company's history. Although the full-size tunnel was the major investment, the initial expenditure would indicate a fundamental change of attitude toward research and development on a modern scale.

The company had frequently dug itself into deep holes with ideas that took on a life of their own and became irreversible. Schairer's ideas tended to develop a compelling momentum. Boeing's managers didn't begin to understand half of what

Schairer said, but somehow felt he was right. The $25,000 was found.

Eddie Allen, who had supported Schairer's case for the tunnel, called in the acknowledged maestro of wind, von Karman. Von Karman had just designed a tunnel for the Army Air Corps research center at Wright Field in Dayton, Ohio. This tunnel was to be big enough to take full-size sections of actual airplanes, as well as models, and it was going to run at speeds of more than 400 mph. Von Karman urged Boeing to build an equally powerful tunnel. Thanks in part to Schairer's superior understanding of the tunnel at NACA, Boeing had won a contract to develop the Flying Fortress's successor, the B-29. This was intended to have a top speed of around 360 mph, and 400-mph-plus speeds for fighters were easily attainable. In 1939 a Messerschmitt 209 racer set a world record speed of 481 mph. Von Karman thought it prudent to go beyond even that, to a tunnel that could handle speeds up to the speed of sound, of 600 mph or more. To many at Boeing, this seemed fantastic and excessive. In 1941, nobody knew how to make an airplane fly that fast.

To the lay mind, the only simple thing about a wind tunnel is the physical law on which it is based, that instead of moving an object through air to see what effect it has, you can move the air over the object. Or—to be a little less simplistic—a fluid passing over a stationary object produces the same interactions as an object moving at the same speed through a stationary fluid. Air is, of course, a very dilute fluid. Moreover, it is seldom still. The sky is comparable to an ocean many miles deep containing many capricious currents (even invisible holes) and great variations of temperature and density.

Since there is no way to reproduce in a tunnel a sample of sky, containing every condition an airplane will encounter, the validity of wind tunnel testing depends on how precisely controlled can be the speed and condition of the air reaching the test section, where the model airplane or section of a real airplane sits. By incrementally changing speed under controlled conditions, a wide variety of the sky's tricks can be simulated in the tunnel.

The plans for the Boeing tunnel were subjected to the scrutiny of some of the country's best aerodynamic minds. They recommended a rectangular test section, twelve feet wide and eight feet high, with a turntable so that models could be tested for directional stability.

For once, being based in Seattle gave Boeing an advantage. The major cost of running a tunnel is its consumption of electric power. The power needed rises roughly by a cube of the speed of the wind required. Doubling the speed costs as much as ten times more in power. The tunnel Schairer wanted needed an eighteen-thousand-horsepower electric motor to drive the fan, with an appetite for electricity that approached gluttony. In many parts of the country the cost of running this would have been ruinous. But the construction on the Columbia River of the Grand Coulee and Bonneville dams had tripled the hydroelectric power available in the Pacific Northwest, and the cost of this power was a third or less what it was anywhere else in the United States.

In August 1941, the go-ahead was given for a tunnel that would be capable of speeds into the high subsonic zone—to within a Mach number of 0.975, Mach 1 being the speed of sound. (In the end, the tunnel cost something less than the forecast $1 million, thanks in part to enforced wartime economies in materials.) To help prepare Boeing for using the tunnel, Schairer hired a young technician from the MIT tunnel, Bob Withington.

At Cambridge, Withington had noticed that of all the companies that brought models to be tested at MIT—each would send a team of up to six people to watch the model and calibrate the results—the men from Boeing stood out. Boeing's team was led by Schairer. At the time Schairer hired Withington, only a handful of people in the country could match Withington's expertise, although he was only twenty-two. In Seattle, Withington found himself working closely with the Texan MIT graduate who had preceded Schairer to Boeing, Bill Cook.

While the young bloods were shaping the magic cave for Boeing's future, the flight testing of the B-29 assumed the characteristics of a recurrent nightmare. The Army had ordered more than seven hundred B-29s, more or less straight from the drawing board. After the first flight, on September 21, 1942, Eddie Allen, who was doing most of the flying himself, was subjected to remorseless pressure from Wright Field, fielding calls every day. And every day there were new problems, the worst of them involving the B-29's Wright Cyclone engines.

In the first twenty-six hours of flying there were sixteen engine changes. The publicity department wanted a picture of the B-29 with all four engines running, but it took days to manage it. The strain showed in Allen. Jack Steiner, who was flying as a performance aerodynamicist on the tests, found himself having to remind Allen of tests to be done—the kind of lapse that in Allen's whole previous career would have been unthinkable. At the end of December there was a serious incident with the second prototype. An engine fire filled the cockpit with smoke, and Allen only just made it back to the field, skimming over a line of high-tension wires.

Under normal circumstances the airplanes would have been grounded. It was totally against the grain at Boeing to try to solve in the air problems that were more safely studied on the ground. But this was war. In Europe and the Pacific, the Army Air Forces were suffering ravaging losses. Allen felt personally the duty of living up to the slogan hyping the B-29 as "the plane that will win the war for America." He decided to press on with the flight testing.

On February 18, 1943, there was a meeting of the executive staff in the administrative building overlooking Boeing Field. The mood was up because at last Flying Fortress deliveries were nearing the target of two hundred a month.

Things were different at the flight test center; a feeling of morbid despair was tangible. Allen was flying the second prototype again. Left behind in the flight test hangar, Steiner was reflecting that the B-29 was not so much a pilot's dream as a military dream. He'd seen one of the flight engineers who had gone up with Allen that morning fling his car keys at his secretary with the stark instruction to give them to his wife if he didn't return.

Steiner could hear over the flight control radio that the B-29 was in trouble. The crew was trying to extinguish another engine fire. Allen was approaching the field from the south, on a day when the traffic pattern was to land from the north. The tower told him he could come straight in, against the other traffic, which they would hold off until he was down. But Allen elected to join the pattern, which required making a wide, sweeping turn over Lake Washington, adding minutes to the approach. It seemed a strange choice, but it was in keeping with Allen's punctilious nature.

He completed the turn and was lining up from the north with the Boeing Field runway when a new fire broke out and reached the fuel tanks. The B-29 faltered for a few seconds and then, suddenly engulfed, fell like a bomb into a meat-packing plant. Steiner, on a roof with other engineers, heard the explosion and saw a plume of dark, oil-saturated smoke rising. The executive meeting had been interrupted by news of the emergency, and Wells and others were also outside, looking grimly toward the smoke. From a school on a hill to the east of Boeing Field a young student called Joe Sutter, like many other kids that day, had seen the crash more graphically. But Joe Sutter was a little different from most. His whole universe—home, school, vocation—was centered on Boeing Field. He would never forget the crash; it conditioned his determination to be an airplane designer with an apprehension of the enormous risks involved.

In one sense, Allen's loss was a deeper blow to Boeing than the men who had died in the Stratoliner. Nobody could match his unique balance of technician and airman. He had personally accrued more of the experience of America's long struggle to achieve supremacy in aviation than any other pilot—far more, for example, than Charles Lindbergh. In another sense, though, Allen left Boeing formidably armed in talent and fundamentally changed in its capacity and respect for research. It was only fitting, therefore, that when the new wind tunnel opened it should be named for him.

And by 1944 one question that could not be answered in 1941 was answerable: how you got an airplane to fly as fast as the tunnel. Two months before Pearl Harbor, with the knowledge of only a handful of people, a highly classified piece of machinery was shipped from England to the United States. It was a jet engine. Some of the best engineering minds in the United States had been taken unawares by the development of the jet. The fact that the British had a jet airplane that was already operational by May 1941 was discovered—by chance—by General Hap Arnold on a visit to England that spring. A prototype engine was shipped to America so that General Electric could build fifteen copies. (For a while, the development was kept secret even from NACA, some of whose scientists had earlier predicted that a jet engine for airplanes was impossible.)

By October 1942, the first American jet-powered airplane, the
Bell XP-59A Airacomet, was flying—a phenomenal achievement
in catching up.

The Germans, too, were developing jets. They already perceived that for high-speed flight the piston engine and propeller
were finished. Some of the best German scientists were devoted
to a tantalizing but perplexing problem: what kind of airplane
could fly as fast as this engine wanted to fly? In America, George
Schairer was wondering the same thing. And then, late in 1944,
he got a call from Theodor von Karman. The air force had asked
von Karman to round up the country's best aviation minds to
advise on the future of flight. One of their missions would be to
go to Germany, as soon as it fell, and assess the work of German
scientists that had been done during the war. Schairer left
Boeing and went on the government payroll in Washington.

The Wing That
Shrank the World

3　■

Nobody at Pan Am could ever be sure what Juan Trippe knew, and when he had known it. Those closest to Trippe at Pan Am played a thankless and delicate game, offering information or withholding it according to their sense of how it would square with his view at the time. Trippe, meantime, edited his conversations with outsiders, like Bill Allen, according to a concept of self-interest that he kept in his own head. For example, Trippe's professed surprise about Boeing's commitment to the 747 in his September 27 conversation with Allen might well have been simulated. Or, on the other hand, it might not. There were men below Trippe who had known for some time that Boeing was serious about the 747. Maybe they just hadn't told him.

Certainly General Laurence S. Kuter knew, and Kuter had Trippe's ear as much as anyone could claim to have it. Kuter was Trippe's centurion, a type Trippe liked to include in the Pan Am hierarchy if only to annoy others. A straight-arrow West Pointer, Kuter had run the Military Air Transport Service with great precision. At Pan Am since retiring from the Air Force in 1962, as the vice president of engineering, he had proved an adaptive student of the Great Dissembler.

In July 1965, Kuter had been invited to join the tail end of a meeting that Pan Am's chief engineer, John Borger, had been holding with two Boeing men, Carl Munson from sales and Don Finlay from product development. During the course of the day, Munson and Finlay had laid out for Borger a surprisingly detailed picture of what they called Boeing's "new-technology airplane." Not yet numbered 747, this airplane, they said, would take what Boeing had already learned from its C5a proposal and go well beyond it, offering not a warmed-over version of a military design but an airplane wholly conceived for an airline like Pan Am.

When the Boeing men left, Kuter said he thought they had been peddling pipe dreams.

In the Pan Am pecking order, there were two men between Borger and Trippe: Borger's boss, Sanford Kauffman (who had also sat in at the end of the meeting with the Boeing men), and above him, Kuter. Kauffman, characteristically, would take his lead from Kuter, and it seemed to Borger that there was nothing he could do but wait to see whether Boeing persisted and if, eventually, Trippe took the bait.

As often happened with Trippe, once he did get a taste for the 747, it was all bells and flashing lights. On October 19, Allen took a call from Trippe that developed a new, urgent tone. It transpired that on the previous night Trippe had dined with a party including another potentate of the aviation industry, Jack Horner, the head of Pratt & Whitney. Horner had told Trippe that Pratt's designers were at full stretch devising an engine for the 747.

Now Trippe pressed Allen: "Is it a problem beyond the reach of the engine manufacturers?"

Allen was sanguine. "No, I wouldn't think so. Maybe both engine companies"—the other was General Electric—"would be willing to step up to this."

Allen had got Trippe hooked; Trippe went on immediately to talk of Pan Am's ordering "a large fleet of twenty-five" 747s. This was too much even for Allen, who tried to slow Trippe down. Boeing, said Allen, had "this high-quality team working this problem just as hard as they can." He suggested that Boeing and Pan Am could sit down and work out "a general expression of intent." Trippe had no patience for vague expressions of intent: "The problem is for us, *how long?* We've just got to step up, we're so underequipped."

Little more than a week later, John Yeasting, the head of

Boeing's commercial division, sent Trippe a five-page letter which, to all intents and purposes, set in stone what Boeing was ready to promise with the 747.

In the end, everything that Boeing aspired to achieve with the 747 became the responsibility of one man, the chief engineer chosen by Wells and Allen for the project, Joe Sutter. By the time of Yeasting's letter, he had been on the job for little more than two months.

When the call came, directly from Allen, Sutter had been vacationing with his family in his cabin on the Hood Canal, southwest of Seattle. He had needed the break. He had been working on the troubled 737 with Jack Steiner. Sutter had always been toiling in Steiner's shadow. At Boeing, Steiner, after the wartime horrors of the B-29, had emerged as an almost dauntingly articulate exponent of jet airliners, and it was Steiner who delivered the commercial division's first real cash cow, the 727 trijet. All over the world, the 727 was a dependable and heavily used medium-range, no-frills workhorse.

In the debate over whom to choose as the chief engineer for the 747, Steiner's claim might have seemed unimpeachable. But Allen had reservations: he acknowledged Steiner's gifts as an engineer, but Steiner had recently lobbied Boeing board members to contest an Allen decision and Allen had been furious. Sutter, on the other hand, had clearly been a good soldier. He had worked only on commercial airplanes, never military, which was unusual. He had never been in research: he was a practical aerodynamicist with a proven skill as the kind of all-rounder that Wells wanted, someone who, like Wells, could never lose sight of the idea as a whole.

Among the engineering elite at Boeing, and especially among those working on the SST, the 747 was already viewed as about as glamorous as a Mack truck. Whoever got to develop it didn't need too much imagination. When the word came that Sutter had been chosen, it seemed right to most of his peers. Joe was a good guy. Let him have his day on the 747, and then, maybe, he could be elected to the pantheon where the great ones had the future in their sights.

Sutter was a small but implacably solid man. He squared off against a problem or an adversary with a steady, relentless application. He had made a personal religion of designing safety into an airplane; the B-29 crash was something he could still describe in ghoulish detail, knowing exactly what design flaws had been responsible. He had endured Steiner with fortitude— "endured" because Steiner never respected the Boeing fraternal rule that there should be no stars, that even a chief engineer should be the first among equals. Steiner had an ego that could cut through metal. Breaking free of Steiner should be like getting a lung full of fresh Puget Sound air.

John Borger, for one, was happy to find Sutter in charge of the 747. They had known each other for twenty years. Sutter was an engineer's engineer. No bullshit. Not like Steiner. Steiner was always trying to put one over. Very few people ever put one over on Borger. And if anyone did, he paid later. As Borger looked at Yeasting's letter listing the performance goals of the 747, he could smell the overarching ambition. An airplane that would carry four hundred passengers and a load of cargo and cruise as high as 35,000 feet with a range of 5,100 miles.

Trippe wanted a quantum advance in airplane economics. This was expressed, quite simply, in one measure: the seat-mile cost, what it cost to carry a filled seat one mile. Every one of the thousands of decisions involved in defining the next generation of airliner came down to this one calculation. Trippe had set Borger a target for the 747: a seat-mile cost 30 percent lower than the best achieved by the 707, 6.6 cents.

There was a long way to go before Borger could be sure whether the 747 costs would hit this target, but another figure jumped off the page of Boeing's specifications for the 747: the speed. Boeing promised a cruise speed of nine-tenths Mach. That meant around 650 mph. That was one hot ship. A thing this size, two and a half times bigger than a 707, flying 100 mph faster than a 707? Borger was very dubious. This was faster than Boeing's B-52 bomber, and the only experience Boeing had with anything approaching the size of the 747 was with the B-52. Even then, it was on the edge. These high subsonic speeds had been achieved only after thousands of hours in the wind tunnel with the swept wing—it was the combination of the swept wing, angled back like an arrowhead, with the jet engine that had shrunk the world. But the swept wing was an inherently wild thing, difficult to domesticate for airline use. True enough, if anyone knew how to tame a swept wing it was Boeing. But nine-tenths Mach? Let Sutter try it.

ST. LOUIS, MISSOURI, 1924

The crowds lining Olive Street in downtown St. Louis were getting restless. They had been waiting an hour for what had been billed as the biggest thrill of the Fourth of July weekend. Then they heard the sound of an airplane engine. The sound was not a reliable guide to where to look, because it was echoing like a rockfall in a canyon. In fact, the airplane that was turning to line up with Olive Street was coming in below the roofs of the offices and hotels. It was leaving a trail of white exhaust, and this helped the crowd to focus. And there, half crouching, half standing on the center of the upper wing of the biplane, like a jockey uncertain of his seat, was a tiny figure in a white flying suit.

There she was, Marie Meyer—the "Daring Aviatrix." It was the gut-wrencher of stunts. The old Standard biplane had no elegance to match the wing-walker. It was a rough-hewn, tired leftover from World War I, and it was very susceptible to turbulence. The pilot, in the rearmost of two open seats, could see Meyer fighting to keep her feet in the stirrups that anchored her to the wing, and he was grappling with an airplane that was beginning to buck from the crosscurrents between the buildings—he had dropped lower and was passing between the *St. Louis Globe Democrat* offices on one side and the Railway Exchange on the other. He began to climb clear of the buildings but was caught in a wind shear. Meyer was thrown off balance, hanging on only by a support wire. They barely cleared a smokestack.

For once the newspapers' hyperbole the next morning seemed justified—"It is unlikely that such a feat will ever be duplicated."

As the Standard flew back to Lambert Field on the fringe of St. Louis, Marie Meyer climbed back into the front seat. Behind her the pilot, her husband, Charlie Fower, was more agitated than she seemed to be. She was always composed and was convincing when she told reporters, "I feel safer in the air than I do on the ground. I'm always afraid of being run down when I cross the street." When it came to the stunts, she was the boss. The Standard bore on the side of its fuselage the legend "Marie Meyer's Flying Circus." At Lambert Field they shared a hangar with a rangy young pilot called Charles Lindbergh. Occasionally, Lindbergh flew with the circus, but he was known more for his prudent flying as a pioneer of the airmail routes then beginning to snake across the country.

Charlie and Marie had a dedicated acolyte waiting on the ground to help service the Standard. In fact, they couldn't shake the kid off. Robert Jones, wiry and elfin, should have been in college, but he had skipped after two semesters to follow the circus, learning to rig wings and fix the engine. He didn't like the beaten-up wings and got some new fabric to patch them up. He looked at the Standard with increasing skepticism, wondering why it held together at all as Charlie dived it straight to earth and then pulled up into a loop over the crowds. He wondered about the parachutes, homemade from cotton from the dry goods store. The "Aerobats" in the circus strapped a laundry basket to the wing, folded the parachute into it, and pulled out the shrouds as they fell.

Charlie Fower could see that Jones was addicted. He was always reading the aviation magazines, soaking up the technical detail, wanting more knowledge than Fower or any of the other pilots could provide. Jones began sending off to the Government Printing Office in Washington for technical papers, ten cents apiece. The mania had begun in Macon, Missouri, where, until he met Marie Meyer, Charlie Fower, a former Army pilot, had driven a cab. One of his regular clients was Jones's father, a lawyer. One day Marie Meyer flew into Macon with a circus and met Fower. She taught him to fly stunts; she had been wing-walking since the age of seventeen and then became a pilot.

You could buy a Standard for $500. They bought one together and began their circus. Charlie left the talking to her. He was content. And when an old taxi client asked if his son could help carry gas or something when they flew out of the cow pasture near the fairground, he was happy to oblige.

The actuarial odds against an extended life in a flying circus were not encouraging. After Lindbergh's transatlantic flight in 1927, Charlie and Marie decided to quit while they were ahead. Robert Jones had to face the future, too. Charlie flew him one last time, to Marshall, Missouri, where he was hired by the engineering department of the Nicholas-Beazley Airplane Company. Similar companies were springing up all over, in Arkansas, Colorado, Kentucky, Kansas, chancing their luck on the boom in aviation triggered by Lindbergh's flight. Nicholas-Beazley's designers were better than most. They produced an advanced all-metal airplane, but their timing was unlucky. Depression overtook the boom and the company crashed.

Robert Jones realized that if he was to amount to anything the roaming had to stop. At the pit of the Depression he arrived in Washington, D.C., and was soon able to write home that he had found "a position in the highest levels of government." He was operating the lone elevator in the old Congressional Office Building.

Everything changed when into the elevator one day stepped David J. Lewis, a small, compact Welshman, once a coal miner, then self-taught in law, a judge, and now a congressman from Maryland. Still striving to round out his education, Lewis was looking for someone to teach him math. He asked the advice of Dr. Albert Zahm, who ran the aeronautical section of the Library of Congress. Zahm, who had encountered Jones as an obsessive student of aeronautics and knew him to be a math wizard, told Lewis to see the elevator operator. Jones set Lewis a study course.

Franklin Roosevelt had Lewis on a list of candidates for his Supreme Court appointments. (Hugo Black, the scourge of Boeing, was another.) When Roosevelt inaugurated the Public Works Administration, Lewis had successfully lobbied for a PWA project to extend NACA's laboratories at Langley Field, which fell within Lewis's constituency. Jones, in the course of guiding Lewis's reading in math, heard of this, and was electrified: his dream was to end up as a scientist at NACA. But there was a problem. You needed a college degree to get a job at NACA, and because he had forsaken college for the flying circuses, Jones did not qualify. However, Lewis was impressed by Jones and used his influence to get Jones into Langley as a temporary PWA hiring. The "temporary" appointment was to last fifty years.

Jones had been taking evening classes at Catholic University, and one of his teachers was a German aerodynamic theorist,

Max Munk. That Munk should have been teaching such a class at all was surprising; Munk's academic pedigree was, by any standards, illustrious. Like von Karman, he had made his reputation at Göttingen, under Prandtl.

Munk's work in the wind tunnel at Göttingen during World War I had attracted notice. Although much of it was classified as a military secret, NACA heard about Munk after the war through the scientific grapevine, and in 1921 he was invited to work in America. It required the personal intervention of the White House to sanction Munk's immigration. At the age of thirty, Munk was installed as a technical assistant in NACA's Washington office, ardently making a case for NACA to invest in a new generation of wind tunnel. His argument centered on the problem of the air's viscosity.

At that time, all the test results achieved with models in a wind tunnel were falsified by the difference in size between the model in the test section and the actual airplane. A true description of the interaction of airplane and air could occur only with a full-size airplane; test results were degraded in exact proportion to the scale reduction represented by the model. Incarnated as a model, the airplane shrank, but the air did not similarly shrink its molecular composition. In other words, given a constant viscosity in the air, it was proportionately thinner the smaller the model was. The air's viscosity as it flowed over a model therefore had values different from those it had flowing over the actual airplane in flight.

Since the 1880s there had been a well-tried mathematical formula for computing this difference in values. By using this formula the wind tunnel technicians could extrapolate the results with the model to fit the full-size airplane. But this was not an exact science. It rendered much testing little better than informed guesswork.

Munk had a solution, and like many flashes of original thought, it seemed astonishingly simple: to compress the air in the test section to reflect, in viscosity, the scale difference between the airplane and the model. He called this brainwave, which he was urging on NACA, the Variable Density Tunnel. In Munk's tunnel the test section would look something like a deep-sea-diving bell, because it would have to withstand an internal air density of up to twenty atmospheres. In October 1922, a handful of skeptical NACA engineers peered through a porthole in a heavily riveted test chamber as the VDT made its first run. Everything Munk claimed for it was borne out by the results. With this one facility, Langley became a world-class research center.

Nothing like Munk had ever hit the engineers at NACA. He was a slight, fragile-seeming figure who got out of breath simply climbing a few stairs, but there was nothing infirm about his intellect: he had held his own at Göttingen, one of the world's most competitive academic arenas. As long as he remained in the Washington office, away from the practical engineers at Langley, Munk's ideas were listened to. NACA's director, George Lewis, was apt to say things like "Dr. Munk believes that we can do this," and people had to respond.

The trouble was, though, that Langley was not remotely like Göttingen. America had no comparable scientific base to draw from, particularly in physics and theoretical mathematics. Langley had a heavy bias toward practical engineering. Its best brains were recruited from the industrialized states of the Midwest and the Northeast, where there was a tradition of engineering schools feeding graduates into client companies. NACA's stars tended to come from MIT, Cornell, Yale, Worcester Polytechnic in Massachusetts, and the University of Michigan.

In 1926, Lewis took a gamble and transferred Munk to Langley to head the aerodynamics division. Munk immediately raised hackles. Engineers brought up on method, who accepted that they had to explain a theory's evolution every step of the way, found Munk unwilling to explain very much. He proceeded by intuition, and he was so confident in his intuitive decrees that he expected others to accept them on his own terms, as some kind of immanent manifestation of truth. Asked later in life to explain, for example, a seminal theory on airfoils, he said, "How do such things happen? They are miracles!" He was describing NACA Report No. 142, "General Theory of Thin Wing Sections," which, in combination with his new tunnel, brought NACA's work on airfoils into the front rank.

At the Langley test center, near Chesapeake Bay, the laboratory doors opened not to a Gothic university campus but directly onto the airfield. Every idea had ultimately to be put into the hands of a test pilot. This was the common forge of American aviation, and the gifts that were characteristically American, of turning ideas into metal and making them work by experiment and test flying, had been exercised at Langley in a confident and self-sufficient way. Munk, with his head stuffed with exotic ideas, was walking culture shock.

Langley's immune system very quickly began the process of rejecting the alien body. To succeed in what became a less than creditable episode in NACA's history, the engineers began to manufacture a Munk caricature, a version of the mad professor from Mitteleuropa. Typical of this campaign was a story that has been remarkably persistent down the years. It described Munk's approach to driving a car.

According to the tale, Munk drew a map of the route between his home at Buckroe Beach and Langley Field, and measured the distance between the curves in the road. For each of these curves, he calculated the movement needed to turn the steering wheel. He took a piece of string and hung it from the top of the steering wheel marked, in sequence, with the amount of turn for each curve. By driving at a set speed, monitored by stopwatch, and noting the tabulated string, Munk could be sure to find his way without trouble.

This traducing and almost certainly fictitious story made a deadly metaphor of the demented eccentric groping with the real world's prosaic tasks. In truth, it probably revealed more of the innate prejudices of the men whose professional tolerance fell short of recognizing in Munk the truly intuitive genius. Munk's refusal to explain himself was simply a factor of the momentum of his mind; once the idea was clear to him he was already out of patience with it. He had to move on. There was no time for going through the motions again, and no time to suffer fools gladly, and it seemed that there were fools at large.

Langley closed ranks against Munk. In 1927 all the section heads of the aerodynamics division resigned en masse. Lewis, who had sent Munk to Langley precisely because he wanted to make the work there more scientific, felt that he had to put the institution above the man, and "reassigned" him. The section heads returned, and the defeat was too much for Munk's pride. He resigned from NACA. Although nobody at Langley would have conceded it at the time, or even later, Munk's curtailed influence at NACA seriously weakened both NACA and the quality of American research in the field for some time to come. It was not until von Karman established himself at Caltech that an equally original intellect was brought to bear and, immediately, broke through the barriers of traditional thought.

While Robert Jones was still a novitiate dreamer living in Macon, Missouri, he had read a book of Munk's, *Fluid Dynamics for Aircraft Designers*—not the kind of title that would come readily to hand in Missouri. When he arrived in Washington he saw an advertisement in an aviation magazine placed by Munk, offering services as a consulting engineer. Jones called on Munk, hoping that he would find him a job. He found a man who did not at all fit Langley's black propaganda. First, Munk was not a thick-accented Germanic crank. His English was fluent and free of strange inflections. (One thing that had enraged the Langley scientists was an offer by Munk to teach *them* English!) Second, he had adapted so well that he had been able to pass the Virginia bar examination and now practiced as a patent lawyer. And third, as Jones discovered by accepting Munk's invitation to enroll in his evening class, Munk was a sympathetic and brilliant teacher. As well as teaching aerodynamic theory, Munk liked to debate philosophy, and, driving Jones home from class (with a firm hand on the wheel), he would discuss Kant and Goethe as well as Russian literature, which he read in Russian.

Although not *in extremis*, Munk was working well below his potential. Patent law brought in a little money, and he worked as a consulting editor for the magazine *Aero Digest*. One can imagine the two of them in the car, Jones full to the brim with half-formed knowledge, and Munk ranging the world of ideas and science in an endless torrent. Jones soon perceived the lingering bitterness over the Langley experience, which tended to color Munk's contributions to the magazine. The stellar German theorist was playing out the role of a marginal, already half-forgotten pioneer, while retaining the mind of a true visionary.

It would be too simple to say that Jones, at Langley, became a covert disciple of Munk's, hoping to find a way to vindicate him. But Munk, through his interest in and encouragement of Jones, had become something of a mentor. Jones saw Munk's key contributions to aerodynamic theory as intense but narrow beams of revelation. In his own work Jones intended to widen those beams, to advance with a great deal more subtlety than was Munk's style, to apply Munk's principles to the numerous torments of the air. He was put to work in a wind tunnel test section as an "assistant scientific aide."

In the summer of 1935, von Karman took a cruise to Europe on the luxurious Italian liner *Conte de Savoie*, as a guest of Benito Mussolini, the Italian Fascist dictator. At the time, the trip seemed memorable only for the excesses of a state-sponsored scientific junket, and for the chance it gave to witness megalomania at first hand, when von Karman, as the leader of a delegation, walked across a hundred feet of marble to be presented to Il Duce.

Officially, it was the fifth Volta Congress on high-speed flight. The world of aerodynamics, as it came together in Rome, had grown into a cozy little village with its private and mystifying lingua franca. Mussolini had his own agenda. He identified world air speed records with national esteem, and was pressing his own airplane designers to surpass the British and the Germans, who kept pushing toward what was then the mark to beat, 400 mph. The Italians showed von Karman a new supersonic wind tunnel which, in a tiny test section, could simulate speeds of up to 2,500 mph. Von Karman wondered what the point of it was: it was like having a Ferrari in the garage that had no engine.

Von Karman was more impressed by a young German, Adolf Busemann, a protégé of the great Prandtl's at Göttingen, who delivered a paper at the conference that seemed of passing novelty. It suggested an airplane with wings that were swept back from the body like an arrowhead.

Sweepback itself wasn't a new idea. As early as 1911 it had been used in efforts to improve stability, and the British had tried it again, unmemorably, in 1930 on a "flying wing." Busemann proposed that a dartlike wing plan would work better than straight wings as an airplane approached the speed of sound.

Von Karman and a few others joined Busemann for dinner that night. An argument developed between Busemann and General Arturo Crocco, the director of scientific research for the

Italian air force. Crocco said that Busemann's paper had been too theoretical for his taste, and he wanted to offer a practical application. As von Karman and Busemann watched, Crocco spread out a napkin and sketched the airplane he thought Busemann was talking about. Its wings were swept very sharply back, at an angle of about 45 degrees, and the propeller blades were also hooked back at the tips. It looked very lean and racy. Very Italian. Von Karman thought that, like Crocco himself, the sketch was engaging but entirely fanciful, and he didn't give the swept wing another thought.

In Nazi Germany an experimental jet engine, developed for a paltry $20,000, was successfully run in 1937. By 1939 the Junkers company was developing a far more advanced engine, the Jumo 004, perceptibly the progenitor of what we know today as the turbojet. The task of designing an airplane for the Jumo engine fell to Willy Messerschmitt.

Airplane manufacture in Germany was more like a series of maverick fiefdoms than an industry. Willy Messerschmitt dominated the company that bore his name, but he was no despot. To an extraordinary degree, the Messerschmitt management style was like the Boeing style. Where Boeing used project engineers—Wells on the Flying Fortress, Beall on the Clippers—who eventually handed over to production engineers, Messerschmitt divided his staff at Augsburg between advanced design, employing a little less than a third of the engineers, and structural design and production. The advanced design team were treated as an elite, unfettered by a budget. As in Seattle, the two engineering teams were encouraged to solve problems by consensus.

No drawing ever went to the shop floor without Willy Messerschmitt's approval, and seldom without his changing it, but every idea had its hearing, every idea had its day, and every problem was tackled with originality. The design team for the airplane being fashioned around the Jumo, the Me 262, was led by an assertive individualist named Woldemar Voigt. One of Voigt's engineers knew of tests made in the Göttingen tunnel on wings using sweepback, carrying on the work begun by Busemann. Voigt had not heard of Busemann's 1935 paper, and he thought the swept wing tests, predicating flight at the fringes of the speed of sound, were too experimental to be of use to the Me 262, which, although intended to fly at more than 500 mph, far faster than any known Allied airplane, was not designed to court the problems of flight at high subsonic speeds.

In fact, minimal use was made of the wind tunnel in shaping the Me 262. It was more notable for the ingenuity of its construction than for its aerodynamics; it closely followed Jack Northrop's cellular approach and was both light in weight and cheap to produce. However, the Jumo engine grew in weight, and when it was slung under the Me 262's wings the airplane was nose-heavy. To counter this, the wings were mildly swept back.

The disconnection between advanced theory, as worked on by Busemann, and airplane development at plants like Messerschmitt was a characteristic flaw of the dispersed Nazi system of management. While the Me 262 was taking shape, Busemann and many of Germany's best aerodynamicists had been sent, literally, into the woods. In 1937, Hermann Goering, master of the Luftwaffe and the ruling Caesar of German aviation, had ordered the construction of a lavishly equipped secret research complex in a forest near Brunswick. The inhabitants of a village called Volkenrode saw strange things happening, but were told to keep quiet. Fifty-six buildings appeared, masquerading as farmhouses and outbuildings, none above tree level and some partly underground.

Once the war began, Busemann and his colleagues were spurred on by accurate intelligence reports on their British rivals. One name, in particular, recurred: Frank Whittle, a serving officer in the RAF who had struggled since 1930 to get backing to develop a jet engine. Whittle had begun work long before the Germans, and if he had seen Volkenrode he would have felt even more bitter than he already did about the meager support he was getting from the British government. In the summer of 1941, German intelligence had picked up vague accounts indicating American interest in the British engine.

NACA was more in the dark than the Germans. Not until a year after the Bell Airacomet flew were NACA's senior engineers officially briefed on America's secret jet engine developments. If anyone should have grasped the implications of the jet for the future of aerodynamic research, and therefore for the shape of the airplane of the future, it was NACA's theorists. In fact, only one of them, Eastman Jacobs, who had studied supersonic airflow since the thirties, realized that neither the British nor the Americans understood the potential of the jet engine for high-speed flight; they were, instead, trying to adapt it to conventional airplanes. Yet Jacobs failed to air his misgivings. He had frequently feuded with other senior NACA engineers, and this was fatal to the exchange of ideas within NACA, which was still locked into the inbred jealousies that had led to Munk's rejection.

NACA, in short, seemed like the least suitable intellectual climate for what would be the most enabling revelation of the jet age, and but for the presence there of the modestly situated Robert Jones it would have been. Since joining NACA, Jones had burrowed into an esoteric corner of research involving guided missiles. By today's meaning of the term, it was a crude art, without the benefit of sophisticated electronics for control and guidance. At NACA it was less glamorous than the mainstream work on conventional warplanes. Nonetheless, Jones's projects involved working beyond the accepted parameters of manned flight into the zone where dwelt the terrible demons of high speed.

A powerfully simple image haunted aerodynamicists as they faced the problems of flying faster: the sound barrier. There is no literal barrier. The popular notion that there was began its life with an innocent remark. In 1935 a British aerodynamicist, W. F. Hilton, was showing a reporter the new high-speed wind tunnel at the National Physical Laboratory near London. Doing his best to escape the arcana, Hilton explained: " . . . the resistance of a wing shoots up like a barrier against higher speed as we approach the speed of sound." Within hours, this phenomenon was described in print as "the sound barrier." It was the kind of sinister, ill-defined danger that popular journalism liked to uncover, and it made tangible something of uncertain form that would spook many people for more than a decade and become an essential part of an heroic mythology.

Here was something nasty in the sky that brave men would go up and seek out, pitting their lives against it. However, as the emotive phrase conjured up a phantom threat, it obscured the real one. Although there was, in reality, no physical barrier beyond which an airplane could not fly, there was, as the speed of sound was approached, a radical change in the behavior of the pressure fields surrounding the airplane—an altered state in the conditions of flight.

Fifty years of wind tunnel research had illuminated many, but by no means all, of the widely varying conditions in the air that governed the control and stability of an airplane. But as the speed of sound was approached, the conditions assumed a sudden violence that none of the conventional flight controls were designed to handle.

Not only airframe designers had a problem. Wind tunnels themselves failed to work at speeds at the threshold of the speed of sound and just above it. At Langley they could get a speed of Mach 1 in the high-speed tunnel when it was empty, but not when a model was sitting in the test section. Shock waves from the model bounced off the tunnel wall and wrecked the monitoring of the airplane's behavior; even in the small experimental supersonic tunnel, which could reach speeds of Mach 2, twice the speed of sound, the air choked in the tunnel around Mach 1. Transonic flight was a dark passage, like taking a boat through a storm knowing that on the other side the waters were probably as calm as those you were about to leave, but knowing also that some uncharted violence lay between.

In the later stages of the war, some of the faster Allied piston-engine airplanes began having sometimes fatal skirmishes with this violence, although at speeds well short of 500 mph. When the Luftwaffe's pilots began flying the Me 262 they moved much closer to the danger zone. In a dive, the Me 262's jet engines just wanted to go faster, but the airplane did not. At around 540 mph it was prone to pitching up suddenly, producing forces the airframe was not designed to survive. Pilots learned not to tempt fate.

Without exception, propeller-powered flight was at its limits. And the jet engine, itself producing no impediment to supersonic flight, awaited an aerodynamicist who could rethink the airplane's shape so that it could follow the engine's inclination. In Germany, Busemann and his colleagues were sure that they knew the answer. In America, thanks in part to the work of his old mentor, Max Munk, Robert Jones was about to stumble on the same solution.

The path by which a fundamental scientific discovery is

made is seldom glimpsed in advance. When the scientists involved look back on it from the vantage point of success they tend to limit themselves to the immediate deductive process. To the lay observer, however, it is the wild flux of life that contains the thunderbolts. For example, if a taxi driver in Macon, Missouri, had not been asked to let a young kid carry gas for a flying circus . . . if Congressman Lewis had not stepped into the elevator looking for a tutor . . . if Max Munk had not been teaching night school . . . and now, in August 1944, if Roger W. Griswold had not met Robert Jones in the laboratory at Langley . . .

Griswold arrived carrying a balsa model of an air-to-ground glide bomb, inelegantly dubbed a "glomb." The glomb had had a long and abortive pedigree, and but for the Griswold-Jones meeting it would have had no issue. It was the glomb's shape that engaged Jones's curiosity. It was like an arrowhead, an exotic and rare planform known to aerodynamicists as a delta wing, and in Griswold's version the wing was unusually thin. In talking to Griswold, Jones realized that the advocacy of the delta wing rested on what were, he suspected, flawed calculations based on a theory of the patriarch of Göttingen, Ludwig Prandtl.

Griswold used the calculations to argue the case of the delta wing's superior lift and drag characteristics, the crucial components of a wing's virtues and vices. When Griswold left Langley, Jones lingered over the problem. He felt he had to have independent scientific proof of the delta's qualities, but what *was* the right method for calculating the lift and drag of such a radically different wingform as this slender delta?

Then Jones remembered Munk. Early in his career, Munk had studied the hulls of the Zeppelin airships and produced a mathematical formula for analyzing the complex flow of air around a hull—Munk called this his slender body theory. In an intuitive flash, Jones recognized an affinity between the slender delta wing and the airship hull, though on the face of it the two would seem markedly different in form. It is important to realize that at this point Jones had no sense of being on the brink of a discovery. He had merely taken a step forward in trying actually to intuit the aerodynamic character of the thin delta wing. He had not perceived that it had any qualities that could propose a solution to the perplexities of high-speed flight.

Using the Munk formula, the picture Jones drew of the delta wing's characteristics had a striking feature, what is called the lift-curve slope. (Aerodynamicists produce very elegant diagrams that, even if they defy understanding, are an art form as satisfying as Egyptian pictography.) The delta wing appeared to have what was, to Jones, a surprisingly virtuous lift-curve slope, suggesting unusually low drag.

Jones began to believe that he was being led in his analysis of the glomb's wing toward a viable new theory of his own. There was the incidental satisfaction of acknowledging that Munk had served as a pathfinder. Although now intellectually as well as intuitively convinced of his putative theory, Jones felt that he was not ready to reveal the discovery in a way that would be acceptable to his peers at NACA. It seemed too glib.

He was also aware that he had a blind spot. He knew very little of a phenomenon called compressibility. Of all the demons lurking in the transonic zone, compressibility was thought to be the most destructive. It was known that as the airflow over a body broke down as the body tried to move from subsonic to supersonic speeds, areas of the flow were compressed and formed shock waves capable of smashing an airframe to pieces in seconds. Under these conditions, all the drilled abilities of pilot and airplane to retain control and stability were, in an instant, rendered useless.

The normal laws of flight were violated and, in some aspects, reversed: on the control stick, up was down and down was up. As a shock wave broke over a wing the wing's inherent characteristics—how it created lift, how it distributed drag, how it altered attitude and direction—were suddenly and violently redistributed. Pressures on the airframe's skin did a crazy dance. Vortexes formed and played on the control surfaces. Turbulence buffeted every limb, and in this redistribution of stresses, the loads that had been exactly allowed for in the structure of the airplane were no longer valid. A new regime of breaking points had been imposed by the new regime of stresses. Some of NACA's best efforts were going into trying to understand and master compressibility. NACA aerodynamicists wanted to be able to suggest how an airplane might be designed to survive its effects. Jones was not engaged in this work. Unveiling his slender wing theory without taking compressibility into account would, he felt, expose him to charges of superficiality. He stuffed his papers away in his desk.

But the theory was not so easily put to rest. As Jones

searched to find more support for it, he recalled a paper published in 1938 by a Chinese aerodynamicist, Hsue-shen Tsien, working under von Karman at Caltech. Tsien had produced an analytical solution to the behavior of the air around a projectile revolving in flight. In this paper, Tsien cited Munk's slender body theory (applied to the airship hull) and—for Jones this was the catalyst—showed that Munk's theory remained valid for air traveling at supersonic speeds. Until this point, Jones had confined his slender wing theory to very low subsonic speeds where there was no compressible flow. Now, prompted by Tsien's thesis that certain slender projectiles had no problem of compressibility when revolving at high speed, Jones applied the principles of his theory to supersonic speeds.

What he then saw was astounding: *the slender wing theory was impervious to Mach numbers.*

Ironically, Jones's relative ignorance of compressibility had left his mind open to accept this conclusion, whereas anyone immersed in the problem of compressibility would have balked— as, indeed, they later did balk—at the idea that Jones's wing could, in effect, cheat the compressibility effect. As Jones was able to reflect, more than forty years later, "If you know too much, it's hard to make progress. You have to know something, and if by accident you know the right thing, it works out."

But there remained one piece of the equation that was elusive: what *was* it about the delta wing (it was, after all, the delta planform that Jones had begun with) that gave it this property? Once more, incredibly, the answer lay with old work by Munk. In 1924, Munk had been working on problems of stability as they were governed by wing planform. One of the forms Munk looked at was sweepback. Looking at sweepback with his impulsive clarity, Munk had barely bothered to elaborate a conclusion he thought should have been obvious. He called this the independence principle, and it was this that Jones now recalled and applied to the delta wing. Munk had said, to put it baldly, that the flow of air over a wing was independent of the motion.

Since we are about to watch Jones reach the moment of revelation, we should appreciate what it is that we are witnessing—the birth of a mechanism which is so totally familiar that we take it as being natural to the art of flight, wings angled back from the centerline. Nothing, alas, would more easily rob this moment of its distinctive *frisson* than to attempt a detailed explanation of the independence principle. Let it be assumed that Jones had to work some abstruse mathematics, and that what they described was clear, if not simple: the wing went to its own fate independently of the rest of the airplane. It was predestined to this fate by its physical form. In this world, the aerodynamicist played God. Evolution and survival were functions of design. And the decisive feature of the delta wing was its angle of sweepback.

How did sweepback defy compressibility and the impact of the Mach number? School textbooks are fond of showing a picture of a speeding bullet in which a sharply angled wave breaks from above and below the point of the bullet. An airplane entering the sonic zone creates a similar wave. The impact of the airplane on the air ahead of it forms a cone of shock waves that break around the airplane. This is called the Mach cone. An airplane with a straight wing hits this cone and is engulfed by it; a wing that is sufficiently swept back, however, instead of being instantly swallowed in the cone, remains behind it. If the cone could think, it would simply decide that a wing was coming, but in the case of sweepback the wing fails to arrive when expected; it always stays behind the cone.

The combination of the slender wing—meaning a wing that is thin in cross section—and sweepback, the two physical characteristics that Jones had now combined in his theory, provided the optimum qualities for a transonic wing, and for a wing that would significantly and safely raise subsonic speeds. This was nothing less than the aerodynamic solution to the most forbidding problem of high-speed flight. But Jones knew that within the conservative culture of NACA he was getting farther and farther out on a limb—or more aptly, perhaps, that he was out on a wing and a prayer.

No one else at NACA had gone down this path. A considerable research effort was under way on the problems of high-speed flight, an effort of high priority consuming expensive resources, but not one thread had pointed in this direction. The work on compressibility, at the center of this effort, was led by a man notorious for his adamantine view that mathematics was the key to everything, and that rigorous mathematical proof was the sine qua non of research. Theodore Theodorsen, the head of the aerodynamics group, was another of NACA's legion of dog-matists, a Norwegian with a face that looked as though it had been fashioned and set by chilling Nordic blasts.

It was Theodorsen who had long feuded with Eastman Jacobs, ostensibly drawing the line between Jacobs as an experimentalist and Theodorsen as the classic theorist, but it was in reality a feud rooted in well-seasoned mutual animosity. As he did with any field he chose, Theodorsen had appropriated compressibility theory as his own sovereign turf. Yet he confined his work on compressible flow to only one element of the wing, its airfoil section. This was rather like believing that you could put out a spreading fire with one hose. By looking at the total wing, Jones had impertinently addressed and contained the larger threat, seeing it as a whole.

In fact, Theodorsen's position at NACA placed Jones and his slender wing theory in double jeopardy. Theodorsen would see the theory as a direct challenge to his sacred methodology. Jones himself had no such adamantine postures; he had kept, in an engaging way, the credulity of the ever open mind of a student, and expected others to do the same, but Theodorsen thought this trait another instance of American lack of discipline. Even more forbidding for Jones was that Theodorsen ran NACA's editorial committee, where every paper was reviewed and none was published without his consent.

Lacking a convincing file of mathematical equations, Jones needed a physical demonstration to support his theory. The only way this could be achieved was by using NACA's model supersonic tunnel. This was of minuscule dimensions, with a test section only nine inches wide, intended more to study the design of supersonic tunnels than to test wing theory. Jones explained his theory to two colleagues, and together they made a small metal model of a slender delta wing. It was only four inches long, with a wingspan of one and a half inches. Under these conditions not a lot could be expected, but the test did, at least, verify Jones's picture of the delta's promising lift-curve slope.

By now, Jones's theory was general knowledge within NACA. On March 5, 1945, as the European war was drawing to its close, he sent a formal announcement to Langley's chief of research, including this key passage very simply stating his case: "... theoretical analysis indicates that a V-shaped wing traveling point foremost would be less affected by compressibility than other planforms. In fact, if the angle of the V is kept small relative to the Mach angle, the lift and center of pressure remain the same at speeds both above and below the speed of sound."

It was impossible to withhold his work any longer from the scrutiny of the editorial committee. Jones combined both his propositions in one paper, the theory of the slender delta wing and the effect of sweepback on transonic airflow. For Jones, the latter discovery superseded in importance the former, and he made the sweep theory paramount in his paper. (He was, of course, right: the delta wing exhibited the virtues of sweepback, but the delta planform was not essential to sweepback.)

Theodorsen fell upon Jones's paper in characteristic style. He was emphatic that supersonic flow was radically different in nature from subsonic flow. Jones's idea that a wing traveling at supersonic speeds could actually have a subsonic flow—an outcome of the independence principle—struck Theodorsen as a particularly reckless heresy. He said he found parts of Jones's presentation *too* intuitive and recommended that he clarify his "hocus pocus" with some "real mathematics." This was familiar Theodorsen code for what he had always regarded as the sloppy ways of the American engineers who rushed into experiments without enough paperwork. But it was for the theory of sweepback that Theodorsen reserved his most withering scorn. It was, he said, "a snare and a delusion."

What then followed seems, in retrospect, to be irrational. Theodorsen decided, and the committee complied, that Jones could publish the part of the paper concerned with the slender delta theory, but *not* the part describing sweepback theory. Since the properties of the slender delta in supersonic flight were a direct demonstration of sweepback, this decision made no sense to Jones (nor did it forty years later, although he was by then able to look on it with the kinder humor of the vindicated).

In the course of the committee's debate over Jones's paper, one of the editors found a copy of Adolf Busemann's 1935 paper on high-speed flight that had been delivered in Rome, a paper that had lain unnoticed in the NACA files. Had anyone realized the significance of Busemann's advocacy of sweepback at the time, of course, Jones would have been beaten to it. But two things conspired to bury Busemann's paper in the heavy traffic of scientific exchanges: sweepback was a small part of his thesis, and there was no imperative to face up to the problems of supersonic flight. Moreover, Busemann had not made the discovery so essential to Jones's case, of placing the swept wing *behind* the Mach cone. In Busemann's paper the wing was *inside* the cone. Finding the Busemann paper did nothing to help Jones.

Deeply frustrated, Jones went over Theodorsen's head to NACA's chief in Washington, George Lewis. He requested that more model testing be done. But before this had any results, a chance meeting with Professor Tsien of Caltech took the idea out of NACA's hands—and, ultimately, put it into the hands of Boeing.

Jones and Tsien met at Princeton as delegates to a conference of mathematicians. During a coffee break, Jones told Tsien what had happened at Langley, and outlined his theory. Tsien had good cause to listen carefully. He knew Jones's reputation, and since his own work had prompted Jones's reasoning he could assimilate the idea easily and with a certain self-satisfaction— Tsien had a well-developed ego. It was a fateful conversation.

Tsien, like George Schairer, had been recruited to von Karman's team of scientists, being held in readiness to plunder the scientific secrets of Nazi Germany. In fact, the choice of Schairer had been attacked, as favoring one company over others, suggesting that von Karman was really choosing Boeing, not Schairer. Von Karman stood his ground, asserting that Schairer was there on his own merit.

The morning after his conversation at Princeton with Jones, Tsien was back in Washington, telling Schairer about the swept wing theory. Schairer knew all about the demons of supersonic flight, and the proposition that they might be exorcised in one stroke got his full attention. He and Tsien decided that together they would figure out whether or not they agreed with Jones, but it was not until two weeks later, flying to Germany, that the opportunity presented itself.

George Schairer Writes Home and Wild Things
4   ■   Happen in the Tunnel

It was the rigors of flying the Atlantic in 1945 that finally allowed Tsien and Schairer the isolation in which they could put Jones's sweepback theory through their own mathematical wringer. They flew in a Douglas C-54, the militarized DC-4, and it was a tiresome route via Nova Scotia, the Azores, and Villacoublay, a military air base outside Paris. Incarcerated in the noisy, wind-buffeted airplane, they scribbled equations on pads, tested every stage of the theory, and eventually brought two others into the debate, von Karman and Hugh Dryden, an aerodynamicist who had been working on supersonic flow since the 1920s and had been at the Volta conference in Rome with von Karman.

Before the airplane touched down in France they were all convinced that Jones was right.

The flight had taken twenty-six hours. As they waited for their bags to be unloaded on the tarmac at Villacoublay, von Karman began pacing with the vigor of an animal released from a cage; pacing was a regular part of von Karman's thought mechanism, and Schairer had known him to pace with such preoccupation that he could pass within two feet of someone and never see him. Suddenly he came to a dead stop in front of Schairer, eyes ablaze. "Now I know," he said, "why you want to go fast!"

Von Karman's team operated under the unlikely code name "Lusty." They had a list of German research centers—and scientists—they wanted to see as soon as possible, even though the war was still rolling over the German plains toward Berlin. The Russians had already taken the prize secret weapons center at Peenemünde on the Baltic, where the V-1 and V-2 rockets had been created and tested, denying von Karman, who had been working on rockets, the most tantalizing revelations. Wernher von Braun, though, the pioneer of the ballistic missile, was held by the Allies in prison at Garmisch, out of the Russians' reach. Von Karman was anxious to get to Göttingen, to seek out Ludwig Prandtl, but the American First Army had not yet secured the city. So he decided to take the Lusty team to another of his old academic pastures, Aachen.

They flew to Maastricht in liberated Holland, near the German border, and arrived on the morning the war ended. The town was *en fête*. Von Karman recalled the emerging anti-Semitism of his last days in Aachen. Now the wheel had come full circle, the terror had come and gone, and the Dutch were free. But what would the German mood be? What had been going on in his old wind tunnel at Aachen?

He had scant chance to find out. They had barely crossed the border into Germany when von Karman had an urgent message from his controllers in Paris. A vast secret German research center had just been discovered in the forest near Brunswick. The fake farm camouflage had served well: Volkenrode had remained undetected from the air through the war, and not one intelligence report had so much as hinted at the existence of what turned out to be German aviation's prize research center. Volkenrode had been run by Hermann Goering's director of research, Adolf Baumker, and more than a thousand scientists had worked there. When von Karman's team drove into Volkenrode in jeeps they could not believe the scale of the place.

There had been some looting by advancing troops, but the laboratories and wind tunnels were largely intact, and had clearly functioned until the last days of the war. The Lusty team split up to follow their own specialties. Von Karman, Schairer, Tsien, and Dryden went to the aerodynamic laboratories, and almost immediately they discovered that the Germans had devoted a large part of their effort to the problems of high-speed flight. They were ahead of the Americans in shaping jets to fly faster than sound. They had a swept wing in the tunnel.

The German scientists were confined to their living quarters, under military guard. The army gave von Karman a list of names. He and Schairer were familiar with many of them, and none was more intriguing than that of Adolf Busemann. The morning after von Karman's arrival, soldiers were sent to bring selected scientists for a first round of interrogation by the Lusty team. Some of the Germans were hostile and unresponsive (tardy efforts had been made to destroy papers); others, including Busemann, behaved as though the war had been almost a distraction and now, once again in the company of their scientific peers, they could catch up on each other's work.

When Busemann faced von Karman he seemed surprised by the urgency of the questions about the swept wing.

"But you must know all about it," he said. "I gave a lecture in Italy in 1935 on the subject." He concentrated on von Karman and Dryden. "You were there. We all had dinner that night. The Italian general drew a picture of an airplane on a napkin. I remember, he called it the airplane of the future. He passed it around. Surely, you remember?"

Schairer and Tsien looked at their colleagues.

"Of course," said von Karman. "I remember."

Von Karman and Dryden never revealed to Busemann that they had forgotten Busemann's theory almost as soon as they had heard it. Nor did they disclose that they had only just been converted to another interpretation of it, thanks to Robert Jones. Schairer already knew, from looking at the German papers, that although they had not put an airplane with sweepback into the air, the Germans were at least a year ahead in understanding how to use it.

On May 10, Schairer sat down and wrote a seven-page letter to Seattle. Hoping to avoid the delay that censorship could cause, he wrote "Censored" on the envelope and signed it in a way he thought might look authoritative. Each page of the letter had "G. S. Schairer" printed at the top, like a memo pad. In a careful, spidery script Schairer wrote to Ben Cohn, who was running the Boeing aerodynamics department in Schairer's absence. After a few pleasantries about the relative comforts of the Lusty team's quarters (Schairer was particularly amused that his electric shaver had been running on Nazi-generated current before Germany capitulated), he crisply described sweepback theory, providing on the third page a simple sketch of a swept wing and the essence of the formula.

No mention was made of Jones. Instead, Schairer told Cohn: "The Germans have been doing extensive work on high-speed aerodynamics. This has led to one important discovery. Sweepback and sweepforward have a very large effect on critical Mach No." And there was one final, morale-boosting salutation to Seattle: "My best to all the gang. They are sure tops in all comparisons." Schairer was aware of the psychological power of the German reputation over the American; it would not have seemed so urgent to explain that Jones already had the same understanding of why the swept wing worked—and urgency was of the essence. Schairer gathered a collection of German data on microfilm at Volkenrode, but he wanted Cohn to get a swept wing into the new tunnel at Seattle right away.

As other Allied scientists fanned out through Germany, they found more solid evidence that the swept wing was very close to being turned into metal. Junkers had been working on a bomber with the wings swept *forward* by 25 degrees; it seemed anomalous, but wind tunnel tests had not then distinguished the superiority of sweepback, and in theory both held out promise. Much more viable was a design found on the drawing boards at Messerschmitt's bombproof development center in the mountains near Oberammergau. This had a sweepback of 45 degrees. Woldemar Voigt, along with other German engineers and a squadron or so of Me 262s, would soon be shipped to America.

Before the Lusty team left Germany there was a disenchanting encounter at Göttingen. The draw to von Karman of going there must have involved some private sense of reckoning: as a Jew he was becoming aware of the appalling fate met by those he had left in Germany; as a scientist he remembered Göttingen University as a remarkably syncretic place where Lutherans, Catholics, Anglicans, and Jews had worked together in fevers of discovery under great teachers like Ludwig Prandtl.

Göttingen University, sometimes called the Georgia Augusta after its sponsor, George II of England, was founded in 1734 on a fairly narrow imperial notion of learning in philosophy, philology, and law, but it had grown into the supreme powerhouse of European mathematics. This, in turn, led to further dominance in the applied sciences. Fluid dynamics, for example, posed the kind of nasty and elusive problems that Göttingen's physicists thrived upon, and by the beginning of the twentieth century, aerodynamics, which was similar to fluid dynamics and equally elusive of solutions, had attracted a hard core of Göttingen's finest minds, like Munk and von Karman.

Von Karman and Schairer found Prandtl. He was complaining that the roof of his home had been blown off by American bombing. In the same breath, he asked von Karman if there was any research he could do for the Americans in the future. Von Karman lost all tolerance, and snarled at his old mentor: "You will work for *anybody*, just like a prostitute."

Prandtl, who had elevated aerodynamics from a speculative pursuit to a consummate science, had no social ethic at all.

While von Karman's team was still in Germany, Jones found a new ally in testing his theory of wingsweep, Robert Gilruth, a young Minnesotan with a strong originality of his own, who ran NACA's flight research section at Langley. Gilruth had instigated a way of testing wing theory in supersonic airflow that avoided all the problems of the wind tunnel—by turning an airplane's wing into a test platform. Pilots flying the P-51 Mustang fighter had reported that under certain conditions, they could see in shadow form the shock waves moving across the airplane's wings. The Mustang had the most aerodynamically sophisticated wing of its time; it was an airplane designed in a hurry that got just about every detail right (it is still much loved today by airplane preservationists), and in a dive at a speed of about Mach 0.75, parts of the air over its wings flowed at supersonic speeds without inducing shock.

Gilruth had been able to deduce this from the pilots' accounts, and realized that if a small model of a wing section could be attached to the right part of a Mustang's wing, complete with the monitoring instruments normally used in a wind tunnel, it would provide valuable data during the brief period of supersonic flow. This was deeply offensive to Langley orthodoxy. How on earth could you ask pilots to dive Mustangs to the limits of their tolerance and get meaningful results from tiny wing sections stuck upright in the slipstream? There was, indeed, a danger to the pilots, so Gilruth fitted the test Mustang with sensors to warn of impending control problems. And, very quickly, he was proved right: the tests yielded a far higher quality of data than any so far achieved in the tunnel.

Gilruth agreed to test a thin, swept wing on the Mustang. Jones waited for the results. And waited. Gilruth was uncharacteristically evasive. He said they were having trouble with the monitoring instruments. Finally Jones realized the problem: Gilruth did not *believe* the results. They showed remarkably lower drag than anyone had seen on any other kind of wing tested at supersonic speed. The thin, swept wing *was* beyond doubt the answer.

Theodorsen was now an emperor without clothes. Later, the editorial committee approved the publication of the crucial wingsweep section of Jones's original paper, and the two papers remain in the archives to this day, separate and in the wrong sequence, with the thin delta wing first.

And what of Max Munk, whose work had led his pupil to what was arguably the most important perception made in aerodynamic theory by an American since the Wright Brothers? Some years later, Jones went to see Munk, who was living near the University of Maryland. He took with him Adolf Busemann, who by this time was working in America. Jones was very keen to convey to Munk how he had extended Munk's slender body theory, and the providential results.

Munk wasn't interested. His mind had moved on. He was polite, but he was wrestling with a new demon, turbulence. The swept wing did not excite him at all. He was still the same Munk, for whom a problem solved was a problem forgotten.

The material uncovered by teams like Lusty was shipped in bulk to the United States for analysis, along with many of its complying authors. A staggering total of more than three million documents, weighing fifteen hundred tons, was microfilmed in Europe and sent to the Bureau of Aeronautics in Washington for analysis and to determine what action should be taken.

Boeing was not the only company with access to this plunder. Two Douglas engineers, L. Eugene Root and A.M.O. Smith, followed Schairer and von Karman to Göttingen, where they microfilmed papers for the U.S. Navy. Early in August, data on German work on the swept wing unearthed by Root and Smith arrived at the Douglas offices in California. Douglas was working with the Navy to develop some experimental aircraft to investigate the problems of flight at high subsonic and transonic speeds.

NACA and the Navy had been critical of Douglas's first designs, which were conceived more with an eye to immediate production than for the peculiar needs of a high speed test aircraft. Under pressure, the design was revised as a prototype, the D-558. It had a straight, not swept, wing. At this point, Jones's thesis on sweepback became known to the Navy, and NACA suggested that the D-558 should incorporate a wing swept back by 35 degrees. Douglas, however, persuaded them that it was too soon to apply the theory to a prototype without more tunnel testing. This attitude changed, almost overnight, with the arrival of the data from Göttingen, and design began on a second Douglas prototype with a swept wing. This became the Douglas Skyrocket, which would join other hot ships to be tested by an elite team of test pilots at Muroc Dry Lake in California.

Jones could not help but notice the reverence with which his colleagues looked at the German data. The Germans were, he reflected with a gentle sarcasm, well known to be the last word in aerodynamics. Indeed, it was as though Herr Goebbels were still directing Nazi propaganda. When NACA's scientists, the Army Air Forces engineers at Wright Field, and the research heads of the American airplane companies gazed at all the marvels conjured up in the German laboratories, from the V-2 rocket to the swept wing jet, it was hard to believe that Germany had actually lost the war.

They had, in fact, won a psychological victory. As the Allied scientists plundered the material, an infatuation set in. It was driven, in part, by an inferiority complex. The American aerodynamicists had walked for the first time into the halls of the medieval universities like Göttingen; it was impossible not to sense the values of European intellectual life as expressed in the texture of these ancient cities. Caltech and Langley had no roots—they were prosaic and purely functional establishments. And what would they have been without their mentors from Mitteleuropa? Even Mad Max had turned out not to be mad at all—he simply demanded more of American imagination than America was prepared to give him.

It was possible from the luxury of such an absolute military conquest suddenly to feel generous about the fallen enemy. It was not the German scientific establishment that had been defeated, but its masters. Few people were in a mood to ask, when beguiled by what they found behind the hangar doors in Germany, whether this really had been a superior scientific performance. For example, a prize swiftly shipped back to America, along with the Me 262s, was the little rocket-powered Messerschmitt 163 Komet. This was a tailless interceptor, literally a "flying wing" that in a short operational life acquired an aura of futurism. The truth belied the appearance: the Komet's rocket engine frequently blew up and the plane was uncontrollable at high speeds. Aerodynamically it led nowhere, and even its creator gave up on the concept, yet it has inspired an enduring fan club and numerous hagiographies.

In America, a plane as lethal as the Komet, if conceived, would never have reached operational service. It would have, rightly, remained an experimental curiosity. The uncritical adulation of things German obscured what American aviation had actually itself achieved during the war. The German research work had been dissipated, not concentrated on the realistic use of the available ideas. The Luftwaffe, for example, had never been provided with a heavy bomber, while the Allies had—as shown by the case of the B-17—committed themselves to four-engine bombers long before the outbreak of war.

As the preeminent mass producer of four-engine bombers, Boeing had come of age during the war. The B-29 was to become, as promised, the airplane that ended the war, over Hiroshima and Nagasaki.

Claire Egtvedt, from his office as chairman, had been running the company since the death of its president, Phil Johnson, in 1944. (Johnson had unsnarled Boeing's plants and built the production lines that had disgorged the B-17s and B-29s.) Egtvedt had no appetite to continue beyond the time it would take to find a new president. He felt that none of the engineers had the broader background now needed to run the company. It was a sensitive problem. The engineers were like a college of car-

dinals gathered around two popes, Wells and Schairer. An outsider would not find these men easily malleable.

Egtvedt turned to the company attorney, Bill Allen, who
had been there for twenty years, fourteen of them on the board.
Allen balked. He felt he lacked the technical grasp that running
Boeing required. He had great respect for the engineers and
failed to see how they would take direction from someone who
could not speak their recondite tongue. Instead of taking the
job, Allen agreed to go around the country looking for a new
president. It was during this hiatus that Ben Cohn received
Schairer's letter from Volkenrode.

Cohn realized at once the immensity of what Schairer was
proposing: not just to prove the swept wing theory in the tunnel,
but to apply it *immediately* to a design then in gestation. Late
in 1943, the Army Air Forces had invited Boeing and four other
manufacturers to submit designs for the first American jet
bomber. By November 1944, four companies—Boeing, North
American, Convair, and Martin—were committed to building
prototypes.

The Army wanted the bomber to fly at a minimum speed
of 500 mph at an operating altitude of between 35,000 and 40,000
feet. Thus were set the objectives for a new generation of bombers intended to optimize the jet engine's virtues of high speed
and altitude (its vice was an insatiable thirst for fuel, which
severely inhibited the airplane's range). No one at Boeing could
fail to see the significance of this contract. Whoever built the
Army Air Forces' first jet bomber would have a commanding
foothold in the dawning jet age.

Schairer's advocacy, at this late stage, of an idea as radical
and untested as the swept wing alarmed Cohn. But when
Schairer—even a Schairer some seven thousand miles distant—
wanted something done in Seattle it was done. The aerodynamicists puzzled over the three pages of the letter detailing the
formula, sensing that somewhere in the numbers a genie was
waiting to be released: as Schairer scrawled out the numbers
his script became compacted, as though wrought with the thrill
of it all. His fountain pen was running out of ink. He sketched
a wing with 29 degrees of sweep and scratched out the equations
that provided the mathematical proof.

At first, in their own paper exercises, Cohn's staff couldn't get the result Schairer claimed. Cohn tried again—and realized that they had not accounted for a fundamental, the changed direction of the airflow over the swept wing (Schairer's letter had pointed this out). Old habits died hard; they were in an unfamiliar aerodynamic regime beyond the established calculus. But, on paper at least, the theory of sweep checked out.

At the time, Wells, who was in charge of developing the jet bomber, was unhappy with the preliminary designs. They were testimony to Eastman Jacobs's complaint that American and British thinking had not adjusted to the demands and potential of the jet engine as rapidly as had the Germans. Boeing's first two outline designs, models 432 and 424, represented the state of the art at the end of the war—conventional, straight-wing airplanes cleaned up for higher speeds; their only outward surprise was the lack of propellers.

North American, Convair, and Martin had gone the same way: you could have replaced the jet engines with piston engines and everything else remained familiar. The Martin XB-48 did have one innovation that interested Wells, a bicycle landing gear arrangement instead of the usual tricycle. Two sets of fat wheels on the centerline retracted directly into the fuselage, leaving the airplane's wing, free of wheel wells, to be thinner. Otherwise all four competitors were too similar for Wells's comfort— Boeing had failed to come up with the edge that had always been expected of it since the B-17.

And now Wells looked at Schairer's letter. Was the swept wing the edge? He knew it would take months, even years, to take this raw theory and build it into a new airplane. And it didn't matter how good an idea like this looked in the tunnel. In the air it was always another story. The three competitors were at the point of freezing the design of their prototypes. If Boeing adopted the swept wing, its prototype, the XB-47, would be the last to fly by as long as it took to master the new wing. Once more, as so often at Boeing, everything was on the line for the sake of one unprecedented idea.

Schairer's wing put the company's fate into the hands of the aerodynamicists more completely than had any previous project, and Wells could see this. The old balance of specializations among the engineers—structures, aerodynamics, power plant, systems, fabrication, production, flight test—had perceptibly shifted. In the early thirties the development of the all-metal monoplanes, beginning with the 247, had placed a new reliance on the structural engineers, whose craft became far more sophisticated and demanded far higher academic qualifications. Since Schairer's arrival, and culminating in the opening of the Boeing high-speed wind tunnel, the aerodynamicists gained primacy.

This involved no petty political squabbles over turf, and no contests for individual power. It was simply that in the evolving science of designing an airplane, primacy passed to where there were the most problems to solve. Designing an airplane still involved a panoply of talents, but they were pushing inexorably into the great darkness of high-speed flight where the first light was carried by the aerodynamicists—or, as they were now being called at Boeing, the aeromen.

This change cast Wells in a role that no company title could signify. In Seattle he was the supreme polymath among the engineers; at Wright Field he was the supreme salesman without any of the glibness of a salesman. The military clients listened because he never wasted a word. At thirty-five he was only chronologically junior to Beall, who was thirty-eight. Beall was beginning to suffer from a common liability among the old-style hustling salesmen. He had a drinking problem.

To the engineers, the ascetic Wells was their leader. And now it was Wells, more than anyone, who kept the delicate equilibrium in which Schairer and the aeromen were allowed to have their run with the swept wing. Wells alone seemed to have somewhere in his bones, free of any scientific reasoning, a sense of where things were going—and a resolve that Boeing should be there.

Bill Allen already recognized in Wells the company's engineering soul. And Allen was agonizing over whether to take the top job himself; his trawl of the country had been fruitless. Other board members had been playing on his fealty to the company. They didn't agree that he was fatally handicapped by his lack of technical knowledge. Allen had *size:* he could represent Boeing's interests on an equal footing with any other company president or any senator. But Allen thought they didn't know him as well as he knew himself. His inclination was dictatorial, and Boeing was not like a law practice—it needed a leader who could influence, not dominate.

It was a desolate time in Allen's personal life. His wife,

Dorothy, had recently died of cancer, at the age of forty-three, leaving two young daughters. It had been a marriage of kindred spirits; she was also from Montana, the daughter of a politician who had made a name there as a progressive Republican, Joseph Dixon. As a senator and then as governor, Dixon had fought the hegemony enjoyed over the state by the Anaconda Mining Company. Allen had married directly after graduating from Harvard Law School, and Dorothy had stoically borne the early years of Allen's frequently dangerous flights on Boeing's mail planes and fledgling airline.

Allen was half Irish and half Scottish. The Scottish part had always been uncomfortable with the free spending at Boeing— free spending, admittedly, not on junketing but on the latest engineering dream. It was not a business in which Scottish parsimony would win affection, as the different corporate climate at Douglas demonstrated. (Donald Douglas had resisted bidding for the jet bomber, frustrating his own engineers, to concentrate on the money-spinning extension of the DC-4 series of airliners.) Financially, a new airplane could be a bottomless pit. On the other hand, Allen had grown up with Boeing, and seen its emergence in the war as a national asset. The Irish in him liked a gamble. He took the job.

In September 1945, a week after Allen became president of the Boeing Airplane Company, a proposal to change the XB-47 configuration to a swept wing went to Wright Field. The aeromen had worked quickly: within a week of Schairer's letter arriving, they had put the first crude test wing in the tunnel. It was a rectangular wing, six times as long as wide, which could swing back to an angle of 30 degrees.

They were looking for the critical Mach number: the speed at which the flow over the wing began its transonic dance. As they increased the angle of the wing, so the critical Mach number rose. QED: the theory worked as well in the tunnel as it had on paper. At once they could see the significance for the XB-47. The bomber was not intended to be supersonic, but by postponing the onset of the critical Mach number they could have it fly far closer to the speed of sound than any straight-wing bomber, so creating an unmatchable margin in top speed.

Another benefit came with the speed. The Army was greatly concerned about range. The early generation of jet engines for which the B-47 was designed had an efficiency roughly proportional to the speed of the airplane; if the airplane flew 50 percent faster it would get 50 percent more miles per pound of fuel burned. The swept wing would render the jet engine more efficient at the bomber's optimum performance.

Wiser heads among the aeromen were not ready to see the swept wing as a paragon. In aerodynamics you seldom get anything for nothing, and a gain in speed of this magnitude looked too easy, too much like a free lunch. It was time to move from the simple test wing, proving the theory, to something much more like the wing that the bomber would need.

It was unusual at Boeing to have done anything that was purely theoretical, and it was typical that its engineers should leap impatiently from the abstract to the practical. (In a research laboratory like Langley, the engineers would have been content to play with the theory for months, refining and extending it, but NACA wasn't in the business of building airplanes and meeting contracts.) And so the process now embarked upon was characteristically empirical. There were no computers to crunch the numbers; some use was made of desk calculators, but the aeroman's instrument of choice was the slide rule (and remained so into the age of computers). If there was a group philosophy at work at this critical point, it was very much shaped by the MIT background that so many of the aeromen shared, and particularly the laboratory style of Doc Draper. They remembered that Draper always preferred to fix a problem in the laboratory and only then write all the fancy equations that went with it—frequently it fell to Draper's brightest students (some of whom were now working in the Boeing tunnel) to compose these post-hoc "theories."

For one of the engineers taking his first look at the swept wing, there was a jolting sense of *déjà vu*. In 1940 the Curtiss Wright company of St. Louis had designed an experimental fighter, the XP-55. It had wings that could be swung backward. A model of these wings was tested in the MIT tunnel, under the eyes of Bob Withington. Tests were run with the wings swept as sharply back as 20 degrees. In fact, the Curtiss Wright designers were worried that in this configuration the airplane would go *too* fast for the safety of its airframe (it was, after all, a propeller-powered machine, not a jet). The tests in Cambridge were run at only 150 mph, and the model was moved to NACA's tunnel at Langley for higher speeds. At Cambridge, Withington had noticed that both the NACA and Curtiss Wright engineers were so concerned about shock waves on the wing that they ignored all data that did not seem related to this. Withington suspected that something had been indicated in the tunnel about the swept wing's properties at higher speeds that was unusual and probably very significant. He pressed the NACA technicians to give him the overlooked data, but they never did. Now, as Cohn monitored the performance of Boeing's first crude swept wings, Withington realized that the key to Jones's theory had almost certainly been buried in the NACA data of 1940.

To lead the half-dozen or so aerodynamicists who would develop the bomber in the tunnel, Wells and Schairer chose Bill Cook. The choice mystified Cook himself; he had never worked on high-speed aerodynamics. But his knowledge of how to use the tunnel, which he and Withington had refined together, turned out to more than compensate for this handicap. The tunnel was the great enabler. It gave Boeing six times the wind tunnel time available to any competitor. Moreover, no prying eyes could see the work. Designing the wing involved literally thousands of decisions that could add up to an invaluable asset, a proprietary store of knowledge. A competitor could look at the wing, measure it even, and make a good guess about its internal structure. But a wing has as many invisible tricks built into its shape as a Savile Row suit; you would need to tear it apart and study every strand to figure out its secrets.

The most consequential decision that had to be taken when theory gave way to a solidified airplane was the angle of sweep. Astonishingly, this decision was left to one of the most junior aerodynamicists, Victor Ganzer. He chose an angle of 35 degrees sweepback on the basis that this optimized both the performance of the airplane and the power of the jet engines. Not long afterward, Ganzer left to teach at the University of Washington, having bequeathed to Boeing, in what seemed relatively casual circumstances, a synthesis good enough to underpin the design of a generation of airplanes, military and commercial.

The secrecy afforded by the tunnel not only preserved successes—it masked embarrassments. And at first, the swept wing created for the XB-47 was an unmitigated disaster. Even though, by raising the critical Mach number, sweepback delivered a huge advantage in speed, it ruined everything else. In its inchoate state, Ganzer's chosen wing was a wild thing—an unleashed mustang that not even the most fearless cowboy pilot would be able to tame or ride. A wing as radical as this violated the equilibrium carefully evolved since the Wrights had figured out how to turn, climb, and dive safely. The normal control surfaces simply could not deal with it—the swept wing had a mind of its own and would flip the plane over in seconds. The wing in the tunnel was unflyable.

The problem of control was compounded by another: where could they put the engines?

The straight-wing model that had evolved in Schairer's absence had four jet engines buried in the fuselage above the wing. The first model to be sketched with the swept wing, 448, had them in the same configuration, with an air intake for all four in the nose. The Army took one look at this and summoned Wells to Wright Field.

Wells was taken to the tunnel, where they had installed a full-size fuselage of a Lockheed P-80 fighter, which had its jet engine behind the cockpit. Holes had been drilled in the engine to simulate gunfire damage. As Wells watched, they started the engine and jets of fire appeared from the holes like blowtorches. The results were dramatic and unambiguous: with only a few hits in the engine, an operational airplane would become a ball of fire. This was a fighter, with one engine. The bomber as Boeing had designed it, with *four* engines adjacent to the crew, would be a flying crematorium. Wells was told to come back with an airplane that could take bullets without frying its crew.

At this bleak moment the two problems, of wing sweep and engine location, seemed intractable and likely to doom the XB-47 before it became anything more than a wind tunnel model. There was little taste at Wright Field for the swept wing. It provoked a hard core of opposition among a group the Boeing engineers called the laboratory mafia, a clique of veteran colonels who were supposed to be the Army Air Forces' eyes to the future. Their sympathy for the XB-47 had not been helped by encounters with Schairer, who swiftly judged them to be dolts. Schairer's contempt was, as always when faced with lesser minds, open and sometimes audible.

These "full bird" colonels had no knowledge of Jones's paper, no knowledge of Busemann's work, and no grasp of Schairer's arguments for the principle of wing sweep. And yet they were the ones who would have to sanction the funding for Boeing to proceed with the change in the XB-47 prototype. They convened among themselves like a Star Chamber to decide the fate of the project—knowing that any one of Boeing's three competitors could give them an airplane that safely represented the world that they knew. The tone of this meeting was set by a colonel who asked why the Air Forces should have to pay for "Schairer's wet dream."

Fortunately for Boeing, it had a covert friend in this assembly. Lieutenant Colonel Henry E. Warden had just arrived at Wright Field to head the bombardment branch of the engineering division. "Pete" Warden was of another generation, promoted rapidly in the war and familiar with the new thinking of the jet age. After the meeting, when it looked as if Boeing would be told to revert to the orthodox straight wing, Warden told an aide to call Wells, explain the problem, and get him back to Dayton.

In one of his finest moments, Wells—emollient where Schairer was abrasive, seasoned at dealing with men he had no more respect for than did Schairer—faced the reconvened mafia and talked them into the swept wing. It was, though, at that point a limited victory. Boeing was being indulged, being allowed to play. Nonetheless, but for Warden's intervention the military could have stumbled at the threshold of the jet age.

There remained the problem of where to put the engines. Flying back from Wright Field with Bob Jewett, Boeing's head of preliminary design, Wells began sketching alternatives. Jewett did the same. There were not that many choices. The Air Forces wanted the engines isolated from the crew and the bomb load. That really left only the wing. But if, like piston engines, they were put inside nacelles which were hung directly on the wing—the solution adopted by their three rivals—an engine fire from bullet penetration would still be fatal to the wing. (Both Wells and Schairer had painful memories of the Flying Fortresses lost over Germany when an engine fire burned through a wing in seconds.)

Wells suggested lowering the engines under the wing, clear

from its structure, on struts. If there was an engine fire the slipstream would carry the flames under the wing, not through it. To describe what followed as empirical research falls far short of its bizarre, almost farcical, appearance. It was the crudest improvisation, carried out with a touch of desperation.

The wing—only the wing, with no other part of the airplane attached—was mounted so that it stuck up from the floor of the tunnel. Two of the wing's characteristics were critically influenced by where the engine nacelles were positioned: the drag of the wing itself and the distribution of what were called the pressure peaks of the wings and the nacelles. The nacelles, essentially tubes encasing the jet engine, had their own aerodynamic profile. There was no previous experience to draw upon in predicting the pattern of this profile, except that it was understood that if the pressure fields of the nacelle and the wing intersected, the aeromen would be facing another nightmare. There was nothing for it but to put the nacelles in a variety of positions under the wing and see what happened. This became known as the broomstick method. The nacelles were stuck on the end of sticks (actually rather more substantial than a broomstick) and set in position. It had been decided to increase the number of engines from four to six, three to each wing. Two engines were mounted in a double nacelle and one engine in a single nacelle.

As they moved the "broomstick" searching for the right place to put each of the nacelles, they realized how sensitive the arrangement was: relatively small changes made things radically better or worse. Gradually, by trial and error, a pattern emerged. When the nacelles were placed forward of the wing the complex flow of air into the engines and around the nacelles sorted itself out without compromising the wing's own airflow— the double nacelle worked best slung forward of and below the wing, about a third of the way out from the fuselage, and the single nacelle could go right out to the wingtip. They had tried around fifty different positions when they settled on this configuration. Schairer put the essence of the solution succinctly: the two of them, the wing and the nacelle, had to go to the high Mach number each in its own way.

Although the aeromen now felt that they knew where to put the engines, the structural engineers had never looked at a

wing like this, with the engine weight slung so low, so far forward, and so far apart. What was "clean" aerodynamically was,
structurally, a new architecture. It seemed unnatural, the engines dangling out there on pylons, the unusually long and thin
wing—nine and a half times longer than it was wide. If this was
the future according to George Schairer, it was like nothing that
anyone could have anticipated.

Out of this arbitrary arrangement, all stemming from the
military client's refusal to have the engines in the body, the
designers, groping for a formula that would reconcile structural
integrity with aerodynamic balance, made their own luck. The
first step was unorthodox. Instead of proposing a rigid wing,
the structures men outlined a wing that would be unusually
flexible, designed to bend with the aerodynamic stresses as it
carried the loads of the underslung engines. This was called an
"aeroelastic" wing, an image that was, if anything, an under-
statement. The wild animal was getting wilder—now they had
a swept wing that danced to its own tune, not only bending but
twisting torsionally. But, as they watched this bucking mustang
of a wing in the tunnel, they were led, purely by luck, to the
solution of their first problem, the appalling control characteristics. The clue came as they tried to master what was called
the pitching moment—how the airplane moved up and down on
its longitudinal axis. Pitching up was the problem—violently
pitching up.

They found they could control the tendency to pitch up as
long as the airplane flew straight. That was not much consola-
tion, since it would have to turn. And every time they tried to
turn it beyond 10 degrees it would go crazy again. The nose
would suddenly rear up. They couldn't stop it. And when it
reared up the whole wing would stall out—lose all its lift. In
the real world, that was it—ZAP!

But when they moved the outer nacelle to the end of the
wing they noticed that under certain conditions the weight of
the nacelle "damped" the tendency of the wing to pitch up.
("Damping" is a favored euphemism in the aeroman's argot,
lending a sense of gentle suppression rather than of desperate
resort.) In a bald sense, the wing was malign, but the effect of
the underslung podded engines was benign. Or, at least, potentially so. Could they actually *fine-tune* this balancing act, so that

the inherent tendency of the wing to buck its way out of control could be suppressed by using the podded engines as a countervailing force? It turned out to be an almost miraculous example of synergy: two ideas, the swept wing and the podded engine, each independently troublesome, made perfect harmony together. The interplay of the flexible wing and the leverage generated by the engine pods acted like an immanent control system, inducing something like a supple muscular movement within the skin of the wing that corrected the pitching moment before it could develop into a stall. It was a breathtakingly sophisticated solution, once realized, but it had been arrived at in a strikingly unsophisticated way.

Incredibly, their luck held when they hit another problem. The bomber's fuselage, which was no part of the aeroelastic regime, was long and tubular and subject to unintended bending when the tail control surfaces were used at high speed. This might well have been a fatal flaw, but it turned out that purely· by chance the flexing in the wings countered the aerodynamic deflection of the fuselage.

Everything can be rationalized after the event to give the impression of immaculate conception. Those who witnessed the birth of the XB-47 knew better. They had improvised their way and been blessed with serendipity. Schairer, however, was not ready to reveal this to the world. Some time afterward, giving a lecture in California on the innovations of the B-47, he left the distinct impression that only superior scientific work could have foreseen the problems and solved them.

As far as the models in the tunnel could indicate, it was beginning to look as if the beast *could* be ridden—or flown. At least, within limits. However, Schairer was not at all sure that it was yet entirely benign. For one thing, they had already decided that the XB-47 would need *three times* as much lateral control as anybody had ever put into an airplane. Then there was flutter, their old and frequently lethal adversary. The B-47 was shaping up to be something of an open love letter to flutter, an airplane that was almost saying, "Come get me." They had calculated that the airplane had more than thirty "modes of oscillation." That nice, neutral term was too neutral. For "modes of oscillation" read "ways in which the airplane can shake itself apart."

The wing wiggled. The tail wiggled. The body wiggled. If any of these wiggles got together you called it flutter. And you called flutter "the end"—a terminal wiggle. None of this language, the clinical technical descriptions, the jokey "wiggle," or the embracing condition "flutter," was vicious enough as a description of the reality. Flutter? Leaves flutter gracefully to the ground. The crash of the Stratoliner, triggered by flutter, was always on Schairer's mind. He had walked into a dead man's shoes. And what flutter had done to the Stratoliner was nothing to what it might do to the B-47, where the speed and the violence would be of a different order of magnitude. If those "modes of oscillation" got together on this ship as it barreled through the sky at something over 500 mph, the pieces would be widely scattered.

5 ■ Falling Apart

The demons the aeromen watched at play in the tunnel at Boeing were challenged with less caution in England. Given their longer experience with jet-powered flight, the British were not so inclined to linger in the wind tunnel as their American peers. In Britain, it was the De Havilland Aircraft Company that sped work to get a swept wing into the sky. De Havilland was, like Messerschmitt, something of a personal fiefdom with its own strongly individual style in design, set by the company's patrician founder, Sir Geoffrey de Havilland. It had built the Mosquito, one of the war's best bombers, and the RAF's second operational jet, the Vampire. Impetuously, De Havilland took a Vampire fuselage, removed its tail, and gave it swept wings and swept tailfin. It looked superficially like the rocket-powered German Komet, a flying wing, but perversely it was given the same name as the Me 262 Schwalbe—the Swallow.

Two Swallows were built, one for low-speed research and the other to test the stability and control of the swept wing approaching the speed of sound—the same zone which the B-47 was being designed for. Geoffrey de Havilland, the thirty-six-year-old heir to the company and a skilled test pilot, decided to challenge the new holder of the world speed record, the British

Gloster Meteor. That meant pushing the Swallow clearly beyond the Meteor's 615 mph.

Here, as it happens, I have a personal recollection. Geoffrey de Havilland was the unwitting agent of my own initiation into the wonders of high-speed flight. Some of the Swallow's trial flights took it over the Bedfordshire village where, as an easily distracted schoolboy, I first set eyes on it. This was not easy. The Swallow came first and its sound followed. I remember its phantom passage—a flash of silver hardly allowing the time to take in its substance, leaving behind it the strangely disembodied, almost plaintive high-pitched whine. The hairs on the back of my neck were electrified. It was mysterious and—I knew this with all the sureness of a dreamer—most certainly prophetic.

On the evening of September 27, 1946, de Havilland took off and headed for the Thames estuary. He was making his last high-speed test flight before the attempt on the record. Half an hour later, people on the shores of the estuary saw the Swallow break apart as it began its run. De Havilland's body was found ten days later. He had pushed the Swallow beyond its critical Mach number and compressibility had performed its deadly dance, shattering the airframe in seconds. In England all manned exploration of supersonic flight was abandoned by government decree. The mythic "sound barrier" intimidated British high-speed research for years, inspiring a movie classic of the same name.

In Seattle the aeromen thought the British disaster proved only the folly of the British approach, cannibalizing an existing jet, flying a wing without finding its vices in the tunnel. Nonetheless, nobody could afford to be overconfident of what they had created in the Boeing tunnel. Not even Schairer, for example, could be certain whether they had given birth to something that would be looked back upon as an audacious experimental prototype, leading nowhere (it happened all the time), or whether it was something more.

The company needed a winner. None knew this better than the man who was beginning to feel his way into its leadership. Bill Allen had thickened into a type, one of those upright, Sinclair Lewis men of probity in a three-piece suit. His hair had receded but left behind dark, thick brows that seemed to concentrate his authority in his eyes—those eyes that signaled by their shade of brown his temper. The internal struggle over his fitness for the job left no trace of irresolution. One thing was as manifest as his conservative suits: his understanding of the Boeing ethic. The company might now be a national brand name (though not yet a generic noun), but its values remained those of a parochially secure and independent community.

Allen faced the crisis of peace: where were the company's best prospects, with the airlines or with the military? To the airlines Boeing remained unproven; it was seen as a company where the military design came first and only then, and with little grace, was a mutation of the military design offered as an airliner. Douglas remained unchallenged as the airlines' favorite; the new DC-6 epitomized the state of the art, carrying 102 passengers in gracious style on the international routes. Donald Douglas did not believe that it was time to invest in big jets. He had resisted bidding for the jet bomber, instead opting to build the D-558 series of experimental ships for the high-speed tests at Muroc Dry Lake in the Mojave Desert.

Although Boeing's wind tunnel seemed like an ace in the hole, Allen could privately entertain a dark doubt: suppose Douglas was right? Suppose George Schairer's "wet dream" was just that? Allen was not a Schairer fan. Schairer was hard enough to understand if you were an engineer; if you were not an engineer it was like listening to a sermon in Urdu, with no allowance made if you were the boss. But Allen respected Schairer's talents and—as long as Wells backed Schairer—had to believe that he knew what he was doing with a large slice of the company's money.

And Schairer was too good an aerodynamicist not to be a realist. The reality was that they could only do so much testing in the wind tunnel. No prototype that the company had ever built would roll out of the hangar with as much wind tunnel time given to it yet with as much still unproven. And even though Wright Field had been talked into funding two prototypes, it was clear that the laboratory mafia, who had been ominously disinterested in the bomber's development, were just waiting for a fiasco to unfold. Their vote was going to the North American B-45, which could clock 580 mph without any fancy swept wing.

As the B-47 moved from tunnel models to prototypes, Boeing adopted the landing-gear arrangement that had first appeared on its Martin competitor: "bicycle" instead of tricycle.

This did nothing to increase pilot confidence. Landing a big, heavy plane squarely on wheels confined to the center of the body, without the stability provided by a main gear spread out from the wings, looked forbidding. In fact, there was no choice. The wing was too thin to take any landing gear.

Then there was the matter of engine power. They had gone from four to six engines because of disappointing performance from the General Electric J-35 jets, which could give only a maximum of 3,750 pounds of thrust for takeoff. Other drawbacks were emerging. The jet engine gave of its best only at high speed and high altitudes. It was slow responding to the throttle. Pilots who were used to gunning a piston engine to get out of trouble during a landing or a takeoff (the prop engine gave you the power instantly) found that jets did not cooperate. There was a potentially fatal lag between calling for power and getting it. Everything about the B-47 had been shaped by the need for speed, but the qualities that made it fast—the thin, clean wing and the slippery body—promised to be penalties in low-speed flight, and especially in landing, with engines that were relatively unresponsive. As the test pilots were briefed for the airplane's audition, they could see that coming into land would be like trying to ride a bullet that didn't want to slow down, or come to earth.

In his efforts to keep the program alive, Pete Warden had used a young aide, Ken Holtby, as his conduit to Wells. Warden made First Lieutenant Holtby the contracting officer with Boeing, and it was Holtby, at the age of twenty-three, who technically *bought* the two prototypes from Boeing for $19 million. In July 1947, with the first airplane being built, Holtby left the Army Air Forces and joined Boeing as an aerodynamicist.

Warden had infected Holtby with his faith in Boeing, but— better than anyone else in Seattle—Holtby arrived knowing that Curtis LeMay, the bomber chief known for wearing two pearl-handled revolvers at his hips and permanently chomping on a cigar, would need some persuading to take the jet seriously as a bomber. The first XB-47 left the plant in September for systems checks carried out in a part of the apron shrouded for secrecy. At the same time, the Boeing pilot already chosen to make the first flight, Bob Robbins, was in California, "flying" a mock-up of the control surfaces in the wind tunnel at the Ames Research Center near San Francisco.

It was nearing Christmas when the airplane itself was ready to fly. The usual last-minute glitches, as well as the weather, brought delays. Not by any masterstroke of public relations, but simply by chance, it happened to be December 17 when Robbins and his copilot, Scott Osler, turned onto the runway at Boeing Field ready to roll, with the small team of aeromen among the hundreds watching. It was the forty-fourth anniversary of the Wright Brothers' first flight at Kitty Hawk.

The pulsing sound of the six jets at full blast bounced off the neighboring hills. A lot of kerosene was burning—as the XB-47 went torching down the runway it trailed plumes of dark smoke. It swallowed up runway without lifting, more like a projectile than a plane, and not like any other bomber that had ever lumbered into the air at Boeing Field. Robbins's and Osler's helmeted heads were visible in the tiny bubble of a cockpit, men borne on a new wind and on a wild new wing. They lifted with a few hundred yards to spare—and lifted fast, heading for a gap in the clouds, leaving a signature of suspended smoke, the acrid smell of kerosene, and a distant crackling of combusted air.

They flew over the Cascades and landed at Moses Lake, in eastern Washington, where the rest of the flight testing was to take place; Moses Lake had a large runway without urban development and, usually, better weather. Few problems had surfaced on the first flight; the flaps had been reluctant to retract but finally did, and an outrigger wheel, important in stabilizing the airplane on landing, developed a shimmy. Within the narrow limits set for a maiden flight, the XB-47 had been surprisingly docile.

Barely two months earlier, Chuck Yeager had flown the rocket-powered Bell XS-1 through the sound barrier at 43,000 feet over Muroc Dry Lake. This was a one-of-a-kind experimental prototype, never intended itself to lead to an operational airplane. The XB-47, in contrast, had been designed from the beginning to pass from prototypes into mass production with as few changes as possible, and was in many ways a more adventurous—even possibly reckless—journey into the unknown. Very soon, though, the aeromen grew impatient with the slowness of flight test results. There were murmurs that Robbins and Osler were flying the plane more timidly than even the usually conservative Boeing regime allowed.

As well as seats for pilot and copilot, there was a position in the nose below them for a bombardier; on the test flights this was usually occupied by an instrumentation engineer. Holtby took this seat on an early flight, watching paper scroll under ink pens that recorded behavior from the wired nerve ends of the airplane and occasionally unsticking the pens. If he climbed up alongside the pilot and peered out the canopy he could see the continual flexing of the wings with the engines bobbing with the movement; the first sight of this was deeply alarming, and called for every reserve of faith in the structural engineers.

A little later, Holtby was in the control tower at Moses Lake with Bill Cook when Robbins reported over the radio that he was experiencing a strange oscillation. He was flying at high altitude, but well short of the upper speed limit. He had begun to feel confident enough to take his eyes off the controls, and was checking his flight plan. Suddenly, he was conscious that the airplane was snaking. He straightened up and then let it free of control again. Of its own volition, the bomber was making a series of S turns, incrementally more pronounced, with the wings beginning to bank. As Robbins described the condition in more detail, Cook said, "We have Dutch roll."

This was a demon that Schairer had feared from the beginning. It was a condition known for more than forty years, and dubbed Dutch roll after a style of skating popular on Dutch canals.

They thought they had designed enough control into the prototype to prevent it. Now they knew otherwise. Left unchecked—or, to use the favored euphemism again, "undamped"—each phase of Dutch roll was an involuntary spasm lasting about six seconds that created a sickening yaw. In its most lethal form, and especially in the hands of a novice pilot, it could rapidly get out of hand and pull the plane apart.

They had detected this tendency in the tunnel. Their failure to design it out of the airplane confirmed Schairer's worst suspicion, that Dutch roll was, in a way not seen before, endemic to the swept wing. In fact, the condition was exacerbated by the podded engines slung on the pylons—in the Dutch roll the engines became forces of moment against the airplane's axis, like weights that wanted to whirl around the sky. There is an inclination to pessimism in physical laws. To put it crudely, physicists get to know that you can't mess with Mother Nature.

If you defy gravity with one device, gravity will find a way of reasserting itself. The aeromen had very nearly got away with it: the swept wing had fooled the Mach number but here revealed, with the Dutch roll, was the price to be paid, the settling of the account in the form of a fundamental of physics, the tendency of a mass to rotate around its axis.

The whole B-47 configuration was in jeopardy. Cook's instincts were shaped by the time he had spent under Draper at MIT, and he recalled Draper's belief that pilots should get as much help as they could from their flight controls. He wondered if there was a way of the XB-47's controls "reading" the onset of Dutch roll and correcting it before a pilot even knew it was there. Cook called Seattle and found Ed Pfafman. The aeromen knew Pfafman as the man to see when they were in trouble: almost entirely self-taught, Pfafman was a magician with mechanical-electrical devices. Cook explained the problem and asked Pfafman if he thought he could produce a gadget that could be interposed between the rudder pedals in the cockpit and the rudder that, without any intervention by the pilot, would sense the presence of Dutch roll and damp it before the pilot had to touch the rudder pedals. Pfafman scavenged around for parts, taking one from the B-29 bomber, another from a local junkyard, another from a helpful local subcontractor.

Within three weeks the XB-47 had been fitted with the device, described technically as a yaw damper, but colloquially at Moses Lake, for no clear reason, as "Little Herbie." It worked. It is true to say that no other single step was as important in granting life to this form of airplane: the large, flexible swept wing would never have become the commonplace it now is without Little Herbie. To this day, every airplane of the same form has one.

Not everybody was happy about this solution. The man who had given Dutch roll its name, Dr. Jerome Hunsaker, another of Cook's mentors at MIT, was an old-fashioned stickler for aerodynamic "purity"—he complained that vices should be designed out of an airplane, not circumvented by mechanical means. There was a fundamental argument here: Dutch roll had not disappeared, it had been suppressed. In that respect, the configuration was inherently unstable.

For the first time in aviation, a potentially fatal vice became acceptable because of the intervention of a device that could act faster than any pilot's brain. When Douglas heard of the yaw damper it put out the story that Boeing's swept wing had a serious flaw that could not be corrected. Unfortunately for Douglas, the military client took Little Herbie to its heart, as a welcome safety feature. Cook and Pfafman collected $50 each for the patent.

As the flight testing of the XB-47 progressed—far too cautiously for the taste of the Army Air Forces—it was clear from the work continuing in the tunnel that the design still had daunting problems. The rigid models the engineers had first used in the tunnel didn't replicate the complex flexing of the wing in flight. What they could not risk in test-flying the XB-47, taking the plane to its limits, they had to find a way of doing in the tunnel. Now, led by the young Holtby, they built aeroelastic models, with wings that did oscillate, and that could be "flown" in the tunnel as they would be in the air.

The torment that now surfaced was flutter. The model was fixed to a vertical rod in the tunnel, with controls operated from outside the tunnel. But only one of the three basic controls, the elevators, could be replicated, meaning that whoever "flew" the model could control only the longitudinal axis—in other words, up or down. As soon as they approached high speeds, beyond eight-tenths Mach, everything went crazy. The aeroelastic wing developed terminal flutter. They could find only one engineer with reflexes quick enough to give some semblance of control as he sat outside the tunnel attempting to "fly" the model. Even so, model after model came apart, with the pieces splattered against the tunnel walls.

Set against the frenetic scenes in the tunnel, the theoretical mathematicians painstakingly struggled to find order in the chaos. They analyzed each of the many conditions of flutter. It took two weeks to complete the work on each condition, using mechanical calculators. This was another, more desperate version of Draper's style in the MIT tunnel: finding the theory after the fact. In this case, theory had to explain the physical phenomena they observed as wing after wing twisted, shuddered, flapped like a bird, and failed.

Even as the aeromen rode the roller-coaster B-47 in the tunnel, an electric change took place in the flight testing at Moses Lake. Despairing of the timidity of the Boeing pilots, the U.S. Air Force (now an independent service) sent Major Guy Townsend to be the first military pilot to test the XB-47. Within a week, Townsend had flown the prototype through its whole test envelope (within the "never exceed" limits set until the flutter problems were resolved). Monitoring Townsend's flights, Holtby learned in that week as much about the XB-47 as he had in the six months of intermittent flying by the Boeing pilots.

Townsend loved the ship; to him it flew like a fighter, not like any bomber he had ever touched, and he soon had a chance to prove his point.

It was a standard game that during the trials of a new bomber the hotshot fighter test pilots from Edwards Air Force Base in California (the name now given to the Muroc Dry Lake test field) would pitch their latest airplane against the bomber, to test its defensive capability. The night before the B-47 faced this challenge, Townsend and Holtby had dinner with the selected pilot, a Lieutenant McCullough. In the tradition of his breed, McCullough was dismissive of the B-47's chances—he was flying a Lockheed F-84 Thunderjet, newest of the Air Force's jet fighters.

"Any time you build a bomber," said McCullough, "there'll be a fighter to shoot it down."

Next day, the B-47 went first—making its usual long takeoff run as the engines slowly gathered their power, and going decorously up to cruising height. McCullough followed.

In a few minutes, Holtby, in the tower, heard a puzzled call from the F-84: "Guy, where are you?"

Came the answer from Townsend: "How in the hell are you gonna shoot me down if you can't find me?" While the straight-winged F-84 had been climbing to interception, Townsend had been slicing through the stratosphere out of sight and out of reach.

Over the radio, Townsend gave McCullough his position and throttled back, coasting along until the lame F-84 caught up. Then, with the two airplanes side by side, Townsend throttled up to full power, leaving the fighter standing.

When they landed, McCullough complained that there had been something wrong with his engine. Townsend had the grace not to disabuse him. Everybody at Moses Lake saw the import of the aerial combat that wasn't: if the Air Force bought the B-47 it would have a bomber that could outfly its best fighters.

Townsend needed no converting, but Allen, Wells, and

Schairer had all picked up signals that the Air Force still saw the XB-47 as a small sideshow, an experimental airplane that fell short of what they needed as an operational bomber.

The long and elaborately plagued research program, in the tunnel and in the air, had so far earned only the $19 million price of the two prototypes, and had cost a lot more. Allen was concerned that the company had no sure basis for a military contract in the future. Even Schairer appears to have wavered in his commitment to the B-47. Cook was dismayed one day when Schairer told him, "You can play with your experimental airplane, but the bread and butter of Boeing is the B-54." The B-54 was hardly the future; it was a reworking of the B-29.

The issue of the B-47's real prospects had to be brought to a head. It was a question of knowing who had the power to change the Air Force's attitude. At Wright Field, Pete Warden's support of the project had been strengthened by Townsend's reports, and more of the senior engineers were converts. But there was no one there with the clout to sway Curtis LeMay, a man not known for changing his mind once it was made up.

It was Allen's instinct that they should appeal to General Kenneth B. Wolfe. Wolfe, invariably known as K.B., had risen through the hierarchy at Wright Field by the breadth of his engineering grasp and the force of his opinions. Wolfe had been the military's point man on the B-29, and had persevered through its many crises. He counted in Washington: LeMay listened to him. And he was on his way to Seattle.

The whole attitude toward military procurement had made a 180-degree turn. Winston Churchill had described "an Iron Curtain" dropping between eastern and western Europe, and the Cold War was demanding a new air strategy. Wolfe was coming to Seattle to order B-50s, the first "stretch" of the B-29. His mind didn't seem engaged by the idea of jets at all. When Allen suggested that Wolfe fly out to Moses Lake to see the XB-47, Wolfe snapped, "We aren't interested in experimental airplanes."

Allen was crestfallen; Warden and Townsend were at Moses Lake with the XB-47 ready to roll. Allen knew that Wolfe and his party were droning around the country in an old B-17. He offered to fly them to Moses Lake in the much faster B-29, arguing that while their B-17 followed they could see the

XB-47 and not miss their schedule. Allowing Allen his ploy, Wolfe relented.

At Moses Lake, Townsend closed the circle. He knew that Wolfe had never flown in a jet. As Townsend stood under the airplane, geared up for what Wolfe had been told would be a brief flyby, he asked Wolfe to go along for the ride. The veteran flyer in Wolfe transcended the bureaucrat. He was zipped into a flying suit and helmet. Pilot and copilot rode in tandem; Wolfe sat behind Townsend. The XB-47 had been fitted with rockets to shorten its takeoff run. They greatly dramatized the experience, giving the plane the equivalent of a smart kick up the rear and leaving a fiery trail before they were jettisoned.

Townsend, talking to Wolfe through the intercom in his laconic Mississippi drawl, read off the numbers: 470 mph at six thousand feet . . . 20 percent cut in power . . . 180-degree turn . . . down to 400 mph . . .

On the ground, Allen turned to one of Wolfe's group, grinning. "Townsend's going to sell him that airplane or he's not going to bring it down."

Behind the joke, Allen knew he was witnessing what could be the most crucial flight in the company's history—certainly a fateful one for his own stewardship of Boeing. Townsend spared nothing. He brought the bomber down low and then lower, barely fifty feet above the runway, at nearly 500 mph, then pulled up the nose and—still on full power—blasted through the cloud cover to break into the arctic blue of the stratosphere with the plane still eating up the sky. Wolfe looked from side to side, watching the peculiar flexing of the wings, with the engines moving in sync on their pods.

Landing was an experience in itself. Brakes alone were not enough to slow the silver bullet. They had adopted a German idea, a ribbon parachute that popped out the tail to add drag. (Its inventor, Professor Theodore Kanake, was a feature at Moses Lake, strutting around in a full-length Luftwaffe leather coat, appalled that Townsend could endure the primitive barracks at the test strip, which he insisted no Luftwaffe test pilot would have accepted for a minute.) When Wolfe climbed down from the belly of the beast after a twenty-minute flight he was inscrutable. They knew the face: it said, so you think you can sell me this thing? Betraying no more, he flew off in the tired Flying Fortress. One of the aeromen asked Townsend what the G-force had been when he had taken that last ride up into the heavens.

"The max," said Townsend. "I figured it proved Uncle Sam needs this airplane."

But Uncle Sam didn't call. A week passed without any word from the Air Force. The feeling in Seattle was anticlimactic. Wells, who knew as acutely as Allen what was at risk, went on vacation. The following Saturday, Schairer was pottering in his den in his small ranch house on the edge of Lake Washington. The letter he had written from Volkenrode was in his desk. He had recovered it from Ben Cohn and filed it away, feeling that one day it might be valued as a piece of history, as the single pointing finger. The phone rang. It was the operator at the Boeing administrative building on East Marginal Way, across from Boeing Field. She said she had a caller who was trying to reach an officer of the company—*any* officer. She couldn't find the chairman, she couldn't find the president. Would Schairer talk to him?

It was Wolfe.

"I would like to buy about ten of your airplanes as fast as you can build them," said Wolfe. "Who can I talk to to sign up to have you do this?"

Schairer knew where Wells was on vacation. He gave Wolfe the number. The B-47 had been given life. Robert Jones's understanding of the powers of the swept wing had proved that American science was a lot better than its sponsors often realized; the production of the B-47 was about to demonstrate that nothing could compare with the American industrial machine once it was animated and directed.

One of the few foreigners to be given an official view of the XB-47 on the apron at Moses Lake was the chief designer of the British Vickers airplane company, George Edwards. He gaped at it. "Only Boeing," he said, "would have the guts to design a plane like that." Nonetheless, Edwards was not moved to imitate it. He designed a bomber for the RAF with its four engines buried in the wing. The British were to pay the price of this in later years, when they did the same thing with a jet-powered airliner, the Comet.

The B-47, looked at as a strategic calculation for the future of Boeing, didn't yet seem a progenitor. At most, it was testimony to the mesmerizing power of a single idea. Once Schairer ac-

cepted the swept wing it became the new faith for the small group
of aeromen working on the project, but to others its application
appeared to be strictly military. Despite all the research and development effort put into the B-47 program, only twenty-eight
engineers were directly charged to it. There wasn't the money for
more. No one had allowed for the cost of the wind tunnel time that
the B-47 was demanding, thousands of hours. However, to the
men in the tunnel, padding about in their stockinged feet and still
scraping up the debris from shattered wings, the swept wing had
a life beyond the B-47. But for a few further tweaks to its handling, they had done what they could with that design. Already
they could see that a more docile wing was possible.

In Allen's first year as President, Boeing was playing two
very different cards: the wild card of the B-47, and the supposedly safe card of a new four-engine airliner derived from the
wings and tail of the B-29, the model 377, or Stratocruiser. In
Santa Monica, Douglas responded with the DC-6 (adopting the
pressurized cabin that Boeing had pioneered with the Stratoliner), and in Burbank, Lockheed responded with the elegant,
curvy Constellation.

Inside the Boeing engineering department the men working
on the Stratocruiser felt left in the backwash of the B-47. Jack
Steiner had emerged as the top aeroman on the Stratocruiser,
but working on the Stratocruiser became scary. There were
problems with the propellers. One propeller failure ripped an
engine right out of the wing and it went spinning over the top
of the airplane. For Steiner it was like a replay of the worst
days of the B-29: each time they tried to get more power out of
the Pratt & Whitney engines and get smarter with the propellers, it was a new load of trouble.

The Stratocruiser's engines were pigs. Each of the four
engines had twenty-eight cylinders, and each cylinder had two
spark plugs—making 224 spark plugs to a plane. If the Stratocruiser was kept with its engines idling awaiting takeoff, all
224 spark plugs gummed up, and the airplane had to go back
for a change of plugs. No wonder that the aeromen on the Stratocruiser should be looking across the hall at the crew nursing
the B-47 through its trials. The jet engine might be in its infancy,
but compared with the engine on the Stratocruiser it seemed
admirably simple and reliable.

Working under Steiner was a new Boeing recruit, a young aerodynamicist called Joe Sutter. Sutter was helping to get the FAA certification for the Stratocruiser, and he soon discovered that while Boeing had its own rigorous engineering conscience, there was one customer who could be ornery about every detail: Pan American. Juan Trippe had come out of the war having established Pan Am as the dominant international airline. When Pan Am bought twenty Stratocruisers, at $1.25 million each, Pan Am engineers, led by a Dutchman named Andre Priester, rode shotgun with Steiner and his team.

Pan Am owed much to Trippe's will, but Priester had been with Trippe from the beginning, and his small cadre of engineers never received public due for their work—not just Pan Am's airplanes, but any airplane they touched was invariably better for it. Small but impressively cerebral, Priester made almost a fetish of airline safety. The engineers he gathered to work with him were indoctrinated with the same obsession.

There was a lot about the Stratocruiser Priester didn't like. To lean on Boeing, he sent John Borger to Seattle. Before the war, Borger had worked on the 314 Clipper flying boats. Like Schairer, Borger had graduated from MIT in the Depression. But unlike Schairer, Borger saw the MIT connection as the foundation of his own freemasonry of engineers, and he made a point of wearing the MIT ring, with its beaver symbol, as though it were the lodestar by which they should all live.

Borger respected the Boeing engineers, but castigated what he called their "Pacific Northwest psychology"—an insular arrogance that he found peculiar to the place. He was a huge, broad-hipped bear of a man, with an astringent tongue, and being upbraided by Borger left its mark. Pan Am had also ordered the Douglas DC-6, and Borger, with intimate access to both companies, told the Boeing engineers they didn't listen as hard to their customers as Douglas did—a complaint that could be heard from other airlines, too.

A case in point was the ailerons on the Stratocruiser. (Ailerons provide lateral control.) The Pan Am pilot assigned to test the Stratocruiser complained that the ailerons were imprecise. Boeing resisted making a change—until Borger arrived. After a full frontal assault by Borger, Steiner assigned Joe Sutter to fix the problem. Borger found he couldn't cow Sutter. Raw as he was, Sutter had an implacable Slavic eye—his father had taken the name Sutter in place of a difficult Balkan family name. Sutter was as fastidious with detail as Borger. The two of them hit it off, and Sutter solved the aileron problem.

In public, the romance lay in commercial aviation. Dependable intercontinental services became a reality. Across the Atlantic the days of doglegging it in a flying boat via the Azores were over. The new generation of four-engine airliners could fly nonstop in sixteen hours. The blue-ribbon transatlantic liners, taking five or six days, having had some forty years of stylish monopoly, faced their nemesis, whether they knew it or not. But this kind of flying remained to most people a luxury. When Pan Am introduced a tourist class, other members of the tight-knit international airline cartel fought it bitterly; it offended their sense that international air travel should be the privilege of an elite, with prices to match. But Trippe prevailed. Pan Am Stratocruisers introduced seats mounted on tracks, so that they could be spaced according to the mix of first and tourist classes. Passengers liked the Stratocruiser. They liked the circular staircase you took down to the lounge. Sleeperettes let the hours drift by; sometimes you could land and take off without waking up. It was also liked for its aesthetics. The Stratocruiser was a distinctive piece of sculpture, a hint of pregnancy in the fat, lower lobe of the fuselage and the pushy, confident proboscis reminiscent of the Stratoliner.

For pilots, it was another story. Even after changes insisted upon by Pan Am, Pratt & Whitney never completely debugged the engines. Allen, who was fond of the plane, admitted that it "flew uphill all the time." Allen had set the first production target at fifty aircraft. Boeing managed to sell fifty-five, but ended with a $7 million loss. And the Stratocruiser did nothing to convince the airlines that Boeing was a serious contender; the plane was all too clearly a compromise, a hybrid—its military variants, the C-97 cargo plane and the KC-97 tanker for aerial refueling, satisfied the Air Force and helped cover the loss on the airliner.

Douglas and Lockheed tailored their planes to the airlines' needs, and it showed. The Douglas DC-6B, a plane given a personal working-over by John Borger, was part of a series that sold six hundred airplanes to forty-four airlines. The Lockheed Constellation, with its elegant, porpoiselike body and triple tail, was stretchable and eventually outflew the DC-6, forcing Douglas to produce the DC-7.

At Boeing there was a growing frustration in always being the also-ran. Allen realized that more was involved than simply talking up a new airliner. It needed a sea change in the company culture to win a respected place in the commercial business. He was beginning to look for another wave of talent, men who were technically literate and, at the same time, personally persuasive. Men who might get Boeing taken seriously as a commercial airplane company.

Among those he had noticed, two stood out. Their characters could not have been more in contrast. One was Jack Steiner, who had borne the plagues of the Stratocruiser well. Steiner had the ability that Wells looked for of seeing the airplane as a whole. The bruising Steiner had taken on the Stratocruiser at the hands of Borger had educated him about airlines—about how much to give them and how much not to give them. It wasn't a good idea to roll over and give them everything, because they would take it. Sometimes, even, Steiner had outflanked Borger.

The other rising star was not an aeroman, which helped keep him out of direct competition with Schairer. Maynard Pennell was a structures specialist. If he had an affinity with anyone, it was with Wells. Like Wells, he was economical with words. But once he had thought out a position he was more openly an advocate of it than Wells had it in his nature to be—sometimes people got the idea that Wells thought ardent personal advocacy a breach of reason. Pennell also fought the corner for structures men. He thought, for example, that the structures man on the B-47, George Martin, who had mastered the gelatinous wing, had not been accorded enough credit—the aeromen had stolen the limelight.

Pennell had come to Boeing from Douglas, and was very conscious of the difference in company styles. At its simplest, it was a picture of one company dominated and driven by one man, Donald Douglas, and another that was still trying to build a management style around its new chief executive, Allen.

Douglas, like Trippe, had taken to conducting much of the company business personally, over the phone. He was growing reclusive and sometimes cranky. At the start of World War II—ironically, in view of his readiness to trade his secrets with

Japan—he feared that the Japanese would soon be bombing Santa Monica, and had all his furniture shipped to Salt Lake City. Douglas still kept a core of first-rate engineers around him, but the atmosphere at the top of the company was uneasy. Douglas's mistress, Peggy Tucker, had joined the company as his personal driver at the beginning of the war. She was soon in charge of all company transportation and its food supplies. Eventually, her name appeared on the company organization chart at the same level as Douglas's. On the executive floor, she gained the influence of a capricious gatekeeper. Disaffected managers left.

In Seattle, Pennell found a far greater openness to ideas and little caution about gambling: Donald Douglas would never have sanctioned a program as risky as the B-47. As Pennell won Allen's confidence, he argued that Boeing had to demonstrate to the airlines a far higher degree of commitment to their needs and a lot less inclination to sell them mutations of military designs. Pennell gained more influence when he was made chief of preliminary design. He decided to begin trying subtly to shift the company's thinking toward an arching step: a commercial jet. The reliability of the B-47's engines had impressed everybody, but they were notorious fuel guzzlers. There were other advocates of a commercial jet in the company, but Allen resisted them all; he thought it was too soon.

The military business was back in a boom cycle, and everything was playing into Boeing's hands. The B-47, unlike its competitors for the Air Force contract, had a bomb bay large enough for the Hiroshima generation of atomic bomb, and had become the backbone of America's nuclear deterrent. (There was, as yet, no triad—no ballistic missiles, no nuclear submarines.) Suddenly, the B-47 was the darling of Strategic Air Command. In military aircraft, none of the other companies came close. "*We are it*," exulted Schairer.

6 ■ The Cowboy and the Scientist

The manner of A. M. "Tex" Johnston's arrival at Boeing in 1949 left no doubt about one side of his character. The company had just instituted a psychoanalytical test for senior appointments. At first sight, Johnston certainly did not fit the solemn mold of Boeing pilots. He had long legs in cowboy boots, a voice like Jimmy Stewart's, a Gable mustache, and roamin' eyes. The psychiatrist chosen to put Johnston through the test turned out to be an attractive brunette with long green nails.

Johnston endured an infantile round-peg-into-round-hole test and patiently explained that he had already been a test pilot for six years. Solemnly persisting, and trying to probe his motivation, the woman asked, "What do you like better than anything else in the world?"

"Copulation," said Johnston—refining his normal vocabulary for her benefit.

This terminated the examination. The doctor declined an invitation to go to dinner.

The Boeing flight test department, imbued with the scientific disciplines set by Eddie Allen, looked askance at the coming of Johnston, who announced that he always bought a new pair of Western boots for every prototype he flew. Johnston had grown up in Emporia, Kansas, and, just like the young Robert Jones, had been intoxicated by the flying circuses. At the age of eleven he saw a pilot put down on a cow pasture and hitched a flight. The plane banked over his hometown, and the world changed. By the time Amelia Earhart landed in Emporia on a cross-country flight in 1929, Johnston was learning to fly. In 1933, at the age of nineteen and already known for his grasp of airplane mechanics, he qualified for a commercial pilot's license.

In little more than another decade, Johnston had become the consummate test pilot—one of very few pilots whose instincts and reflexes became an extension of the machine, the brain it didn't have. In 1946 he flew a hot-rod Bell P-39 fighter to victory in the Thompson Trophy, setting a new world speed record of 373.9 mph for closed-course air racing. However, he had other credentials that explained his selection by Boeing. He had been the first American to fly a swept wing airplane, a propeller-powered experimental Bell L-39 used to feel out the swept wing's low-speed habits. This was an NACA program, forced on NACA by Jones's work and the incoming German data. The L-39 was a handful, but it did help the development of the first American swept wing jet fighter, the F-86 Sabre.

There was, however, a well-suppressed chip on Johnston's shoulder that the psychiatrist's fatuous tests had not located. While Johnston was flying for Bell, Bell had built the X-1 rocket ship in which Chuck Yeager became the first pilot through the "sound barrier." That flight, Johnston felt, should have been his. But Bell had chosen a younger wartime combat hero, Chalmers "Slick" Goodlin, as well as Johnston, to test the X-1 at Edwards Air Force Base, and Goodlin—according to Johnston's reasoning—had flown so poorly that the Air Force had taken over the program, denying Johnston his moment of glory and giving it to Yeager. Disaffected with Bell and having roamed awhile, Johnston came to Seattle to ride the B-47 in the wake of Townsend, who had returned to Wright Field.

By then, the XB-47 had claimed the only victim of the test program. Scott Osler had died in a freak accident: coming in to land, he had opened his cockpit canopy for ventilation and it had slammed back and decapitated him. The plane was safely brought in by the copilot, Jim Frazier. Neither Osler nor Bob

Robbins had ever felt at home in the XB-47, and Frazier had quit flying it after the accident.

It had taken five years of intensive flight testing and more than three thousand hours of continual work in the wind tunnel to domesticate the B-47 to a point where it could safely be placed in the hands of Air Force pilots. But Boeing was not simply proving the serviceability of a bomber. The plane had become the triggering spore in the breeding process of the company's next generation of aircraft—military and commercial.

When Johnston arrived, the prototype had flown for fewer than fifteen hours. Some people talked of the plane as though it were jinxed. Everybody in flight test knew it was still a bag of tricks, not all of them yet revealed. To the cynics among them there did seem a certain poetic justice in the fact that a plane with the character of a treacherous mustang now had an authentic cowboy in the saddle.

But it was not as simple as that. It was true that Johnston, although an avowed family man, had a seemingly inexhaustible appetite for partying. It was also clear, from the moment that Johnston took control of the bomber, that the man of the night was always, come the dawn, gimlet-eyed, with reflexes the equal of every quirk that an airframe or an engine might unleash. In fact, represented in the paradoxes of Johnston's character and skills was a long-running cultural conflict peculiar to aviation in America.

The conflict was between aviation, as an institutionally organized science, and the driven individualist—spiritually if not actually a cowboy—who proved essential to challenging the orthodoxies. Each decade threw up examples: Billy Mitchell, the rebel general and advocate of bombing; Lindbergh; Yeager. It was as though some mutation of the cowboy ethic, encouraging acts of aggressive heroism over collective order, had been translated to the skies, to be emboldened by the conquerable vastnesses of the land below.

In Europe, on the other hand, aeronautics was seen from its theoretical infancy as—if not carefully directed—a wanton science always trying to reach beyond what was properly understood and explicable. (Keeping science in the grip of intellectual rigor was what Göttingen's priesthood had insisted upon.) Yet it was in America, against all the scientific odds, that manned flight began, from no more than a bicycle workshop. This insolent dynamic reached its apotheosis in Lindbergh, who respected science but saw it merely as the means to an end. In America it was understood that in the end, a man had to ride the machine. And so as the cowboy disappeared from the plains and prairie, the cowboy ethic lived on in the pilot's seat. To this day it has never been entirely eradicated, witness the Sam Shepard version of Chuck Yeager as horseman in *The Right Stuff.*

Tex Johnston took to the XB-47 like a natural. He rode it hard. Hard enough to discover, very quickly, that it had another nasty habit. The test flying had moved from Moses Lake to Wichita, where the production B-47s were to be built. The XB-47 had been refitted with more powerful engines. Johnston was making a demonstration flight for Air Force officers. He followed Townsend's barnstorming trick of coming in very fast and low and then pulling up into the kind of climb that left the spectators agape. Using the extra power, Johnston flew across the field at 525 mph and, without losing speed, began a climbing turn to the right. At least, that was what he intended—but the bomber rolled to the left. Johnston slapped the throttles closed; as the speed fell the airplane stabilized. What had happened was that Johnston's lateral control, through the ailerons, had actually been reversed. At high speed the ailerons actually twisted the flexing wing the wrong way. Johnston gave the trick the playful name "wing windup."

The aeromen listening to Johnston realized immediately that the airplane was in the hands of a different class of pilot. Over the radio, Johnston's detached, laconic voice explained the event as though he were watching the model in the tunnel, not flying the XB-47 itself. He was systematic and analytical. Johnston flew with a cowboy's panache, but he thought like an engineer and talked like an engineer. His flying brought the aeromen more data per hour flown than they had ever known.

It was the kind of day that exemplified the virtues of Wichita over Seattle for test flying. The Kansas corn was as high as an elephant's eye and the August sky over the plains seemed clear all the way to the moon. The shadows of cotton-wool clouds moved lazily over the blanched concrete of the runways at the Boeing plant, where the first B-47s were being built. It was the high summer of 1950.

For nearly three years, Bill Allen had watched Schairer's

"wet dream" turn into the bomber that restored the company's fortunes and reinforced its reputation with the military, which would eventually buy more than two thousand B-47s. He had listened to Tex Johnston's rhapsodic accounts of the plane's performance; he had seen Pennell's thesis on the future of the jet as an airliner; he knew that Boeing had already acquired a body of knowledge about large jets that was unrivaled. But he was not yet certain how they could exploit this advantage.

In the popular mind, jets were still demonstrably machines of war. They had manners to match—they were thunderous in sound and left smutty trails behind them. It required a leap of imagination to think that they might be house-trained to the point where they could use civilian airports without befouling them and scaring the neighborhood out of its wits.

And so, on this perfect day, Allen came to Wichita to take his first flight in a jet—in a production version of the B-47. It was typical of him that if people were passionate about something, as they were passionate about the cause of the jet, he would want to sample for himself the experience that bred the passion. Allen was zipped into the one-piece flying suit the test pilots wore and given a helmet rigged with an oxygen mask and microphone. He kept his well-waxed executive shoes. He was posed for photographs, helmet under his arm, with one foot on the retractable aluminum ladder that hung vertically from under the bomber's nose. He looked as a malleable father might look when invited by his son to try a ride on a Harley—like a man slightly out of his element but making a show.

The pilot, Doug Heimburger, climbed up first. The copilot, Ed Hartz, strapped a parachute onto Allen and installed him in the navigator's position, below and ahead of the pilots in the nose. It was a spectacular, if scary, seat to ride, with a Plexiglas cone at the nose giving a wide view. Hartz explained what would happen if they hit trouble and had to abandon the plane. A hatch above the navigator's seat would blow, his seat would be armed, and—if the seat was triggered—Allen, strapped into the seat, would be ejected through the hole above. The two pilots would follow after jettisoning their canopy.

They taxied out and turned onto the end of the runway. Heimburger held the brakes until the six jets were up to full power: the new J-47 engines each delivered six thousand pounds of thrust. For anyone riding a jet for the first time, a radical change in the experience of flying now registered itself emphatically. If Allen had been sitting in a Stratocruiser instead of the B-47, there would have been a lot more vibration as the piston engines came up to power, and the noise would have been more intrusive.

When the brakes came off, Allen—much closer to the runway than the pilots—had an intensified sense of speed with the skyline coming at him. A Stratocruiser would have accelerated faster and left the ground sooner, the propeller wash buffeting the plane as it rose. The B-47 needed six thousand of the ten thousand feet of the runway before its wheels lifted. In the prop plane you felt as if someone had given a big push from behind and then stopped pushing; in the B-47 you felt as if someone had his hand between your shoulders and kept pushing, increasing the force all the time.

The bomber took off at around 150 mph. It continued at climb power until, in minutes, it was at ten thousand feet and traveling at 520 mph, where it leveled off. Everything had been uncommonly smooth, with none of the laboring familiar to Allen as the Stratocruiser clawed into the thinner air. Heimburger paused to get Allen's reaction over the intercom. The flight was a revelation. He didn't need any technical commentary to assess the new dimension he had entered. Heimburger and Hartz hadn't, like Allen, flown in the old Boeing Model 40-A, carrying just two passengers. In those days gravity had seemed reluctant to let go; gravity didn't keep much of a hold on the B-47.

With very little climb power, Heimburger took them up to the bomber's normal operational height of 35,000 feet, more than ten thousand feet above the ceiling of a Stratocruiser. Here everything was at peak efficiency: the engines and the swept wing. They edged up to the subsonic, to 0.88 Mach. Allen looked down. The world was displayed as he had never seen it. The Great Plains had diminished to the proportions of a map. To the south he could see the Arkansas River wandering into Oklahoma; to the northeast was the Missouri and Kansas City.

There were no barriers left. Not mountains, not weather. Once, way back, flying in the old Boeing trimotor, he had put down at an emergency strip called Locomotive Springs, on the northern edge of Great Salt Lake, nothing there but a shack and a radio. A blizzard had closed in. The plane froze; Allen went duck hunting. Now, no barriers were left, but something was lost. What? The beginning. Humility, probably. Yet there was a thread running way through to this surge of adrenaline as they cut effortlessly through the sky. Not knowing what you couldn't do.

Heimburger was calling Wichita for clearance to enter the pattern. They went down in an extended shallow dive. When the old Stratocruiser throttled back she went willingly to earth. When the jets went to idle this lean and clean machine just wanted to go on flying on momentum. Only when the landing gear and flaps came down did you feel any aerodynamic braking, and then not much. She hit concrete at 140 mph, gently settling on that centralized bicycle gear, two fat wheels ahead, two behind, and the antlike stabilizing legs out there on the inboard engine pods finally settling those Jell-O wings. The strip raced by Allen's feet, and then, with wheel braking, she was just rolling, back to the taxiway with the engines idling in their shrill, high register.

Some months earlier, Pennell had gone public with his case for the commercial jet. An interview he gave to the company magazine raised skeptical eyebrows at Douglas and among Boeing's other competitors. Having suggested some of the features of the jet, Pennell said, ". . . the American turbojet transport is indeed ready to leave the drawing boards and move into the factory."

This was not the case. More than half the people at Boeing with any voice in the issue were against attempting a commercial jet. This was largely the sentiment of the military camp, which felt that thanks to the B-47, Boeing had ahead of it a huge captive market that needed no converting to the new religion of the jet, unlike the airlines, which measured everything in dollars and cents and were highly skeptical of jets.

It became a battle for Allen's ear. For Pennell, his close relationship with Wells was crucial, since Wells—as everybody knew—had more sway with Allen than anyone else. But Wells was always hard to read. He was not openly partisan either way. He was always as deeply engaged in the military designs as in the commercial.

As chief of preliminary design, Pennell could use as much

drawing-board time as he liked in trying to adapt the swept wing, podded engine configuration to fit the operating envelope of an airliner. But it was only paper. Even a man Pennell admired greatly, George Martin, the structures man on the B-47, remained lukewarm toward the commercial concept. Where stood Schairer, the greatest influence among the aeromen? The aeromen were caught straddling two increasingly different disciplines. Steiner, by nature a propagandist for whatever he happened at the moment to be working on, was stuck on the Stratocruiser track, stuck with propellers. So were younger and equally able talents like Sutter. Schairer's maestros of the wind tunnel—Cook, Withington, and Holtby—were translating the lessons of the B-47 into the outline of the next generation of jet bomber, with only secondary thoughts about how much closer these ideas might bring the commercial jet.

Schairer, in his late thirties, was assuming the mantle of a high guru. This manner is caught very well in a photograph taken for a story on Boeing in *Fortune* magazine. Most of his hair has gone. He outstares the camera through his rimless glasses. He manages to swagger, though standing still—hands thrust deep inside the pockets of pleated pants, jacket pulled open to reveal the glory of a very loud tie. But the fixing feature is the line of the mouth: set in a well-used sneer.

He stands locked between the wings and the tail of an oversized model of the B-47. You feel it is implicit that he knows that his place in aviation is secure. This is his machine. And the machine is the law according to Schairer. Apart from possibly the tie, there is nothing meretricious in this performance. There was no personality cult at Boeing, and Schairer was never a publicity-seeker. This is the high priest on his private mountain, serenely confident.

Schairer would never again be so completely identified with one airplane as he was with the B-47. Henceforth, he would preside within his own spiritual domain, running things according to his own capricious lights, inspiring and enraging as he went. His touch was a form of magic, sometimes black magic. Boeing—and particularly Ed Wells—arranged that they could suffer Schairer for the sake of his magic.

When Allen returned to Seattle from Wichita, there was no immediate emanation of a vision. That would not have been his style. But Pennell soon had the perfect opening for pressing Allen again on the commercial jet. The two of them led a small group of Boeing executives on a trip to the annual British air show at Farnborough. For a while they had known that the British were developing the world's first jet airliner, the Comet, and here, suddenly and with great impact, it was flying over Farnborough. The Comet represented a very different philosophy—a more cautious one—than Boeing's. It had negligible sweepback and its four Rolls-Royce engines were buried inside the roots of the wing, anathema to the Boeing engineers. It carried fewer passengers than a Stratocruiser and had a far more limited range.

Nonetheless, the Boeing men had to concede that the Comet, modest though its ambitions were, did show how the jet would transform airline travel: it cruised at nearly 500 mph at 35,000 feet. This was precisely the leap in performance that Allen had himself experienced aboard the B-47.

"How do you like the Comet?" Allen asked Pennell.

"We could do better," Pennell answered confidently.

Just how much better became amply evident when the Boeing men went to the De Havilland plant where the Comets were being built (the plant that had produced the doomed Swallow). Compared with Seattle, it was like looking at a small-town auto repair shop. There was nothing recognizable as a production line. The Comets, in Allen's words when, back in Seattle, he described the plant, were "just sort of hammered up. With the lack of tooling they had, you fellows couldn't even build an experimental airplane." It reminded Allen of the Boeing plant of the early thirties, when the company's ideas were ahead of its capacity to produce airplanes in any volume. De Havilland had always, like Boeing, been a venturesome company, and it had built some fine aircraft. But it was critically undercapitalized for the business as it now was.

Pennell realized that the Comet was no persuader. It violated the safety standards Boeing had insisted on from the start, particularly by putting the engines where any turbine failure would compromise the integrity of the airframe. The Comet's wing flap system was rudimentary, giving it poor airfield characteristics; even worse, the British had not invested in the rigorous research and test program that was mandatory at Boeing.

(Despite this critical view of the Comet, no one in Seattle then realized how fatally flawed the airplane would prove to be.) Outsiders were asking Allen whether Boeing was going into commercial jets.

"We're reviewing it," he said, without elaboration. He wanted time. He was still educating himself into the job. His family life had been reinvigorated by a new marriage, to a friend of his late wife's, Mary Ellen Field, known exclusively as Mef. Proposing marriage, Allen had explained that he proposed to do all his business entertaining at home, and wanted to know how she felt about that. She said she would manage just fine, and over the years enchanted many an airline chief into the Boeing embrace.

At the start of the marriage, Allen and Mef spent two or three hours every month visiting a Boeing plant, walking the floor with an engineer who would explain how things worked, although this habit tailed off as things became familiar. Allen made a point of being approachable; he listened. The precision of the work as he peered at it was extraordinary. These vast airplanes were fashioned to microscopic tolerances. Each B-47 required six thousand bolt holes, to be drilled with an accuracy of two thousandths of an inch. The aluminum wing skin was milled from a thickness of five eights of an inch at the center to three sixteenths of an inch at the tip in a continuous taper more than fifty feet in length.

There was a drawing for everything, however minute. The weight of everything counted. Separately the parts seemed so fragile. Then, when they came together, the seamless metal enclosed the inner maze and gave it order. The more of it you saw, the more you marveled at the virtuosity.

Every night he took a briefcase full of papers home, and after cocktails and dinner he would retreat to the papers. Mef soon felt that Bill Allen wasn't going to change Boeing. Boeing was changing him. The lawyer was giving way to a more judicial cast of mind. The roles had reversed: instead of being an advocate, he had to rule between advocates. And at the end of the day he left behind the clamor to seek his own counsel. Making up his mind was done in private.

Allen knew that the decision to develop a jet airliner would imply more than might be apparent. It would send a signal that

Boeing was through with propellers. It was already through with the Stratocruiser, but it still had heavy commitments to develop its military derivatives. Would that be the end of it, the end of the first age of aviation, the age of the propeller? It was a tough call. Donald Douglas, for one, showed no sign of giving up on the propeller. Now he was designing a DC-7, an airliner to extend the company's hold on the airlines beyond the hundreds of DC-6s.

As a company strategy you could look at the jet decision two ways. Either in one leap you would leave the opposition looking archaic—or you would end up with a speculative airplane, one no airline had asked for, that would involve changing every detail of operations from maintenance to airport handling, and that would have to get safety certification according to rules that did not yet even exist for jets. Certainly, there was the Comet to worry about, but there was no real evidence that the world was ready to switch to the jet.

So the question hung there: would they bet that the propeller was finished?

At the end of 1948, Joe Sutter had checked in one morning to find a new notice plastered everywhere: "Life is too short to work on propellers.—Ed Wells." This had lifted Sutter's spirits. They were still debugging the military spin-offs of the Stratocruiser, still living in the backwash of the B-47. What had happened to make Wells so sure?

The explanation was remarkable and eventually became a legend within the company, albeit a slightly garbled one. It lay in events over a few days in Dayton that fall. This episode provides a rare instance of being able to pin down a sea change in Boeing's philosophy to one conversation, and it also offers a textbook case of how a company's fortunes can turn on a dime.

Since 1946, Boeing designers had been failing to satisfy a military specification for a large, high-flying intercontinental bomber—twice the size of the B-47. It was to be powered by turbo-prop engines, gas turbines used not as jets but to power large propellers. By the fall of 1948 the work had reached an impasse. No one could find a way of coupling the turbine to a propeller and having the propeller stay in one piece.

The XB-47 had been flying for ten months. German scientists imported to the military research center at Wright Field

(Woldemar Voigt, mastermind of the Messerschmitt 262, was one of them) had been urging Warden to abandon the turboprops and make the big bomber a jet. With the striking performance of the XB-47 backing them up, Warden listened.

On Thursday, October 21, 1948, Schairer and a small group of Boeing aeromen filed in for a meeting with Warden, about to tell him the turboprop was a dog.

Warden barely glanced at the papers they gave him. "You have to come up with a better airplane or your contract is going to come to an end," he said.

Schairer knew what he meant: every design they had proposed had fallen short of the B-36 bomber that was already flying. Then Warden dropped the other shoe. "Make it a jet."

On the face of it, such a change meant months of reworking the big bomber design. Yet only five days later, Warden had on his desk a detailed proposal for a new large jet bomber, the XB-52, plus a 120th-scale model of it neatly boxed for a journey to the Pentagon.

The airplane that became the B-52, with a career stretching from Vietnam to the Gulf War, was designed in a suite of the Van Cleve Hotel in Dayton over the course of a long weekend. That, at least, is the company legend. In truth, it wasn't that simple. When they left Warden, Schairer called Wells in Seattle, and Wells took a night flight to Dayton. Three other Boeing men happened to be in Dayton that week: Pennell, representing structures, and two aeromen, Bob Withington and Vaughn Blumenthal. They had been conferring at Wright Field on yet another bomber, the B-55, a jet. This was about the same size as the B-47, but far more sophisticated.

On the Friday morning, Wells called in these three to join him and Schairer and another aeroman, Art Carlsen. On the line was possibly the biggest military contract the company would ever see. What they decided to do—it was the only way to preempt a new competition for the contract—was to double the size of the B-55. By luck, the airplane then matched in dimensions what the Air Force was asking for. Blumenthal and Schairer went out to buy balsa, glue, and model paint from a hobby store. Wells bought drafting equipment.

Withington and Blumenthal expected Schairer—who was, after all, one of the world's best aerodynamicists—to make all the crucial estimates of performance, which was a far more elaborate series of calculations than simply doubling the numbers for the B-55. But Schairer told them to get on with it. He sat in a corner of the suite with the balsa wood and carved a model according to dimensions called out by Wells as he drew them. The model was made peculiarly to the 120th scale simply because Schairer had a twelve-inch ruler and carved the model on the basis of one inch to ten feet.

None of them would ever have to worry about propellers again. Warden took the model and the proposal to Washington within a week, and Boeing secured the contract. The B-55 was never built, but as it was reincarnated as the B-52 its design introduced ideas that took Boeing much closer to what would be needed for a jet airliner.

The XB-52 did not fly until April 1952, with Tex Johnston at the controls. This was unusually long for the period between concept and first flight, but the airplane's development was paced by that of the new Pratt & Whitney engines, and they, too, would bring the jet airliner a lot closer. After a few flights, Johnston was able to demonstrate that the bomber's performance came within a whisker of the numbers calculated in the Van Cleve Hotel.

In the summer of 1950, when Allen climbed out of the belly of the B-47, he already knew that the qualitative advantages of jet flight would, sooner or later, prove irresistible. Within a few months, he decided it was time to feel out the market for a commercial jet. Steiner was released from the bondage of propellers and, with Pennell, drew up the configuration for Boeing's vision of the future of airline travel. It was called the Model 473-60C, and it was a clear statement of the Boeing philosophy, with swept wings and podded engines.

When Steiner was let loose on the new jet, his intense competitiveness—everybody around him felt its impact—made him ideal as a salesman. He was, instantly, the True Believer in the Model 473-60C. However, he and Pennell were given a serious disability in making their pitch to the airlines. They could talk only hazily about the airplane's engines—not because there was anything wrong with them, but because they were a military secret. The Pratt & Whitney J-57, an engine that would become a classic of its generation in both its military and civilian versions, was being developed for the B-57. In designing the airliner, Pennell and Steiner had simply scaled down the bomber's wing to half size and attached two of these engines in a double nacelle (again from the B-52) to each wing.

They were, after all, selling an airliner that, like the B-52, would fly at high subsonic speeds and cruise at 35,000 feet. They pitched it to U.S. airlines and then took off for Europe. Each time the question of the engines came up, and each time they became oddly evasive. They were trying to look confident that the engine would do what they said, but if they gave away any of the technical details of the J-57 they would have violated military secrecy, so they invented an imaginary engine.

They even tried to sell the airplane to the Russians. Here they found a willing audience, especially when it came to the engine. The Russians, who had digested their own German aerodynamicists, knew all about the swept wing but were weak on turbojet technology. Again, the Boeing men clammed up.

In the end, zero sales. The Douglas DC-7C was being sold convincingly as the state of the airliner art. It had long range, it was economical to operate, and Douglas was trusted. It might have propellers, but that's what the airlines liked about Douglas: nothing fancy, everything well proven. Boeing, by comparison, was pushing the future too hard, before it seemed palatable.

Even Steiner was deflated. He tried selling the plane to the Air Force as a tanker, but got nowhere.

Pennell took another look at their proposal. The 473-60C was not an impressive concept. The airlines recognized in it the old Boeing failings of partly cannibalizing a military design and of not thinking an airplane through, from scratch, to fit what airlines needed. To be a serious contender, Boeing would not only have to show its unquestioned mastery of swept wing technology, but marry that to an airplane that would be economically irresistible to the board of an airline—not easy to do, with the thirst of jet engines all too apparent.

Some people thought that Pennell had given up everything else and staked his career on getting Boeing into the jet airliner business. But Pennell made no apology: he knew he had to change the whole natural disposition of the company. When it came to selling an airplane, most of Boeing's senior executives

knew only the military bureaucracy. They understood that lab-
yrinth well. It had certain fixed and friendly features—men like
Warden and Wolfe.

The airlines were very different. They were run by—often
dominated by—aviation pioneers with strong tastes and prejudices of their own. Several of the men who had come well out
of Postmaster Brown's mergers of the 1930s were still there:
Cyrus—C. R.—Smith at American, Rickenbacker at Eastern,
and W. A. "Pat" Patterson, who had taken over United in 1934
and was small but lethal with his tongue. Even though Patterson
had broken into the air transport business (from the Wells Fargo
Bank) via Bill Boeing's airline, he was no fan of the Boeing
Airplane Company. He had looked over the Stratocruiser's cabin
and fingered the cloth trim. "What's this?" he barked, and answered his own question: "Coffin cloth. It's coffin cloth. A *dead*
airplane!" Boeing had no reputation at all with United. And then,
at the top of the hill, was Juan Trippe of Pan Am, a truly imperial
temperament and unquestioned czar of the international air
routes.

How could Boeing win the confidence and then the business
of men like these? Fortunately, Pennell's determination to gain
commercial credibility was helped by Allen's growing public stature. What might have handicapped him inside the company, his
technical illiteracy, was more than compensated for outside the
company by his social graces and sagacity. He was the best
ambassador Boeing had had since Bill Boeing himself. Allen
cultivated the airline chiefs. It helped that they were mostly of
his generation, and that he shared values and sometimes tastes
with them; he and C. R. Smith shared a passion for Charlie
Russell's Arcadian paintings. Trippe was the hardest to fathom,
but Allen found a rapport even with him.

Allen made it clear that he wanted Pennell's next proposal
to reflect the best the company could do; he now called for a
total commitment to the jet. But first there was a ritual to
perform that often, within Boeing, carried an almost superstitious aura: they had to pick a model number. The Stratocruiser
was numbered 377, and the 400, 500, and 600 series were already
assigned to missiles and nonaircraft products. There was a persuasive symbolic reason for marking a clean break between the
age of the propeller and the jet, and so, because it had a certain
resonance, they picked the number 707.

And, as the 707 evolved, it began to look at last like a plane designed for the airlines, from the ground up, not a nimble assembly of bits from a bomber.

Wells and Schairer, now playing into the role of the two wise men, vetted the ideas as they coalesced into the outline of an airplane. Only a trace of the Stratocruiser remained in their thinking—the width of the passenger cabin, 132 inches, based on the Stratocruiser's comfortable two-plus-two seating. Gone were the two-deck cabin, the downstairs lounge, the cocktail bar. Jets would slash traveling times. There would be no need for elegant distractions—in its belly the 707 would carry baggage and cargo. Boeing had taken to heart an airline dictum: payload meant load that paid.

Schairer kept a close eye on the wing. The 707 was going to be very fast—passengers had ridden nothing like it—and the wing set the speed. There would be no loitering around 500 mph like the Comet. The 707 would cruise at something approaching 600 mph, sneaking up on high Mach with the same angle of sweepback as the B-47, 35 degrees. Only six or so years before, this would have been unthinkable, and in 1952 it was still radical to believe that you could breed into the swept wing an essential further stage of docility, so that an airline pilot could regard its handling as routine.

The 707's engines would hang out there separately in four pods, two spaced out over each wing. But there was a problem in tailoring the 707's wing with the finesse that would normally have been demanded by Schairer. The Boeing wind tunnel was shut down for an extensive conversion, designed by NACA, that would greatly improve its transonic work. Before the tunnel was closed, they had tested a wing for an airplane of about the same size as the 707, a tanker that was never built. But the tanker wing had only a 25-degree sweepback.

For the 707, it seemed expedient to take the tanker wing and simply rotate it another 10 degrees. This design solution was somewhat cruder than they would have liked, but there was no time to begin from scratch. The higher sweepback implied a substantial difference in handling characteristics. To check these out, and to do what further refining they could, they put the wing into the wind tunnel at Purdue University, in Indiana, whose engineering college was second in size to MIT, and whose tunnel happened to be free when Boeing desperately needed it.

Allen was coming to a decision that would be unprecedented for Boeing. To overcome the airlines' skepticism of both the company and the jet, Boeing would build a prototype out of its own pocket—a prototype that itself it would never be able to sell because the design included too many innovations that had to be proved before it could be developed into a production airplane. There was, however, a way of hedging this risk. The Air Force's B-52s would need aerial refueling from tankers as long-legged as they were, and such a tanker might spring from the chrysalis of the prototype jetliner.

Six days after Tex Johnston took the XB-52 up for the first time, in the spring of 1952, Pennell and Schairer presented Allen with the detailed 707 design. The accountants put the cost at between $13 million and $15 million (it would be $16 million). On April 22, Allen put the proposal to the board. By now, his wish was their command, and the program to build a prototype was approved.

Allen made one curious change, illustrating the gravity given to model numbers. He withdrew the number 707 from the prototype and renumbered it the 367-80; 367 was the series number of the military freighter version of the Stratocruiser, the KC-97. To try to throw competitors like Douglas off the scent, Allen added the -80 to suggest nothing more than an extension of the Stratocruiser's genes. The new number was such a mouthful that in the patois of Boeing Field the jet became known as the "Dash-80," and was to be immortalized as such.

The Dash-80 decision has become an oft-touted piece of Boeing lore, exemplifying the spirit of boldness, innovation, and high risk. Bold it certainly was, and innovative on a broad front. But the risk has been exaggerated. Boeing at that time was the country's largest defense contractor. It had three lucrative contracts with the Air Force: for the B-47, for the KC-97 aerial tanker, and, coming up, for the B-52, a twenty-year cash cow. The government always paid its bills on time.

In truth, Boeing was saddled with an excess profits tax, weighted in a way that peculiarly penalized it. The tax was calculated on the difference between a company's prewar profits and the profits made on the war contracts. Since Boeing had been deeply in the red before the war, the wartime bonanza loaded the formula for assessing excess profits. When the board

A heretic at NACA: Robert Jones, a largely self-taught aerodynamicist, realized that he had stumbled on a fundamental key to high-speed flight, the swept wing. But the NACA establishment disbelieved his theory. Jones was finally proved right and was vindicated by data brought back from Nazi Germany at the end of the war.

Not-so-mad Max: Max Munk was recruited to America from Germany at the end of World War I and built a revolutionary wind tunnel at NACA. Munk's style did not fit with NACA's senior staff, and he was forced out. Munk's work later inspired Robert Jones's work on high-speed flight. Late in life, Munk was still promoting new ideas but never recovered the status he held briefly at NACA.

The formula emerges: These three wind tunnel models crafted in 1945 show the evolution of the XB-47 bomber. Two have conventional straight wings, the center model with engines buried in the fuselage. As the U.S. Air Force objected to buried engines, this led the Boeing engineers to put them in pods, suspended from the wings on pylons. The combination of swept wing and podded engines became an almost universally adopted formula.

All in a weekend: George Schairer holds the balsa model of a bomber that he crafted over a weekend in a hotel suite in Dayton, Ohio. Schairer and Ed Wells, fourth from left, were the two dominant engineers of their generation at Boeing. In Dayton, Wells drew the configuration details of the bomber as Schairer cut the balsa. The model and a hastily devised specification went to the U.S. Air Force and became the basis for the B-52 bomber.

Origin of the species: a wind tunnel model of the XB-47 bomber in the Boeing wind tunnel. This first expression of Schairer's belief in the swept wing was at first uncontrollable in the tunnel. An engineer, left, chosen for his lightning reflexes is trying to "fly" the model, but it would often go wild and disintegrate. Only after thousands of hours of testing was the design finally made tractable, transforming high-speed flight.

■

Mentor and tormentor: George Schairer was the prime gatherer of Boeing's engineering elite and, to the end of his career, an irascible taskmaster. In 1945, Schairer sent a note to Seattle from Germany outlining a theory for a new kind of wing. From that moment, Boeing took the lead in large aircraft with swept wings. The 747 is a direct descendant of those aircraft, and all of Boeing's family of commercial jets bear Schairer's influence.

The true believer: Maynard Pennell, a specialist in airframe structures, joined Boeing from Douglas after World War II. Once Pennell saw the depth of Boeing's knowledge of high-speed, subsonic jet flight, gained from building bombers, he became the company's leading advocate of launching commercial jets. Boeing had a poor reputation with airlines, who were lukewarm toward jets. Pennell, however, persisted and the Boeing 707 followed.

Moment of revelation: Boeing's boss, William Allen, steps up into the belly of a B-47 for his first taste of jet flight at Wichita, Kansas, in August 1950. Allen had flown airliners since the 1920s, and had never known anything to equal the experience that the B-47 provided. From that moment, Allen was ready to listen to the idea of transferring the technology from bombers to commercial jets. Allen's leadership was to take Boeing to the top in jets.

COURTESY THE BOEING COMPANY ARCHIVES

The future appears: rollout of the Dash-80, May 15, 1954, prototype of the 707 airliner. The 707 launched the Boeing family of commercial jets, and posed a serious threat to the company then dominating the airliner business, Douglas. Boeing was forced at the last minute to make the 707's fuselage wider because of Douglas's challenger, the DC-8. And without a later change to the 707's wing, Boeing might well have lost its lead in jets.

■

The man with the golden touch: Jack Steiner, fourth from the left, and the team he led to develop the Boeing 727. This trijet became the first real cash cow of the commercial division, flying domestic trunk routes around the world. Joe Sutter, third from the left, worked closely with Steiner on the 727. Steiner was flamboyant and tended to steal the limelight. Sutter, as adept an engineer as Steiner, finally got his big break with the 747.

COURTESY THE BOEING COMPANY ARCHIVES

Nose in the dirt: The Dash-80 prototype lost its brake power on landing and careered across Boeing Field, finally stopping only when the nosewheel hit a piece of concrete and collapsed. Test pilot Tex Johnston was later reprimanded when he twice rolled the Dash-80 like a jet fighter over the crowds during hydroplane races on Lake Washington. Johnston had total confidence in the airplane and countered that he had never put it at risk.

The first man up: Tex Johnston (*left*) preparing to test-fly the B-52 bomber. Johnston also tested the XB-47, the Dash-80 prototype, and the 707. He later stepped down as chief test pilot after disputes with the management over changes to make the 707 safer to fly.

■

The makers of Boeing: Ed Wells, Bill Allen, and George Schairer at the B-52 plant. Allen depended on the two brilliant engineers to keep Boeing at the cutting edge of design. And they depended on Allen's nerve and commercial judgment.

COURTESY THE BOEING COMPANY ARCHIVES

Enter the jet set: Frank Del Giudice (*third from left*) virtually invented the modern jet airliner cabin. On his left are Maynard Pennell, Ed Wells, and Milt Heinemann of Boeing—Heinemann and Del Giudice collaborated on every Boeing jet from the 707 to the 747. Here they stand at the door of a wooden mock-up of the 707's interior that was built in a coffee warehouse in Manhattan.

COURTESY WALTER DORWIN TEAGUE

Setting the rules: Frank Del Giudice briefs airline stewardesses in the uncompleted 707 mock-up. The stewardesses had to deal with many more passengers than before.

The pioneers: Cyrus R. Smith (*left*) built American Airlines into a major carrier. His ideas led to the Douglas DC-3, the prewar airliner that eclipsed Boeing's 247. Smith and Boeing's chief, Allen (*center*) later became close friends, and Smith's order was crucial for the launch of the 707. Frank Kolk (*right*), American's chief engineer, urged Smith to order a twin-engine wide-body, but Smith balked. The idea later flowered in the European Airbus.

■

The world shrinks: Boeing's first brochure to introduce the jet age pictured a Norman Rockwell style of family adventure, but the truth was that at first jet flight remained beyond the reach of most people, who identified it with the elitist jet setters.

Come aboard THE 707

voted on the Dash-80 it knew full well that around 70 percent of that investment would otherwise have gone to Uncle Sam. At a real cost of $4-5 million, the Dash-80 was no more than a reasonable risk to take for the chance of transforming Boeing's prospects in the one market where its performance was lamentable.

As it took shape, the Dash-80 was virtually a hand-built airplane. With no production line laid down, every part was custom-made. There were no flashy trimmings. It was a test airplane, and equipped only with the instrumentation needed for that role. The cabin was lined with cheap plywood paneling, not very effective insulation against the sound of four turbojets. Tex Johnston, between flight tests of the XB-52, watched over every detail of the Dash-80's flight deck. This was a new kind of bird to fly—it was like trying to build a car with the power of a hot rod and the manners of a limousine.

In spite of the deception of the model number, there was no hope of effectively preserving the secrecy around the Dash-80. It was being built in a former wartime satellite plant at Renton, on the southern edge of Lake Washington, and there was just too much of a buzz coming from the assembly shop. Nonetheless, the two competitors most likely to respond, Douglas and Lockheed, seemed to show little awareness that Boeing was set on a challenging new course. To some extent, a series of fatal crashes of the British Comet had poisoned the well. (A weakness in the fuselage had caused explosive decompression when the Comet neared its cruising altitude.)

And when the Dash-80 was finally wheeled into sunlight, you didn't need to be as conservative an engineer as Donald Douglas to think that it was a hairy idea. It was rolled out of the plant on May 15, 1954, to a brass band and in view of an honored guest—William E. Boeing, a vigorous seventy-two-year-old. The jet was painted in a bilious combination of brown and yellow. Boeing's wife, Bertha, broke a bottle of champagne over the nose and christened the ship "airplane of tomorrow, the Boeing Jet Stratoliner and Stratotanker."

It did look the part, from its wind-tunnel-molded nose to the sharply swept tail. Here was an extraordinary metamorphosis of the formula fashioned from Robert Jones's theory and Schairer's beast of a bomber. Boeing's aeromen were acutely conscious of how far they had come—and how fast. It was almost nine years to the day since Schairer's letter had arrived from Volkenrode. Aviation had never known a decade like it. Some of those standing in Schairer's shadow had come much of the way under his maverick tutelage, through the trials of the war, the short postwar euphoria, and the new Cold War. Others, like Joe Sutter, had thought solely of the airliners. For Sutter, working under Steiner on the Dash-80 was a baptism of a kind, imbuing the vision of a world suddenly rendered much smaller.

A week later, Johnston was taxiing gently along the apron at Renton, getting the feel of the plane on the ground and testing the brakes, when the Dash-80 listed suddenly to the left, like a ship sinking into a trough. He shut down the engines. The left landing gear had collapsed. It was a significant structural failure, and Wells himself bore down with ferocity on the investigation. A design flaw had been compounded by a faulty metal forging. It cost the program six weeks and the engineers some esteem, the kind of basic goof that wasn't supposed to happen with supposedly the hottest designers in the business. But the delay brought its own serendipity: Johnston declared the Dash-80 ready to fly on the company's thirty-eighth anniversary, July 15.

As was his ritual, that morning Johnston slipped on a new pair of cowboy boots. He had completed the high-speed taxi trials. The ship had a kick in it; the controls were responsive, everything felt right. He walked around the plane as the engineers completed their checks. Allen arrived. Johnston had got to know Allen in all his moods—he had flown him on an XB-52 test flight and seen his upside. This was the downside—Allen was bent and worried. Johnston went over to Allen and made the required speech, in his plummy, soothing Kansas drawl: "Bill, you don't need to worry about this airplane. It's a hell of a good airplane. We've done all we can do. We've got to fly it now."

Douglas Redux: Decided by Inches

No airline had shown more than a passing curiosity in the Boeing Dash-80, and since it was a single-copy prototype, none was being asked to order it. The few thousands of people regularly flying around the world on piston-engine airliners like the Lockheed Constellation, the Douglas DC-6, and the Boeing Stratocruiser—airplanes that were then glamorous and often carrying movie stars—imagined that they could hardly travel in higher style. The leisurely cruising speeds, seldom more than 300 mph, and restricted range of these aircraft were not seen as a hindrance to the experience, since the one allowed for elaborate gastronomic pampering in the air and the other for exotic way stations during refueling—Athens, Cairo, Tehran, Bombay. It was all a well-mannered kind of traveling that set its adherents apart from ordinary mortals; flying in this way, without trepidation, was very chic. It would be some years before this community of comforts would be undermined and then eradicated by an urgent, spreading egalitarianism of movement, but the first flight of the Dash-80 was, without fanfare, the beginning of the end.

As Johnston buckled up in the cockpit with copilot Dix Loesch he could see Allen on the apron, still locked in gloom, the embodiment of a Scotsman whose whole fortune was invested in something he feared would go up and disappear. Johnston, however, from the moment he released the brakes, knew in his bones that the Dash-80 would do what it was designed to do: demonstrate that high-speed flight was no longer the sole province of military aircraft. They climbed up over Lake Washington, did a few basic maneuvers so that Johnston could be sure of the controls, and then came in for an approach over Seattle and into Boeing Field, where the flight testing would take place.

A few days after Boeing celebrated its auspicious birthday, Johnston took the Dash-80 up for its second flight, and let the jet loose. No airliner had ever felt like this: she was eager and nimble, and, like the B-47, the higher and faster she flew the more at home she seemed. There was, however, a less comforting reminder of the precursive bomber. The first intimations came with a familiar tremor. Johnston knew the signs. He had gone over it so many times with the aeromen that he could almost see the unseeable. A yaw began, just a rocking of the swept wings. As the yaw increased, the airflow over the wings would suddenly become asymmetrical: the air would move normally over one wing but over the other it would begin slipping sideways, in the direction of the span. And as this airflow bled away, the wing lost lift and turned the yaw into a roll. The Dash-80 had a marked inclination to Dutch-roll.

Johnston himself could handle it comfortably, suppressing the roll before it got out of control, and under most flight conditions Little Herbie would suppress it before a pilot even knew it was there, but nonetheless Johnston found it worrisome. It was one thing for a skilled test pilot to know the signs and not get into trouble, but the airliner had to be safe in the hands of pilots whose competence would vary greatly and who would have no previous experience of flying jets. At the end of the second flight, Johnston noted in his log that the directional stability of the Dash-80 was barely acceptable.

Astonishingly, the implications of this comment were neglected by the flight test supervisors, possibly because of a near disaster with the airplane soon afterward. Johnston had been worrying about the Dash-80's braking abilities. To reassure himself, he had done some high-speed taxiing with hard braking. The brakes had held up well, and he took off for a short flight. But when he returned to Boeing Field and applied the brakes, nothing happened. They had lost pressure, invisibly, during the testing and completely failed on landing. With the engines cut, the end of the runway was coming up frighteningly fast. Johnston's only resort to save the airplane was to attempt what was called a ground loop—steering the Dash-80 off the runway and into a wide arc through the grass to dissipate speed, hoping that he didn't hit anything before he rolled to a stop. It required great nerve and skill. Everybody on Boeing Field seemed to hold his breath. The pride of the company was disappearing into the rough in a cloud of dust, and she nearly made it. With only a few feet left to roll, the nose gear hit a slab of concrete lying in the grass and collapsed. The Dash-80 settled with her nose inelegantly resting in a ditch.

A few days later in Seattle, Jack Steiner had to deliver the keynote lecture to a conference of his peers in the airplane industry. His theme was the coming of jet transports. Steiner remembered the advice of an industrial designer whom Boeing had called in to advise on cabin interiors: if you can't hide it, paint it red. He opened his lecture with a slide of the Dash-80 with its snitch in the ditch and said, "There are several ways of stopping large jet airplanes. This is one."

It brought the house down.

In the audience were some of the best designers from Douglas and Lockheed. Once the Dash-80 was in the air, Boeing's design philosophy for jet transports was exposed for all to see, even though what was under its skin was a treasury of knowledge that could only be guessed at. In a real sense, a great technical watershed of this kind could only be first assessed and judged by an innermost coterie with the appropriate knowledge and a vested interest in understanding its import; the public response to pictures of the Dash-80 was simply that it looked unfamiliar in a futuristic way. As they listened to Steiner, Boeing's competitors were impressed that the gamble had been made, but they needed to know more. They asked Steiner if they could take a look at the airplane.

Allen consented, and they walked into the hangar where the Dash-80 was coddled in scaffolding while the nose gear and other superficial damage were repaired.

The man from Douglas was an old and distinguished rival, Bailey Oswald—the same Bailey Oswald who had seen the

Boeing 247 being tested in the Caltech tunnel, worked on the DC-1, and then joined Douglas as the alchemy of the DC-3 was wrought. Until Oswald stepped into this hangar, he had not absorbed how far ahead of Douglas in domesticating the jet transport Boeing was. The Dash-80 might never fly a paying passenger, but it looked alarmingly like an airliner—like the next generation of airliner. Others, like the men from Lockheed, thought that Boeing was out on a limb, and that the Dash-80 was another Boeing hybrid with one eye on military orders and the other on the airlines, but Oswald went back to Santa Monica looking shaken.

Oswald and another of the originators of the DC series, Arthur Raymond, backed by Douglas's chief engineer, Ed Burton, argued with Donald Douglas that they had to catch up with Boeing and develop a jet with some urgency. Douglas, however, could not be swayed. He was under pressure from C. R. Smith of American Airlines to produce the DC-7. The production line was so busy filling orders for as far ahead as the eye could see that to Donald Douglas a jet seemed a distraction from the business of making money. His company's lack of a wind tunnel of its own played into his argument: the DC-7 would need all the technical resources they could hire.

Douglas's private life had also been distracting. In 1951 his wife, Charlotte, finally, after twenty years, acknowledged the existence of Peggy Tucker and sued for divorce. Douglas married his mistress in 1953. He was four years from his intended retirement at sixty-five, and his son, Donald Douglas, Jr., was pressing his claim to succeed. None of this was reassuring to the surviving members of the brilliant team of engineers that had built the company with the touchy patriarch.

Another venerable figure in the world of aviation was far more able to see that the Dash-80 was the writing on the wall for every airliner then flying. Lord Hives, the head of Rolls-Royce, was shown the airplane by George Schairer.

"This is the end," said Hives.

Schairer was puzzled. "The end of what?"

"The end of British aviation."

Hives explained that the Comet crashes had discouraged the British from building further jets and that they were, instead, concentrating on turboprops. Now Hives realized that as far as the international airways were concerned, the turboprops would lead nowhere and the future belonged to the big jets. He was, in essence, right: although the British would go on to build a variety of successful airliners using both turboprops and jets, they never produced a big jet to equal any of the Dash-80's progeny.

One of the summer's highlights in Seattle was the Gold Cup race for hydroplanes, held on Lake Washington just north of the Renton plant. Allen decided to use the 1955 race as an opportunity to promote the commercial jet, and Boeing invited airline chiefs and other industry notables to watch the hydroplanes from a company boat. During the course of the event, Tex Johnston would fly over the lake in the Dash-80.

The race was on a Sunday. On the Saturday before, Johnston turned up at the flight test center at Boeing Field and told the engineers, who set the performance limits for each stage of the prototype's test flights, that he wasn't happy with the restrictions then placed on the Dash-80. He said he wanted to make a low, high-speed run over the Gold Cup course, but the airplane was not cleared to do this. The Dash-80 had not completed the critical testing for flutter, but the flight engineers reviewed their data and were persuaded that they could allow Johnston his high-speed run.

By the time Johnston took off, a crowd of some 200,000 was gathered at the shoreline watching the races. Air traffic control cleared the sky of private planes so that Johnston could make two runs over the course. Every face turned up at the sound of the approaching jet. Most people in Seattle were used to the sight of the Dash-80 now, but it still had a magic effect on them, as it did for the visitors who were seeing it for the first time. Johnston brought her in low enough so that the spectators could see the trademark livery. The nose lifted a little. A wing waggled. And then, with a kind of lazy majesty, the whole airplane turned on its axis. Johnston was performing a barrel roll, a stunt normally limited to jet fighters or aerobatic teams. Allen couldn't believe his eyes. *A barrel roll, for God's sake!* For a few seconds as it passed over the VIP boats the airplane was actually *upside down!* The podded engines stuck up above the wings instead of hanging down. Cool as you like. Allen was turning puce.

Johnston finished his run with a wide, banking turn and came toward them again. And again he went into the languorous roll. Everybody around Allen was applauding, but he turned to a friend, Larry Bell, who always carried pills for a heart condition. "For Pete's sake, Larry, give me one of your pills." Bell, an aviation pioneer whose company had once employed Johnston, was enjoying the show. For the crowds along the lake the stunt momentarily eclipsed the hydroplanes; Allen was apoplectic, but realized that everybody else assumed the maneuver had been planned.

The next morning, Johnston was testing the Dash-80 again, and landed just before noon, to find himself summoned immediately to the executive building on Marginal Way. He was directed to Allen's office, where Allen sat flanked by Wells and Schairer. Even then it took him a few seconds to perceive that it was not an occasion for congratulations.

"Tex," said Allen, "what on earth did you think you were doing yesterday?"

Wells and Schairer glowered.

"Wait just a minute, Bill," said Johnston, using his best Jimmy Stewart drawl. "I want to tell you guys something so you understand. That was a barrel roll. A one-G maneuver. The airplane never knew it was doing anything but flying straight and level, with aileron deflection."

Allen waited, wanting more.

"I started at about four hundred feet. Applied up elevator, held the one G, put the aileron in. After the roll I was at sixteen hundred feet, climbed out during the maneuver. This is not risky. If you hold one G you don't uncover the fuel pumps. You don't uncover the hydraulic pumps. There's nothing that can happen to the airplane. Believe me, Bill . . . I wouldn't do it if I didn't know I *could* do it."

Allen pounced. "You've done it *before*?"

"Sure. This is a good airplane. There's nothing that can happen to the airplane."

"Well, Tex," said Allen, "you know that. Now we know that. But just don't do it anymore. The whole future of this company is in that airplane."

Chastened more by the atmosphere than by anything Allen had said, Johnston nodded, in respect rather than in contrition.

"By the way," said Allen, "Eddie Rickenbacker is coming to my house tonight for a stag dinner. You're invited."

"Why, thanks, Bill." Johnston relaxed.

Johnston never realized how close he had come to being fired. He persisted in thinking that all was forgiven. Hadn't Allen asked him to the party? And a lot of other parties? Didn't everybody love those barrel rolls? If you wanted to show you really had an airplane, that was what you did. Just ask the competition.

But Wells and Schairer hadn't needed a lecture on the airplane's capacity to survive a roll. They, like Allen, were worried about the reaction of the airline chiefs who had come to the Gold Cup—Boeing didn't want people to get the idea that its airliners were tested by cowboys. Airlines didn't buy airplanes the way the Air Force did.

Only Allen's feeling that Johnston was probably the best experimental test pilot in the business had saved him. Later— a lot later—Allen told a conference in Seattle: "It has taken twenty-two years for me to reach the point where I can discuss the event with a modicum of humor."

Johnston never absorbed this; he never accepted Allen's contention that he had put the whole company at risk, and he never really understood Bill Allen, who had a very fixed view of propriety in the air as well as on the ground, and a very long memory. Allen filed his feelings away when it suited him, but he kept a score. If the score got too high, pragmatism gave way to action.

Someone more attuned than Johnston to the corporate politics of Boeing would have seen in the troika convened to deal with him a neat diagram of how Allen was now running the company. When it came to anything technical, Wells and Schairer were Allen's satraps. Neither was hobbled by having to run a department. Wells tended to be the bridge between the company and its customers, whether the Air Force or the airlines, working problems as they arose. Schairer buzzed like a tireless wasp over the rump of technical output, principally over the aeromen, diving and stinging at will.

In fact, Schairer exercised a pervasive (and often abrasive) influence on a whole generation of some of the company's best minds. When he joined Boeing in 1939 there were fewer than ten men in the aerodynamics unit. By 1943 there were nearly sixty, and the number continued to rise steadily as the wind tunnel became Boeing's scientific powerhouse. Few of these appointments were made without screening by Schairer, and most were the result of his own talent-scouting across the country. Sometimes, however, being chosen by Schairer and getting a job with Boeing were not quite synchronous.

Take, for example, the case of W. T. Hamilton, who was to become perhaps the best mind at work on wing design that the company would ever see. Although Hamilton graduated from the University of Washington in 1941, he defected from Seattle in favor of California, to work at a new NACA research center at Moffat Field, near San Francisco. There, in the high-speed wind tunnel, he helped solve a number of serious glitches in wartime airplanes. By the end of the war, none of the Boeing aeromen had acquired as much hands-on tunnel experience with as many types of operational airplanes as Hamilton, and Schairer, hearing about Hamilton on the grapevine, called him to say that Boeing would like to hire him. They set a date.

When Hamilton turned up at Boeing, Schairer was away at Wright Field. Hamilton went to the personnel department and insisted that he had already been hired by Schairer.

"Schairer's nuts," they said. "We're laying people off. We're not hiring anybody. Just forget it."

Hamilton went back to California. A few months later, Schairer called again, apologized, repeated the offer, set a new date, and said that if he was away Hamilton should see his deputy, Ben Cohn. This time when Hamilton arrived neither Schairer nor Cohn was there. Again, he went back to California, convinced that either Schairer, the Boeing system, or conceivably both were indeed nuts.

It was a year before Schairer called again.

"We really need your help," he said, explaining the problems with the aeroelastic wing on the B-47. "I'll make a deal with you on the phone."

Third time lucky—for Hamilton, and for Boeing.

Hamilton progressed from the B-47 wing to the B-52 wing, and his California experience gave him insights that put him at the center of the wing team. From the beginning, he was bemused by Schairer's eccentric, improvised way of supervising the program and his impatience with any formal allocation of skills—it was as though, in the middle of a football game, the manager not only called out the plays but kept switching the players' positions. But Hamilton came slowly to see that there

was a devilish kind of reason at the heart of the madness—
Schairer was deliberately pushing people over boundaries to see
how they could handle it.

Hamilton's turn for the treatment came with the B-52 wing.
This was a big floppy wing. A very big floppy wing. The aeroelastic principles Boeing had worked out on the B-47 wing, which
was a good deal less than half the size, were supposed to operate
in a far more subtle (and supple) way on the B-52. Schairer was
pondering the effects of all this elasticity on the controls. It was
the toughest work of calculation they faced, and the most critical.
He asked Hamilton to do it.

"George," said Hamilton, in his unflustered, amiable way,
"I'm an aerodynamicist, not a structures man. I'll go get the info
from the structures guys."

"No," said Schairer. "That isn't what I said. I want *you* to
sit down and do it. Calculate your own. They've got a wing laid
out. That's fine to take that wing. But *you* calculate how much
it's gonna flex, how much it's gonna twist, and what's gonna
happen when you use the ailerons and the spoilers and things
like that. Show me what it looks like when it flies."

"Show you what it looks like when it flies?"

Hamilton gaped. He remembered what it had taken on the
B-47. One man, a theoretical structures man, had cranked away
at his mechanical calculator for months. Mounds and mounds of
paper. A very meticulous job. But that wasn't what Schairer
wanted this time. Schairer wanted someone to sit down and put
it together in weeks.

The structures men were doing the work anyway, Hamilton
knew that. They were doing it in their own real time, not
Schairer time. Hamilton turned to them for help, but they all
knew Schairer too well. "If George said do it, do it yourself,"
they said, with pitiless grins.

The ticking clock for Hamilton was on the shop floor, where
they were laying out the massive jigs for the wings. The jigs
were the finite point in building a wing, the cradles in which the
wing took shape, like a series of vises that had to be placed
accurately to zillionths of an inch at critical points all the way
out on the enormous span. The way a wing left the jigs was the
way a wing ended up meeting the sky. *Show me what it looks
like when it flies.*

Hamilton knew that it would be six months before the structures men had their numbers, and they were building the jigs *now*. He went to the shop floor. They wanted to talk jig lines; they could do nothing until he figured that out. He was on the spot, exactly what Schairer had wanted. He went back to his office and started the elaborate calculations. Once in a while, Schairer would look over his work. "Don't change a thing," said Schairer. "Just keep on going."

He kept on going. He had no choice.

Hamilton's papers went out, the jigs were lined up. The first B-52 wings took shape: the anchoring spars, the delicate lattice of ribs and skin, all the internal artistry.

One morning somebody stopped by Hamilton's desk. "Hey! We got the final answers on those wings from the structures guys. Guess what? They're all within half a degree of what you had!" Hamilton had jumped through the hoop. But the ringmaster was still holding the hoop, waiting.

If Schairer had an *idée fixe*, it could involve a huge commitment of time and resources before he was satisfied, one way or the other. The Wright Field engineers had been developing an idea called boundary-layer flaps. The boundary layer, the thinnest membrane of air on a wing, was a favorite playground for aerodynamicists, but, as Hamilton knew from experience, it had never yielded more than a series of theoretical false dawns. The boundary-layer flap, Hamilton was sure, was another.

But Schairer had fallen in love with it. He barely heard Hamilton out as he tried to explain the flaws in the concept.

"Don't give me that old crap," said Schairer. "The people at Wright Field have done a lot of work and they think that's a real good deal. So you keep right on working on it."

Hamilton didn't think the idea was worth a diddly. Nonetheless, he had to oblige. Schairer ordered that the flap system be put on a model and tested in the tunnel.

As they put the model through simulated takeoffs and landings it was soon clear that Hamilton had been right all along— the touted boundary-layer flap introduced more problems than it solved.

At this moment, Schairer appeared, with a three-star Air Force general in tow. They watched a run of the test, and then, without any embarrassment, Schairer spent thirty minutes giving the general the critique that Hamilton had originally given Schairer. The new flap system was dead.

Hamilton held his tongue; he couldn't be sure whether Schairer had been playing devil's advocate all along, a role that was second nature to him.

From the outset, it was never easy to assess a Schairer idea; linguistic problems were involved. Understanding Schairer required interpreters. Bob Withington, his early recruit from the MIT tunnel, had the knack of seeing through the riddles to the meaning, and for fifteen years became accepted as the man who translated Schairerspeak to the other aeromen.

"He'd hold a meeting," says Withington, "and he'd wing out all these ideas. If you took him literally, he was wrong. We'd always hold a second meeting, right afterward, with all the guys except Schairer. We'd discuss what the hell Schairer really meant. We knew he was right, but we weren't sure he'd said it right. What he really wanted you to do was something different from what he actually told you to do. Remember, this was one of the smartest aerodynamicists in the world, and we usually figured out what he wanted—it wasn't hard if you thought about it a little bit."

Withington probably fell into this thankless vocation as Schairer's interpreter because Schairer never intimidated him; in order to function in the way he chose, Schairer needed at least one man by him who didn't feel intellectually mugged every time they had a dispute. Schairer was the reason Withington had come to Boeing; to Withington any company that could arrange itself around a man like Schairer had to be as unusual as Schairer himself.

Schairer's effect on Jack Steiner was more complicated. Steiner so openly paraded his conceits ("Here comes Jack," they would say, "still walking through walls") that he presented Schairer with an irresistible target.

Looking back after he retired, Steiner felt that Wells and Schairer were the unchallenged intellects of their generation at Boeing, and even as he speaks with pain of Schairer—"Ask my wife how I suffered under George Schairer; she'd say I almost died"—there is an unvanquished reverence in his voice. Nonetheless, he says, "you either had a supportive wife or you got out."

One of Steiner's worst experiences with Schairer was a classic devil's advocate episode, and one with a great deal hanging on the result: how to develop the Dash-80 design into a viable commercial jet, the 707.

All the best engineering talents were now engaged in adapting the layout of the Dash-80 to what they supposed the airlines would want. It was becoming clear to Pennell and Steiner that although the airlines might concede that Boeing had defined the jet of the future on the outside, what happened on the inside was a different game. The company still had a lot to learn about seeing an airplane the way an airline manager did.

It was Wells, more than Schairer, who saw this weakness and moved to correct it. There was nobody at Boeing with a real grasp of the function and aesthetics of cabin design. Pennell agreed with Wells, but then, to fill the gap, chose an engineer with no background at all in cabin design. Milt Heinemann had been a systems engineer on the B-47; its seating arrangement for the crew of three was spartan, and its payload was nuclear bombs. A bemused Heinemann took the assignment, but after reflection went back to Pennell and said he was scared—he didn't have the resources or the depth of experience to carry the job through.

Two days later, Wells called Heinemann. He'd realized that Heinemann was right, he said. If they didn't get smart the airlines would soon be talking them into ideas that they had no means of challenging. "We have to know more about everything than the airlines do," said Wells. For this reason, he said, he had just hired an industrial design firm, Walter Dorwin Teague, to introduce jet age cabin design. It would be Heinemann's job to manage the shock to Boeing's introverted culture of accepting outside consultants.

Wells's briefing to Heinemann reveals the subtlety of Wells's hand—his mastery of the company ego, his emollient instincts, his own readiness to accept imperative change.

"Your job is going to be very difficult," he told Heinemann. "I'll give you some guidelines. Don't ask the consultants' design team to do any production work. Assure the production engineering department that they're going to do the engineering. The consultants are going to consider everything, all the little details that make for a composite design unity, which sells a product like an automobile or a camera."

In time, Wells's decision and choice of designers would create the bedrock of the company's ability to deal with airlines as astutely as it had with the Air Force, but almost immediately Heinemann, because he was working with Steiner, ran into a brick wall: Schairer.

Steiner had decided that the width of the Dash-80 cabin, 132 inches, while it replicated the generous comforts of the Stratocruiser's two-plus-two seating, was too narrow for the 707. To carry an effective payload, the 707 would need six-abreast seating. The Air Force tanker being developed from the Dash-80 already had a wider, 144-inch body, and that—Steiner argued—should also be the cabin width for the 707, since it would allow six-abreast seating with a center aisle.

Schairer thought the Dash-80 cabin was just fine as it was. On past experience, Steiner decided to retire from this first encounter without a fight, to prepare a detailed argument. Armed with this, they returned.

This time, Heinemann felt like an infantryman who had never faced live ammunition before. He kept quiet, while Steiner and Schairer argued. By the time they left Schairer's office, Steiner was verbally eviscerated.

Heinemann said, "I've never in my life seen anybody abused as you were abused in that meeting."

Steiner shrugged. "Milt, you don't understand how this game is played. Next week George will be with the management, using all the arguments that I gave him today to change the body diameter." Heinemann was still shaking his head in disbelief. But Steiner was right.

In Santa Monica, Donald Douglas had finally been forced to recognize the threat from Boeing. The evolution of the Dash-80 into the 707 had described the first viable jetliner, and it was evident that Boeing had become far more responsive to what the airlines were seeking. Every airplane Douglas was building was obsolescent. Douglas faced up to the unpalatable prospect of having to spend probably hundreds of millions of dollars to catch up.

And yet when word reached Seattle that Douglas was talking to the airlines about a jet, the DC-8, nobody was particularly rattled. Despite the punishment Boeing had taken from Douglas in the past, there was a complacent feeling, a tone well illustrated by a joke circulated at the plant.

A Douglas engineer is asked: "How could you build the airplane without a prototype?" He answers, "The prototype is in Seattle."

Surprisingly, Boeing had no patent on its basic formula, the swept wing and the podded engines. (Some people at Boeing wondered why Allen, with his covetous legal instincts, had not tried to patent the engine pod and pylon design—it would have been open to patent protection, and the French had successfully sought and enforced a patent for a much simpler engine layout on their new jet airliner, the Caravelle.)

Douglas still had one salient advantage over Boeing: the respect the company enjoyed with virtually all of the world's major airlines. While Douglas engineers would have to second-guess Boeing on the aerodynamics, they would, as they always did, go out and *listen* to the airlines, let the airlines help them design the jet.

Douglas was also helped by a delay in the development of the 707. By selling the KC-135 tanker to the Air Force, Boeing incurred a penalty: Pentagon permission would be needed if tooling paid for by the Air Force was used to extend the line to build the 707. Months of lead time over Douglas were lost trying to appeal this restraint, and in the end Allen had to talk directly to Air Force Secretary Harold Talbot. Talbot relented only after Boeing agreed to help pay part of the tooling costs.

During these months, Douglas had been convincing the airlines that it was now a serious contender to supply a jet that could reflect the decades of its experience in the commercial business. It was easy for Douglas to tell the airlines that once more, Boeing was offering an airplane compromised by trying to satisfy both the Air Force and the airlines, while Douglas — as it always did—was thinking only of the airlines. In fact, had Douglas known it, the point was still somewhat valid: although Steiner had won his case over cabin width, Boeing had still not taken sufficient account of what the airlines would want.

The outcome of any campaign to sell a new airliner hinges on the quality of the launch orders. For the 707 there were at least three customers from which orders would give credence to the idea that Boeing had truly launched the age of travel by jet: Pan Am, as the prime international carrier, and United and American as the domestic carriers. Solid orders from any one of these would trigger a chain reaction among competitors anxious not to be left out of the revolution.

John Borger of Pan Am, whose long experience of working with Boeing, as well as his qualities as a technical critic, made him the man to cultivate at the airline, stopped by in Seattle to see Steiner as Boeing was beginning to talk details and court sales for the first 707s. He was surprised to find Steiner vague on the final configuration; Borger suspected that Boeing was still a house divided. What he didn't tell Steiner was that in his own Pan Am flight bag, sitting by his chair as he talked, was a far more precisely detailed specification for the Douglas DC-8 that he had collected in Santa Monica.

Just how tough a fight Douglas would give Boeing only came home when a posse of Boeing engineers, led by Pennell, went to San Francisco to make a pitch to United. Feisty little W. A. "Pat" Patterson—he of the coffin-cloth jibe—led them straight into a trap. Patterson had built mock-ups of short sections of the cabins of the two contenders, separated in the center: you walked into the DC-8, and then into the 707. The DC-8 cabin was 147 inches wide; the 707 was still at the width of the KC-135 tanker, 144 inches. The three inches made a difference out of all proportion to the numbers, and the Boeing men were visibly deflated.

The geometry of the cabin, essentially a circle intersected by the floor, was critical at shoulder height. Douglas had set its cabin floor so that both shoulder room and headroom were strikingly superior to the Boeing layout. (Ironically, this had been decided partly by anachronistic reasoning, to allow space for upward-folding sleeping berths, which were superfluous in view of the airplane's speed.) In the battle of inches, three inches was a decisive margin of victory in providing a cabin that the airlines would favor.

Not only was the Boeing cabin demonstrably smaller, but the floor was too high, restricting headroom and the room for overhead bins. In cross section, the 707 (and KC-135) fuselage was not circular. It retained a vestige of the Stratocruiser's "double bubble": it was slightly nipped in at the waist, like an egg sitting high in an egg cup. The floor was set at the waistline, with the smaller lower lobe making the cargo hold, as well as accommodating parts of the airplane's systems.

One reason why the 707's floor ate up space was that Heinemann had intended to have hot air blown through it to heat the airplane, an innovation that required the floor to be around two inches thick.

As usual, Patterson enjoyed Boeing's embarrassment. The Boeing men had gone to San Francisco feeling that they were already the proprietary masters of the jet age. The sale wasn't yet quite lost—United's board had to meet in Chicago—but Patterson was unambiguous in his contempt for Boeing and transparent in his joy in seeing Douglas come from behind to score a coup of this magnitude, once again, in United's eyes and those of other airlines, showing that it was Douglas, not Boeing, that naturally spoke the language of payload and passenger appeal.

Pennell and his men went to Chicago to await the United board's decision.

Allen realized how seriously they were in trouble. Yet even now, neither Wells nor Schairer felt that the airline orders could be settled fairly on the issue of cabin size. Didn't Boeing's far greater experience with big jets count for more? As far as they could see, the DC-8 was still a paper airplane. Superficially, it looked like a clone of the 707, but how would Douglas know how to fine-tune that swept wing; how would Douglas understand all the subtleties of podded engines and high-speed controls? The DC-8's angle of sweepback was slightly less than the 707's, which suggested the caution of men who had simply not had enough time in the tunnel to be bolder.

The United order went to Douglas. Patterson dominated his board and raged away at Boeing: not only would he reject the 707, but he wouldn't buy any airplane numbered 707. He just didn't like those numbers.

The loss of United was a stinging public rebuke to Boeing; its whole reputation as America's pioneer of large jets had been compromised by its failure to listen to airlines before turning ideas into metal. It was especially mortifying for Pennell, the man with a past at Douglas. This shrewd and far-seeing engineer had won over Allen and the senior Boeing executives to the cause of the commercial jet with the insistent but engaging force of his reasoning. He was a natural leader who had converted the many skeptics in his own generation of engineers as well as the newer stars like Joe Sutter.

Even as he was flying back from Chicago, Pennell saw that

they had to change the 707. The next sales call was to Tulsa, where the board of American Airlines was to choose between the two contenders.

During the flight, Pennell's team agreed that whatever else happened, they would lower the 707's floor. Heinemann abandoned the under-floor heating, but worried about how they would keep the passengers warm at 35,000 feet. That, said Pennell, we can fix. The pivotal decision, which only Allen could finally authorize, was whether they could widen the fuselage. Pennell wanted to trump Douglas by going one inch better, to 148 inches. They all realized the financial consequences of this: the 707 fuselage could no longer be built on the same lines as the KC-135. But Pennell didn't care what it took. He was fighting for the 707's life.

For Allen, the trauma was not just a financial nightmare. As well as anyone in the company, he remembered the ignominy of the Boeing 247 and the DC-3. The specter was chilling: would Douglas pull that DC-3 thing all over again? Was there some enduring flaw in the Boeing psychology? You didn't forget. Douglas had bought thirty years of leadership with that one trick.

It wasn't up to Allen to grasp the engineering implications of adding four inches to the 707's waistline, he just wanted to know what it would cost. The degree of structural disturbance to the design work already done—and therefore the cost of making a change—centered on one point, the crease between the upper and lower lobes of the body. The integrity of the fuselage at this point was reinforced by a beam, called the crease beam. It was a very tricky thing to change.

The morning after the loss of the United order—to be precise, at 6:00 A.M. that morning—a young Boeing administrative assistant named T. Wilson arrived to find the light showing from under the office door of his boss, George Martin, who was the head of structures on the 707. Wilson opened the door. Martin was on his hands and knees on the floor, with a huge metal template. As though fearing that the defeat in Chicago had deranged Martin, Wilson asked, "What the hell are you doing, George?"

"There was no way I could get this template home with me," said Martin, still noting measurements.

Martin was designing the intersection of a new crease beam and the enlarged fuselage. Wells was waiting to know if it could be done. And later that morning Martin was able to tell Wells that it was feasible to make the change without unraveling the whole fuselage.

"Right," Wells told Martin. "You go and convince Allen."

By the time Pennell arrived in Tulsa, Allen was on his way to lead the Boeing team. He had agreed to the change. It would now no longer be just a battle settled by promising to go the extra inch in cabin width. It would come down to Allen's rapport with Cyrus R. Smith, to the two with their hearts in the West. But Smith was no Patterson; he was harder to read, there would be no tantrums about not wanting a transport developed from a military tanker, yet he was hardly likely to accept an airplane inferior to one already ordered by a major competitor. Here, the deal was going to be done, if done at all, man-to-man. Pennell and the engineers waited while Allen was cloistered with Smith. In a while, the two of them came out, arm in arm, and beaming. Boeing had the American order.

Boeing already knew that Pan Am would buy some 707s, simply to be first with a jet—Trippe understood the iconic significance of that. But Pan Am was likely to buy DC-8s, too. Winning the American order, as far as domestic airlines were concerned, was the turning point for the 707. For the moment, at least, it was still a two-horse race.

Smith had told Allen that he had never doubted that Boeing had, technically, the better airplane. In his mind what still had to be proved was whether Boeing really meant it when it said that henceforth, like a reformed recidivist, it would do what airlines wanted, instead of telling them what they were going to get. He didn't want to be bothered with engineering details. If Boeing said the 707 would be bigger than the DC-8, he would buy it. The issue of size had been a test. As far as Smith was concerned, Boeing had passed it.

A profound change now occurred in Boeing's public demeanor: it came out singing and dancing. To sell their new 707, the backwoodsmen went to New York and staged an extravaganza. For three weeks, airline chiefs from all over the world were wined and dined and given a knockout show to introduce them to the jet age. The feasting took place at the Waldorf Astoria; afterward the guests were wafted by limousine to an incongruous location in lower Manhattan, an old coffee ware-

house that occupied a whole block on Eleventh Avenue. There
they ascended eight floors in a monstrous freight elevator, with
stale Colombian aromas wafting in the air.

A yellow door led from the elevator. Suddenly, beyond this
door, they entered the jet age. They were in an avant-garde
airport lounge, and the departure of the "707 Superjet" was
being announced. They paused for a breathless description of
the flight to come, then went through another door, directly into
a mock-up of the new 707 cabin. They took their seats and buckled up to the sound of the four engines starting up. Chic stewardesses served cocktails, and the "captain" gave cruising
altitude (35,000 feet) and cruising speed (590 mph).

All this had cost half a million dollars, and it was a style
nobody had suspected from Boeing, a company always devoid
of flash, always seeming to hold its nose when the tasteless winds
of ballyhoo wafted its way. It was a lot to do with Allen, who
had never liked sales hoopla. Boeing's airplanes should be good
enough to sell themselves; he didn't want anything that smacked
of what he dismissed as "Hollywood." But times were changing.
Douglas was putting on jazzy presentations of the DC-8, and
Wells had persuaded Allen to upstage Douglas.

The 707's cabin had subtle pastel colors, carefully sculpted
seats, and a new cabin environment stripped of heavy steamship
drapes and Edwardian standards of lighting—it was bright,
clean, and suggestive of something the airline moguls really
liked: efficiency. It had been carefully planned to use every inch
of space without seeming oppressively packed.

Many of the details of this airplane cabin of the future had
been argued over during flights in the airplane cabin of the past.
Heinemann commuted weekly from Seattle to New York, out
on Monday, back on Friday, riding Stratocruisers. The grinding
din of the pistons had never effectively been deadened in the
cabin, nor could the vibrations be suppressed. They knew from
the Dash-80, although its cabin was jerry-built of plywood and
scraps, that the 707 cabin could be tuned to a new sound regime;
the slipstream might be more audible than the engines.

Because jet engines needed far less maintenance, the airplanes could be turned around faster and spend longer in the
air. The greater the utilization, the better the profits. The need
to clean the airplane faster and more thoroughly brought a rad-

ical change for the cabin: no more soft walls, no more "coffin cloth." The cabin that no passenger would ever see (and the hidden logic behind the winning aesthetic of the New York mock-up) was a hard-walled tube that could be hosed down. All the seats were quickly removable and on tracks so that passenger density could be altered at will. The airplanes might be flying for twenty years, and no one knew how many configurations of seating they might need: first class, tourist, cargo.

Windows were smaller, but more numerous. The old windows were sixteen inches wide and twenty inches high. The 707's were ten inches wide and twelve high, and closely spaced so that wherever the seats went there would always be a window view—a distinct advantage over the DC-8, in which the traditional, more widely spaced windows left many rows of seats with just a wall to stare at. Heinemann invented a movable cluster of controls, called the Passenger Service Unit, which would appear on every subsequent jet. But his most ingenious innovation was the plug door.

The principle was simple enough. The structural integrity of the pressurized fuselage was greatly enhanced if the cabin doors, instead of closing in the old way from the outside, closed from the inside and formed a pluglike seal. As the differential increased between the pressurized air inside the cabin and the air outside, the security of the door seal increased. The problem was that if the door closed from the inside, the movement of the swing ate up the equivalent in cabin space of a row of seats, or six passengers. The prevailing wisdom was that it was impossible to design a plug door that did not cost six seats.

Heinemann, and a colleague named Bud James, thought otherwise. They designed a door with a gymnastic, double-jointed movement. It partially opened inward and then changed dimension vertically, to hinge outside. It was an effective plug door, and it did not cost a single seat in space. Heinemann and James took out a patent, and the door was adopted universally, even by Boeing's two closest rivals, Douglas and Lockheed.

While the engineering solutions of the new cabin came from Boeing, as Wells had ordained, the ergonomic and aesthetic revolution represented by the New York mock-up was masterminded by a designer from Walter Dorwin Teague, Frank Del Giudice (pronounced "Del Judis"). In the 707, Del Giudice was handed the chance to style something that awaited definition and personality, and it is doubtful whether any designer has fashioned a more pervasive machine-age aesthetic than he did in his work for Boeing.

In the moment that they entered the cabin of a jet, passengers' eyes would register far more than just their place in the airplane. The first impression would describe a break with the whole experience of flight until that moment. Car designers could fantasize the lines of a car, they could play with chrome and make an interior look like a brothel or a boudoir, but they couldn't make the car function differently or suddenly travel twice as fast or far. Architects could play with vernacular, revere function over form or vice versa, but they couldn't levitate a building's occupants.

Del Giudice realized that he was dealing with a truly transforming machine. He could have indulged Buck Rogers fantasies, but he did not. He respected function, where space was at a premium, and he countered the inherent risk of claustrophobia with clever optical illusions to flatten the tube's edges and avoid making a tunnel. He understood that an experience that would certainly be unnerving for many people needed soothing, almost anodyne colors, not surfaces that seemed aflame. Raymond Loewy, the great fantasist of car styling, was hired by Douglas to design the DC-8's interior, but chose to be far more conventional than Del Giudice, whose work for Boeing had lasting significance.

One night in New York, the legendary past met the embryonic future. Wells called Heinemann and said he should be waiting at the mock-up—alone—at 7:00 that evening. He was bringing someone down to the coffee warehouse. He couldn't say who, but if Heinemann recognized him he was not to show any reaction. Heinemann waited on the eighth floor, peering out a window. A limo drew up. Heinemann felt like a character in a mafia movie: Wells got out, followed by a figure in a black topcoat and fedora, keeping his face from the light.

When they came out of the freight elevator to the yellow door, Heinemann was waiting. He recognized the visitor before Wells introduced him, and tried hard not to gape. It was Charles Lindbergh.

Lindbergh had been a longtime consultant to Pan Am, had flown as a pathfinder for some of its Pacific and European routes, and was a confidant of Juan Trippe's (it took an enigma to know an enigma). Though discredited by his gullible flirtation with the Nazis, Lindbergh had never lost his standing with aviation engineers, nor with the pilots' fraternity: Tex Johnston had been thrilled to give him a ride in the Dash-80.

Heinemann would come to know Lindbergh well. On this first encounter, he led Lindbergh around the 707's interior with Wells, and then they sat in a row of seats, with Lindbergh at the dummy window. He drummed a finger on the sidewall.

"What's this?"

"Aluminum vinyl laminate," said Heinemann.

"You mean it's *metal?*"

"Yes, sort of."

"That's going to be cold."

"Maybe," said Heinemann, "but it will wash nice and quickly."

Lindy, whose face seemed to uncrease with curiosity, absorbed the details. He fell silent as Wells talked of journey times, the passenger service arrangements.

Finally, surfacing from thought, Lindbergh unwound from the seat and gave Wells some advice that Boeing would have cause to remember: "Whatever decisions you make now, always bear in mind that airplanes get bigger. Don't make a decision now that doesn't allow you to increase the capacity of your airplane. Don't limit yourself. Get the most out of the airplane."

The three-week carnival in New York had upstaged Douglas, and Allen was reconciled to the idea that, in future, it would pay the company to be a little flashier in its style. But he was never reconciled to extended stays in New York. It would be the first and last mock-up Boeing would build there. In future, the mountain would come to Mohammed, and Mohammed was in Seattle, where he belonged.

8 ■ Something Nasty in the Way It Wiggles

On December 20, 1957, Tex Johnston slipped on a new pair of cowboy boots. The 707 was ready to fly. (His Dash-80 boots were by then a little worse for wear; during a bout of daytime roistering in a San Diego club, Johnston had dived fully clothed from the high board into the pool, boots and all.) The 707 was eighteen months behind the KC-135 tanker (Johnston had waived new boots for that first flight, and let Dix Loesch, the project pilot, have the left-hand seat, while he rode as co-pilot in the right-hand seat). But it was still a year ahead of the DC-8.

Boeing was delicately balancing the security of its military business with the risks of developing commercial jets. The KC-135 tanker gave them for decades a profitable companion to the B-52 bomber, whose deep thirst it was designed to slake. (There is a dreamy sequence under the opening titles of Stanley Kubrick's Cold War satire, *Dr. Strangelove*, in which a B-52 noses up to the rear of a KC-135 and the gas line mates with the bomber, two vast birds copulating in the heavens.)

The extensive testing of the Dash-80 and the KC-135 really left only the safety requirements of the FAA to be met. There were, however, no guidelines for the Boeing engineers to use.

They were writing a new book. The jet changed all the safety parameters: number of passengers in a cabin, evacuation procedures, structural integrity at high speed and high altitude. Rather than designing FAA regulations into the 707, they found themselves recasting the FAA rules to encompass the 707. Little by little, the new rules were proposed and reviewed in the company and then submitted to the FAA inspectors who rode in the plane and watched over things like the evacuation drills.

The most serious vice revealed in the handling of the 707 was Dutch roll. Very early in the flight testing, Johnston discovered that the problem he had identified as inherent in the Dash-80 had been passed on to the 707, like something ineradicable in the DNA of the Boeing jets. The 707, though far more worked-over than the Dash-80, was still worryingly skittish in its directional stability. Johnston made no attempt to conceal this from the FAA inspectors; he took the airplane to cruise altitude, encouraged it to yaw, and then turned it loose. Each time it oscillated violently into a Dutch roll. By now, he had a polished technique for regaining control (helped by the power of his lanky legs and a kick on the rudder pedals from his cowboy boots). Johnston showed the inspectors how it was done, and then handed over. After two or three tries, the FAA men mastered the problem, and certified the airplane as safe. They were, of course, very experienced pilots.

Johnston went on to make spectacular demonstration flights before potential customers around the world, without revealing the plane's proclivity to roll. But at Pan Am, the first customer and still the most crucial to the airplane's future, there was growing disenchantment with the 707 for other reasons. John Borger, who had ridden shotgun for Pan Am during the 707's development, felt that he was running into a bad case of what he called the "Northwest corner psychology." Pan Am wasn't happy with either the payload or the range.

This dispute had rumbled for months. Borger did not accept that the 707 could truly qualify as an intercontinental jet—it ran out of fuel too soon. American Airlines was having the same problem. When it put the 707 into service between the coasts, the westbound flights, if they met strong headwinds, had to put down at Phoenix for refueling.

Borger knew the essence of the problem. It was the wing;

it simply wasn't big enough. The airplane needed more wing—
more of several things, wing, fuel capacity, and seats, but pri-
marily wing. Borger's critique was, however, intractably resisted by the man who was, to Borger, the Northwest
psychology incarnate: George Schairer. Borger could not move
Schairer, who was, he said, pushing the 707 wing much too far.
Borger was forced to take his concern directly to Trippe. And
when Trippe called, Boeing jumped.

Allen flew to New York with Wells, Pennell, Steiner, and
other engineers. Borger and his immediate boss, Sanford Kauffman, went to Allen's suite in the Ritz Towers Hotel on Park
Avenue. They were characteristically blunt. Pan Am had told
Douglas it would take twenty-five DC-8s, when they were ready;
it was committed to only twenty-one 707s, and only six of the
first 707s as they were. Pan Am was buying more DC-8s because
the DC-8 would have better range and better payload. Borger
knew how to hit home, how to smash through the Northwest
psychology. The 707, he said, was a half-great airplane. But
half-great wasn't going to be good enough. Boeing might sell
sixty, eighty, even a hundred 707s just because it was first, but
if it didn't fix the airplane, that would be the end of it—another
of those short-lived innovations from Seattle that the airlines
had seen before.

After the Pan Am men left, Wells felt the same urgency to
respond that he remembered from the weekend in the Van Cleve
Hotel in Dayton. But this time, instead of being invited to throw
a design out the window and start over, they had been given an
unmistakable warning. They would have to come up with a new
wing for the 707, whatever it cost.

Allen agreed, and Wells returned to Seattle the next morning to put the work in hand. At the same time, Allen told Steiner
to get over to Pan Am and tell Borger they were going to compete head-on with the DC-8. Not just compete with it, but beat
it. Lest Pan Am have any doubt of Boeing's commitment, Allen
left Steiner in New York to stay close to Borger.

Wells knew that, in effect, he had been sent home to do
something unprecedented: to overrule Schairer. To those around
them, Wells and Schairer had always seemed to be in lockstep.
If they had differences, they worked them out in private. For
all his bombast, Schairer had his own sense of propriety—he

would always acknowledge that Wells was, in the end, his boss. Wells was the only person at Boeing Schairer deferred to. Open clashes of authority between them were unknown.

This time, too, there was no open dispute. But everybody knew Schairer had gone out on a limb with the 707 wing. And everybody waited to see who Wells would get to fix it.

He called in Hamilton.

"We're going to give Pan Am an airplane that has more wingspan," said Wells. "More performance, take bigger engines."

"That sounds great," said Hamilton. "You're going to design a new wing?"

"No," said Wells. "We just told them we're going to cut off the old wing at the body, move it out six or seven feet on each side, and build a structure like a bridge in there, and cover it over so it looks like a wing. And that's it."

"It won't work," said Hamilton.

Wells appraised his challenger. There were echoes from his own youth, particularly an argument with Montieth over the wing of the Flying Fortress, in which Wells had prevailed. Hamilton, sitting before him now, had the beatific composure of a young bishop, and carried a kind of holy certitude. People were listening to him more; Wells knew he had a growing reputation as a wing doctor. On the B-52, he had shuffled around in the wind tunnel in stocking feet, fussing over every contour of the wing like a lapidary. He had come through Schairer's trials of fire with no visible damage. He clearly thought Wells was proposing voodoo aerodynamics.

"I'll tell you what," said Wells. "You've got a good record on this stuff. You've got six weeks to tell us what will work."

"I'll need full use of the tunnel," said Hamilton. "Whole time, twenty-four hours a day. It's going to take a lot of experimental tailoring."

"You've got it," said Wells.

Hamilton was not quite the innocent he seemed. He had already had to spend a lot of time listening to complaints about the performance of the 707; more had been promised than had been delivered. The shortcomings of the wing were, perhaps, traceable to the hasty testing in a rented tunnel. Hamilton resolved that any wing *he* designed was going to under-promise;

he would design more performance into it than anyone would expect from it. In fact, to all intents and purposes, instead of fixing the old wing, this would be virtually a new wing—designed in six weeks.

The wind tunnel went to three eight-hour shifts. Two models were built, so that while one was being tested the other could be changed. The "tailoring" metaphor adopted by the aeromen to describe this kind of work hardly portrayed the intensity of the calculations. Hamilton more or less lived at the tunnel. He would monitor the models' behavior on every run, and review all the analysis as it was computed.

In spite of being given a seemingly impossible deadline to meet, Hamilton realized that it was actually a golden opportunity to distill everything Boeing now knew about swept wings into something like an optimum. Drawing on his experience with the B-47 and B-52, Hamilton sensed that it was possible to reach a new level of scientific elegance, a marriage of virtues in one wing that had, until then, been dispersed over several. And the urgency bestowed unusual freedoms: there was simply no time for the usual second-guessing, for the peer group reviews and getting all the departmental ducks into line.

Hamilton drew on two details of the B-52 wing. The first was where to position the engines on the wing, a decision that could have a more broadly governing influence on the wing's performance than any other. On the B-52, Schairer had intervened in a dispute over how far forward of the wing the engines should go. Hamilton had advocated putting them farther forward than on the B-47, and Schairer had backed him. It had proved to be the better idea, and Hamilton adopted the same principle for the new 707 wing.

The second refinement carried over from the bomber was far more complex and virtually invisible to any but the trained eye. It concerned the way in which the wing's cross section, its airfoil, evolved outward from the junction with the fuselage. A substantial part of the old 707 wing was discarded: Hamilton's changes extended to the outer engine position, a distance of around forty-five feet. The wing underwent an almost fluid and immensely subtle series of changes in profile. The result revealed a finesse worthy of comparison more with sculpture than with "tailoring."

The purpose of this sensitive engineering was not, however, to satisfy the eye, although it did. Aerodynamicists are oblivious to aesthetics, and Hamilton was intent on function. His aim was to defeat a tendency in the swept wing to become aerodynamically unbalanced. It was a state in which the outer wing lost lift first and stalled, pushing the nose of the airplane violently upward. Hamilton intended that when his wing stalled, instead of pitching up the airplane would gently pitch down. He had done it on the B-52, and was confident he could do it on the 707. Docility at the stall was essential to safety.

Hamilton completed these ambitious changes in the allotted six weeks. This new version of the airplane was given a new model number, 707-320.

Ken Holtby had been appointed the chief aerodynamicist of the commercial division. Hamilton had run his own analysis of what the new wing's performance was likely to be, and he revealed the results to Holtby. Neither could quite believe them. They agreed to perpetrate a deliberate deception. Hamilton wrote into the contractural commitment on performance that they would make to the airlines a conscious underestimate of 2.5 percent. For once, Boeing would promise less than an engineer felt that he could deliver. Holtby agreed to this, and not even Wells, Schairer, or Pennell was told.

"If these numbers are right," said Holtby, "we have Douglas beat."

Douglas, however, was not yet beat. Pratt & Whitney, under pressure from airlines to improve the first-generation jet engine on the 707, and virtually blackmailed by a threat by American Airlines to switch to General Electric engines, produced a new engine, the JT-4 fanjet. Douglas immediately adopted the JT-4 for the DC-8.

John Borger could see at one glance that a JT-4-powered DC-8 would seriously outperform not only the original 707 but also the new 707-320. It didn't take much arm-twisting to get Boeing to see the same threat. With only a few other minor changes, the 320 was equipped with the new engines and designated the 707-320B. When delivered to Pan Am, it had a longer body, more fuel capacity, more seats, and greater range. Immediately, Pan Am discovered Hamilton's cushion. To Borger, getting an airplane from anyone that was superior to what had been promised was a minor miracle; getting it from Boeing suggested that, at last, the Northwest psychology had undergone a radical therapy.

The 707-320B was so good that Pan Am went on buying them, in batch after batch. Eventually it had sixty. Even at full stretch, the DC-8 could not come close. Borger, a man sparing with praise throughout a long and distinguished career, made no bones about it: Hamilton's wing had not only given Boeing the lead in jets, it confirmed Boeing as a company the airlines could believe in.

An important lesson had been learned at Boeing. As things turned out, it would take fifteen years to better the efficiency of the wing that Hamilton had engineered in six weeks.

Even though starting from behind, Douglas had deployed its considerable talents and very nearly caught up. The effort cost more than $200 million. In some respects—its understanding of metal fatigue, for example—Douglas was ahead of Boeing. But, in the end, Douglas had failed where Boeing's technical memory was superior, with the wing. The DC-8's wing was more conservatively designed, and according to a formula which Douglas expected would provide an edge, but it was at least 5 percent less efficient than Hamilton's 707 wing. This was not a marginal difference. The future of the two companies was as fatally shaped by it as it was by the difference in the inches of the cabin width. Jack Steiner came to drill into his colleagues a personal maxim: "The wing is where you're going to fail."

Between 1957 and 1961, Douglas sold only forty-seven DC-8s; in the same period, Boeing sold 172 707s. The fight was not yet out of Douglas; its family motto was *jamais arrière*— never behind. But now, for the first time, Douglas was behind. Seattle had surpassed Santa Monica.

Other problems had debilitated Douglas. In 1957, Donald Douglas, according to intention, elevated Donald Douglas, Jr., to the presidency, while himself remaining chairman of the board. The heir immediately violated the tenets of his father's regime, trying to rebuild the house in his own aggressive way. Ten vice presidents left in short order, and with them much of that part of the company's brain that had grown from the triumph of the DC-3. Among them was Arthur Raymond. Occasionally, the old man would step in and veto one of his son's decisions, but this merely compounded the damage.

At Boeing, in the meantime, Bill Allen was just hitting his

stride. He knew that while the 707 might look to outsiders like a money machine (it was for the airlines), for Boeing it was, in truth, generating nothing but red ink. Notionally, as far as the Boeing accountants were able to predict, the program should break even after around three hundred airplanes had been sold. But this assumed that development costs would end, that the design would stabilize and thereafter just keep selling.

But the design did not stabilize. It seemed that Boeing was ready to indulge almost any airline's whim. There was, for example, the strange case of the Nadi Bump. Qantas, the Australian airline, wanted to use 707s between Fiji and Honolulu. The airfield at Fiji—Nadi—had a short, humped runway (hence the "bump") that required peculiar performance certification for a jet the size of the 707; a standard 707 just could not deal with it. To give Qantas an airplane that could handle Nadi, Boeing cut a chunk out of the fuselage of the 707 and Pratt & Whitney delivered a specially rated engine. Only seven of this model of the 707 were built—no other airline ever bought one.

What Allen was knowingly doing (it was a kind of conspiracy-by-consent within the company) was what a later generation of managers would recognize as buying market share. It was no more than the Japanese would do in seizing a bridgehead for their cars in the United States. Yet, in the late fifties and early sixties, it was an extremely risky and bold thing to do with a company the size of Boeing, and would not have been possible without the safety net provided by the military sales.

Even when 707 sales surged on beyond the three hundred mark, the break-even line kept slipping away like a mirage. But, taking the long view rather than one shaped by quarterly earnings, all the chopping and tailoring and tuning did buy Boeing world supremacy. Qantas, for example, went on to buy twenty-one later-model 707s. And Boeing was able to relish the day when Pat Patterson of United finally capitulated to reason and bought twenty-nine 707s, though his peculiar superstition was respected—Boeing renumbered these aircraft the 720.

However, before the 707 became established as the world leader, it had to survive a serious crisis of confidence among airline pilots. The problem was the persistence of Dutch roll. It surfaced in 1959, as airline crews were being trained to fly the first 707s. It was a big leap in technique and procedures to move from the pistons to the jet. Few realized that within the decorous procedures for flying the 707 there remained, if unleashed, the temperament of the B-47. Tex Johnston's test-flying, and the certification program carried out with the FAA, had produced a flight manual that assumed—as all flight manuals had to—a basic level of competence in the pilots. The feeling at Boeing was that the 707 had been refined to a point where it was safely manageable by average piloting skills in every situation likely to be faced.

It is part of crew training to get the airplane into trouble, under monitored conditions, so that the pilots will learn how to recover. But this idea went disastrously wrong while an American Airlines crew was training on a 707 over Calverton on Long Island. According to procedure, they aborted a landing, repositioned for another approach, and then sharply reduced power on the two starboard engines, simulating a multiple engine failure. Coming out of a left turn, the 707 suddenly began to yaw to the right—the unmistakable onset of Dutch roll. Within only fifteen seconds the 707 flipped onto its back and hit the ground upside down, exploding on impact. All the crew died.

The accident was assigned to pilot error—failing to correct the yaw. But the pilots were unaware of the 707's propensity to roll within seconds of yaw developing, and should have been more closely watched. Tex Johnston and another Boeing pilot, Jim Gannett, were sent to supervise further pilot training at American. They took off one morning from La Guardia with a regular instructor alongside the student pilot, Gannett in the rear jump seat and Johnston standing behind. The instructor deliberately initiated Dutch roll. The student pilot went too far, the instructor lost control, and Gannett had to grab the controls and close all four throttles to regain control. It was nearly fatal. Johnston, appalled at the instructor's performance, insisted that in future no American Airlines pilot should allow a 707 to cut loose—to let the degree of roll go beyond a yaw angle of 15 degrees.

But not long afterward, a Pan Am 707 got wildly out of control on a training flight near Paris. Again, as it had in the Long Island incident, a Dutch roll turned the airplane upside down and an outboard engine sheared off and fell to earth. But the pilots were high enough to regain control and landed safely on three engines. The same thing happened to an Air France 707. Notwithstanding these incidents, Johnston felt that stricter training could solve the problem—after all, none of the accidents had involved passenger-carrying flights.

Johnston's view changed on October 19, 1959.

Boeing pilot Russell Baum was nursing a Braniff pilot through the regular training pattern above the Olympic Peninsula. Once again, a Dutch roll got out of hand. But this time the maneuver was so violent that the airplane threw off *three* of its four engines. Baum regained control and began a crash-landing approach over woodlands and lakes. He told four of the eight men on board, including another Boeing instructor, to get to the back of the airplane, where they would have a better chance to survive. Baum held the 707 in a shallow dive, with its wheels up. It clipped into trees and broke apart; the four strapped into seats in the rear survived, Baum and three others died.

Johnston felt the loss personally, although in Baum's place he would have chosen to ditch in a lake, rather than in the heavily wooded area on the north fork of the Stillaguamish River. Johnston listened to the survivors' accounts and reviewed the earlier incidents. He began getting disturbing phone calls at home, people saying, "I thought you'd tested that airplane." Three days after the crash, he asked for a meeting with Wellwood Beall, Wells, and Schairer.

Johnston didn't realize that he was precipitating a divisive argument in the top ranks of Boeing. Allen and the financial officers felt that Boeing had delivered a safe, certificated airplane to the airlines and that if they followed the cautionary training instructions it would stay out of trouble—it was the responsibility of the airlines to follow the manual. But Johnston had, with some misgivings, concluded that Boeing had expected a higher competence from the airline pilots than was actually evident. To allow for this, the 707 needed better directional stability. The problem he had noted from the earliest flights of the Dash-80 should have been taken more seriously.

This was, of course, tantamount to admitting Boeing liability for the accidents—an attitude that was firmly resisted by the company's lawyers and accountants. Beall, Wells, and Schairer listened to Johnston's ideas: more hydraulic boost for the rudder, particularly so that short-legged pilots could kick in full rudder more easily; a small "ventral" fin under the tail and more vertical tail. Schairer nodded.

Wells said, "We will fix it."

The Braniff crash had unnerved Boeing's customers around the world. Johnston was sent off to talk to managements and pilots and reassure them that modifications would cure the problem. In London, the treasurer of British Overseas Airways had only one question: "Who's paying?"

Johnston remembered what Wells had said—"We will fix it." He looked confidently at the treasurer. "We are."

After London came Paris, and then other capitals. As soon as Johnston said Boeing would foot the bill, everybody was happy, and the scare receded.

When he returned to Seattle, Johnston had a call from Bruce Connelly, vice president of the transport division.

"Did you tell those people Boeing would pay for the modification?"

"That's what Wells said—we'll fix it."

Johnston never heard another word about it. The changes made to insulate pilots from the risk of getting into a violent roll, and other modifications, led to a cost overrun of $150 million on the first batch of 707s, and Connelly paid a personal price— he was demoted. Arctic fissures were opening up between the managers and the engineers. Johnston, for example, remained unaware that Maynard Pennell, the acknowledged father of the commercial jet program, had himself been locked in an argument over responsibility for the Dutch roll incidents. Pennell had insisted that the cost of the new parts be paid for by Boeing, while the airlines paid the relatively modest costs of installation. John Yeasting, the commercial division's financial chief, was appalled, but Pennell said that if he was ever called to give evidence in a court case and was asked whether there had been a deficiency in the design of the airplane, he would have to say there was.

Yeasting, provoked to fury, said Pennell's company loyalty was in question.

This was too much for Pennell, a fanatic about the structural integrity of every airplane he had been involved with. He told Yeasting he thought his company loyalty was right where it should be—"I'm proud of this company, I'm proud of its products, and our airplanes are going to have to stand on their own."

Allen agreed with Pennell, and Boeing paid. But so, in the

end, did Tex Johnston. From the time of the telephone call from Connelly onward, Johnston felt that his old open and easy relationship with everyone from Allen down was, in some unstated way, compromised. Without any charge actually being leveled against him, he sensed that his freewheeling style no longer sat comfortably with the new corporate army that had emerged to run the burgeoning commercial business.

In 1960, Boeing placed Johnston under a manager and cut him off from direct access to Allen.

Had Johnston, as he suspected, become the fall guy for the 707's problems? If so, it was partly because he had seriously misread two men: Wells and Allen. Wells would not have welcomed the fact that Johnston had taken one of his lines out of context and invoked it as the executive authority for a decision as large as paying for the 707 modifications. Wells's engineering conscience was as highly developed as Pennell's, but he carried no financial authority. Then there was Allen's reaction to the barrel rolls with the Dash-80—whatever Johnston imagined from the stag-party side of Allen, on the other side of Allen's personality only so much rope was allowed.

Soon after the managerial coup, Johnston quit as head of flight testing and moved to the aerospace division. A whole piece of aviation history—the age in which it had been possible to reconcile the roles of the cowboy and the scientist in one man— left with him. It was ineffably sad; character was slowly yielding to corporatism.

Dutch roll never jeopardized any 707 on a passenger-carrying flight. It remained one of the more exotic hurdles that a pilot in training had to experience and master. The changes made to the 707, on Johnston's suggestion, ended the accidents, which had been a part of the cost of crossing the threshold to the jet age, and a remarkably small cost in view of the quantum leap in airplane performance. Without any airline passengers knowing it, Little Herbie was always there, doing the job. And still is.

In October 1958, when a Pan Am 707 left New York for its first scheduled flight to Paris, it could carry nearly sixty more people than a Stratocruiser and cruise almost twice as fast, at a height 70 percent higher than the average propeller plane of the day, well above the onerous weather. In the subsequent decade the jet airliner transformed not just travel but the attitude of people toward travel. In the most obvious terms, the jets diminished the size of the world and made circumnavigation, that word with so many illustrious navigators behind it, seem routine. But there was more to it than that. The way you left and arrived was different. The trappings left over from ocean liners seemed pretentious and suddenly archaic. Like dressing for dinner, dressing up for travel when crossing the Atlantic in a third of a day instead of five or six days had become too elaborate. If you were a snob, you lamented the passing of a certain elegance. An ocean voyage was the occasion for display, a modish parade of the celebrated among the hoping-to-be-celebrated. But if you were simply concerned with getting there, the jet stripped things to the essentials—and, very quickly, it brought the end of all the great ocean liners.

The appearance of the Boeing 707s and Douglas DC-8s at airports that had previously been colonial backwaters or little more than gas stations for piston-engined airplanes suggested a new urgency in the Western way of life. Eventually jets would introduce a new class to advertise Western prosperity, tourists who wore their flight bags like trophies, decal-stamped just as an earlier generation's steamer trunks had once been plastered with the labels of ocean liners and grand hotels. It is salutary to realize that up to 1939 only around thirty aircraft had ever crossed the Atlantic. Even so, the bearers of the pervasive values of the jet age were fewer than two thousand machines. Boeing delivered just under one thousand of all versions of the 707, and Douglas fewer than six hundred DC-8s; there were a handful of other jets, but none of anything like equal consequence. Each jet carried, on average, between 150 and 180 people. On the whole, they did it dependably, safely, and with relentless frequency.

This was an American-led revolution. And, being American, it had little patience with elitism. The economics of the jet, in any case, favored a leveling equality: the more seats in an airplane, the better the payload. (After a debut with five-abreast seating, the 707 swiftly regressed to six-abreast, and with a lengthened fuselage the payload rose by a third.)

Nonetheless, for a while the publicly touted image of the

jet age was personified in the camera-hogging jet set—an importunate group made up of business moguls, politicians, well-heeled society figures deserting the flashbulbs of the transoceanic piers for the flashbulbs of the airport lounges, along with Hollywood stars and rock musicians and would-be swingers of all ages.

For the average traveler, flying an ocean to another continent remained a dream, a once-in-a-lifetime adventure, even though it could now be borne on a swept wing. Fares were controlled by the International Air Transport Association, a cartel in no hurry to extend cheaper fares beyond closely prescribed numbers of seats on each flight. Trippe had fought IATA's fare regime since 1945, when he tried to introduce a tourist-class fare from New York to London. He cut the round-trip fare by more than half, to $275, but the British closed their airports to Pan Am flights with tourist seats, forcing him to land in Shannon, Ireland. Thwarted in Europe, Pan Am introduced cheap flights from New York to San Juan, Puerto Rico. The one-way fare on a sixty-one-seat DC-4 was $75, and the flights were packed. It was not until 1952, long before jets were in service, that Trippe's incessant bombardment of IATA forced all the airlines to accept the age of the tourist fare. That summer, Pan Am introduced a round-trip fare between London and New York of $486. This was still hardly within reach of the common man, but it compares strikingly with what it cost to fly on the first Boeing 247 service between Newark and San Francisco in June 1933: $160 one-way, about equal to $2,000 today.

In the sixties, international air travel grew by 15 percent per year. If it continued at this rate, the airlines would face problems of capacity. Trippe, for one, worried about how to catch the tide at flood. And then, through one of those confluences of independently conceived technical attainments that find common purpose, an answer suggested itself. It offered a quantum leap in airline economics of the kind Trippe had long hoped would fall within his lifetime. An outline formed of the truly transforming machine, a jet so much cheaper to operate that it would bring air travel within the means of millions more people. At Boeing, this dream took the shape, almost literally, of a shadow thrown by the 707, similar in profile but of a wholly different order of scale.

THE FORMULA *circa 1946*

Basic Dash-80 Layout Inherited from B-47 and B-52

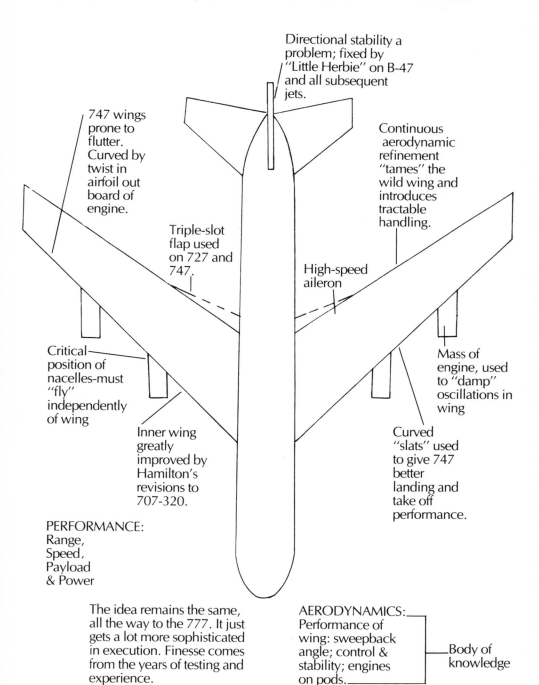

Directional stability a problem; fixed by "Little Herbie" on B-47 and all subsequent jets.

747 wings prone to flutter. Curved by twist in airfoil out board of engine.

Continuous aerodynamic refinement "tames" the wild wing and introduces tractable handling.

Triple-slot flap used on 727 and 747.

High-speed aileron

Critical position of nacelles-must "fly" independently of wing

Mass of engine, used to "damp" oscillations in wing

Inner wing greatly improved by Hamilton's revisions to 707-320.

Curved "slats" used to give 747 better landing and take off performance.

PERFORMANCE: Range, Speed, Payload & Power

The idea remains the same, all the way to the 777. It just gets a lot more sophisticated in execution. Finesse comes from the years of testing and experience.

AERODYNAMICS: Performance of wing: sweepback angle; control & stability; engines on pods.

Body of knowledge

Part Two

*Two Old Men
Have a Final Fling*

9 ■ We Wuz Robbed

Charles Lindbergh liked riding in the back of airplanes watching how people settled into the habit of flying. He always checked in under an alias, and could usually reckon on remaining anonymous, since the image of him in most people's minds remained that of prairie-faced hero. Trippe had lured him away from his old association with TWA. No airline wanted to be called "the Lindbergh Line" any longer; there was the lingering stigma of his German problem. Lindbergh's value to Pan Am was that he had something Trippe himself could never bend to: he had, if not a common touch, a common eye. "Slim" Lindbergh, assessing the passengers' responses to an airplane, listening to what they said about service, was always in his mind projecting the experience forward to when it might truly be termed a commonplace to use an airplane as casually as a bus.

An incessant theme of Lindbergh's to anyone who would listen was the counsel he had given Wells and Heinemann as they sat in the mock-up of the 707: always allow for the airplane to get bigger. Ironically, Douglas had taken this into account better than Boeing. Douglas had given the DC-8 a new lease of life by stretching its fuselage by thirty-six feet, more than doubling its passenger capacity. Boeing found, to its chagrin, that the 707 could not be stretched so easily. The main problem was its landing gear. It was not long enough to give sufficient clearance for a stretched fuselage on takeoff—the fuselage would hit the runway. The DC-8's gear was lanky and the stretched DC-8, like a flying pencil, had no such problem.

The 707 still outperformed and outsold the DC-8, but Boeing had seen very little return on its 707 investment in more than a decade and after nearly a thousand airplanes had been delivered. The dilemma for Allen now was whether it was really worthwhile to sink any more cash into the 707 for what could only be relatively small gains. Trippe, though, kept stressing to Allen that he simply didn't have enough seats to meet what he expected to be the demand. He talked about an "elongated subsonic or some other double-decker" that would serve the needs of the 1970s until his ultimate machine, the supersonic transport, arrived. But the larger subsonic jet remained a vague notion without the one thing needed to empower it, the right engine.

In April 1965, Trippe sent Lindbergh and a team of Pan Am executives to the Pratt & Whitney plant at Hartford, Connecticut, to look at a new, advanced version of the fanjet that powered the latest series of the 707, the JT-3D, designed to deliver 21,000 pounds of thrust, the kind of power that a stretched version of the 707 would need.

But, rather than reawakening Pan Am's enthusiasm for the idea of stretching the 707, Lindbergh's visit to Hartford effectively killed that proposition, for at the end of the presentation on the JT-3D, Pratt's chief engineer, Art Smith, revealed details of a new engine unlike anything Lindbergh had seen before. It would have virtually doubled the power of the JT-3D: a boggling 41,000 pounds of thrust. Pratt had entered this design in competition with General Electric to power the C5a, the Air Force's new leviathan transport. The Pan Am men realized that this was the engine missing from Trippe's stopgap airliner. Lindbergh did not, however, equate this engine with a jet transport designed exclusively around it by Boeing or anyone else; like Trippe, he expected that they would have to wait until whoever won the C5a contract got around to adapting an airliner from the military design.

Four months later, one Sunday afternoon in the summer of 1965, Ken Holtby, Bob Withington, and a few others were summoned to Bill Allen's home in The Highlands, a private estate to the north of Seattle on a bluff overlooking Puget Sound—a place that lived up to its name by being a fair approximation of a landscape that would make a Scottish laird feel at home, shadowed by firs and gently irrigated by mists. It was unusual for Allen to convene a meeting on a Sunday, but a crisis had blown up that weekend.

Boeing had been told by the Air Force that the price it had tendered for the C5a was too high—by hundreds of millions. There were three overriding reasons why Allen coveted the C5a project. Two of these were publicly known: it would put Boeing back into a line of military business it had neglected since the old C-97 version of the Stratocruiser, and—far more delectable—the C5a would help break the ground for what was now inevitable, the similarly huge commercial jet.

It was not, however, public knowledge that the whole idea for the C5a had originated with Boeing, not the Air Force. Boeing had even helped write the budget paper submitted to Congress to get the project started. This made it particularly galling to be told, now, that Boeing was in danger of losing the contract. The Air Force's program evaluation officers at Wright Field had told Boeing that Lockheed was undercutting it by a margin as large as $300 million. None of the Boeing team, who had worked on the project for three years, found this figure credible.

Withington told Allen that if Boeing priced its airplane that low, "we will lose the company."

They had been through the numbers many times; they went through them again. Howard Nefner, the head of contract administration, pressed to lower Boeing's bid substantially. Allen was reluctant, despite the stakes. He saw the same specter as Withington. Finally, he said, "Let's lower it a hundred million, but if it takes more than that, there's probably some better use for our resources." A cut of that size would, in effect, wipe out all profit on the first batch of airplanes. The gamble was that follow-on orders would, in a euphemism of the defense contracting business, help Boeing to "get well."

Holtby and Withington, who had lived with the C5a program and made many visits to Wright Field, knew that the Boeing airplane was comfortably ahead of both rivals on the technical scorecard used by the Air Force. The man Boeing kept at Wright Field on the program, Don Sachs, was sure that the generals wanted the Boeing C5a. They knew that Douglas had gone in with a price very similar to Boeing's, but suspected that, under pressure, Douglas might crack to match Lockheed.

However, the Pentagon's inclinations were more opaque. Allen feared that Boeing's intelligence network in Washington was weak. Many of Boeing's misgivings centered on one man, Robert McNamara. The regime that McNamara initiated as Secretary of Defense under John F. Kennedy, and then extended under Lyndon Johnson, rested on his reputation as the archetypal super-technocrat. His reformist doctrine went under the fashionable banner of cost-effectiveness, and it was according to these lights that the C5a had been conceived.

In 1962, Maynard Pennell was searching for a way to get Boeing back into military transports. Pennell, Holtby, and another engineer, Bill Hamilton (not W. T. Hamilton of the wind tunnel), listened to McNamara's sermons and designed a big, long-range strategic transport to fit the scenario. Boeing had no argument with any rationalization of the procurement process; on the contrary, it had always felt disadvantaged by being based in a state with little political clout.

The enabling instrument for a plane this large was a revolutionary new jet engine, the high-bypass-ratio turbofan. Much of the credit for developing this engine goes to a prolific German-born engineer, Gerhard Neumann, the general manager of General Electric's aero-engine division. Neumann had become a jet engine specialist after a piratical war with American special services in the Far East. His admission to the United States, like Munk's after the First World War, had required a presidential intervention.

On a Monday morning in 1963, Neumann turned up at the Washington office of General Marvin Demler, head of research and development for the Air Force, for an audience requested by phone the night before. He had stressed secrecy. Behind closed doors, Neumann unfurled a scroll, stretching from wall to wall, which they had to examine on the floor. It was a cutaway diagram of a new jet engine that GE had just test-run. Neumann claimed the engine would deliver twice the power of any existing engine yet use a third less fuel.

The engine's novelty lay in the size of its fan. All you see when you peer into the throat of a jet engine of a parked airplane *is* the fan; if there is a wind on the field the fan blades may be gently windmilling. The fan is similar to a multibladed propeller, with each blade subtly warped. The early turbofan engines that gave the 707-320 its new shot of energy had comparatively small fans that left the engine nacelles almost imperceptibly larger in diameter. Neumann's engine had massive fans that suddenly transformed the engine nacelle into the bulbous drum that you see on all today's big jets.

The giant fan greatly increased the volume of air being sucked into the engine. It boosted power in two ways—by increasing the thrust of the exhaust gases, the original form of jet power, and simultaneously by acting as a propeller and literally sucking the airplane through the air. The air drawn into the engine was divided between the flow taken into the hot and faster-moving core, and a large volume of cooler, denser air flowing between the core engine and the engine's outer cowling. This outer, cooler stream of air not only added enormous extra thrust but significantly helped to deaden the sound of the hot core. It was a seductively simple principle, but it presented horrendous engineering problems, most of them concerned with extremely high turbine temperatures.

The two areas of stress that endanger any high-bypass engine are the fan blades and the compressor. The fan blades have to survive the impact of ingesting, along with air, any impurities up to and including a flock of geese; the compressor has to hold together under temperatures that would melt many metals in seconds. GE had made the task harder by devising blades that were internally cooled by drilling tiny holes into them to circulate air; only adventurous technology of this order made the high-bypass engine possible.

Neumann's engine and Boeing's C5a concept had been waiting for each other to happen. The engine was a more demanding challenge than the airframe. From the days of the B-29, Boeing had had good cause to honor the maxim that a new engine and a new airplane are bad chemistry; a minimum rule of thumb was that an engine took at least a year longer to make work than an airplane and often, if there were serious bugs, a lot longer.

GE had a jump start in high-bypass engines, but its main competitors, Pratt & Whitney and Rolls-Royce, were working on the same principle. Pratt had at first been dubious of the whole concept (its engineers thought the turbines would melt) and slow to react. Nonetheless, the Air Force was obliged to invite the two American companies to compete for the C5a contract. Astonishingly, it insisted that Boeing make the final choice. Wells did not like this at all, but had to accept it, and Withington helped write the letter recommending the General Electric engine.

Over the years, Boeing had shown great confidence in Pratt & Whitney jet engines, and something of the filial association from the days of the old Boeing conglomerate lingered on in the minds of those able to recall it, like Allen. Pratt engines had powered hundreds of 707s, and a later version, the JT-8D, was used on the ubiquitous 727—and more than 70 percent of the world's short- and medium-range airliners.

That Boeing should choose the GE engine for the C5a sent a very clear signal: this was no time for sentiment, and a company's technical supremacy could disappear overnight. (The engine Smith had revealed to Lindbergh at Hartford was Pratt's prototype and the engine Boeing had rejected.)

The degree of Boeing's involvement in fashioning the C5a and in the selection of its engines made it seem improbable that either Douglas or Lockheed could wrest the prize away. Every detail of the airplane had been exhaustively "iterated" ("iterating" a design, a rare but correct usage of the word, was a standard part of the Boeing engineers' lexicon). The complete C5a proposal sent to the Air Force had required an entire airplane, a chartered DC-6, to deliver it. The Air Force wanted thirty copies of everything. (The technical paper that had secured the B-52 contract for Boeing had needed only thirty-three pages.)

The core team of engineers was called to Wright Field to hear the Air Force's technical debriefing. Normally, this would be the last scrutiny of the proposal before the choice was made. And, normally, it would be rigorous.

The engineers filed into a dingy conference room to face a civilian evaluator, Cal Hodges. There was a stack of notes on his desk, scrawled on a yellow legal pad. Hodges shuffled the notes, looked up, and said, "This is your technical debriefing." He paused, as though teasing them with the suspense, then said, "You guys have a hell of a good proposal. Let's have a cup of coffee." And that was it—apart from a few questions about the airplane's weight, which seemed readily satisfied.

The airplane that Boeing had first conceived, and then designed, had virtually to defy the laws of gravity. It was more than twice the size of any existing transport (a fuselage as wide as a two-lane highway, a wingspan of more than two hundred feet, and a loaded weight of over 700,000 pounds); it had to carry troops, tanks, armored personnel carriers, and jeeps over long distances and then safely put them down on short airstrips in forward battle zones. This was the strategic athleticism that so appealed to the McNamara doctrine: instead of prepositioning heavy equipment or waiting for it to be carried by sea, these goliaths of the air would deliver it, plus troops, anywhere in the world where there was a four-thousand-foot runway.

At the heart of Boeing's confidence in its design was the C5a's ability to perform one particular mission that Boeing knew carried a heavy weighting in the Air Force's system of points awarded in an evaluation. It was called the "long-range austere mission," in which maximum load had to be flown four thousand miles and delivered to a crude, "unimproved" airstrip. This mission virtually defined the airplane's capability. To fulfill it, Boeing had developed what was called a "blown flap" wing. The normal lifting force of the flaps was augmented by blowing engine exhaust into the flaps. This system greatly reduced the huge plane's landing speed and therefore enhanced its ability to get down on small strips.

From what they knew of the Lockheed and Douglas designs, the Boeing engineers were sure that the blown flaps had, in fact, blown Lockheed and Douglas out of the air.

But, unknown to Boeing, the Air Force had moved the goal posts. The long-range austere mission was devalued in points. By the time Boeing discovered the change, it was too late to respond. Lockheed, on the other hand, had known of the change much earlier, and adapted to it.

In the late fifties, a group of Boeing engineers under Ken Holtby had been secreted away in a telephone building in the Seattle dormitory town of Bellevue to work on the design of a supersonic transport. After two years, it was clear that the research and development costs would be beyond the resources of any single company, and the SST team broke up. Holtby moved to the C5a project.

But by 1964 the SST program came back to life. The Johnson administration funded a design competition, entered by Boeing and Lockheed, for an airplane that would be twice the size of the Concorde and a generation ahead in technology (the Concorde was essentially a product of the 1950s). From the inventions of its resourceful "skunk works," Lockheed had far more experience with supersonic flight than Boeing, but this was military work, subject to none of the environmental policing that would increasingly govern a supersonic airliner. Instead of being put under the Pentagon, which, despite all its delinquencies, had a long-established system for evaluating new projects, the SST program was put under the Federal Aviation Administration, answerable to the Department of Transportation, which had no background in programs of this complexity.

In April 1964, Trippe and Allen were called separately to state the case for the SST to the FAA. Before he left for Washington, Allen, well aware of Trippe's propensity to promise the moon, called Trippe to check on what he had said to the FAA and to make sure the two of them would seem to be in step. Trippe knew that Boeing's SST proposal had a swing wing—a conventional swept wing for takeoffs and landings that folded back to become an arrowhead, or delta wing, for supersonic flight, while Lockheed's design had fixed double delta wings.

No one romanced the SST more than Trippe. He told Allen that he had predicted that an American SST could be worth $7 billion in exports. Allen must have known that this was fanciful, but he was in the booster business, too. Within Boeing, there were people as evangelistic about the SST as Trippe, and none more than Maynard Pennell. Between them, Pan Am's engineers and Boeing's were fashioning a conventional wisdom that by the 1980s all major international airline traffic would be supersonic. Anything else would be a stopgap.

One of the few warning voices about the SST was Lindbergh. In later life, Lindbergh had become planet-sensitive, an early "green." He thought the SST would be profligate in its fuel consumption and polluting. This had no impact on Trippe, nor on many of the best minds at Boeing, Pan Am, and the FAA, who were mesmerized by the SST. Men who were normally sagacious and prudent—Pennell at Boeing and Borger at Pan Am, for example—were almost religiously credulous. Allen, however, did try to impose some caution on Trippe. The FAA had told Trippe that it was prepared to award an SST contract to what would be, at that stage, still a paper airplane, yet it expected the prototypes to have so few bugs that after testing they could go straight into airline service. Allen disabused the FAA (and Trippe) of this notion. An SST prototype would have to be regarded as an essentially experimental airplane. The FAA eventually accepted this course.

Boeing finally learned that it had lost the C5a contract via Juan Trippe. Trippe's personal intelligence network had kept very accurate track of the state of the contest. By August 1965, his spies reported that in the C5a runoff Boeing had the better airplane but Lockheed was going to win, even though the Douglas design was ranked second by the Air Force. The result happened to be announced on September 30, when a delegation of Boeing engineers was in New York talking to John Borger and his boss, Sanford Kauffman. This was the meeting to discuss the just-emerging 747 concept that Trippe had forsaken for the golf tournament, as he had confessed to Allen on the phone, but on or off the golf course Trippe got the word first. He immediately called Courtland Gross, the chairman of Lockheed, in Burbank, California. Gross's pleasure was qualified by annoyance that his staff seemed to be the last to know their own good fortune. Trippe, wasting no time, said he was ready to start working with Lockheed on an airliner they would derive from the C5a; Gross said he would think about it, and call Trippe back. He never did.

Boeing faced the result with cynical disaffection. If Trippe had listened to Allen on the phone with more acuity, he might have sensed that Allen's urgency to discuss the 747 reflected that by then Allen expected to lose the C5a. Whose hand had cheated Boeing? History pointed to McNamara. Among the Boeing engineers, the Secretary of Defense was an old *bête noire*. His crime was bean-counting compounded by technical illiteracy. It all stemmed from a project called the TFX, a tactical fighter-bomber that McNamara had ordained should be common to both the Air Force and the Navy.

The TFX was the first great test of McNamara's cost-effective doctrine: one airplane fits all. But the operational demands of the two services were as different, literally, as a ten-thousand-foot runway and the heaving deck of an aircraft carrier. To design an airplane that could fulfill two wholly different missions was virtually impossible. Yet Boeing had come ingeniously close to doing so. As it did later with the C5a, it shaped the Pentagon's own specifications. With the help of NASA, Boeing had designed a swing wing to combine high supersonic speeds with the kind of low-speed handling the Navy demanded.

The Pentagon ran four rounds of evaluation, lasting a year, between designs by Boeing, General Dynamics, and Grumman. At the end of the first round, Boeing knew it was ahead by a large margin. But as Boeing was called to successive questioning, often by McNamara himself, it began to seem that McNamara was searching for flaws that could justify awarding the contract elsewhere.

Wells was called, as the only permitted Boeing spokesman. That evening, Withington, Holtby, and others joined him for dinner. They had never seen him so angry. The measured, contained Wells, whose whole engineering life had been built on rational analysis, had been given what he called "the idiot treatment." Normally abstemious, he had three martinis with dinner. Afterward, he went up to his room and wrote the testimony he would give the next day, hoping that logic would prevail.

But McNamara, clearly a man of intellectual range, had certain fixations. On the TFX, one of these was the number of parts to the airplane. His optimum was, quite reasonably, a design with as many parts as possible common to both the Air Force and Navy versions. So McNamara personally counted the parts, and found that the Boeing airplane had far fewer common parts than its competitors. At least, that was how it looked, by just counting the part numbers.

Boeing tried to point out that it was using an innovative technique to machine the parts, called "dollar-sign tooling." Different weights and gauges of parts could be shaped without changing the tooling, simply by telling a computer to, for example, alter the thickness of the wing skin for the lighter land-based airplane. It was a highly efficient system, which allowed two markedly different versions of the airplane to come off the same production line. But the variation in part specifications showed up as differently numbered parts, and by that measure alone the Boeing technique violated McNamara's doctrine.

Nothing could persuade McNamara that there were compensating virtues in the Boeing system. And he had another count against Boeing: titanium. Boeing had used this metal, for its superior strength-for-weight qualities, in the variable-sweep wing of the TFX. Again McNamara counted, this time the amount of titanium. Titanium bugged McNamara: Lockheed was blaming the difficulties of machining it for cost overruns on its skunk-works spy plane, the supersonic Blackbird. It was true that airplane manufacturers had not yet mastered the application of titanium (they would quickly do so), but Boeing's use of it in the TFX was conservative.

Nonetheless, on the issues of part count and titanium, McNamara was immovable.

The TFX contract was awarded to General Dynamics in Texas and Grumman in New York. These just happened to be two constituencies of immense importance to Lyndon Johnson's Democratic power bases. Against them, the Pacific Northwest might as well have been Mars. Wells, who maintained an element of provincial innocence throughout, was appalled. Allen had personally intervened to try to get McNamara off his fixations. He got nowhere. On the airplane home to Seattle, Allen was visibly burned up. The engineering team were apoplectic. They had been robbed, and they wanted to raise hell. But Allen counseled buttoned lips. They had to take it, he said. That was how it was. It wasn't the government's job to keep Boeing in business.

And now, with the C5a, it had happened again. Boeing had been even more flagrantly robbed. In the end, Lockheed's winning strategy had little to do with the relative merits of the three designs; a Pentagon civilian who had followed the contest all the way revealed later that the Lockheed technical proposal never rose higher than third place. The chairman of the Senate Armed Services Committee was Senator Richard Russell, of Georgia. From its beginnings, Lockheed had been essentially a California company; that was its base. This time, though, it had promised to build the C5a some 2,500 miles from California: at an old World War II plant in Marietta, Georgia.

Boeing had certainly been ingenuous about the political real-ities of both these large military contracts. Its lobbying in Wash-ington and its intelligence system were no match for Lockheed's. But Boeing personnel were what they were: dedicated engineers who thought that it was enough just to be the best. It is doubtful that the contracts were ever solely in the gift of the Pentagon; the awards were transparently constituency-driven. And Allen was right, in one sense: nobody in government owed Boeing any fa-vors. If, by Washington's lights, Boeing was going to get smart, squawking in public wouldn't redress the injury. You never knew when you might next need the hand that had robbed you.

In the event, the men who had created the Boeing C5a—men like Pennell, Wells, Holtby, and Withington—could later take a grim satisfaction in the consequences of giving the C5a to Lockheed. The program established a record, of a kind. It was the first to produce a $1 billion overrun (that innocent, sanitary word can somehow make it seem like a joke). The wings developed cracks, and rebuilding them cost another $2 billion. The program was terminated in the early 1970s with only the original eighty aircraft built.

At Wright Field, there was an ironic twist to the Air Force's problems with the C5a program as it got under way. One of the officers responsible for insisting that the airplane deliver its promised performance was the man who had first flown the B-47 to its limits, Guy Townsend. Now a general, Townsend tried to hold Lockheed's feet to the fire. But the program was too delinquent, and the company too politically well connected, for there to be any cure other than taxpayer dollars. Townsend was bypassed and overruled.

Ken Holtby should be allowed a last word: "In retrospect, the C5a was not that wonderful an idea. A big airplane is terribly vulnerable to small-arms fire. They don't risk that big an asset in a forward base. They're operating from rear bases and they don't really need all that landing gear."

In the 1991 Gulf War, the C5a flew huge amounts of equip-ment and many troops to Saudi Arabia. It was kept safely out of the war zone, and was successful in a mission that had few similarities to the one it had been designed for.

The team of engineers brought together for the C5a were now without work. The orphans of a program—of any program, but particularly one of this size and duration—suffered the engineering equivalent of coitus interruptus. Without stretching the metaphor too far, designing an airplane generated an energy not unlike the libido. (Many Boeing wives could testify that if their husbands took a mistress, more often than not it was an airplane.) This prolonged concentration of creative energy on one objective had been denied consummation. Their airplane would never fly. It was immensely frustrating to a career.

Bob Withington drew up a list of names and called it the Hungry Hundred, the pick of the team. Some could move directly to the SST, and some to the 747. The SST seemed to be the priority; it needed all the help it could get. Nothing about it was conventional. It was not evolutionary: you couldn't refigure anything you'd done before and bolt it to a new shape. From the landing-gear tires to the tailpipe, the SST was tomorrow's stuff. The high-bypass engine didn't fit. The operating cycles of a turbine that rammed this metal through the air to the point where you could fry an egg on its skin were of another order.

When it came to career choice and reputation, what was the 747 worth? Who would get it? Who would *want* it? After all, this was the Mack truck with wings, *not* the cutting edge.

Allen looked over the names with Wells. There were programs other than the SST and the 747 to consider. The 737, cobbled together in a hurry to compete with a new Douglas airplane that Boeing had seriously underrated, the DC-9, was a mess. Just thinking of the 737 gave Allen the vapors: it reminded him of Jack Steiner. For the 737 had involved Steiner in a high misdemeanor—as high as it got at Boeing without summary execution to follow. In fact, Allen had been sorely tempted to chop Steiner for it, or, at least, to cut him down to size. Probably all that saved Steiner was that he had fathered the highly profitable 727 trijet.

To minimize the new work necessary for the 737, Steiner had taken the 727 fuselage and greatly shortened it; he was notorious for transferring parts from one airplane to the next. Unlike the DC-9, which had its twin engines at the tail, the 737 had its engines slung very closely under each wing (inadvertently reminiscent of Woldemar Voigt's Messerschmitt 262), and was designed to fly from grass and gravel strips as well as runways, an ambition that complicated its development.

Steiner put his heart and soul into selling the 737 concept, but the airlines were resistant to its charms. After getting no U.S. sale, Steiner finally won the promise of a small launch order from Lufthansa, the German airline. Allen was not impressed; unless Steiner could get either United or Eastern to commit to the 737, he wasn't prepared to sanction production.

Steiner knew that the Boeing board was due to meet in New Orleans. The board had never gone against Allen. Undaunted, Steiner decided to covertly lobby some of the outside directors. He argued that if Boeing dragged its feet on the 737, a lucrative slice of the airliner market would be left to Douglas. One of the most influential directors was the chairman of Du Pont, Crawford Greenwalt. Steiner got to Greenwalt through another director, a Seattle real estate developer named Ned Skinner; Skinner and Steiner lived a half mile from each other on Lake Washington, and Steiner's children played tennis on Skinner's private courts. Allen went to New Orleans intending to veto the 737 program. He returned outvoted. The board said that if Lufthansa confirmed its order, it should be taken as sufficient cause to launch the 737.

Previously, when Allen was unsure of a decision, he would listen to the engineers, and principally to Wells. This time he had been coerced by men who weren't even in the airplane business. He was mad. Madder than anyone remembered. And he soon discovered who had stage-managed the boardroom reversal.

He called Steiner to his office.

"Are you aware of what happened in New Orleans?" he asked.

Steiner said he had heard some accounts.

"Jack, how many outside directors did you talk to?"

Steiner confessed to his transgression.

Allen jabbed a finger at him. "Jack, *never* do that again."

For a fleeting moment, Steiner gave a convincing impression of being chastened. But it was not in his nature to sulk in his tent. When it came to the 737, he was a True Believer. He would just go out and sell it harder.

Now, as Allen considered who should lead the 747 program, Steiner's behavior on the 737 still rankled. The 747 would need a galvanic leader, and Steiner was certainly that. It might lack the glamor and sexiness of the SST, but it posed production and logistical problems as large as its likely size; for one thing, Boeing had no plant big enough to build it in. The 747 would need a plant to itself. Steiner had grown up with the successes of Boeing's commercial jets, from the Dash-80 through the 707 and the 727. The only engineer with as much experience in jet airliners was Pennell, but Pennell was clearly consumed by the SST.

And yet Allen hesitated. Perhaps it was too soon to commit full management resources to the 747. The preliminary design work was still tentative. The ultimate investment would be the biggest the company had ever made. There was no customer in sight; he knew that Trippe was still playing the field.

Wells scanned the Hungry Hundred list again. Whoever eventually came to run the design of the 747, the preliminary design team already needed stronger leadership. He was looking for a chief engineer. He didn't see any name among the hundred that seemed exactly right. They were all good men, but none exactly fitted what he thought the 747 team was lacking. They were not lacking in ideas; ideas were spilling out of them. But the 747 needed a catalyst, someone to balance the competing interests, to make an airplane of it.

And so it happened that during the closing stages of the C5a imbroglio, two panaceas had taken hold: the prospect of a giant subsonic transport with dramatically reduced seat-mile costs, and the second-generation supersonic transport that would reduce the world to the size of a pea. This was, after all, a euphoric time in American technology, the can-do culture. The country had come back from the scientific humiliation of Sputnik and was within two years of putting men on the moon. American aerospace companies (Boeing was now one of them) were enjoying unchallenged supremacy. Pan Am, the world's most experienced airline, was the benchmark of its business and the acknowledged national flag carrier.

Trippe had good reason to feel bullish. The forecast for 1965 was that there would be 35 million people flying the international routes, and sober forecasters were predicting a 200 percent increase by 1980. It was getting a lot easier to keep jets in the air and turn them around quickly on the ground. The jet engine had reached an astonishing level of reliability: the Pratt & Whitney JT-8D on the Boeing 727 could operate for seventeen thousand hours, nearly two years of continuous service, between over-hauls. (The best piston engines had managed only 2,500 hours between overhauls.)

Once the design of the 747 was under way, Trippe was still hoping to goad Boeing along by getting Douglas to compete. Borger knew that Douglas was building a mock-up of an airliner with a double-decked fuselage, and it already had a number, DC-10.

On the surface, Allen still had cause to fear Douglas. While Douglas had been outgunned by Boeing on the DC-8, with the DC-9 it had found and brilliantly filled a gap in the market that Boeing had neglected, for a short-range, intercity airliner. It seemed uncomfortably like the DC-3 all over again: airlines couldn't get DC-9s fast enough, and Boeing was provoked into an uncharacteristically chaotic bid to catch up.

But everything at Douglas was not as impeccably ordered as it looked. If the company's 1965 balance sheet had reflected Donald Douglas's conservative accounting, and particularly if the company had written off development costs as they occurred, the year would have shown a loss. But his son, more recklessly inclined, had changed the accounting philosophy.

In truth, the company was being bled dry by success. Douglas had seriously underpriced the DC-9. The first twenty to be built were budgeted to show a loss of $750,000 each; in fact, the loss went well over $1 million. The development of the DC-9 had cost $100 million. Instead of writing this off as it occurred, as his penny-wise father had done, Donald Douglas, Jr., postponed the write-offs and listed them as an asset under deferred charges, waiting for the program to become the gold mine it should have been. But the company's plant at Long Beach had been poorly prepared for volume production. (Ted Conant, the head of manufacturing, had joined Raymond in the exodus following the elevation of Donald Douglas, Jr.) There were expensive delays in delivering planes. Such tangles would have been unthinkable under the old regime, but Donald Douglas's heir went on digging himself into a deeper and deeper hole.

None of the men at Boeing, however, knew that the rival they feared most was in such jeopardy.

10 ■ Row Brown Closes the Circle

In the summer, as they often did, Allen and Trippe, with their wives, had gone fishing in Alaska. They rented an elegant old classic of a yacht, the *Wild Goose*, owned by John Wayne. Between arguing about the relative merits of Atlantic and Alaskan salmon or the spawning habits of trout, the two industrial patriarchs reviewed the progress of the businesses that were their lives' work. This was the atmosphere in which the 747 was conceived and, in due course, became a commitment, an idea transmuted from a whim into an imperative almost without formal acknowledgment. It was put into the terms of a dare. Trippe said, "If you build it, I'll buy it." And Allen responded, "If you buy it, I'll build it." The sense of there being a valedictory urge was inescapable. Perhaps they felt, as a definition of the kind of power that they each enjoyed, that there was no thrill to beat the one of betting their companies on an all-consuming idea. That would be a swan song of the highest order.

In their defense, however, it could be argued that such a suspicion traduces the essential character of each man. They were practiced and determined visionaries, not mindless gamblers. A decade earlier they had finely calculated their respective investments and interests in launching the jet age, and they had lived to see the payoff. The conception of the 747 may have seemed, at this point, just the inevitable second act of a well-rehearsed drama.

To those down the line, however, it seemed anything but well rehearsed. Years afterward, the memories—good and bad—were still able to trigger bursts of reflective adrenaline. Tex Boullioun, in 1965 one of John Yeasting's two assistants and a flamboyant character who would find himself severely tested by the 747 program, puts it simply: "The two of them decided that it was absolutely necessary to have an airplane like this. Everybody said, it's too big, and we can't build it. They didn't pay any attention. They said, you're gonna build it and you're gonna have it done in five years."

It was rare at Boeing to be able to put an individual signature on an airplane. Many of the men involved—each of them creative within his own disciplines, and few of them interested in glory—would have disapproved of any attempt to do so. The case of the 707 shows very well the virtues of the collegiate regime. Maynard Pennell drove the concept; George Schairer ordered what was, in effect, an aerodynamic mutation of the two bombers, the B-47 and the B-52. Jack Steiner refined the configuration and poured his ego into the cause. Much of the structural integrity was husbanded by George Martin, the man who had worked the body template on his office floor. And finally, W. T. Hamilton gave it the new wing that transformed its performance and ensured its future.

There was room for iconoclasts, like Bill Cook, who had been there from the days of the B-17. Cook's ingenuity had been shown in the incident that had created Little Herbie for the XB-47 (he had married the sister of Scott Osler, who died in the XB-47). Cook liked to work a problem according to his own counsel. Milt Heinemann, dropped into the deep water of cabin design without preparation, had survived to gain an international reputation. There were others like these, who moved from airplane to airplane, advancing their arts. If anyone in the delicate comity of Boeing was likely to make an issue of parentage, it was not Schairer, who, despite his combativeness, never advertised his achievements.

The engineer incurably given to self-promotion was Jack

Steiner. Steiner had every cause to put his signature to the 727, but he was so insistent on doing so that he disaffected even engineers who had not been on the program with him. "You weren't alone when you designed the 727," he was told. "A lot of people worked for you. And some with you."

The truth was that Steiner did less than justice to engineers whose work had given the 727 qualities that marked it out. One was, without doubt, Bill Cook. Any 727 passenger sitting at a window behind the wing can see Cook's unnerving creation in action as the airplane comes in to land. It is called the triple-slotted wing flap. On final approach it looks as if the whole wing is coming apart at the seams; in fact, what you see is a remarkably sophisticated piece of engineering that gave the plane the agility to fly from short runways like New York's La Guardia, more an aircraft carrier than an airport.

Cook was too independent-minded to worry much about Steiner's self-aggrandizement. It was not the same with Joe Sutter. Sutter had been enduring Steiner's style of leadership since they had worked together on that intractable dog the Stratocruiser. They had both been in at the creation of the commercial jet age, but it was Pennell who had led that cause, and if Sutter revered anyone it was Pennell, a father figure for the men of Sutter's generation.

Steiner, on the other hand, rather than seeing such men as mentors, thought of them as competitors. He yielded only to Wells and Schairer—"In my career," Steiner told me, "I came across only two superior intellects, Wells and Schairer." It was probably no accident that these were the only other men in the company who had indelible claims to the authorship of particular aircraft: Wells of the B-17 Flying Fortress and Schairer of the B-47.

The case of the B-17, however, is instructive because it did not begin its life as Wells's concept. The project engineer was a man far more senior in rank than Wells, Giff Emery, who was, in turn, under the supervision of Monteith, the chief engineer of stubbornly conservative inclination. Under the pressure of a deadline set by the Army, Emery floundered and Wells very quickly emerged as the prevailing hand in the bomber's evolution. This was not, like Hamilton's wing for the 707, a case of giving a final touch with a magic wand. Wells was enough of a generalist (in fact, Wells remained, more than anyone else, what was defined by the original term "aeronautical engineer") to lock the whole design together, capping the achievement by winning the argument with Monteith over giving the bomber wing flaps—not, by any means, a minor detail, since it made the plane far more tractable.

In fact, it took several years of evolutionary change to make the B-17 into the legend it became, including a crucial contribution from George Schairer on the vertical control surfaces. But nobody at Boeing would ever want to challenge the view that the reputations of Wells and of the B-17 were indivisible.

Of equal stature are the reputations of the B-47 and George Schairer. The circumstances were, however, very different. By this time, the design of any large airplane required a numerous and diverse legion of engineers. And the B-47 was not just another large airplane, it was forced into being against a formidable body of opinion that held that the whole concept was demented. This airplane was a heady combination of a theory totally lacking empirical support and a machine whose performance went way beyond the experience of any of the men who created it.

Given this, Schairer's signature is, indeed, deserved—by the uncompromising force of his argument and will, the airplane was created and *made to work*. Three thousand hours in the wind tunnel! Persistence, and a team of men too young to know what was supposed not to be possible, bludgeoned the resistance into submission. In ascribing credit, the character of the achievement leads unmistakeably to the character of the man, take him for what you will: dogmatist, tyrant, gadfly, maverick, mentor, or magus.

Whether an engineer ever gets the chance to express his own vision in an airplane is, inevitably, influenced by luck. The way that the design of the B-52 coalesced in the Dayton hotel suite mitigated against any one engineer's being able, later, to say that the bomber was his, although many who were not present in Dayton that weekend left their handprints on the design— Martin, Holtby, Hamilton were just a few.

The truth is that some of Boeing's finest minds had to complete long careers without the satisfaction of parentage, if parentage meant that an airplane carried their personal stamp. Pennell is, perhaps, the most arresting example. In both the company's military and commercial developments, Pennell was an inspirational leader and steadfast custodian of the company's values. Pennell and others—Holtby and Withington are notable cases—often labored long and creatively over designs that never left the drawing board, through no deficiency of theirs. Indeed, some gifted engineers were fated by ill luck to spend their most fecund years moving from one design to another which, because of intrigue and dissembling in Washington, or because the design was not commercially propitious, never went beyond the wooden mock-ups.

Is any law discernible that might explain how luck breaks in this way? It helped to be under the gun. In the cases of the B-17, the B-52, and the 707-320, the life-giving force was the kind of concentration of the mind that comes in desperate times. The B-47 was not under a similar deadline pressure, but it moved from crisis to crisis in a way that simulated a series of deadlines, and so could be enlisted to reinforce the point. The B-29 (an instance of failure becoming an orphan?) was brought to the edge of disaster by the demands of a deadline. And the Stratocruiser, sharing the same flawed genes, encouraged nobody to raise a hand and claim it for himself.

By the time Joe Sutter moved to the 737 with Steiner, he liked to characterize himself, simply, as an airplane *developer*, as someone trying to follow the Wells tradition of seeing the airplane as a whole. People came to recognize in Sutter the qualities of a hard-nosed realist who worked an airplane from the inside out, starting with the basics of payload, range, and airfield performance, and then finding the outline of an airplane by "iterating" the options. This had been done with the 737.

To begin with, Steiner had taken the 727 fuselage (which, in turn, had been a direct descendant of the 707 fuselage) and truncated it. Around this was hatched an "all-square" airplane: wingspan of a hundred feet, fuselage length of a hundred feet, and capacity of a hundred passengers. The 737 had been framed in this way to exploit a weakness that Steiner had sensed in the Douglas DC-9. The DC-9's engines were at the rear. The basic airplane, Steiner foresaw, would have to be stretched into larger versions, and each time it was stretched the nose would have to get longer to counter the weight of the engines. This, in turn, meant that most of the extra baggage would end up in holds forward of the wing. Eventually, the DC-9 would become difficult to load in a way that retained its central balance.

On the 737, Steiner and Sutter put the engines on the wing so that when it was stretched it could be done by simply adding "plugs" to the fuselage, in front of and behind the wings, and the balance would always be retained and the baggage loading would not be critical. It all sounded fine, but this elegant symmetry unraveled when the first 737 rolled out. The engines were fitted with defective thrust reversers—an essential braking device on an airplane designed for short runways. When the reversers were modified their weight toppled the airplane backward on its landing gear.

By the early summer of 1965, Sutter could see himself enmeshed in the 737 like a man condemned to a backwater, while the refugees from the C5a program were picked up for the 747 and the cutting-edge men like Withington and Holtby were joining Pennell on the SST. Steiner was clearly looking around for another, larger plate of raw meat. Steiner was the dean of the subsonic jets, and the 747 looked like a nice plateful and, if it worked, the maker of an international reputation.

Sutter, prone to be a workaholic, had not had a break for a long while and took off with his family for their simple cabin on the Hood Canal. It was there that Allen found him, with the call that changed his life.

"I'd like you to head up the studies on the 747," said Allen. Allen's call had left a lot of things unclear—like, for example, who would be in ultimate charge of the 747.

Since the 1930s, the development of every Boeing airplane had been controlled through a binary system of checks and balances. There was the project staff, which was responsible for the preliminary design work and which, if the design "closed" for production, would be expanded to take on the design of every component down to the last rivet. And there was the technical staff, which reviewed the work of the project and was consulted for assistance when technical problems arose—the technical staff was, in one of its roles, the gateway to the wind tunnel, where critical elements of the design, and especially the wing, would have to be rigorously tested. The technical staff reported independently to the management, providing one way for the senior management to keep watch on a program.

For the designer of any airplane, the decisive point of power was the authority to release drawings. Normally, it was the chief engineer of the project who had this power—a power with heavy financial consequences, since the release of a drawing to the shop began the process of material consumption, of ordering and cutting metal. The fiscal controls at Boeing were, therefore, in the end dependent on an engineer's decision to release drawings, and although budgets were set and directed from on high, it was beyond the competence of the company's financial officers to question how well or how tightly the release of drawings was managed.

Steiner had always been sensitive to the power bestowed on the designer by his authority to release drawings. In explaining to me his authorship of the 727, he said of Sutter, "He didn't have the authority to release a goddam thing to the shop. He was head of the technical staff. He didn't have much to do with the fundamental design, although he had a lot to do with the development of the airplane."

In a company dominated by engineers, it was natural that such an essential instrument of management as the authority to release drawings should have devolved in this way. The principle of profit centers and micromanagement by accountants could never have been embraced in this culture. If major arguments broke out between the project and technical staffs they would, in any case, climb the ladder and be intercepted at the level of Wells and Schairer, whom Allen trusted to resolve them. Other company elders, like Pennell, Cook, and Martin, could be drawn in. This was stuff for men wearing the MIT beaver ring, not MBAs. For them, the bottom line at Boeing was not a line of numbers, but would the airplane be better for it?

When Joe Sutter took his seat behind a desk to pick up the 747 as a work in progress, he was making $29,565 a year—a handy sum by 1965 standards, but somewhat less than competitors might have paid for a man with such a depth of experience in commercial jets. Boeing was not then a big payer; in California, where there was always another aerospace company to go to, there was a more active market in top engineers, but in Seattle defections were very rare—company loyalty was part of a tie to the city and its way of life.

Allen certainly set an example in conservative salaries: in 1965 he was paid $99,600. (During his tenure as president of

Boeing, Allen never took home more than $150,000 a year, whereas Donald Douglas was paying himself $120,000 way back in the middle of World War II.) Wells, surely the company's single most valuable human asset and at the peak of his career, made $77,100. Nor was it a company stacked with vice presidents. Although Sutter had been asked to take a job in which his judgment might well involve the very survival of Boeing, there was no prospect of his being given a vice presidency. The commercial airplane division had only nine vice presidents, including the top of its shallow pyramid, the general manager and his two assistants. (Wells ranged over the whole company, military and commercial, as vice president of product development.)

On the 747, Sutter reported to the vice president of engineering, George Snyder, a longtime manager who had risen by seniority rather than by any significant flashes of brilliance. Sutter could ask for particular engineers he wanted, but another engineering vice president, Dick Rouzie, was handpicking engineers for the 747 from the C5a orphans, including those on the Hungry Hundred list, and Sutter was expected to take whoever came.

The commercial division's lean hierarchy ran a nondescript collection of offices and plants in Renton, a singularly featureless town that had originally grown out of a mining settlement. The headquarters complex at Boeing Field, apart from the one Deco flourish allowed in the late thirties, had never been better than merely functional; the Renton sprawl, divided from Boeing Field by a thin ridge of hills, was (and still is) even less prepossessing. One senses the art of arrogant self-denial. A statement is being made that the business in hand is too serious to permit distracting corporate frills.

Certainly, the birthplace of the 747 program was not spiritually arousing. Sutter and his team had the second floor of what was called the 1085 Building in Renton, no more than a basic Boeing drawing office, with metal desks and strip lighting, which clearly granted no right of permanence. Programs and people came and went, some leaving no trace. In such a place it was inevitable that in the fall of 1965 the hundred or so men working with Sutter had the sense of being transients, headed either for glory in the big sky or another false dawn.

Of the men already in place when Sutter arrived, the one

he was most glad to see was Row Brown, who ran a small team charged to explore every possible configuration for the airplane. Brown was the polar opposite of Jack Steiner, a man who retreated from the faintest beam of limelight. But Sutter regarded him as the best airplane developer he had ever known. Like Milt Heinemann, Brown had gradually emerged as a man with a forte of his own; he originally worked as an aerodynamicist on the B-47 wing, and later moved into preliminary design. Brown's configuration group had been switched to the 747 from the C5a as soon as Allen was told Boeing had lost the contract. "We had been sitting around with the blues," one of them told me, "but by two o'clock in the afternoon we went to work on the 747."

Configuration men were always the first over the threshold of a new program. Their objective was to size the airplane according to its intended payload. They considered the implications of the load it had to lift, both in passengers and cargo, and how it would be manageable on the ground. Everything that was subsequently required of the design grew from this chrysalis. The airplane that Carl Munson from sales and Don Finlay from product development had discussed with Borger and the skeptical General Kuter back in July had remained amorphous until Brown's unit was assigned to it. Boeing had talked to Pan Am of a "new-technology" airplane. As well as the engines, this included, in their minds, the work done at Boeing on large structures in developing the C5a.

Configuration was a process best carried out with an unsentimental eye, relentlessly fixed on numbers. The 747, as proposed to Brown, was expressly utilitarian—first a large-capacity airliner with generous space for cargo, then, when the SST supplanted it, capable of being used solely as a freighter. Or, in the words of one of Brown's staff, the job was to "sell 'em, build 'em, use 'em, and change 'em."

But within days, before Sutter had had a chance to assess the ideas that had been sketched out for the 747, he found the range of his own role being challenged. Rouzie called to say he was sending over a hundred more engineers from the C5a. Among them were specialists who, if the program accelerated, would lead teams on things like the power plant, controls, and systems. One was openly more ambitious than the rest, Fred Maxam. Maxam had worked with Sutter on the 727. During the development of the C5a, Maxam had worked under the eye of Wells (few key decisions on the C5a were taken without Wells's blessing), and Sutter now realized that Maxam was acting like a man who believed he was a Wells favorite.

Maxam, although reporting to Sutter as his assistant, announced—implying that he was speaking for Wells—that because Sutter had developed a good rapport with the airlines, and particularly with Pan Am, Sutter should be the outside face of the 747 program, while Maxam got on and designed the airplane.

This was news to Sutter. "Jeez," he said, "is that what you heard?"

Not only that, but on the basis of the very first sketches done by Row Brown's configuration group, Maxam had already made up his mind on the 747's configuration: it should have a double-deck fuselage. This was the simplest way to more than double the passenger capacity of the 707, six-abreast seating on two decks. Even then, to provide the 350 to 400 seats they were talking about, the fuselage would have to be very long. Two long, narrow tubes.

Sutter didn't like this idea on sight: to evacuate the airplane in an emergency would require escape chutes on two levels, with passengers on the upper deck facing something like an Olympic bobsled ride.

But Maxam had support for his concept from outside Boeing. Juan Trippe had leaped at the very phrase "double-decker," which to him had the ring of a great marketing slogan. Douglas was also talking double-decker. In fact, the conventional wisdom of the hour had really never considered anything else—the engineers were inclined to see the six-abreast cabin as a standard, and to add seats you either did the big stretch, as Douglas had with the DC-8, or you put another deck on top.

Sutter's gut feeling was that the double-decker was misconceived. A gut feeling, however, did not amount to a viable technical argument. Sutter couldn't kill the double-decker without an alternative idea, and—since it was the only idea they yet had—the double-decker was unchallenged all the way up to Wells.

The translation of performance targets into an airplane was a process that invited many arguments. An airplane of this size was unprecedented, and the arguments multiplied. Palpably overhanging every idea that Sutter explored was the responsibility for potentially putting at risk more than twice the number of lives that any designer had ever had on his conscience. Sutter was known for being ultraconservative on structural integrity, always positing the worst-case scenarios and wanting "redundancy"—an extra margin that might never be needed but if it ever was would avoid catastrophe.

As well as the concern for safety, an airplane of this size— even as an intangible notion—carried political liabilities. As Sutter pondered the 747 configuration, he knew that there was hardly a single technical step that did not carry a political consequence. Noise, for one. Jets of the 707 generation left a rasping and penetrating wake of sound as they took off, and airport noise had provoked an increasingly powerful backlash from communities under the flight paths. These same jet engines were also dirty: they trailed sooty ribbons of imperfectly combusted kerosene.

But perhaps the most contentious matter was the impact the 747 would have on airports and air traffic movements. The global boom in air travel had already overpowered the capacity of many airports. And in a lot of the municipal airports around the United States, Boeing 727s and Douglas DC-9s came with such frequency and with such loads that they stretched out in lines waiting for takeoff like cabs on a rank. How would a monster carrying three to four hundred people help this?

Every 747, went the rehearsed answer, would remove the need for up to two out of three smaller aircraft. But the 747 was a transcontinental and transoceanic jet, and would not reduce aircraft numbers on the congested domestic hops. Never mind, went the Boeing refrain, on the long-haul routes 747s could cut the number of individual departures by nearly 40 percent, and anything is better than nothing.

Sutter had arrived too late to stop the production of scale models demonstrating the virtues of the double-decker. There were several versions, and Sutter had a word for all of them— turkeys. One had a midwing arrangement, in which the lower deck was actually interrupted by the wing structure. Sutter had long ago memorized every detail of the 247 fiasco and recalled that one of its most serious flaws had been the main wing spar running through the middle of the passenger cabin like a giant step. Some guys never learn, steamed Sutter. He didn't like the low-wing version of the same design any better—it looked ungainly and top-heavy.

There was another model showing three engines instead of four, all three clustered at the rear as on the 727, with a high T-tail. (Wells, for some reason, always liked T-tails even though they involved tiresome aerodynamic and structural complications.) This one looked rear-heavy, a big pain in the butt. But the most peculiar proposal was a model they called the "anteater" because its flight deck was actually placed *under* the passenger cabin. Passengers at the very front had windows curving around the nose, so that they would be sitting where the pilots normally were, looking forward! Below them, the pilots would find themselves enjoying an uncomfortable intimacy with the ground on takeoff and landing.

Yet, of all these models, the anteater had redeeming qualities. It was not a double-decker. If you overlooked the aberration at the nose, it was far sleeker than the others and had the kind of natural balance to it that Sutter always looked for. (A maxim from the earliest days of flight was "If it looks right it will fly right," and Sutter had no argument with that.) Moreover, there was method of a sort in the madness of the nose. If its future after the SST was to be a cargo carrier, getting the flight deck out of the way of the main passenger cabin was an inspired stroke. Cargo could be front-loaded through a hinged nose. As far as Sutter was concerned, the anteater was still a no-no, but it was suggestive of an idea.

The airplane that the Boeing team had talked about to Pan Am on September 30 was no more tangible than the one suggested in the July meeting. Nobody had expected that it would be, and the 747 remained evanescent in John Yeasting's five-page letter to Pan Am at the end of October. Boeing was offering an envelope: so many passengers, so much range, such a cost per seat-mile. The detail that caught Borger's eye, a cruising speed of nine-tenths Mach, had not given Sutter pause. Of the many things on his mind, it didn't seem an issue.

Fred Maxam, however, *was* an issue. Sutter was tired of hearing how Maxam was going to run the project. He called Rouzie with a simple choice: "It's either me or him." Within two weeks, Maxam had gone—to the SST team. To the few hundred engineers now gathered in the pastures of the 1085 Building, there was no lingering doubt about who was in charge. And beyond Sutter's team, it was a detectable signal that the 747 was being driven by a single-minded engineer who wanted no ambiguities in lines of responsibility.

Sutter had been picking his core team.

One Friday afternoon Milt Heinemann was slipping a round-trip ticket to Alaska into his briefcase. The saga of the 737 had taken yet another turn. Ward Air, the Canadian company that serviced the Alaskan North Slope oil explorations, was pressing to know if the 737 would be able to use the gravel runways that had been laid down in Alaska. Boeing's technical staff balked. Throw rocks into a $2 million engine? No way. Heinemann was going to find out whether gravel runways could somehow be dealt with. It was the kind of problem he liked.

Rouzie came into his office. Sutter wanted him on the 747—right away. There was no appeal. Somebody else could go and test the gravel in Alaska.

As the authority on cabin layout, Heinemann found himself dropped into the center of the argument about the double-decker. Although Maxam was gone, the double-decker had gathered alarming momentum. A brochure featuring it had been prepared for the airlines. Its advocates pointed out that airports were running out of space and that it would be a lot easier to turn around an airplane that was twice as tall than one that was twice as long—length and height were, significantly, the only dimensions anyone seemed able to project.

Like Sutter, Heinemann distrusted the double-decker on sight. And he voiced his concern: two hundred or more people up thirty-five to forty feet from the ground and *he* had to have them all evacuated within ninety seconds—the time laid down by the Federal Aviation Administration as mandatory—without injury? Just how was that going to be done? Nobody had an answer. It was his problem. They were already building a wooden mock-up of the double-deck fuselage to show to the airlines.

But Heinemann knew that he enjoyed one inviolate instrument of power over the project—Boeing would withhold approval of any design until he was prepared to take responsibility for the evacuation of the passengers by the ninety-second rule. Sutter knew that Heinemann would never compromise on that. It was one of the reasons Sutter had had him pulled from the 737 program. And Sutter had another ally against the double-decker.

Row Brown was iterating the configuration like mad, never seeming satisfied with the results. Torrents of drawings spewed forth: Brown was approaching his two hundredth attempt at reconciling the payload with the performance. He was thinking of cargo as well as passengers. Word had come down from Allen, reemphasizing that if the 747 went ahead, "all the family jewels" would be tied up in it, that the engineers would have only one shot to get it right, and that included making sure that they made the design as flexible and versatile as possible. That meant not losing sight of its destiny as a freighter—this was the Mack-truck epithet given tangible form.

Allen's emphasis on the freighter came directly from conversations with Trippe. Trippe had told him that as a passenger carrier alone the 747 "would be very difficult to assimilate." Pan Am had presciently figured that if seat-per-mile costs were as drastically reduced as Boeing said they would be, so also would be the cost of shipping cargo, and that there was a large world-wide demand for the rapid delivery of liftable freight.

The double-decker didn't impress Brown as freighter, any more than it impressed Heinemann as a way of safely seating four hundred or more passengers. In the minds of Sutter, Brown, and Heinemann it was coming down to one decision before all others: the cross section of the fuselage. If they got that wrong, it wouldn't matter what else was right.

There were lots of uncomfortable phantoms in their technical memory beyond that of the 247. Heinemann and Sutter could recall full well the crisis days of the 707's cross section, and the difference between success and failure then had been measured in inches. Allen's injunction about the family jewels concentrated their minds powerfully. In a large bay at the back of the executive offices at Renton they looked at the completed wooden mock-up of the double decker. It generated excitement by its sheer scale. Maybe this was a glimpse of the future, but to Sutter it was still a turkey, just a very large one.

At Pan Am, Trippe was turning the screw. He wanted the

big jet as fast as he could get it. Nobody had so far calculated what a 747 might cost. Pan Am was even now buying more 707s, the model 321B, at $7 million apiece. The crudest extrapolation, that the 747 would be two and a half times larger, suggested that it could not cost less than $17 or $18 million. So, in talking of an initial order of twenty-five 747s, Trippe was breezily talking about committing Pan Am to an investment of $450 million in one airplane. That excluded the cost of spares and the conversion of airport piers and maintenance plant that would be needed. No airline had ever talked in such terms before, and this was an airplane that did not exist, that as yet had no engines, that no airport was equipped to take.

Trippe was, however, riding the euphoria of a good year. Every indication was that for the first time, Pan Am's earnings would top $50 million. (It had been a long journey: in its first year as a mail carrier, Pan Am had lost $300,000; by 1931 it turned its first profit, $100,000, but Trippe had always spent lavishly on new airplanes.)

Allen understood full well that Trippe's talking of such a large initial order was a coercive step, in keeping with his manner of doing business. In effect, Trippe was offering the launch order. Two things would inevitably follow: Trippe would want sufficient priority in deliveries over all other airlines to establish an early dominance with the 747, and Pan Am engineers, led by Borger, would be crawling all over Boeing's engineers as they designed the airplane.

In Yeasting's October letter there was only one mention of engines, that Boeing and Pan Am would resolve the engine selection by January 3, 1966. But the truth was that there was no engine for the airplane. Trippe wanted Gerhard Neumann's big fan engine designed for the C5a. Its development was being paid for by the military, and Trippe was always anxious to ride on the back of a Pentagon program. Furthermore, Trippe knew that Pratt & Whitney's management was nervous about what it would cost to get into the race with GE. He was doubtful that Pratt could handle further development of its engine.

John Borger, who was in no position to question openly Trippe's preference for the GE engine, nonetheless knew that it just would not fit the 747 as Boeing was describing it. For one thing, it was designed for the C5a's lower cruising speed of

.78 Mach, and an engine designed for one cruising speed could not simply be "tweaked" to fit another. Borger also suspected— rightly, as it turned out—that in meeting the unsentimental military criteria the GE engine would be a "smoker," and noisy. Although Pratt *was* fearful of the investment involved, and sensibly dubious that its first big fan could be developed at the same speed as a new airplane (all the historical evidence being to the contrary), it did make a philosophical decision about its design that was astute.

The GE engine had a very high bypass ratio (the ratio of the uncombusted cool air to the hot core air) of eight to one. Neumann's confidence that his engineers could figure how to hold this engine together had been well placed. Pratt, on the other hand, felt that it could get a more flexible engine, and one more suited to the commercial ambitions of the 747, with a lower ratio. Pratt chose a ratio of five and a half to one. And so, by the end of October, Pratt, like Boeing and Pan Am, was suppressing its best instincts and marching to the tune of Juan Trippe—step by step into the bold new world of the megajet.

Between them, these companies were making a financial commitment beyond the bounds of anything known outside of a military program. John Kennedy's invocation that America would put a man on the moon by the end of the decade testified to one aspect of the national spirit and will, that which was ready to restore America's pride at any price. There was no such simple and clearly defined objective to the 747 program, but the fiscal insouciance behind it was certainly heroic. Only the company treasurers were quaking in their shoes.

Row Brown persisted with the 747's freight-carrying role. A new international standard for freight containers had been arrived at: a cross section of eight feet by eight feet. This was done to achieve commonality between road, rail, and ship cargo—the containers could vary in length according to conveyance, but not in width and height. The average container was built to be indestructible, as far from the finesse of airplane construction as the Brooklyn Bridge. Brown knew that these monsters could never be levitated by an airplane. But it seemed to him that there was a lot to be said for designing the light-weight containers for air cargo to the same common dimension, the eight-foot square. Cargo could then simply be switched from one container to the other without being reconfigured.

How would this fit into the cargo hold of an airplane? Idly sketching, Brown drew an outline for the belly of a 747 around one freight container, but it looked a little lonely. Brown drew in two, side by side. He figured out the required width of the cargo deck's floor. Then he drew a circle to fit snugly around the deck and the containers.

Sutter, Heinemann, and Brown looked at Brown's circle. And then they looked at each other. It was a fuselage. A very *wide* fuselage—more than twenty feet across at the level of the passenger cabin, sitting above the cargo deck. Nobody had ever dreamed of a passenger cabin as wide as this—nearly twice as wide as the 707. Boy, was it *wide*. Without consciously registering the moment—there was no cry of *Eureka!*—they knew they had iterated their way to the most daring solution of the 747's configuration problems.

It might seem odd that it had taken Brown so long to arrive at this solution, because he had previously configured another airplane with a similarly fat body, the C5a. But that was a military transport, constructed for very different loads. Although there was a superficial similarity between the C5a's fuselage and the 747 that had now evolved, it had never occurred to anyone to start with a fuselage of this dimension for the airliner.

It was Sutter's inclination, given the pressures on him, to design the 747 well within Boeing's accumulated body of knowledge. To his mind, the 747 was inside the skin of the 707, waiting to burst out. The basic outline of the 707 was too good to fool around with. Sure, they could tailor it better with the latest wind tunnel tricks, but to hell with T-tails, anteaters, and all the other turkeys. If you scaled up a 707 and superimposed on it Row Brown's wide body it didn't get out of scale. It looked right.

Outside the mock-up shop in Renton it was a character-istically dank January day. General Laurence S. Kuter, Juan Trippe's martinet aide, led a team of Pan Am's top technicians—Sanford Kauffman, John Borger, test pilot Scott Flower, and two senior captains—who were taking their first look at Boeing's 747 mock-up. What they saw was the double-decker—by Sutter's definition, a turkey. The cross section was clearly a descendant of the Stratocruiser. It was more than ever like an egg sitting in an egg cup: two intersecting lobes, the lower lobe the larger, and the upper deck beginning where the lobes met at a seam, roughly two thirds of the way up.

This double-decker was larger than the one Maxam had promoted; on that version the upper deck had been just over fifteen feet from tarmac level. In the version now unveiled to Pan Am, the upper deck was more than twenty-five feet above the tarmac, and for Milt Heinemann, fretting about evacuating passengers, this was a serious regression. It might be true that inside the airplane he could see one improvement. For the first time, the passenger cabins had two aisles, making it easier to get to the exit doors in an emergency. But outside it was a different story—the upper deck was at a dizzying height.

Pan Am was looking at an airplane with eight-across seating on the lower deck (allowing for the aisles, three-two-three) and seven-across seating on the upper deck (two-three-two). The Boeing brass, including Wells and Yeasting, were strangely free of hyperbole, as though the 747's size would speak for itself. Kuter, Kauffman, Borger, and Flower had come to Seattle from California, where they had seen the Douglas mock-up derived from Douglas's C5a proposal. The Pan Am men shared a reservation about whether an airplane of this size could really be digested by the airlines.

Hard hats were handed out. Rather rickety ladders led to the upper deck. When the Pan Am party got up there, it was stiflingly hot. The mock-up was virtually brushing the roof of the badly ventilated building. It might be Seattle in January outside, but on the upper deck it was Miami in August. Heinemann had arranged for a demonstration of emergency evacuation by a chute, and the Pan Am volunteer who took the ride didn't enjoy hurtling to concrete from that height.

More crucially, Borger was underwhelmed by the mock-up. He looked under the lower deck, at the cargo space. For the size of the plane, it seemed miserly. Sutter and Heinemann were lurking in the background. Something was going on.

Wells began talking about a different cross section. He unveiled a drawing, pinned to a blackboard. It was a single circle. The passenger deck was a more comfortable sixteen feet from the tarmac, and there were *nine* seats across, with two aisles— the cabin was spectacularly wide, about twenty feet. This was new. But what Borger liked most was the cargo space. There was room for two eight-by-eight containers, side by side. Trippe had insisted that in future cargo would be as important as passengers, and Boeing had listened.

Kuter, as usual, was hard to read. Kauffman didn't make a career of open enthusiasm. Scott Flower was interested in flight decks and a lot of other questions that a fuselage mock-up couldn't answer. Borger knew that in spite of that capacious cargo hold, Trippe would take some persuading to abandon the double-decker, which with him had become something of an *idée fixe*. But it was clear to Borger where Sutter was headed. The whole double-decker show was a charade, designed not to sell this version of the 747 but to kill it. Even the ladders. How could a group of fastidious engineers come up with ladders like that? They still felt queasy as they walked away.

At that point, Kuter, Kauffman, and Borger were among the very few people inside Pan Am who knew that Trippe had already signed up on the 747. Being favored with this knowledge was like getting an invitation to the Christmas party at Trippe's Park Avenue apartment: you knew you were doing fine if you were invited. If you weren't, you wouldn't know why. At the 1965 party only a few people knew about the negotiations with Boeing on the 747. In fact, on December 22, Trippe had signed a five-page letter of intent. It was a slightly elaborated version of Yeasting's October draft. Indeed, one marvels that the document formally launching the largest commercial aviation project in history is briefer and a good deal less prolix than the average mortgage agreement.

It was not, however, binding on either side, and it was Boeing and not Pan Am that was as yet spending serious money on the 747, but the letter did have an inexorable quality. Borger scribbled in the margin of his copy, "Not airplane shown by Boeing." It was smaller than the 747 he had expected from earlier meetings. He questioned the promised nine-tenths-Mach cruising speed, and thought the range of 5,100 nautical miles a little short of what he would have liked (Pan Am's yardstick route for range was New York-Rome, easily managed by its 707-320Bs), but otherwise the airplane as outlined seemed to him to be close to what he would ask of it.

Trippe had not questioned the performance details. He was exercised about the delivery schedule. Signing of the letter, which should have occurred on December 17, was delayed until he received a revised delivery priority, cabled to New York, guaranteeing Pan Am all of the first five aircraft built, five of each of the first three batches of ten, and five of the next fifteen. Boeing had been reluctant to go this far, for fear of disaffecting other customers, but Trippe wanted every ounce of flesh for his commitment.

Boeing, in its turn, had front-loaded the payments due from Pan Am, calling for half the total price of each aircraft to be paid *before* delivery in gradually escalating amounts, "due to the substantial financial investment required." The tone of the transaction was set by these first demands of each company on the other—a tone that would eventually sound like mutual desperation.

By the time of the vertigo game with the double-decker, Sutter was convinced that Row Brown's single circle was the only viable form for the 747 fuselage. Recalling the moment, Sutter says, "It was a brilliant decision, based on damned few facts." They had refined the wide-body configuration in no more than a month, with sketches and hand calculations (similar studies on later Boeing airplanes would stretch into years and involve elaborate computer models). One serious disadvantage did emerge: the single-deck fuselage was heavier, by as much as twelve thousand pounds, than the double-decker, because of the structure required to give it rigidity. But in Sutter's eyes the wide-body's virtues more than compensated for the weight penalty.

Sutter gave Brown the credit for making the concept convincing enough to win over people like Wells. In fact, Brown was the best evidence that Boeing was no longer a company that did not listen hard enough to airlines—on the 747, he had patiently assimilated the wish lists of all the potential customers for the airplane. Sutter says that Brown had the rare ability to listen to advocates of every interest and satisfy them all without injecting any personal bias.

With Wells persuaded, someone had to begin the process of weaning Trippe away from the double-decker. Sutter now knew that Borger, swayed by the cargo capacity, favored the single deck. Sutter decided that Milt Heinemann, whose manner manifested a nice balance of the venal (payload) with the steadfastly moral (safe evacuation), was more likely to get Trippe's attention than someone from the sales staff.

In his own mind, Heinemann was convinced that the wide-body was a kind of divine revelation: it made the job of seating so many passengers—his job—much easier, and it would have clear advantages when it came to persuading the FAA that emergency evacuation had been carefully considered. But persuading Trippe was never based solely on such rational principles, and Heinemann pondered how the concept might be demonstrated with one striking, diagrammatic stroke. It was then that he went out and bought the hemp rope—"not knowing how I would use it." Even after the knotted rope had revealed that the dimensions of the Pan Am boardroom were tantalizingly close to those of the 747's proposed cabin, he was nervous about facing Trippe, not sure whether he could carry it off. At all.

After telling Trippe that he was, in effect, sitting in the 747's cabin, there were more detailed questions for Heinemann to field, about payload, cabin layout, and, most of all, safety. Heinemann pointed out that the single-deck cabin would have two aisles and be far easier to evacuate than the double-decker. He knew that Trippe felt that the 707 was the finest airplane Pan Am had ever bought, and he stressed that the 747 was, in principle, a scaled-up 707, that Pan Am should see the wide-body as part of that principle, and that there were going to be no surprises. Warming to his theme, he said that Boeing would never give Pan Am cause to doubt even an airplane of this size on the grounds of safety.

Heinemann left New York feeling that although Trippe was hard to read, Pan Am's engineers, and particularly Borger, were swinging to the wide-body.

The gestation process that Sutter now followed in developing the 747 had, as its embryo, the least graceful guts of the airplane. Given the portly stature of the body, the airplane's central balance had to be figured out first. The crucial junction of structure was where the wing met the fuselage. All the stresses converged here: the aerodynamic and load stresses of the wing, the payload's center of gravity, and the impact, passed through the landing gear, of the massive airplane touching down on the runway. As was his way, Sutter worked the 747 outward from this core.

The landing-gear configuration was critical. The airports were being promised that an airplane that was then expected to weigh around 600,000 pounds would be able to use the existing runways, without reinforcing them. What governed this was the weight borne by each wheel, the "footprint." Sutter faced proponents of three different configurations: two-, three-, and four-legged main landing gear. For the 747 to have had the traditional two-legged landing gear would have meant legs like tree trunks, with all the impact stress channeled into only two load-bearing points. A third, central leg was a compromise. But, in the end and after remarkably little time spent on the choice, Sutter opted for four legs and sixteen wheels. In this way the load on the

runway and on the airplane was better diffused, and the wheels and tires were reduced to the same size as those in use already on the 707. The characteristic attitude of the 747 on the ground— it waddles like a pregnant goose—was thus fixed.

The mechanics of the landing gear were ingenious and rhapsody enough to give pleasure to a man who had been regarded as the connoisseur of landing gears since he had designed the gear on the Flying Fortress, Ed Wells. Wells always insisted on having a personal scrutiny of landing-gear design. What he saw this time was more elaborate than anything before. The load was shared between the body and the wings, and the four legs were staggered, two ahead, retracting into the wings, and two behind, retracting into the body. With sixteen tires, a 747 could suffer blowouts without jeopardizing its safety, and the spread of the wheels made it extremely stable on the tarmac. Only one error was made and remained for later correction: the main landing gear was not steerable by the pilot.

In Sutter's words, once this core of the airplane was shaped, "the wing and the engines sort of fall out of that." Confident that the core was right, Sutter sketched wings that, superficially at least, followed the lines of the 707. There were, however, two big differences: size, and—because of the ambition to fly at nine-tenths Mach—the degree of wing sweep. As far as the size and the structure of the wings were concerned, work on the C5a wing had given the structures men confidence that a 747 wing was well within their skills. (This assumption would prove to be too optimistic.) Wing sweep, however, was a different matter.

Wing sweep involved the naggingly persistent bogey of Dutch roll. Eventually, Dutch roll had been successfully suppressed on the 707 and had never endangered a single passenger. More than a decade of further experience in the wind tunnel and advances in theoretical work, accelerated by computers, suggested that this potentially lethal vice was, if not history, permanently incarcerated within the safety regime. Developments in electronics had made "Little Herbie" into what was now less chummily called the SAS—the Stability Augmentation System.

But if you took the term literally, this was a euphemism. Stability had to be augmented because if it was not the 707 was, under known conditions, inherently unstable. However, the SAS now available to Sutter was greatly enhanced and—as he would insist for everything—part of a "belt and suspenders" philosophy, with its own backup, and working independently of other control systems.

And yet Sutter was being very sporty in going after nine-tenths Mach. He was seeking to reconcile two regimes of contrasting intent: large load and high speed. Could you begin with this great, bloated body and then sharpen it into a rocket ship? Borger had said nothing when he saw nine-tenths Mach on the specification, but—like any other airline engineer—he would be eagle-eyed when it came to the 747's handling characteristics, and everybody knew that you couldn't get to nine-tenths without more wing sweep. And more wing sweep put lateral control into question. It made the wing more prone to yaw, and yaw triggered Dutch roll.

Just imagine a thing this size gyrating like the ill-fated 707s, throwing off engines and tearing apart! It had to be considered. The 707's wing was swept back by 35 degrees. An argument encompassing another 5 degrees broke out over the 747's wing. It was not simply the radicals versus the conservatives. Engineers with a lifetime of vocational rectitude behind them thought it reasonable to go to 40 degrees of sweep, giving the 747 the most rakish wing of any airliner.

One of these was Everette Webb, the head of the technical staff. Occupying this position, Webb was, by the lights of the Boeing checks-and-balances system, one of the most influential policemen of the 747 program. Physically, Webb was strikingly similar to Sutter, compact and slightly pugilistic in appearance, and also very direct in his views and fluent in argument. A trust had grown between Sutter and Webb. Both believed deeply in the value of intuition, and in each other's intuitive talents. Webb, like Sutter, was cautious in his faith in computers and felt that computers tended to encourage in engineers a worrying loss of intuition.

Webb liked to "surround a problem analytically." The question of the 747's wing sweep was a case in point. He felt that the nine-tenths Mach was safely attainable with a 40-degree sweep. Airfoil design had progressed to make the wing more manageable—more susceptible to tailoring—and he felt they could have provided the controls to enable an airline pilot to handle it with ease.

There was another respected advocate of the 40-degree sweep: W. T. Hamilton (by now it was part of the Hamilton legend that his initials stood for Wind Tunnel). Hamilton was accepted as Boeing's preeminent wing designer. He was a believer in the competitive edge given by the higher speed, and every degree of sweep translated into more speed. Like Webb, Hamilton had no fears that the faster wing could be tamed. He had experimented in the tunnel with a 40-degree sweep on the B-52, and it had looked good.

Sutter respected these two authorities, but he was caught between them and less intrepid views from above, particularly those of Schairer and Wells. From the beginning of the 747 program, Schairer and Sutter shared the belief that the design should stay within the boundaries proved by the 707. Wells, in his role as salesman, was sensitive to airline pressure not to go as far as 40 degrees. The debate on wing sweep—which, like everything around the 747, had to be disposed of quickly because of the pressure coming from Pan Am for a settled configuration— was not a minor issue. It had the elements of a classic theological dispute among the aeromen, and one audible enough to attract the attention of Jack Steiner.

At the end of 1965, Steiner had been made vice president in charge of product development, replacing Pennell, who became program director of the SST. Steiner's new power granted him no automatic right to intervene in the design of the 747; Pennell had left Sutter to make his own way, knowing that if he wanted help he would call for it. Product development was a strategic concern, encompassing the commercial division's whole market. Steiner, however, was not Pennell. Steiner took product development to include 747 development.

The choice of the wide-body, the most seminal step in the evolution of the 747, had been made without reference to Steiner. With Wells's support already pledged, there was no need to involve Steiner in that decision. The wing, however, was another matter. Steiner decided that the right answer for the wing was a compromise, lying exactly halfway between the 707 and the sporty 40-degree sweep, 37.5 degrees. The higher speed was still attainable, and there was less risk of courting stability problems.

Who actually settled on this number is a matter of dispute.

The competitive memories of Sutter and Steiner admit no place for each other—Sutter says that Steiner was not involved, Steiner claims the decision as his own. Hamilton and Webb believe that once Wells and Schairer turned against the 40-degree sweep, Sutter had no choice but to compromise. Here, in fact, is a textbook example of the Boeing consensus producing what was virtually a disembodied decision. Politically and intuitively, Sutter played safe. Reputations were not made or broken on 2.5 degrees of wing sweep, even though egos were fully engaged. And Sutter was still able to give the 747 the fastest wing out there.

That is, if Boeing could find an engine. Despite Trippe's preference for the GE engine, Neumann said that his engineers were too embroiled in getting that engine up to performance for the C5a to even think about modifying it for the 747. There were only two other companies capable of obliging, Pratt & Whitney and Rolls-Royce. No body of engineers had a higher reputation than those at Rolls-Royce, and Rolls's experience of jets went back further than any American company's. But Rolls's research was underfunded, and Rolls engineers were inclined to let their ideas get beyond their capacity to manufacture them. As the wide-body 747 emerged, Pratt was really the only contender. And, by working to a lower bypass ratio than GE, Pratt felt that it was able to promise an engine that would fit the criteria that Boeing, in turn, had promised to Pan Am.

Trippe only reluctantly accepted that GE could not deliver its engine. Borger had no influence on this decision; his contacts with Pratt were known to be far closer than with GE, and Trippe ordered him to stay out of the engine selection process. However, Borger found himself importuned by other suitors. Two senior Rolls executives on an American tour had picked up news of Pratt's commitment, and they targeted Borger for a sales call. Over lunch in New York they pumped him about what the 747 needed in power. They insisted that they should not be counted out, and said they had a high-bypass engine in development. As usual with Rolls, they promised innovations. Borger heard them out but felt that Rolls was promising too much too soon.

Borger was now involving himself in the intimacies of the 747 design, beginning a process that meant that for two years Sutter would rarely pass a week without seeing or hearing from

Pan Am's engineering conscience. Enthused by the wide-body's cargo capacity, Borger argued insistently for a feature that would give the airplane its distinctive profile. He wanted the freighter version of the 747 to have nose-loading. The main deck would swallow huge amounts of cargo, and it made sense for the nose to hinge upward for the containers to be fed directly inside the fuselage, instead of being loaded from side doors.

Sutter's problem was, if the nose became a giant door, where did the flight deck go? The anteater had put it below. Why not above? Sutter did a rough sketch. The flight crew would certainly have commanding views, more than thirty feet above the tarmac. Like the widened body itself, this extra flourish looked right and helped make the nose as sporty as the wings. By elongating the basic circle into an egg-shaped cross section at the front it gave the 747, from a head-on perspective, a more slippery look. To smooth out this hump, it was faired gradually into the line of the body behind. Sutter thought that space inside the fairing would be useful for installing systems, like air conditioning. Borger mused that it might be handy for a crew rest area.

The definitive outline of the colossus was now visible. Although the issue of wing sweep was settled, one more fundamental change was made to the wing. Wells, in reviewing the design, recalled Boeing's painful experiences with airplanes that did not stretch with the demands of the market. He decided that the 747's wing was too small. It was easy to extend a fuselage by the expedient used on the 707, inserting "plugs" that added rows of seats. It was a far more expensive process to change a wing. Recalling Hamilton's wing on the 707-320, Wells demanded a wing that would be as good as Hamilton's from the beginning and large enough to lift a stretched fuselage.

A critical parameter of airplane design is wing loading: the overall weight divided by the wing area. As a rule of thumb, the smaller the wing, the greater the wing loading. And the greater the wing loading, the faster the airplane—though the penalty for speed achieved this way is that the airplane is more of a handful on takeoffs and landings. Wells thought that the risk of making the 747 slower with a bigger wing was discounted by the advantages it would bring in stretchability and in airfield performance. The original wing had an area of 5,200 square feet.

It was enlarged to 5,500 square feet. (The 707's wing was 3,000 square feet.)

Within a few months, decisions that might normally have been taken only after extensive analysis and testing in the wind tunnel, not to mention haggled over by rival theocracies, were fixed beyond appeal. Allen, locking his company into the commitment, lacked the technical background to understand how adventurous this all was. Consider the sequence: the first wide-bodied commercial jet; a faster wing than any manufacturer had so far risked; a unique body profile with the flight deck as high as a four-story house; a sixteen-wheel main landing gear—all depending on an engine design that was speculative.

Yet the schedule was slipping. Boeing had originally proposed the date of March 1, 1966, for a more binding agreement with Pan Am, including the detailed specification, price, and delivery dates. Late in February, this was changed to April 1. Trippe goaded Allen with a reminder of their "If you build it, I'll buy it" pact, but Allen responded with a one-sided bet: if they weren't building the 747 by August, he would pay Trippe $10 million.

Even so, Allen was sobering up about the financial commitment involved. In March he had revealed to his own board what the program was likely to cost. There was a growing complicity between Allen and Trippe to get their respective bankers on board without being forced to show too much of their hand in public. Allen sent Yeasting to New York to reveal Boeing's estimates of the funding required—he called Trippe to point out that "we have never done this for a customer before." It wasn't a sales pitch, he said (here was the voice of probity from the Pacific Northwest trying to disarm Trippe's innate suspicions), but "the facts as we estimate them—our analysis of the cost situation."

Trippe understood very well that he was out way ahead of most other airline chiefs in his passion for the 747—he told Allen that there were "twenty airlines hoping that nothing would happen." When his industry peers asked him about the 747, he cagily answered: "We are watching what's going on out there with great interest." In the same breath, he was pressing Allen to delay deliveries of the 747 to foreign airlines for six months, to block off the competition until Pan Am had cornered the wide-body market. Yet he knew that Allen needed those customers for two reasons: to hold the loyalty created by the 707, and to stress the worth of the program to the country in foreign earnings.

The political value of a program of this size to the U.S. balance of payments was no small matter. The economy was overheating and Washington was—in the personal temper of Lyndon Johnson—turning a beady eye on large new commitments of capital by American corporations. As Trippe was drawn into what was clearly going to be a conspicuous exercise in raising capital, he began to fear that Johnson would apply pressure to stop the 747 program. Versions of what followed tend to be colored by Trippe's lifelong advertisement of his manipulative skills in Washington. The truth is that Democratic administrations, in particular, had grown leery of Pan Am's incessant lobbying and its preference for cartels rather than competition.

The suspicion in this case must be that Trippe was colluding to create a crisis that he could then get the kudos for solving. His unwary accomplice was Boeing's *bête noire*, Robert Mc-Namara. The Secretary of Defense, sharing Johnson's concern about overcooking the economy, thought that the new large commercial jet should be grown out of the C5a, thereby minimizing the research and development costs. Trippe took it upon himself to explain to McNamara that the roles of the two airplanes were irreconcilable. According to Trippe, McNamara was, for once, humbled to have found himself so ill-briefed.

Allen, in Washington for a Business Council meeting, was then dragged into the endgame. Through McNamara, Trippe got into the Oval Office to have the President himself verbally sign off on the 747, and pitched the case that in both technology *and* its potential contribution to the balance of payments, the 747 was, like the space program, essential Americana. Allen, bemused by the audience and happy to let Trippe have his day, agreed. Later, Trippe was at pains to claim that his intervention had saved the 747. This is strongly contested by people around Allen at the time, who say that he would have treated with contempt any attempt by Washington to dictate Boeing's commercial policy. After its TFX and C5a experiences, Boeing was hardly likely to respect any request coming from McNamara, and the Air Force's dependence on the B-52, an essential instrument in the Vietnam War, which was being continually up-graded, made Boeing immune to at least this kind of Pentagon coercion. The issue was never forced. Trippe was allowed his delusion.

In Renton there were now two plywood mock-ups of the 747, the double-decker and a nose section of the wide-body. After Heinemann's presentation, Trippe decided to fly to Seattle and make the final choice on the spot. The rickety ladder was still there. Allen led him to the upper deck. Both men showed their age, and both were tremulous. Sutter felt that as soon as Trippe's feet touched the ground the argument was over. Trippe, however, kept them in suspense. A firmer set of steps led to the wide-body, and Trippe was shown the cavernous main deck. Sutter explained how the nose on the freighter would open for cargo loading.

It is important to recall how Allen and Trippe had already set limits on the useful life of the 747. In their minds, they were not looking at an airplane with decades of life ahead of it, an airplane that would become—ironically, in view of Trippe's visionary belief in the age of the common man as voyager—the world's traveling machine. They were only convinced of the 747's utility by seeing its capacity to become the airborne equivalent of a tramp steamer. Somewhere nearby, in the shrouded drawing office of the SST program, Pennell, Holtby, Withington, and many of Boeing's best engineers were, at that moment, they believed, hatching the future blue-ribbon ship of the air.

Sutter led Allen, Trippe, Borger, and other luminaries of both companies up into the hump and explained the flight deck layout. Trippe remained inscrutable. In the relatively cramped space of the flight deck, people were almost falling over each other to get a sense of what an airfield might look like to a pilot from such a height. The Boeing photographer, Vern Manion, a veteran of mock-ups and first flights, struggled to get a decent picture out of the milling mass. Trippe led the way back behind the flight deck, where the space under the faired hump felt claustrophobic, like a small, curved tent.

"What is this for?" Trippe asked Borger, suddenly inquisitive. Borger said he thought it would make a good crew rest area. Before Trippe responded, Sutter could see that Borger had made a big mistake.

"Rest area?" barked Trippe. "This is going to be reserved for passengers."

Sutter looked at Heinemann. This was typical Trippe. Already figuring out fancy parlors, cocktail bars. Show Trippe an empty space and what do you expect? And then Sutter realized—he's just bought the wide-body.

Indeed he had. Back on terra firma, Trippe acknowledged: "You made the right decision."

But his fancies were not stilled. He looked up at the great bulging proboscis above. The line of cabin windows stopped a few feet short of the nose. As on all jets, the space inside the nose cone was reserved for the radar scanner that picked up the pattern of weather ahead and helped the navigation.

"Why don't you just put me some windows right across the front of the airplane, so the passengers can see where they're going?"

The abandoned anteater had had this feature, although Trippe had never seen it. Sutter hated the idea. For one thing, there was no place else to put the radar. For another, front-facing windows would have to be proofed against bird impact, and that would add hundreds of pounds in weight.

You didn't argue with Juan Trippe on the spot. Sutter said they would look at it.

On April 12, Trippe got the Pan Am board's approval to sign the purchase agreement for the 747. (On the same day, Pratt & Whitney committed itself to develop the engine.) Each of the twenty-five airplanes would cost $18 million. With the revelation of Boeing's own cost projections before them, the board was not sandbagged without understanding the scale of the commitment. Nobody carped. Trippe was all-persuasive when it came to the culminating dream of his career. And Trippe's belief was shared by the singularly influential voice of Lindbergh, who had been involved in many of the briefings on the 747 given by Boeing since its inception.

Knowing Lindbergh's interest in the 747, Allen wrote to him inviting him to sit at the head of the table at a dinner in Seattle to celebrate Boeing's fiftieth anniversary on July 15. Lindbergh replied from his home in Darien, Connecticut. He graciously set out for Allen the reclusive principle on which he based his life—"It is now more than a decade since I have made

an address at a dinner, or anywhere else"—and said that if he
made an exception for Boeing it would "open the floodgates."
He finished with a eulogy to Boeing's engineers, pointing out
that he had flown Boeing airplanes since 1927. Wistfully, he
recalled Bill Boeing telling him that what he would have liked
most to do was to "put four-wheel brakes on time."

And, indeed, the passage of time was catching up on Allen.
In his seventieth year he had the appearance of an esteemed
but anachronistic figure. His vested suits retained a thirties
severity in their cut. His face had the concentrated vigilance of
a man who had seen too much cynicism and corporate duplicity
seeping into the way business was done. His financial management was delegated to a very few trusted hands (two, in particular, were the vice president of finance, H. W. Haynes, and
Jim Prince, the corporate secretary) who held their tongues and
kept from public view while he fulfilled people's expectations of
what a sound bookkeeper should look like.

It was a very successful charade. Boeing would not have
made a convincing model for a business school study of the sophisticated management of a high-technology enterprise involving risks of the size of the 747. But Allen had had no difficulty
carrying his board of directors into the 747 program. Their assent was little more than a formality. After all, his one setback
with the board, the Steiner-engineered campaign for the 737,
had not demonstrated their timidity but their gung-ho tendency.

Within a week of the signing of Boeing Purchase Agreement
No. 189 between Boeing and Pan Am for the 747, there was an
epochal retirement from the Boeing board. Claire Egtvedt had
been the titular chairman since 1939, although since Allen's selection as president in 1945 Egtvedt had had no executive responsibility. He was a gracious and courtly man, the very
personification of the fiber from which Boeing was cut. Like
Allen, he was a seeming contradiction: a bearer of the old and
almost extinct rectitude in a business of relentless modernity.
His life was nearly the entire lifespan of aviation in America.

Allen, unlike Trippe, had seriously pondered his own succession. He was realist enough to look for someone with the
several disciplines needed to master the organism that Boeing
had become. Inside Boeing, the succession inspired speculation
as factional as that of the election of a pope. There were those

who sensed that it would be more than a change at the top. A sea change in the style of managing Boeing was likely. Would it remain a company built around the gratification of engineers? It was difficult to see how bean-counters could displace engineers when engineers were the company's bedrock.

Many felt that Wells had earned the presidency many times over. To every engineer in Boeing, Wells was already the pope. Every catechism of Boeing doctrine bore Wells's mark. Maynard Pennell was one of the few people who knew that Wells fervently hoped to succeed Allen. Wells was a strange balance of self-effacement, conceit, and ambition. His technical fluency came so effortlessly that it never needed vigorous advocacy, though there were times when others, like Pennell, wished he would take issue and bark. In a sense, he was so assured—this was where the conceit came in—that he expected to prevail without imposing himself.

If Allen was considering Wells, he was telling nobody. Younger and openly aggressive men were brought into the boardroom. Two were conspicuously lacking the somber, gray manners of the Seattle school of business and social intercourse.

E. H. "Tex" Boullioun, one of the two vice presidents reporting to Yeasting, had acquired a brilliant record in the guided missile division of the company before arriving in Renton. He had a face like a young Marine colonel: cropped hair, broad chin, and a suggestion of ribaldry in the set of his mouth (although he alleged that at one point in his youth he had seriously thought of becoming a priest). Boullioun was born in Arkansas, but acquired the handle of "Tex" during many nights spent playing poker. He was formidably numerate, with a memory like a computer.

Boullioun made it known that he didn't want his success to typecast him as an operations man. He wanted to sell. There was little doubt of his aptitude: people felt that in another age Boullioun, who looked a lot younger than his forty-seven years, would have moved record quantities of snake oil.

And then there was Thornton Arnold ("T") Wilson, newly installed as the vice president in charge of operations and planning, and universally known by his single initial. Wilson had come a long way since his spell as George Martin's administrative assistant, where he had witnessed the early-morning revision of the 707's fuselage template. Not far enough, alas, for anyone who felt that a company vice president should be clean-mouthed and socially smooth. Wilson was incontinently profane. He simply could not help himself. Every technical treatise he delivered—and he delivered them often and with a mesmerizing grasp of detail—was peppered with crude barnyard epithets, rather in the manner of Lyndon Johnson. This was not the usual Boeing style. But Wilson, hawk-nosed and with eyes of feral acuity, still talking in his fruity native Missouri timbre, intellectually dominated most of his peers.

Wilson had been an aeroman on the B-47, Dash-80, and B-52. The rule was normally "Once an aeroman always an aeroman": technical careers were distinct from management careers. Technical men set up programs but never managed them. Allen, however, had different ideas for Wilson. In 1952 he sent him on a Sloan Fellowship to MIT for a year, to absorb industrial management. Some years later, Wilson's personal grasp of the tight micromanagement of high-tech work stamped itself on Boeing's Minuteman missile project. Wilson had proved himself able to step outside the scientific preoccupations of the aeroman and effectively manage a complex plant.

Allen clearly kept close watch on Wilson and recognized his value, but just as evidently despaired of ever seeing him sufficiently house-trained to grace the tables of the great and good. In 1965, as the 747 was taking life, Wilson was still feeling his way through the sprawling and flaccid headquarters organization at Boeing Field. To the engineer in him, the place was full of heroes. But few of these heroes had ever heard of—or had any time for—the managerial disciplines that Wilson lived by, like, for example, how to cost a project by the man-hours per pound of airplane.

On April 18, Allen wrote effusively to Trippe that the 747 was now under way "on many fronts." In Lindbergh's stead, Trippe had agreed to make the keynote speech at Boeing's fiftieth-anniversary dinner. People watching Allen and Trippe as they were swept up in their vision compared them to a couple of drunks. The project had now broken cover. *Aviation Week*, always well informed on Boeing, had reported late in February on the rival double- and single-deck configurations, including the first mention of the hump, but the 747's final configuration did not leak out until after the Pan Am deal was signed. By then, other airlines were getting details from Boeing. TWA, second only to Pan Am in Boeing's priorities, was briefed before the end of April.

Some key domestic airlines thought the 747 was too big for their markets. C. R. Smith of American, for example, wanted an airplane tailored for transcontinental, not transoceanic, routes. He liked the wide-body but he wanted only three engines, not four. He had supporters inside Boeing. The three-engine 747 that had been configured before Sutter's arrival was the kind of airplane Smith wanted *and* the kind of airplane there was a solid market for. But Borger, who never knew of this faction in Boeing, says that Pan Am would never have looked at the smaller airplane.

Douglas, on the other hand, decided, with C. R. Smith, that the domestic market for the wide-body airplane was more attractive. They agreed that the 747 was a bigger airplane than almost anybody but Juan Trippe really wanted. Though still more tentative than Boeing, Douglas decided to go where it thought the market really was, for a trijet wide-body. The other potential contender, Lockheed, had its hands full with the C5a and the SST, with which it was competing head-on against Boeing in the FAA-funded contest. In February, Lockheed was openly talking in extravagant terms of converting the C5a to an airliner: a *triple*-decker able to carry *nine hundred* coach-class passengers. But this was fanciful disinformation. Lockheed was about to plunge into a large chasm of its own making.

In a sense, the divergence in the philosophies of the three companies came down to this: Douglas (and later Lockheed) decided to satisfy a market that was there; Boeing decided, far more dangerously, to *create* a market—a market that could only be defined by the airplane itself.

There is a danger of making this choice look both less and more sophisticated than it actually was. It all rested on one quantum advance, the high-bypass engine. This engine promised to redefine airline markets through economies of scale. Although proven in principle, the engine yet had to show that it could meet the same standards of reliability—that it was as *safe*—as the first generation of fanjets. How designers sized their airplanes at this point was bound to be cautious. For example, nobody was yet ready to risk a wide-body airplane with only two engines, yet this would, within a decade, prove to be an extremely profitable formula.

In sizing his airplane, Sutter had to trust that the Pratt & Whitney engine would give him the margins that were demanded when around four hundred passengers were involved. No calculation, of the millions involved in creating the 747, was more definitive than this one of sizing. It was here where the most intensively sophisticated reasoning was supposed to hold sway. There is no way of minimizing the crucial nature of sizing, just as there is no way to make more sophisticated than it actually was the simple directive that launched the 747. As Tex Boullioun put it, describing Allen's role: "His only decision was, we'll do it."

12 ■

Black Parachutes Dropping

An airplane was being designed which no Boeing plant could digest. The hunt for a site for the 747 plant was, from the outset, something of a shell game, orchestrated by the company secretary, Jim Prince. No one in the Boeing company was closer to Allen than Prince. They had been partners in the same Seattle law firm, Holloman, Mickelwaite, Marion, Prince & Black, a firm with long-standing business ties to Boeing. Seven years after Allen took over at Boeing, Prince, the preferred courtier, moved into the Boeing headquarters, two floors below Allen, and remained there. Prince was the only man to whom Allen would comfortably leave a strategic business decision. In the delicate zone where finance, politics, and the narrowest company self-interests mingled, Prince was the keeper of the secrets. Together, Prince and Allen looked like a species waiting to be invented: the Northwestern WASP.

Wherever Boeing chose to put the 747 plant, it would be a delicious political plum: a huge piece of tax-generating real estate, a gargantuan feast for construction firms, and a generator of well-paid skilled employment. It would need upward of seven hundred acres. The assembly building required an unprecedented combination of volume and uninterrupted flow space. At one end, subassemblies and parts would come together; at the other end, after sequences of assembly, the whole airplane would roll out the doors. The doors alone would need to be as large as a football field.

Looked at dispassionately, there was no reason why the plant *had* to be either in the Seattle area or, even, in Washington state. There was, for example, the instructive lesson from Boeing's C5a defeat. Lockheed had disregarded its California allegiance and put the C5a into Georgia. The 747 would be an industry in its own right. None of Boeing's existing plants would have more than a marginal contribution to make to it, and in any case, well over half of its construction would be subcontracted and dispersed all over America.

But how dispassionate about its home state could Boeing really afford to be? Sentiment remained a powerful factor. The company had clawed its way out of what was, to the rest of the country and most of the aviation industry, the distant backwoods. Civic and company pride had been astutely merged to the benefit of both Seattle and Boeing. Geographic isolation may have made Boeing obtusely inbred—Pan Am's Borger certainly thought it did—but it also purified Boeing in a way that its engineers were actively conscious of: they had an ethic that was contemptuous of bottom-liners, bean-counters, and Wall Street investment analysts.

But with the 747 plant they had a piece of persuasive political patronage to dispense. Boeing always made sure that wherever it put work, no matter how small a slice of subcontracting, local congressmen were duly beholden. It had not yet gained coercive influence in Senate committees, but it had absorbed the salutary lessons of failing to have it. And with this in mind, the attractions of California surfaced again. Prince was persuaded that Boeing should look at a site at Walnut Creek, east of Oakland and the Berkeley Hills.

Walnut Creek had been surveyed before, for the plant to build the Bomarc missile, but that, in the end, had remained in Seattle. There was an attractive pool of high-tech industry and talent in this part of northern California. With Stanford and Berkeley nearby, there was also a greater concentration of intellectual resources than could be mustered at the University of Washington. Most of all, there was the cynical feeling that in the corridors of the Pentagon and the Senate, "California will always win." A big slice of subcontracted work on the 747 was already assigned to Northrop in California. Adding this to a plant at Walnut Creek would have made Boeing, virtually overnight, the equal of any Californian aerospace company in political leverage, giving battle to Donald Douglas on his own turf.

Within the Seattle area, the industrial center of gravity had always been to the south of the city, and—because the flat terrain encouraged it—it had continued to drift in that direction, creating an urbanized belt that merged with the suburbs of Tacoma. While still toying with California, Prince was attracted to a site south of Tacoma, bordering McChord Air Force Base. It had clear virtues: they would be able to contract with the Air Force to use the large runway; it was near enough to Seattle to be kept under the control of headquarters without moving senior managers; and they would be able to draw from a labor force whose unions were already used to the ways of Boeing's management. However, some of the land needed for the plant was owned by two women who, once they realized that Boeing was prospecting, sat tight to drive up the price.

Both Walnut Creek and McChord were credible choices. But while they were still being evaluated (some of the engineers were found to be surprisingly attracted to the idea of moving to California), Prince was covertly scouting another site thirty miles north of Seattle, the Snohomish County Airport on the edge of the water at Possession Sound. This was also a lightly used military base known as Paine Field, with a 9,500-foot runway that could easily be extended.

The airfield sat atop an escarpment, actually a glacial moraine, formed as the ice had gouged out Puget Sound and the other great fingers of sheltered water between the Olympic Peninsula and Canada. At sea level there was a layer of clay, and the hills and escarpment were gravel sitting on the clay.

To forestall speculation, Boeing sent in teams masquerading as geologists on a soil-testing exercise. In a way, they were—but with bulldozers. The problem was apparent and enormous. If Paine Field was selected, they would have to move over four million cubic yards of earth to grade a site large enough for the plant—as much as was moved to build the Panama Canal *and* the Grand Coulee Dam combined. The tests showed that the gravel went down five hundred feet. In theory, it was movable. But once the site was graded, provision would have to be made to drain it. Given the climate and the geology, draining the plant and the airfield would need something *like* the Panama Canal to channel all the water.

In June 1966, a month before Trippe rhapsodized the 747 as the future liberator of global travel at Boeing's fiftieth-anniversary banquet, Prince took an option on the land adjoining Paine Field from the owners, the city of Everett. Everett was an old lumber-mill town, its air permeated with the sour-sweet smell of logging. The site had at least three obvious attractions—relatively low land values and taxes, the convenience of being on Interstate 5, and the proximity of a railroad line, although this ran below the plateau along Puget Sound. But there was a political value, too: Everett was the hometown of Washington's two veteran Democratic senators, Warren Magnuson, an old Roosevelt New Dealer, and Henry "Scoop" Jackson. Both senators had kept a gymnastic balance between the traditional bucolic ethic of the Pacific Northwest and military interests, and both were sympathetic to Boeing's local value.

The burghers of Everett woke up with alacrity to what was in prospect. In one stroke they could acquire a clean, high-tech industrial base that would transform what had essentially been a working-class town, as well as stimulate the city's business life. Prince played them along by suggesting that McChord and Walnut Creek were hardening possibilities, although by then he and Allen favored Everett, despite the mammoth earthworks involved. Succumbing to the gambit, Everett offered Boeing a sweetheart deal, including the construction of an interchange with I-5 that was large enough to feed traffic and civic egos for generations to come.

A decision to keep the 747 plant in Washington State made it seem as though Boeing's heart had always been in the right place. Despite California's almost mystical political clout, it was highly doubtful that Allen would have wanted to make his last and largest investment in real estate anywhere other than in Washington. And so the small city of Everett won, and never again would Boeing flirt with California. Instead, Boeing set out to acquire the kind of political sophistication that only astute lobbying could provide. This hardening of its determination to become a player in Washington, D.C., really marked a final rejection of the ivory-tower disdain that Bill Boeing had shown for the pork barrel. Bill Allen didn't like it any better than Bill Boeing, but he had been burned once too often, and in any case the generation that would succeed him did not seem to be so squeamish.

Constructing the plant was, from the beginning, paced by the same manic schedule that Sutter had accepted for the airplane. The 747 was not one program but three, simultaneously: designing the airplane, developing the engine, and building the plant. All three were propelled by a reckless hubris emanating from the two men who left the reality to others, Trippe and Allen.

To build the plant and plan the 747 production line, Allen reached out for a man who was a rarity at Boeing, someone from a radically different industrial culture. Mal Stamper was a Motown boy, Detroit-born and General Motors–reared. He had joined Boeing in 1962 with a reputation as one of the ablest of GM's new generation of manufacturing technicians. In 1965, as the 747 bandwagon began to roll, Allen chose Stamper to amputate an ailing corporate limb, Boeing's gas turbine division. This he did with celerity, selling it to Caterpillar. As his next task, Stamper got the dubious prize of Everett.

The plant was planned around the one main assembly building. The single roof, going to a height of ten stories, would span sixty-three acres and contain the largest volume, by far, of any building in the world: 205 million cubic feet. It was so large, in fact, that it would have its own internal microclimate. Given its location, it would need neither air conditioning nor heating, but, under certain humidity conditions, it was likely that clouds would form *inside* the building. After one look at the time he had left to build the plant, Stamper realized that the first 747s, if they followed the ordained schedule, would have to be assembled before the building was anything like finished: without a roof, with production jigs set in place as the concrete dried.

Even after four years at Boeing, Stamper was still considered an outsider. His first two jobs, in the aerospace division and then winding up the gas turbine business, had not prepared him for the old, clannish alliances of the Seattle headquarters or, in particular, of the commercial airplane division at Renton.

Credentials earned in Motown, no matter how glowing, did not impress aeromen. To them, Detroit was as scientific as a drop hammer. The exceptions in this wall of vocational hauteur were the few who had, like Stamper, been cutting their teeth outside the cabal of aeromen, in aerospace and missiles, managers like T. Wilson and Tex Boullioun.

In Renton, the martially cropped Boullioun was a fast read. Having joined Bruce Connelly as one of John Yeasting's two gatekeepers, Boullioun was already noted for his social stamina—for the kind of leather-lined stomach and irresistible charm that were essential for any airplane salesman, combined with his easy technical fluency and political adeptness. For Stamper, Boullioun was the outsider's insider: he could talk aerospeak, but he could also talk manufacturing. And Boullioun could count. He knew the magnitude of what Stamper was attempting. Just as he knew the bulldog Sutter and all of *his* problems.

Then into Boullioun's office came Steiner. Everyone was adding up something. Stamper was adding up tons of gravel. Sutter was adding up engineering staffs—adding and adding. The 737 program had been "demanned" to feed the 747. Taking into account the design work being done by subcontractors, it looked like the 747 was going to take upward of *six thousand* engineers before every rivet was home. Now Steiner was adding up everything—the whole caboodle.

This was not the wired Steiner, fighting for turf, talking aerospeak.

"Tex," he said, "you're facing an overrun on this program the likes of which you've never seen."

The "you're" was a signal Boullioun understood.

If Steiner was unloading on Boullioun, and he certainly seemed like a man who wanted to unload on somebody, he was bringing to a head an embarrassing ambiguity in the line management of the 747 program. From the moment he had become vice president of product development, Steiner had assumed that part of his job was to turn the 747 into an airplane that the airlines would buy. That, after all, was what he did best.

But, very quickly, Sutter had come to so dominate the development of the 747 that Steiner was marginalized. Had Steiner been of a different temperament, he would have been glad to leave Sutter with the fearsome problems of designing the airplane. After all, Steiner had the 737 and 727 to watch over as well as the 747. But he was *a designer*, dammit. He loved the job. What could beat it? You began with a few sketches on a pad and you ended up with this incredible machine, *your* incredible machine, and you took it all over the world, selling it, selling yourself. What could be sexier than that? And now Sutter had the 747—Sutter *possessed* the 747.

A look at the organization chart of the 747 program did not suggest that Sutter could be as dominant as he was. He appeared under the title of director of engineering, as one of ten managers of equal standing at the second tier. Above these ten was the vice president of engineering, George Snyder. People liked Snyder, but his limitations were becoming obvious. He was supposed to be up there as a figurehead, but he seemed overwhelmed by paper, desperately trying to keep account of the money gushing out. All the available research facilities were drawn into the suction of the 747 effort. Webb's technical staff searched for wind tunnel time all over the country. The program was spending millions of dollars a day—nobody seemed to know just how much. At the center of this dervishlike activity, one thing was plain: no detail of the 747 was fixed without Sutter's scrutiny and approval.

Steiner had painted himself into a corner. Rebuffed by Sutter, but still dying to get his hands on the drawings, he had at last lifted his head above the intramural combat and grasped the scale of the risk. It was the manufacturing specter that broke his nerve. "You don't have manufacturing under control at all," he told Boullioun.

This was an unfamiliar Steiner. He was in misery.

"Well," said Boullioun, "maybe you're not the right guy to manage it."

These were the words that Steiner wanted to hear. He gave up any further claim on managing the 747, but the cost to his pride was as high as his ambition had been to put his name on the airplane. Allen, who didn't enjoy internal warfare and scrupulously kept above it, was sufficiently fond of Steiner to ask him for his assessment of the 747. He got faint praise: it wasn't a very refined design, but it was satisfactory. It would fly. The problem was in manufacturing. They didn't have the time. They didn't have the money. It was horrible.

This was not what Allen liked to know. The 747 was his last

great gamble with the company. It had better be in the hands of true believers. The kindest thing to do with Steiner, like a valiant soldier who has suffered shell shock, was to give him a rest. Steiner saw the rivalry between engineers in gladiatorial terms; he felt he was a "worthy adversary" of Sutter's and, even now, he thought he would get a chance to prove it. Wait long enough, and a chance was bound to come. Steiner had supporters. An important one was Jack Waddell, the test pilot who had been assigned to live with the 747 through its development (he had been project pilot on the C5a). Waddell was an aeronautical engineer as well as an experienced test pilot, and he knew the trouble Steiner always took to design an airplane that *airline* pilots liked to fly. Waddell felt strongly that he, for one, still wanted Steiner around the 747, breathing on it.

But Stamper was now immutably in charge of the 747 program. All ambiguity was gone; Allen made it plain that the buck stopped with Stamper. And people found Stamper unaccountably sanguine. He didn't seem to subscribe to the cynical wisdom that "if you can keep your head when all around you are losing theirs, you simply don't understand the situation." Instead of bending under the bombardment of problems, Stamper presented a spongelike calm. There seemed no limit to how much of other people's distress he could absorb. Still, the petitioners went away wondering, "*Does* the guy understand the trouble we're in?'"

None of Sutter's team saw much of the summer in 1966. With the signing of the purchase order, and with little regret, the engineers had left the transients' floor at Renton and crossed to the other side of a wooded ridge to Boeing Field. They moved into the upper floor of what was called the 201 Building, which sat to the north of the corporate headquarters. The 201 Building had been built in the 1950s on Air Force money, for design work on the B-52, and had subsequently served as a catchall. It backed onto the slummy Duwamish Waterway. Within view to the northwest, on the other side of the river, was the site of Plant 1, literally the launching ramp of the company in 1917. And across East Marginal Way, to the east, was the field itself, constantly resonant with the passage of 707s and 727s from the flight test center.

With Steiner gone, Sutter could breathe more freely.

Stamper hardly knew an aileron from a spoiler. But Milt Heinemann liked Stamper's style from the beginning. It was simple. He told Stamper what he needed—"It has to be instant. I can't wait for a subcommittee to interpret what I want"—and he got it. The glue-and-haywire mock-up, for example, which looked good enough to survive long into the program. It was a small section of the cabin, but the effect of a whole cabin was created by a mirror wall at one end. Before anyone stepped into the cabin he was briefed in a lobby on the 747's mission. But nothing prepared them for their first steps into the wide-body.

Frank Del Giudice, freed of the narrow tubes of the 707 and 727, exploited the feature that Heinemann had pointed out to Trippe in the Pan Am boardroom: the 747's cabin was so big that the wall curvature was greatly lessened. It was no longer a tube, but a room. The high ceilings could be molded to amplify the feeling of a spacious and gently rounded salon, with diffused lighting and generous overhead luggage bins (it would be a while before the bins were free of rattles).

Although each airline chose its own interior colors and upholstery, and the layout of galleys, it was Del Giudice who gave the 747's cabin its framing aesthetic, removing the airplane finally from the influence of the ocean liner and the railroad car—the wide-body was itself generic, and would, in turn, be mimicked in hotel lobbies and corporate suites across the world. For Trippe, there was one touch of *déjà vu* in the 747. When Heinemann and Del Giudice considered the upper lounge decreed by Trippe—at this stage it went by the grand nautical title "the stateroom"—there were problems providing access to it. At first they tried straight stairs with two right-angled turns. It looked clumsy and—more serious—it swallowed too much space. Then they remembered the Stratocruiser's circular staircase. Feelings about the Stratocruiser at Boeing had always been mixed: mechanically it was a dog, but it was fondly remembered for its swank fittings. The looping stairway was adopted for the 747, and Heinemann felt it was a nice salute. That stairway would, in fact, become part of the 747's signature, belonging in style to one of those Manhattan duplexes in a Sinatra movie.

One of Trippe's oft-uttered strictures was that every airplane Pan Am had ever bought had been too small by the time Pan Am had to sell it. (The disposal of old fleets was important down-the-line income for airlines and created a second-tier market in countries too poor to buy new.) At Boeing it was often felt that an airplane was already too small at the time of its delivery—the first 707 was a case in point. Just before he signed the purchase agreement with Boeing, Trippe told Borger he wanted an eighty-inch extension in the 747's body.

It was one of those moments when Borger judged he had to risk opposing his chief. "Gee, I don't think we can handle it," he said.

Borger did a quick calculation. Allowing a thirty-four-inch pitch between the seats in the tourist section, another eighty inches would yield either two and a half or—at a squeeze—three more rows of seats, giving between twenty-three and thirty more seats depending on whether they were nine or ten abreast. And thirty more passengers would mean, if you accounted for the extra structural weight, that the plane would have to carry another 7,500 pounds.

Trippe didn't want to listen. He talked to Wells.

"Wells was always a sucker for Trippe," recalled Borger. "All of a sudden Ed was promising him something he didn't quite know how he was going to manage."

Sutter had to add the eighty inches. And, eventually, the extra seats would help the airplane meet the original target of reducing the seat-mile costs by 30 percent.

As for the shape of the butts in the seats, Pan Am had its own ideas on those, too. Lindbergh and Borger had often ruminated that Americans, men and women, were outgrowing the fifties generation of airline seats. (Lindbergh, always known as Slim to Trippe, wasn't typical, but Borger, generously spread himself, knew of what he spoke.) As it happened, one of Borger's staff found, from anthropological studies carried out at Harvard, a scientific basis for these subjective views of rear ends and thighs. The average American *was* growing taller and wider, and the word "Lite" had not yet been coined.

The Pan Am engineers sketched out the kind of tourist-class seat they wanted in the 747 and sent it to Boeing. The three-seat units in the 707 (and therefore in its successors in body width, the 727 and 737) were 59.6 inches wide. (This odd number was a product of necessity; it was all the room left after the mandatory aisle width was settled.) The unit they wanted for the

747 was sixty-five inches wide and allowed almost two more inches for derrieres. Even this was a tight fit for many on the typical American diet, but the advantage was later sacrificed for payload in 747s that went to ten-abreast seating in tourist.

Given the space in the cabin, the temptation was to provide passengers with as many distractions as possible to the ennui of hours in the air confined to the serried rows. The airplane became an entertainment center. For the first time, there was ample room for movie screens in each class. But as well as headphones for the movies, the seats had to be equipped with call lights, reading lights, and music channels. This meant taking four or five wires into each seat's console.

When Heinemann's electricians laid out the wiring trees, allowing for up to ten seats abreast, they were looking at a spaghetti mountain. Each stem of wires had to be bundled and then routed, and by the time they were all gathered for connection to the power sources it had become an unfathomable maze—and heavy. Too heavy.

It was a problem that arrived more or less simultaneously with its technical solution, or at least the hope of one. The old wire system was impossible. But a new system called Multiplex enabled a single wire to "time-share" signals—in theory, it could take as many as twenty separate signals by sending each one in increments. To use it for the four or five signals needed for each 747 seat seemed well within the technology; instead of the maze there would be a digestible network of single wires. There was no choice but to assume that Multiplex would work. When every pound of weight in the airplane was reckoned to cost $100, Multiplex saved something on the order of six hundred pounds. As it turned out, it took years to debug this system—years in which 747 passengers and cabin staff jointly endured dying movies, overlapping music channels, and imbecilic flashing lights.

Sutter's approach to problems like the cabin wiring was to leave them with the people, like Heinemann, who were expected to fix them. Sutter held design review meetings, in which a decision like the adoption of Multiplex would be talked out and then agreed on. But the essence of Sutter's system was to trust the men he had chosen, as he, in turn, expected to be trusted by those above. In spite of the money he was spending. You could—if you were as detached as Allen was—look on this as rather like a military arrangement in war. If you had a Patton or a MacArthur or a Montgomery you gave him what he asked for and didn't attempt to question the disposition of his tanks or which beach he would land on. As long as he kept on winning.

At Allen's level there seemed only one recurrent problem, Trippe. Trippe behaved as though the entire future of commercial aviation in America was his personal charge. And Pan Am's. If it wasn't the 747, it was the SST. Never mind that Pan Am would be more than $500 million in hock to Boeing on the 747. Trippe didn't leave any doubt that his policy was to use the 747 as a stopgap until the SST came on line. There should be no craven ears bent to the chorus of critics who questioned whether an SST could ever be either economically viable or environmentally acceptable.

In a call to Allen in August 1966, Trippe was blunt: "We can't afford not to go ahead with the SST."

Some senators—notably William Proxmire—had been trying to cut the SST development budget from $280 million to $80 million. Trippe was particularly incensed by editorials in the *Wall Street Journal* and the *New York Times*. "It's a damn shame," he told Allen, "that such an important project as this could be so little understood by people that ought to know better."

"It is that," said Allen. "The longer we work on it, the more enthusiastic we become."

Trippe did not want his own board to be contaminated by the nay-saying (Lindbergh, isolated on this issue, was kept discreetly quiet). Trippe pressed Allen to provide a drum-rolling movie on the SST that he could show at a board meeting in October. Allen, in turn, was pressing his SST team to get a mock-up built so that the government money would have a shape to it.

On the face of it, the impression is of the two men being continually inebriated by their own propaganda. But they were in different businesses, with different competitors. The more Allen followed Trippe's memorializing design for Pan Am, the more likely it was that he would lose sight of where the interests of Boeing and Pan Am might part. Boeing needed new product. Its competitors were less venturesome, but they were looking at markets that seemed to be begging for new airplanes. For those who kept their vision soberly clear, it was now obvious that any failures with commercial jets were not technical but marketing misjudgments.

With the 747, Boeing was addressing, albeit with brio, the replacement of one of its products that had run out of time, the 707. But it was neglecting a high-growth market which it had so far monopolized with the 727: the main domestic trunk routes. The 727 had failed to grow with the market. And it was by no means sure that the smaller 737 would ever curtail Douglas's hold on the feeder routes with the DC-9.

Allen was trapped in a hole that Trippe had helped him dig. The domestic carriers had grasped the appeal of the wide-body, Boeing's invention, and were talking to Lockheed and Douglas about wide-body airplanes more sized to their routes than the 747, and they were frustrated that Boeing seemed unable to upgrade the airplane they had loved at birth, the 727 (American Airlines presciently foresaw the market for a twin-engine wide-body, although it was eventually to be exploited first by the European Airbus consortium).

The SST was a dangerous distraction. Of all the American carriers, only Trippe was committed to the SST without qualms; TWA, the other global carrier, was lukewarm. This distraction was compounded by the extent to which the 747 was absorbing more and more of Boeing's resources, to the exclusion even of the troubled 737.

No part of the 747 concentrated Sutter's mind more than the wing. The initial confidence that work on the C5a wing had mastered the structural and aerodynamic challenges of the big wing was evaporating. The C5a wing was not analogous: it was mounted high, not low; it had less sweepback because it was designed for a lower cruising speed; the engines were hung differently. When it came to the critical positioning of the engines on the 747 wing, Sutter followed the exemplary model of the 707.

But there was a lot more to it than just scaling up a 707 wing. There was no neat law by which you could extrapolate the behavior of the 707 wing and expect the 747 wing, nearly double in area, to follow suit. Until it was tested, the dynamic responses of the larger wing could not be accurately predicted. The masses were beyond anything Boeing had any experience of handling. To meet the deadline, tests were dispersed at eight tunnels across the country. At the very least, it would take fifteen thousand hours in the tunnels to tailor the wing.

Then, in the middle of this effort, Wells became aberrant. Always susceptible to a new idea, Wells wanted to test a 747 wing with what were called "splitter" engine nacelles. Astonishingly, this involved abandoning a Boeing hallmark, the podded engine on the pylon, which Wells himself had helped father. The proven formula was at the core of their proprietary knowledge. The splitter involved, instead, mounting an engine ahead of *and in direct line with* the wing, with the hot exhaust gases passing over the wing. From a safety standpoint it looked like lunacy. Any debris from an engine failure would tear into the wing, and fuel tanks in the wing would have to be kept away from the exhaust gases, meaning wasteful "dry bays" and an insulated structure in the wing. Wells, however, believed that the splitter had alchemic qualities, that it would deliver an increase in performance of between 12 and 15 percent. Two months were lost while it was proved that the gains would be nothing like as large, and the risks to safety were unacceptable.

With Wells's whim indulged and disposed of, it became evident that even the orthodox wing was going to prove temperamental. The high-bypass engine on the 747 made the 707's engines look, by comparison, attenuated. The new Pratt engine would have a far bigger mass, and this changed the fit of the engine and its nacelle within the old, well-practiced geometry of nacelle, pylon, and wing.

In the wing itself, the load-carrying members were supposed to work in harmony with the non-load-carrying members. They were of different materials and construction, and would not fall into step with each other without extensive tuning. One of the new materials introduced on the 747 was fiberglass. On the wing, it was limited to unstressed panels—that is, panels that did not carry loads. Yet it turned out that some of the fiberglass *was* inadvertently stressed, and panels had to be modified. The dense and intricate balance of forces, dynamic, aerodynamic, and structural, was elusive.

It is hard to believe that the engineers would have so clearly failed in an area where there was such a deep body of experience—the wing was Boeing's great craft—if the deadline had not been so stringent. The aeromen and the structures men were pushing themselves to the limits of their concentration and stamina. Yet the great wing would not settle down as it should. It flexed and oscillated in an unruly way of its own. This wing would not fly.

For Everette Webb, it was agony to watch the wing in the tunnel. At high speeds the outer wing failed to flex according to Boeing's aeroelasticity principle and created stability problems. The airplane showed a worrying tendency to lift its nose by 2 or 3 degrees. And, ominously, the wing had a strong inclination to flutter, the worst F word you could use around an aeroman.

Webb had a dual loyalty. He was both Sutter's friend and the company's technical watchdog on the 747. Although Sutter and Webb were sure they could fix the wing problem themselves, given time, it was serious enough to need passing up through the system to Wells and Schairer, and from them to Steiner. As soon as Steiner heard about the rogue wing, he moved. After all, who was it who always warned, "It's the wing where you're going to fail"? Steiner decided to give them a new wing, his own.

Not for the last time, Wells agreed that every spare engineer should be thrown at the 747 to help get Sutter through his troubles. And when you wanted someone with the intensity of a blowtorch to attack a problem, you sent for Steiner. Incredibly, Wells was prepared to have two groups reworking the wing simultaneously: those who had designed it in the first place, working with Sutter and Webb, and a rival team assembled and directed by Steiner.

It was not an arrangement that Sutter cared for, with or without Steiner involved in it, and he did what it was his habit to do when faced with second-guessers: he ignored them.

Steiner, on the other hand, employed a graphic guerrilla image to describe his mission: "You call yourself a black parachutist. You drop in at night and you cut your way through a wall of human flesh."

In more prosaic terms, what Steiner did was to move into the 201 Building over a weekend, occupy an auditorium, rip out all the seats, and install new lighting and drawing tables for the fifty engineers he hijacked from the SST program.

Steiner told the black parachutists that they didn't have

much time, maybe two months. They would have to work day and night. And they had to come up with a wing that was so improved that the company would be prepared to take a delay in the program while the new drawings were issued. (The drawings for Sutter's wing had already been released.) But Steiner was not going to stop at the wing: they would take a shot at redesigning the nose, too. Steiner had heard George Martin, whose word on structures he took as gospel, complaining about the shape of the 747's nose and, particularly, the structure of the body immediately behind the nose identified as Section 41. All Boeing airplanes were numbered into sections according to a system of assembly, and traditionally Section 41 was where the cockpit or flight deck was. (The adjoining nose itself was, illogically, Section 44.) On the 747, when the flight deck and its hump were enlarged to accommodate Trippe's idea of putting passengers up there, the contour of the body at that point was significantly changed. In cross section, the original classic circle of the wide-body became elongated at the top, rather like a piece of clay on a potter's wheel that starts life as a perfect sphere and then develops into an egg.

Aesthetically, this was pleasing, since it gave what would otherwise have been an uneventful profile its distinctive character. There was an aerodynamic bonus as well: the nose and hump looked more slippery, shaped for the aspiration of a cruising speed of nine-tenths Mach. But purists among the structures men took a closer look at the elongated section and hated it.

From the waist point of the circle upward, where the body was surmounted by the hump, the curvature of the body panels was greatly reduced. Around the main passenger door, beneath the hump, and at the bulkiest part of the fuselage, the panels were barely curved at all. And as nature abhors a vacuum, structures men abhor slab-sided fuselages. The circle was the optimum for pressurization, since it equalized the stress over the whole inner surface. Every degree of departure from the true circle complicated the distribution and containment of the pressurization stresses. The 747's body had departed so far from the round that the fuselage skin would want to bend with every pressurization cycle, and the only way of giving it the structural integrity it needed was to clad it with panels so thick that they might almost have been armor plate—adding a lot of weight.

George Snyder, Sutter's immediate superior but not normally inclined to intervene, had echoed Martin's criticism. Steiner's approach was to use the formula well proven on the 707, on which, with the double-lobe fuselage cross section, they had put a reinforcing beam at the junction of the lobes, a crease beam. Steiner reasoned that with a crease beam at the level of the 747's upper deck floor, to take the stresses of the pressurization cycles, they could shed some of the heavy skin panels, getting more strength for less weight.

"This was radical, just plain radical," Steiner told me. "Sutter hated us. He wanted us all to die."

Boeing's doyen of wing design, W. T. Hamilton, was summoned along with the other firemen. He sat with Waddell in the flight simulator at Renton, the "Iron Bird," as they reproduced the high-speed pitching upward of the nose. Hamilton didn't feel that it was alarming, but agreed that the problem had to be fixed. It seemed to him, and to Steiner's team, that to get the wing to flex as it should the whole wing would need twisting—a subtle, incremental twist so that the aerodynamic and structural forces would come into balance. It was the most elegant solution, but it would also be an expensive one, involving extensive structural changes.

Webb, meanwhile, had not given up on the original wing. He was looking for an easier fix, for a compromise that would be acceptable to both the aeromen and the structural engineers. Was there, he wondered, a way of changing the load distribution over the whole wing without completely reengineering it? It was all too clear that—as the black parachutists advocated—the wing would have to be twisted to some degree, whatever the consequences.

"Twisting" is a disarmingly simple word for what was actually involved. Imagine holding a small plastic model of the 747 and, while gripping the body firmly, taking the left wing between thumb and forefinger, about a third of the way in from the tip, and twisting it counterclockwise so that the outer wing flexes downward at the front. Now imagine trying the same trick with the real airplane, where each wing is nearly one hundred feet long, and fifty-four feet wide at the root.

The core of the wing's torsional strength is the wing box, a box in name but actually an interlacing of the main load-bearing spars and ribs. In the aeroelastic wing, the limits of the flexibility are fixed by the wing box, in the same way that an earthquake-proofed skyscraper's resilience is limited by the ability of its steel frame to flex. To have twisted the 747's wing over its entire span would have meant redesigning the wing box, in effect unraveling the wing's entire spinal system. Staring this grisly prospect in the face, Sutter and Webb devised a compromise. Instead of twisting the whole wing, they would twist it only from the outer engine to the tip. It would mean a barely perceptible break in the line of the wing's leading edge. They had never done anything like it before. It certainly was not elegant. But, together with other changes to redistribute the loads over the wing, the outboard twist—if it worked—would involve a lot less reengineering and, therefore, a lot less money and time.

Webb and Sutter, seeking to build a consensus that would forestall the need for Steiner's new wing, put their idea to W. T. Hamilton. He thought it was a promising solution, and well worth testing. In the tunnel, the outboard twist was, in fact, enough to get the wing to fly according to the rules of aeroelasticity. The structural integrity was not compromised. It was, however, too early to know whether the dreaded F word would loom again. Only flight testing could finally reveal a wing's true flutter characteristics.

The black parachutes had dropped into the 201 Building to no avail. Neither Steiner's new wing nor the reengineered nose saw the light of day. Sutter had rendered all Steiner's work redundant. In fact, Martin's worries about Section 41 would be borne out later, when fatigue cracks appeared. They were costly to fix, and this was the one part of the design that carried a long-term penalty for the haste in which it had been conceived. And, ironically, the airplane never flew at the speed for which the nose had been molded.

As Borger had suspected from the beginning, nine-tenths Mach was beyond the ability of both Pratt & Whitney's engine and Boeing's payload technicians. Aerodynamically the airplane would have had no problem cruising that close to the speed of sound, and eventually an engine tuned to that speed would have emerged. But the economics would have been terrible, particularly in fuel consumption.

When the purchase order was signed by Pan Am in April 1966, the cruise speed had come down to Mach .877. Not long afterward it was revised down to Mach .86. In airline service it fell to between .83 and .84, translating to around 600 mph and, twenty years later, still faster than any other airliner. There was, whimsically, a benefit in the nose that never made it to nine-tenths Mach. It was so aerodynamically clean that the people who get to fly in the front of the main deck, almost always the first-class passengers, are sitting in the quietest cabin of any. When Sutter flies a 747, he always tries to secure an aisle seat in row three. He knows.

Sutter had been reminded that his writ was not absolute—peer scrutiny could intervene at any time Ed Wells felt that it should.

Among the engineers who knew about it, the outboard twist became a legendary fix, eventually known as the "Sutter twist." When I discussed the episode with Everette Webb more than twenty years later and casually gave it that name, he was—for a second—disconcerted. "Oh, Sutter got that one, ha?" he said. There were still residual investments of ego among the winners in the battle for the 747's wing, but no dimming of the ego of the loser. Steiner never, in his heart, hung up his black parachute.

13 ■ Don't Let the Russians Near the Bible

The Russians always watched Boeing closely. After all, Boeing's B-47s and now its B-52s were permanently loaded with nuclear weapons and targeted on Soviet cities. But in the mid-1960s the Russians were suddenly revealing a great interest in the 747. Their own aircraft industry had been instructed to become as competitive in commercial aircraft as they were in military. At the Paris Air Show in 1965 they unveiled a model of a supersonic transport. It was far more like the Anglo-French Concorde than the SSTs being developed by Boeing and Lockheed, and rapidly became dubbed the Concordski. But the Russians' more urgent interest was in subsonic transports.

Joe Sutter knew that his counterparts in Russia were able men. In 1945, the Russians—like Boeing—had drunk deeply from the well of captured German research data, including the swept wing material. But Russia's formidable intellectual resources, particularly its strength in applied mathematics and physics, had always flowed into its aviation industry, and its designers were never to be underrated. The problem in Russia was that the military programs devoured the research capacity and preoccupied the best engineers.

The sprawling Soviet Union was, though, rendered functional as a modern state to a significant extent by its domestic airline network. Given the vast distances, only Aeroflot could provide essential daily links between cities large and small, not simply for the convenience of citizens, which came low as a priority, but for the movements of thousands of party function- aries and the dispatch of documents. *Pravda*, the party's daily essay in Orwellian truths, was delivered by air, sometimes even dropped by parachute. To give Aeroflot the modern fleet it needed, Russian designers were inclined to take the easiest course: copy the West. The trick was, whom to copy?

The Boeing engineers were not inclined to play the nice guys in this process. Sutter, for example, knew the Russians were developing a jet of around the size of the 707, the Ilyushin 62. He also knew that instead of hanging the four engines on the wing in the Boeing manner, the Russians were clustering them at the rear of the fuselage, two on each side, as the British had done with their VC-10. To Sutter the Russians and the Brits were fatally penalizing their designs with this choice, but he wasn't about to point this out. In the case of the Russians, it was likely that they just did not have the wind tunnel data and the engineering sophistication to hang engines on pods. In the case of the British, there was less excuse. The Il-62 was prin- cipally for Aeroflot's international routes, including the heavily used flights from Moscow to Havana, Cuba. For the internal routes, Russian designers were producing two workhorse jets with a striking resemblance to American precursors: the twin- engine Tupolev 134, a clone of the Douglas DC-9; and the three- engine Tupolev 154, which was so close to Jack Steiner's Boeing 727 that it seemed that the Russians must have climbed all over it with a tape measure. If imitation was the sincerest form of flattery, Steiner was entitled to overdose on it.

But cloning airplanes is a dangerous game. There are so many proprietary secrets under the skin. After all, although Douglas had deployed its extensive talents to clone and improve upon the Dash-80, it had failed in the end because of extremely subtle and expressly immanent qualities in the 707's wing. The Russians made literally fatal errors with the first version of the Ilyushin 62's wing, as they did with the Concordski. The two Tupolev workhorses, for their part, lacked the finesse that American knowledge would have given them, but they were more bugged by Russian aviation's serious and persistent handicap: its brutish and appallingly "dirty" jet engines.

So when, during the development of the 747, Sutter heard that a party of Russian aeronautical engineers was calling on Boeing to talk about the wide-body, he was on guard. In Washington there was a cautious diplomatic tolerance toward Russian expeditions of this kind. Military programs were off-limits, but there was a feeling that if commercial deals could be struck without violating any technological embargoes they ought at least to be explored. The Russians were invited to Boeing as potential buyers of the 747 and treated as would be any inquiring airline. "They were making love to us," Sutter commented.

There were thirty-two of them in the delegation. As usual, it was easy to spot, through the common tongue of aeronautics, the genuine engineers. And it was easy to spot the KGB minders and the party functionaries representing Aeroflot. For three days they were given presentations on the 747's specification and performance, and for three days they asked a succession of pertinent questions—with a visibly growing annoyance. Finally, the head of the delegation complained to Sutter.

He had two frustrations. First, he expected to talk to experts on the 747, so where were they?

You talked to them, said Sutter.

"They can't be the experts," said the Russian. "They're too young."

"You talked to the head of aerodynamics," said Sutter.

"Mr. Johnson?" said the Russian.

"That's right," said Sutter.

The Russians realized that Sutter was sincere, and he realized that they had suffered a severe cultural shock.

"So what's the second problem?" said Sutter.

"Mr. Luplow," said the Russian, "told us about this book you have—it is called *Design Objectives and Criteria*, I think?"

"He did?" said Sutter, suddenly and openly alarmed. "Well, that was a mistake. I wish to hell I'd been smart enough to tell them not to tell you about that book. That's Boeing proprietary information. We don't show that book to anybody."

The Russian looked at Sutter. "Maybe, for a million dollars?"

At first, Sutter thought it was a game. But by the time he

had got the Russians out of his office the price had reached $10 million. As soon as they were gone he called the engineering office and ordered every copy of the book recovered and put under lock and key until the Russians were well clear of the plant.

He had good cause. The book, *Model 747 Design Objectives and Criteria*, was the Bible of Boeing's technical knowledge, the storehouse of every lesson learned about designing commercial jets from the 707 onward, the accumulated wisdom of the world's best team of aeromen, structures and systems men, anyone who had ever contributed to the design of anything from a cargo hold door lock to the new-technology inertial navigation system. It had the heft of the thickest phone books, 457 pages. $10 million? It was without price.

The Bible was the final sanction for every decision taken on the 747 as well as the definition of the principles on which every engineering decision was to be based. The most frequently used word in its pages—no principle was stated without it—was "shall," used in the imperative and legal sense. One example, taken at random: "Wing fuel tanks shall be baffled to limit effects of airplane attitude and wing flexibility on fuel center of gravity movement."

Laid out on these pages is the ethic of Boeing. Although it is a densely technical document, it is permeated by a voice. It is as though some ghostly conclave has assembled to look over the shoulders of its mortal heirs and is repeating an elaborate litany of vows and instruction. There are certainly present the spirits of those who died in the cause: dominantly in the mind of Joe Sutter, for one, was the legacy of Eddie Allen, who built the discipline of rigorous testing into the company's engineering regime. Wells and Schairer could think of Jack Kylstra, the chief engineer, and Ralph Cram, the chief aerodynamicist, who had been killed in the crash of the Stratoliner. Somewhere implicit in the data now digested in the Bible for the 747 was the knowledge those men had died acquiring.

The sophistication and breadth of the undertaking facing Sutter and his engineers would have been a source of wonder for those pioneers. But if the principles—the holy writ—were directly traceable to them, the instrumental body of data in the 747 Bible was not. The founding layer of the palimpsest, even now discernible through the succeeding tracery, was the B-47. And the begetters of the B-47 were still vigorously corporeal. Schairer, though not directly involved in the 747, was sufficiently close to intervene if need be, and Wells had already backed the choice of the wide-body and specified the larger wing.

Although it was Sutter's staff who compiled the Bible, every line had to have the final approval of the chief of technical staff, Webb. This was a clear expression of the checks and balances in action. As the pages came together, they were continually open to revision, and each revision had to be approved either by Webb or by the heads of the groups making the revisions.

Revisions were inevitable because the body of empirical knowledge, the static content, was being updated and supplemented by the ambitions of the moment, the dynamic content. Other revisions came from problems encountered and then solved, like the twist in the wing. Their knowledge was always in a molten state. Throughout the program, Sutter would have to hold the fine balance between what was conservatively the limit of an engineering decision and what was a desirable advance. Arguments would rage daily and at many points about how far the 747 could truly be the "new-technology airplane" that Boeing had, through its more hyperbolic voices, promised Pan Am. It would never be possible absolutely to "close" the design because something could always be done better. The real test of the design would be to get the basics so right that they would allow evolutionary improvement over a reasonable life-span without drastic change of the airframe.

In one respect, the essential boundaries of the design were inclined to be elusive. Every airplane built in the United States had to conform to Federal Air Regulation 25, which listed the governing dicta for safety. To be certified by the FAA for airline service, the 747 had to meet the requirements of FAR 25 as defined on February 1, 1965. Although the FAR was regularly amended, as the 747 design evolved it outstripped the FAA criteria—just as the 707 had done. The principal change was size. It was not just that an emergency required the evacuation of well over twice as many passengers as there was any experience of handling: FAR 25 had to encompass the problems of the airplane's handling qualities and its ability to survive systems failures, to withstand structural damage and failures, and to fly out of "touch-and-go" emergencies on takeoff and landing. Though all of these factors were in themselves familiar enough, no one had any experience of how they might show up in an airplane of this size and weight, or knew whether size itself introduced unforeseeable vices.

Buried deep in the 747 Bible was the governing Boeing attitude to what Sutter had to achieve: "The airplane handling qualities shall be equal to or better than those of the current family of Boeing jet transports." It was the "better than" that exercised his mind the most. Far from falling short of FAR 25, Sutter intended to have the regulators catch up with *his* ideas of safety. There would be serious outbreaks of hand-to-hand combat as he persisted with this ambition.

The commitment to safety overrode everything. It was spelled out in the opening pages of the Bible: "Safety is the prime design objective of the 747 Design Program; it shall be given first priority in all design decisions. The designer shall insure attainment of this safety objective."

Although this could leave no doubt of the intention, and although the intention was inculcated in the engineers from the beginning, if taken literally this was a counsel of perfection that could never, in fact, be without scope for dispute. This is not to say that the intention was, in any sense, cynically stated. Aircraft designers value their ability to sleep with a clear conscience, knowing that what they do every day can, by dint of the slightest oversight, have catastrophic consequences. Nevertheless, as a design progresses, finite judgments of safety become harder because of intrusive pressures.

Of these pressures, the weight of the airframe is invariably the most irksome. Weight is, fundamentally, the incarnation of both virtue and vice: it measures the structural integrity of the airplane, but it also measures its basic commercial liability—the amount of airplane that does not pay for itself. There is a hint of stigma in the term used to describe this liability: manufacturer's empty weight, MEW. To an accountant, MEW is the bottom line in the debit column, a figure to be remorselessly attacked. To the designer, MEW is his last line of defense, beyond which there is no permissible compromise. (The operator's empty weight, OEW, the margin between what the manufacturer installs and what the airline includes as part of its own "house style" down to the cutlery in the galley, is a bloody battleground between seller and buyer, as we shall see, but not as critical.)

No airplane ever loses weight during its development. As it gathers weight the choice has to be made between what is held to be the optimum engineering solution and a permissible compromise to save weight. (In an agonizing struggle to save two hundred pounds on the Boeing 247 a lavatory mirror was discarded.) The leeway allowed in each of these decisions is usually defined by dollars. In the 747 Bible it was cautiously quantified:

"Items that reduce weight but result in an increase in cost between $100.00 and $150.00 per pound are to be considered carefully. Acceptance of such items shall have the approval of the applicable Senior Project Engineer.

"Normally those items which reduce weight and do not increase the cost by more than $100.00 per pound will be acceptable."

Early in the program, Sutter realized that if the 747 was really to become the "new-technology airplane" it should include, as part of its weight-saving regime, the use of titanium. Titanium would provide far greater strength for a given weight than aluminum, but, as Lockheed's experience with the Blackbird had demonstrated to McNamara, it was a difficult metal to work with. The 747 Bible, however, was adventurous: "It is essential that the weight reduction potential of titanium be developed and utilized to the maximum practical extent so that the 747 airplane will hold a competitive position. . . . "

Sutter had in mind particularly the massive twenty-two-foot landing-gear legs. No one had used titanium in such a highly stressed component before, but if its virtues were as claimed it would be an ideal solution to achieve the required strength without a heavy weight penalty. Boeing engineers, however, lacked the experience of working with titanium that would have given them confidence to use it in this way.

Bob Withington, although on the SST program, was involved in the debate on the use of titanium on the 747 because he was equally anxious to use it on the SST. And he knew where they might find the expertise they needed: in Russia.

The Russians' attempt to get their hands on the Bible,

How it was: Inside the 1947-vintage Boeing Stratocruiser there were only four seats to a row, and drapes on the windows.

The inside story: This 707 cabin looks spacious and elegant, but the five-seat coach-class row soon regressed to six when the airlines realized how many passengers they could pack in.

The high-roll gamblers: Bill Allen of Boeing (*left*) and Juan Trippe of Pan Am bet their companies on the 747. Boeing survived and prospered, but Pan Am was too much the creature of Trippe to adapt to a harsher economic climate and eventually succumbed.

■

Birth of the wide-body: How the cross section of the 747 fuselage evolved from two versions of a double-deck fuselage to the wide single deck, with containerized cargo below. At its widest, the double-deck cabin measured sixteen feet six inches. The wide-body measured nearly twenty feet—nothing like it had been seen before.

■

Waddell's Wagon: Test pilot Jack Waddell, the man chosen to be the first to fly the 747, had this contraption built to simulate maneuvering a 747 around the tarmac. The flight deck was far higher than any with which pilots were then familiar. At first, it was thought that the 747 could be steered on engine power, but during taxi trials the exhaust blast blew away a car. On Waddell's insistence, the 747 was given steerable landing gear.

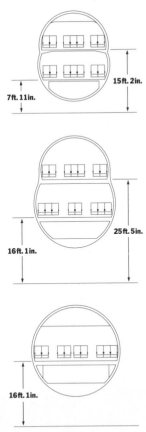

The master builder: As chief engineer of the 747, Joe Sutter fashioned the world's first wide-body airplane. His team became known at Boeing as Sutter's Runaways: The 747 was consuming the company's money at the rate of $5 million a day. Some people tried to get Sutter fired, but he stuck doggedly to his own goals for the 747 and was vindicated by its performance. Eventually, almost as an afterthought, Sutter was made a vice president.

The company patriarch: William Allen took charge of Boeing in 1945 after conducting a fruitless search for a successor to the previous chief executive. Allen was a lawyer of conservative inclination. However, after he had let the engineers have their say, he was ready to take increasingly large gambles on new airplanes. The largest of all, the 747, nearly broke the company. But before Allen retired, the 747 had created its own market.

The family: Jack Steiner with the Boeing jets (counterclockwise): the 747, 707, 737, and 727. "Go talk to Steiner, and he'll tell you he designed every airplane, including the 747," said one of his peers. In fact, Steiner intervened in the design of the 747, proposing a new wing and nose, but his plans were never adopted.

Three flights of fancy: When Frank Del Giudice first sketched interiors for the 747, he had extravagant ideas. The first-class lounge had a sunken well and cocktail bar; there was a cinema with a raked floor; and a library and reading room. None survived the space-conscious airline bean counters.

COURTESY THE BOEING COMPANY ARCHIVES

Putting on the style: Before the 747 rolled out from the plant, stewardesses from every airline that had then ordered the airplane paraded in their uniforms. Only a sari and a kimono deviated from the trend to jet-age chic.

COURTESY THE BOEING COMPANY ARCHIVES

The jumbo's temple: The town of Everett, north of Seattle, was chosen over two other candidates to be the site for the 747's assembly plant. When work began, endless rains caused mud slides that cost $5 million to clear. To get parts into the plant, a railroad spur with one of the steepest gradients in America had to be built. Assembly of the first 747s began before the building was completed. Managers worked around the clock, refusing to go home.

Into the sun: The 747 saw the light of day for the first time on September 30, 1968. Rollout day is a mandatory ritual for all new airplanes, even though they might not be anything like ready to fly. It was another four months before N7470 made its first flight, for a myriad of technical reasons. But on rollout the world was able for the first time to take in the scale of Boeing's revolutionary traveling machine. And call it the jumbo.

COURTESY BOEING PUBLIC RELATIONS

What's wrong with this picture? These were the largest gliders in the world, 747s without engines. Planes were coming out of the Everett plant faster than Pratt & Whitney could produce engines fit to fly. At one time, the powerless 747s on the tarmac represented more than the Boeing company's net worth. The first engines used in the flight test program were so temperamental that a light wind up the tailpipe was enough to shut them down.

Back to base: The first 747 lands at Boeing Field after initial tests at Everett. For the first time, Seattle saw the airplane that would nearly bankrupt the company—and ravage the city's economy.

The three Ws: Test pilot Jack Waddell, flight engineer Jess Wallick, and copilot Brien Wygle jubilantly come to earth after the 747's first flight on February 9, 1969. The flight was curtailed by a minor technical problem. Later testing was plagued by persistent trouble with the engines. Waddell also had to nurse the 747 through serious aerodynamic flutter problems with the wing. When flutter hit, it was "like falling off a cliff."

New man in the hot seat: Najeeb Halaby (*left*), having taken over Pan Am, was given the rare privilege of taking the captain's seat and flying the 747 with Jack Waddell (*right*). Halaby threw the airliner around the sky like a fighter. He also came down hard on Boeing for not meeting Pan Am's performance goals on the first 747s.

Laughing into the abyss: Mal Stamper, Thornton (always known as "T") Wilson, and Tex Boullioun knew the 747 program was taking the company to the edge of bankruptcy. Wilson, inheriting the company leadership and the crisis, initiated savage cutbacks.

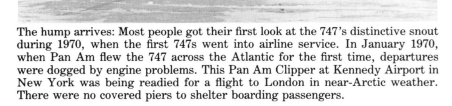

COURTESY THE BOEING COMPANY ARCHIVES

The hump arrives: Most people got their first look at the 747's distinctive snout during 1970, when the first 747s went into airline service. In January 1970, when Pan Am flew the 747 across the Atlantic for the first time, departures were dogged by engine problems. This Pan Am Clipper at Kennedy Airport in New York was being readied for a flight to London in near-Arctic weather. There were no covered piers to shelter boarding passengers.

■

Twenty years, eleven billion miles: The first and the latest 747s flying in formation over Seattle. The original 747 had a range of 4,600 nautical miles; the 747-400, launched in 1989, had a range of 7,100 miles and was 25 percent more fuel-efficient than the first 747s. By the time the 747-400 flew, 747s had carried 780 million passengers over 11 billion miles. The basic 747 configuration is still capable of refinement and larger capacity.

COURTESY BOEING PUBLIC RELATIONS

the first episode in the gavotte of *détente*, had not been encouraging. (Their overtures about buying 747s had been exposed as a sham.) An opportunity to try again came with the next Paris Air Show, where Boeing knew the Russians would be present in force, boosting their SST and their next generation of commercial transports. Word was sent ahead that Boeing was interested in a trade-off: Russian know-how on titanium in exchange for Boeing's engineering formula for hanging engines on pods. (Sutter knew that despite the Il-62's rear engines the Russian designers were coming around to the idea of pods.)

The two parties met for dinner at a Paris restaurant, in an upstairs *privée* where the hospitality could be uninhibited and—they hoped—the technical exchange could be confidential. The Russians showed little interest in the finer points of French cuisine or the subtle balance of wine and food. They laced into vodka and launched into the usual series of effusive toasts to mutual collaboration—"acting like good old Joes," says Sutter, who had been there before.

They were, however, as good as their word. They had brought their titanium experts, and agreed to make their disclosures first. Withington had a prepared list of questions. After an hour, he had answers to every one.

He turned to Sutter. "Okay, I'm satisfied."

Comrade Genrikh Novozhilov, who had succeeded the legendary Sergei Ilyushin as chief designer of the Ilyushin design bureau, and his colleagues now listened to Sutter, making notes and pressing with questions. Sutter began sketching on the tablecloth. He explained the structural and aerodynamic amity of the aeroelastic wing—how the weight of the engines was used to work in harmony with the swept wing's flexibility and how this geometry helped the stall characteristics of the wing. It took an hour and a half. At the end of it, the exquisite sense of the Boeing formula had demolished any lingering skepticism in the Russians. The tablecloth left with them.

The next Ilyushin design, the Il-86, was, like the 747, using the first high-bypass engines. If these engines, with their bulbous nacelles, had been rear-mounted, as originally intended, the airplane would have looked like—as Sutter inimitably expressed it—"a dog." The dinner in Paris effectively killed rear-mounted engines for Ilyushin. Not only that, but the first, double-deck version of the Il-86 became a single-deck wide-body. No wonder that when his new airliner eventually flew, Novozhilov had a brass plaque cast of it flying over Moscow, with its podded engines, and gave it to Sutter. He was a hero of the Soviet Union.

For their part, the Boeing team went home to Seattle well satisfied. They were now confident that they could use titanium in the 747—and the SST.

Their aim, as expressed in the Bible, was that the 747 should be "a new generation of subsonic aircraft developed to reflect the 1969 state-of-the-art." Thus they were setting themselves a target of having the first 747 airborne in less than three years from when the configuration was settled. There was an inescapable tension between this deadline, onerously short by all historical measures, and the aspiration that when it flew the 747 would truly be at the cutting edge of subsonic design. The safety net under this high-wire act was the 707—the Bible was built on 707 experience—but the 707 was, in many essential details, technically outmoded.

There had been great advances in avionics, some of them direct spin-offs from the space program and some from military programs. The 747 would especially benefit from radically improved navigation equipment, including some arising from the work of MIT's "Doc" Draper for the Apollo moon missions. A 747 pilot would have an inertial navigational system that would know the airplane's position anywhere in the world at any time, within a tolerance of error of two miles in any hour. The system needed no ground-based references. It programmed the route from takeoff to landing, including the amount of fuel required and the rate that the fuel would be burned, and that, in turn, took into account changes in the aircraft's trim (the distribution of its loads) during the flight.

Nonetheless, for all the irresistible technical advances that could be adopted, none could be allowed to compromise the airplane's underlying safety regime, and this limited how far the first 747s would—given the pressures to deliver them—truly be "state-of-the-art." In everyone's mind was the least-tested innovation of them all: the engines. The engines could not be deferred.

The safeness of an airliner is not, of course, in the designer's hands alone. Once in service, it is exposed to the human frailties of pilots and air traffic controllers, among others. The most the designer can do to minimize those dangers is to avoid giving the airplane vices that make the pilot's life harder than it needs to be, and to give the airframe the ability to survive a certain level of structural damage.

In this respect, the sheer size of the 747 became an asset. Sutter treated its underbelly as potentially a great impact-absorbing safety cushion. For one thing, it was cargo, not people, which would first take the impact if the landing gear failed; for another, if the landing gear collapsed into the 747's belly there was room to preserve the integrity of the adjacent fuel tanks and therefore avoid the familiar and dreaded sequence that had often turned a crash landing into a pyre.

Loaded with fuel, any airplane is virtually an instantly combustible bomb. To limit this risk, the structure is divided into zones, and the zones most prone to fire are, as far as possible, isolated. On the 747, zone one was the fire zone—the place where there is a permanent fire, the engines. The objective is to seal off an engine in the event of a fire and to surround it with effective fire-extinguishing devices. The podded engine greatly enhanced this way of dealing with what had become, in any case, a very rare event.

A second zone, the combustible zone, was spread throughout the wing tanks and in the wing root, where the integral fuel tanks were. The objective here was to contain leakage of fuel or vapors and to eliminate any potential source of a spark that could ignite them if they did leak. An elaborate system of seals and discrete compartmentalization had been evolved. Sutter could recall the details of the fatal wing fire in the B-29—"the fire got into the leading edge of the wing and the wing came loose, right on final approach," he says, describing the crash that cost Eddie Allen his life. "That was a traumatic deal. You don't fool around with safety," he says. "You try to get it to zero, you never do, but you sure as hell better try."

The 747's size made it easier for Sutter to give the airplane four separate control systems, a high order of redundancy. The Bible decreed that the failure of one system would not implicate another, and that the 747 was to be controllable if only one system remained. (It was: not long after it went into service, a 747 pilot took off from San Francisco on the wrong runway, which was too short, and as the airplane barely lurched off the end of the runway its belly was ripped out by rows of landing lights. Three hydraulic systems were lost, but the fourth survived, and the 747 got back to earth with only a few injuries.)

Every main control surface—rudder, elevators, ailerons, flaps—was split into separate systems so that if one failed there would always be a substitute. Although there was no strictly structural need for it, Sutter added a third spar in the wing to help hold the wing together if it was torn up in a midair collision. The extra spar cost only 150 pounds in weight, and it was weight that Sutter adamantly refused to shed. Several distressed 747s have survived thanks, in part, to that decision.

When it came to the resident specter of Dutch roll, Little Herbie's successor was also duplicated—it functioned through two independent channels. If one failed, the airplane would still be certified to continue a flight normally; if both failed, the 747 had to be "capable of being safely flown with acceptable handling qualities"—although, in that event, the pilot would follow a constrained flight pattern to touchdown.

These were all things only the flight crew would know. Ideally, passengers should remain in blissful ignorance of them. Passengers, for example, would probably prefer not to know that they were sitting in fire zone three, although it was designated as "nonhazardous."

Taking a boldly enlightened view, one could contend that the more a passenger knows about the trouble taken on his behalf, the more relaxed he should be—an informed airline passenger is a happy airline passenger. Would that it were so simple. Flying induces in many people (most?) a completely irrational loss of nerve. It is irrational in part because the statistics show flying to be safer than getting into the car to drive to the supermarket (but statistics are what happen to other people, not you), and in part because no other means of transport have been so saturated in technology aimed at making it safer.

Be that as it may, fear of flying is ineradicable and a common phobia. Its victims feel that once they pass through the door of an airplane, they lose control of their fate; that they are part of an involuntary and collective ordeal. In the spring of 1966, when the means of greatly multiplying the companionship of this phobia were being devised, there were roughly 200,000 seats flying around the world attached to commercial jets. Half a million people were using these seats each day (the average flight lasted two and a half hours) and left them with varying degrees of composure.

These people, and their state of mind, preoccupied Milt Heinemann's waking hours. It had barely dawned on the traveling public what was in store, but early word of the size of the 747 caused alarm. FAR 25 prescribed cabin evacuation arrangements only for loads of up to three hundred passengers. In its highest-density form, the 747 would carry five hundred.

When Heinemann extrapolated the existing rules to cope with the additional two hundred people, he had an airplane with twenty-four doors in it. Each door that goes into an airframe is one door more than a structural engineer's ideal—the simplest and strongest fuselage would be one with no doors at all. The two principal stresses on the fuselage are aerodynamics and pressurization. As the Comet had shown, failure to effectively seal a fuselage to withstand the unequal inside and outside pressures ends in catastrophe. The plug door that Heinemann had created for the 707 greatly helped the integrity of the fuselage under pressurization, but *twenty-four doors?* It was a structural nightmare. The body would be like a sieve.

There had to be a better way. Heinemann and his team analyzed the U.S. records of eighty-seven airplane evacuations that had taken place, under varying degrees of emergency, between 1959 and 1966. They found that the more modern the aircraft, the better the results, but fewer than a third of the passengers were getting out in under ninety seconds, and the FAA had given Heinemann ninety seconds as the goal for evacuating an entire 747. A curious quirk showed up in the analysis: most people wanted to get out the door they had entered by, rather than the one nearest to them.

These incidents were, of course, all in narrow-bodied airplanes with a single aisle. FAR 25 limited these cabins to three seats on either side of the aisle. The 747 had two aisles, but— whatever the number of seats in each row—the center row would have four seats in coach. Unless Heinemann found a new philosophy for evacuating the 747, the wide-body was in trouble.

At the same time, airlines wanted to see a mock-up of the 747's interior, because they were not about to buy an airplane without knowing what its cabin would look like.

Heinemann was trying to satisfy safety according to as yet unwritten rules for what was rather euphemistically called "unassisted egress" and, at the same time, build a mock-up out of glue and haywire that would be sexy enough to win more airline sales. It was a tradition that the airline bosses would arrive with their wives, and the wives would be picky about cabin decor, as though they were choosing the fabrics for their own boudoir. (An exception was Trippe's wife, Betty, who kept whatever counsel she enjoyed in private.)

When the FAR rules had been rewritten for the 707, the FAA had been pliant because it was Boeing that had the experience with jets, not the FAA. This time the regulators made it clear that they would not yield so easily. They understood jets a lot better, and they were conscious of political and public wariness of the idea of so many people in one airplane. Heinemann was caught between the FAA's harder nose and Boeing's structures men, who wanted the doors kept to a minimum.

Part of the solution came in a single stroke: if there were fewer doors, the flow through each door had to be increased. So why not a bigger door? Heinemann proposed what he called the double-width door, but it was not quite that. It was seventy-two inches tall but only forty-two inches wide—not wide enough for two people shoulder to shoulder, but given that people would not evacuate in military file, fudging the term was permissible. It seemed almost as innovative as the plug door. Heinemann sketched in five of the new doors on each side of the main cabin. If they organized the junctions of the twin aisles with cross aisles at each door, ten doors would, they calculated, make it possible to get everyone out in ninety seconds.

But when the structures men saw the plan they balked. Heinemann had put two doors, one on each side, over the wing—as it happened, at one of the most critically stressed parts of the structure. The loads borne by the wing were transmitted into the body at precisely this point. To take the stress the body skin was at its thickest, measured in quarters of an inch rather than tenths. It was inimical to structural doctrine that a door—and a *double* door at that—should puncture the skin right there. Sutter was called in to adjudicate.

"If that's what he has to have, give it to him," he said. As far as Sutter was concerned, it was Heinemann who had to answer for the safety issue, not the structures men. They went back to the drawing board and added more heft, muttering that the 747 was beginning to feel more like a tank than a plane.

Charles Lindbergh maintained his interest in the 747, and was apt to have concerns based on his past knowledge of the kind of trouble a pilot could find himself in with a jet flying at its limits. He had followed Boeing's early struggle with the swept wing and knew that because of certain Mach effects on the wing as it neared the speed of sound, around the cruising speed of the 747, there could be problems of stability. In particular, he was worried about the phenomena called "tuck-under," a sudden urge in the airplane to pitch its nose down, and "pitch-up," a more violent form of the problem W. T. Hamilton and Waddell had watched in the 747 simulator, when the outboard wing panel stalled out and the lift of the inboard wing pulled up the nose.

Lindbergh had two private meetings with Sutter, each time arriving under the pseudonym of Stewart (perhaps a droll allusion to James Stewart, who played him in *The Spirit of St. Louis*?). Sutter was able to reassure him that the 747 could now cruise smoothly at high speed—at least, in the simulator. Lindbergh had, of course, been right in suspecting that pitch-up would appear, although it had been exorcised by the twist in the wing. Tuck-under never did appear.

Lindbergh, like many others, was also concerned about what it would be like landing an airplane of this size. It suggested an orientation problem: everything—the approach path, the runway, the taxiways—remained the same, but the scale of the pilot's environment was radically altered. Sutter told Lindbergh that the approach and landing speed of the 747 would be the same as the 707's. To achieve this, they had taken Bill Cook's triple-slotted wing flap, first used on the 727, and refined it for the 747, as well as using a device on the leading edge of the wings that was coupled with the flaps to give the airplane good low-speed characteristics.

Like the 727's, although on a much more spectacular scale, the 747's wing would look to a passenger staring out at it to be opening up at the seams to the point where you could look through gaps and see the runway coming up beneath. Here, in fact, was a wing designed to fly faster than any other airliner's that would also, remarkably, be a model of deportment at low speeds—a feat that nobody, including Lindbergh, would really be able to credit until the 747 flew.

As the 747's test pilot, Jack Waddell would be the first to know if these devices worked. He, too, was concerned about judging a landing from a cockpit so much higher than he was used to. He had the engineers make him an ungainly contraption that became known as "Waddell's Wagon," a mock-up of the flight deck and part of the nose that was mounted at the actual height of the airplane on top of a rig of the sixteen-wheel landing gear. It was towed around Boeing Field by a truck, as Waddell sat in the "cockpit" and got used to seeing the runway from altitude. Waddell's Wagon, orange with a ludicrously grinning Halloween mask painted on its front as on a routed-out pumpkin, was the first public manifestation of the behemoth. Although a comic fragment of the whole, it somehow summoned the personality of the airplane, as a deft caricature catches a face with a few lines.

Mock-ups, wagons, fabricated cabins, flight simulators: it was all groping for a sense of a dimension, for an understanding of the transformed scale of the flying experience—for the pilots, for the passengers, and for the airports.

From the 201 Building, Sutter could see his old high school up on the ridge to the east of the field. But there was no time for sentimental reflections about this biographical landscape. Sutter was driving everyone else as hard as he was driving himself: ten-hour days, six-day weeks, no vacations. Children were growing up seldom seen by their fathers. Wives were getting to know another numerical mistress, 747. Libidinal metaphors were not happy, given the circumstances. The men were exhausted. On the ground floor of the 201 Building there was a workshop with drop hammers. Every time the hammers fell, they shook the floor above, and the engineers' drafting tables, as though in an earthquake.

One day, Sutter set off to walk two miles along East Marginal Way and see the 747's power plant engineers, who had been installed in an old Ford factory. A freight train was clanking down the track that skirted the road and the Boeing plants. Sutter was so preoccupied that he didn't hear it coming, and was very nearly run over.

The engines were always on his mind. He, Snyder, and Heinemann had been to the Pratt & Whitney plant at Hartford, Connecticut, to check on progress with the first JT-9 engines. The engine had still to make its first test run. They were shown what then existed, just the compressor. Sutter looked it over, but didn't say much until the three of them were riding back to their hotel. Then he put into words what was preying on all their minds: "Can you believe that the success of our entire program depends on that one piece of machinery working?"

14 ■ Death by Chicken

Each Thursday afternoon Sutter would be faced by department heads bringing lists of the engineers who would have to work through the weekend. It seemed that virtually everyone was making the lists. The budget for overtime had ceased to have meaning. At the same time, George Snyder was looking at the mounting engineer population and growling at Sutter, "Do we really need all these guys?"

"Every week," said Sutter, "we need 'em more."

Finally, Allen noticed the numbers. The issue of how many engineers the 747 needed to design it came to a head. Allen gave warning that in three weeks there would be a showdown. All the program's senior managers would have to answer for their budgets, and he wanted cuts. Substantial cuts.

Sutter was warned by Snyder that instead of recruiting more engineers, they would have to shed some.

Sutter asked for some ground rules. They set out to examine every department's manpower and relate it to the production schedule. Sutter then gave these rules to each of his department heads, but stressed his caveat that they should honor their engineering consciences above their budgets.

"Tell me what you need to finish the design of this airplane," he said.

When he ran over the first returns from the departments, Sutter called Snyder. "George," he said, "we have to meet. You're not gonna like the numbers the guys are bringing up."

Not catching Sutter's tone, Snyder said, "Well, I know you're not going to meet our goals, but you'd better do the best you can."

"It's worse than that," persisted Sutter, but Snyder didn't want to listen.

Then, a week before the scheduled meeting, Snyder called to say that Allen was leaving town and wanted the meeting that day—in forty-five minutes.

"Jesus," said Sutter. "You haven't reviewed the figures."

"Get down here," said Snyder.

Sutter was in Everett, and the meeting was in the Renton headquarters of the commercial airplane division. He stuffed all the papers into a bag and drove like the wind the forty miles down Interstate 5.

When he arrived, Allen, Wells, Stamper, T. Wilson, and Boullioun were waiting in a second-floor conference room. Snyder was in the lobby. Sutter pulled out the tallies of the engineering staffs and graphs he had drawn plotting the 747 schedule against the engineering man-hours needed to complete the design.

"You'd better take five minutes to look at these," said Sutter.

But even then, Snyder didn't want to know. "Get up there," he said. "Gotta get up there and do it."

So, without any rehearsal and sweaty from the driving, Sutter faced Allen and his henchmen and matter-of-factly read off his figures.

The result was that he needed eight hundred *more* engineers.

"You can't have them," said Wilson.

"I *know* I can't have them," said Sutter, almost out of patience. "I've been trying to get them for two years. That's why we're using overtime and working like hell, ten hours a day."

Allen looked at Stamper. Stamper looked at Snyder. Everybody looked at somebody. Sutter sat down.

The meeting was a watershed in the program. For the first time, the engineering demands created by the deadline were fully aired and, reluctantly, accepted. Until then, nobody above

Sutter had been able—or, perhaps, willing—to translate Allen's grand ambition into a realistic assessment of the manpower required to execute it. Sutter got the extra engineers; at its peak, the 747 was employing well over half of the twelve thousand engineers on the Boeing payroll. Thereafter, the 747 team became known as Sutter's Runaways. Nonetheless, the experience cemented in Sutter a conviction which he preached for years to come: edicts from on high should always be challenged when they left a program undermanned.

The Allen meeting was a turning point in other ways. It demonstrated that T. Wilson, with the title executive vice president, was emerging more and more as Allen's understudy. Very little had been achieved in smoothing out Wilson's tongue, but the 747 program was providing him with a living laboratory for the study of crisis management.

W. T. Hamilton buttonholed Wilson and said, "Sutter's having a tough time with some of those guys above him who don't understand what the real problem is."

Wilson was characteristically brisk: "Sutter's doing a much better job than those guys—it doesn't make any difference."

"Well," said Hamilton, "it makes a difference to him."

One of the irritants Hamilton had in mind was Snyder. After the showdown on staffing, what little influence Snyder held over Sutter evaporated. There was also an edgy new tone in the relationship between Sutter and Stamper—because of Snyder's dereliction rather than Sutter's, Stamper had been left sitting before Allen with the feeling that he was the emperor with no clothes. Stamper had talked to Snyder about dropping as many as a *thousand* engineers, without getting any argument. Sutter had derailed that plan, and in the heat of the moment Stamper blamed Sutter.

After this, the balance of power over the 747 program became defined more by personal styles than by formally designated authority. Stamper's lack of background in aeronautical engineering seemed to paralyze him when he was asked for a decision bearing on the design of the airplane. Even when Sutter made presentations to Stamper with the hope of getting approval for more resources or a change in the schedule, Stamper would complain about overruns, but still leave Sutter dangling. Sutter had neither the time nor the inclination to work around Stamper, so, more and more, he made the judgment calls himself.

Boeing's management of the program was also colored by the intrusive Pan Am involvement in the 747's design, on a level unknown with any other airplane. Dealing with Pan Am was worked at two levels, divided by an improvised *cordon sanitaire:* contractual disputes (which were of increasing intensity) were fielded by the senior executives and the lawyers of each company; detailed differences over the design were confined, as far as possible, to Sutter and Borger.

This Sutter-Borger axis was often all that stood between the continuing development of the 747 and a total rupture between Boeing and its principal customer. ("That probably pulled us through," allowed T. Wilson, when I asked him about it.) As the relationships at the upper levels deteriorated, the two engineers worked things through in their own way. Consciously or unconsciously, two different games were in progress. Each company unleashed its licensed "bad guys" in the executive suites, while the two extremely willful engineers made their own peace.

Borger and Sutter, though, could not always remain pure. Each had his own masters to answer, and at times each had to play the bad guy in open combat. Borger, at the peak of his career, had not lost any of his unforgiving acerbity. Any Boeing executive rash enough to think that he could pull something on Borger inevitably retired with compound psychological injuries. For his part, Sutter arrived at an understanding with Borger that certain issues of engineering integrity were immutable, but if Borger wanted more than his pound of flesh, Sutter would draw the line for Boeing and not yield.

Pan Am's distress with the 747 *was* mainly measured in pounds. The airplane had been gaining weight by the week. In 1965, the first tentative proposal had been for a takeoff weight of 550,000 pounds; Boeing's first contractual specification had put the weight at 655,000 pounds, then it had moved to 680,000 pounds and by the summer of 1967 to 710,000 pounds. There was no way the original Pratt & Whitney engine could provide enough power to get that much airplane off the ground and carry the payload promised. Pan Am calculated that for a New York–Rome flight the 747 would have to shed fifty-eight passengers, losing $20,000 of revenue.

Executives on both sides were often unsure of their ground because of the freewheeling way their two bosses used their own back channel. Trippe was the worst offender. It was his policy to be able to disclaim in private what his staff had been instructed to say in negotiations. Allen did not believe in deceiving his own executives, and he took care to tape all his phone conversations with Trippe (Trippe *never* left a trace of his), but things were said between the two of them on fishing trips and in other places that were simply washed away in the rain.

Of course, it was an accepted gambit for chief executives to hold themselves above the squalid small-arms fire of negotiations so that, if needed, they could descend to adjudicate with clean hands. But such was the heat and confusion of the wrangling over the 747 that even this device broke down. Just how difficult it could get was shown by a long and taxing call Allen made to Trippe one afternoon in October. An exasperated Allen complained that "the story you get from your people isn't the story I get from my people, and the story I get from my people doesn't indicate the same type of thinking on the part of your people that you recount to me."

In calmer moments, each was inclined to say things like "My people will get on to your people" and so neatly distance himself from unpleasantness.

But if you were one of those "people" it was different. Trippe's hapless front man in most of the meetings with Boeing was General Kuter. Inevitably, Kuter was given to dealing with Boeing as though he was running a military campaign. He used military metaphors: taking over a suite on the eighth floor of the elegant Olympic Hotel in Seattle for a prolonged round of meetings with Boeing, he called it his "command post." Kuter seemed unaware that most of the participants on both sides were far more seasoned in this kind of horse-trading than he was, and knew each other intimately.

Kuter was particularly impatient with John Yeasting, the head of the commercial airplane division. Yeasting had been dealing with Pan Am since 1959. He was respected in both camps as a man who would never commit Boeing to something he thought it couldn't deliver. In fact, in the summer of 1967 Yeasting was a sick man, and the 747 turmoil was wearing him down. To save his energy, Allen promoted him to executive vice president and replaced him with Tex Boullioun. To Kuter, Boullioun looked like the kind of sharp staff officer from West Point with whom he could do business.

That, however, was just one side of Boullioun's adaptable personality. Another was that he was able to work easily with Sutter. He knew that Sutter was gathering enemies, and that some of them wanted him fired. When Sutter hit the ceiling, Boullioun would kid him. "Come on down, Joe. Stop looking like that." They were very different—Boullioun the personable polymath, Sutter the burdened dogmatist—but they trusted each other and Boullioun could deliver what Stamper didn't, a decision on any part of the airplane. Boullioun had also become a true believer in the 747. He had a hunch that it was the airplane the world's airlines were waiting for—even if they didn't yet quite know it.

Of all the trials of the 747, the one that nagged at the conscience the most was whether they were moving too fast. Should they take a delay? Could they *dare* to delay? The first airing of this concern had been as Steiner was designing the new wing. Some of Steiner's supporters argued that it would have been worth nine months' or a year's delay to have the more elegant solution. Now, as the weight problem got worse, there were renewed arguments that it would be worth waiting a year to get a more powerful Pratt engine.

What little experience there was with the high-bypass engine—and remember that Pratt had not yet run one—proved that it yielded at least a twofold increase in power over the smaller fans. That was the first payoff simply from the principle. But getting still more power, the kind of increase that would come only from experience and refinement, was a slower process. The 747 had passed the line where the initial advance in power would be enough.

The 747 now needed nearly 45,000 pounds of thrust from each engine. All that Pratt felt that it could safely deliver was the 40,000 pounds of takeoff thrust of its first design. (Takeoff thrust is the ultimate test of any engine. There is an enormous difference between the thrust required to get the airplane off the ground and the thrust it needs once at cruising speed: Boeing's 747 now needed more than 44,000 pounds of takeoff thrust, though at cruise it would need only 9,500 pounds of thrust.)

Both Boeing and Pan Am choked over the idea of delay. The financial soundness of Boeing's investment in the 747 depended on keeping the production line moving; any delay at all could, they calculated, cost them as much as $400 million. Pan Am was due to pay Boeing $230 million by early 1969, and the interest payments on that would cost them $2 million every month, and the longer the delay the more deferred would be the revenue. Though both companies were reporting record earnings (Boeing's net earnings for the year would be $83.9 million), the 747 gave every indication of flying right through the $1 billion barrier, an unprecedented sum for a commercial program. A delay was unthinkable. Neither Allen nor Trippe seemed yet to realize it, but the financial survival of their companies was inexorably tied to the 747.

And yet Trippe's appetite was not sated. He bombarded Allen with demands for a larger and toughened-up 747 that he wanted as a super-freighter. Allen's hounded engineers had to make a detailed project study just to demonstrate to Trippe that this airplane would involve an extensive redesign—and engines so much more powerful that they were beyond anything Pratt could deliver for years. Jack Horner, the head of Pratt's parent company, United Aircraft, arguing over lunch in New York with Kuter about the bigger engine, did a rough calculation on the back of a menu. Its development costs came out at $350 million. Trippe's behavior had reached the stage of megalomania. Pan Am and Boeing executives had no course but to try to placate him, while knowing that the basic 747 was in such trouble that the big freighter was a pipe dream.

For Boeing, the only hope now of matching the airplane and the engine was to cut weight. The airframe had to lose fat wherever fat could be found. Every pound—every ounce—counted. The trouble was, who could tell what the airplane weighed? It had never been an exact science. Guidelines had been set from experience. The weight of the airframe was estimated by using a parametric method, extrapolating from one constant to another *supposed* constant. That, at least, was the theory.

It didn't work for the 747. The old laws of scaling could not be adapted to an airframe this much larger. You couldn't take the 3,000-square-foot wing of a 707 and extrapolate to the 5,500-square-foot 747 wing and then know what it would weigh; the structure and mass were too different. Another measure was "wetted area," a nice archaic term from the days when canvas was stretched over wood and painted with dope to shrink it. It meant all the skin surfaces. These were not susceptible to a scale law, either. There were many different gauges of metal. There were hundreds of miles of wire. There was tubing of different materials.

On weight, Sutter couldn't get straight answers, and he had to be pulled down from the ceiling again.

"The weights group," said an engineer who suffered along with Sutter, "was not a place where our geniuses wound up." And then, with seasoned fatalism, he added: "When the engineers finally get down to designing the thing, it weighs what it's going to weigh." Put at its crudest, all they could do was tear away at the airframe and weigh what they removed and deduct that from what they *thought* the whole ship had weighed to begin with. All very well. But they weren't cutting weight from a fixed object.

Up against a wall in the first corner of the Everett plant to *have* a wall (the roof was not complete) was a spectacular, glinting foretaste of the airplane to come. It was a full-length 747 fuselage mounted on jigs. Not a fuselage that could ever fly, but the engineering mock-up. The first parts made from drawings, the first metal to be cut, went to make just this one mock-up. It was the only way the engineers could check, literally, that everything fitted together. It often didn't. There were things that drawings could not predict, or even figure out. For example, whether the wiring tracked as it should without snagging on the metal; whether the plumbing interfered with the primary structure.

The engineering mock-up's decisive moment was called the "mock-up buyoff." There was always a bells-and-whistles celebration for this, when every design engineer turned up and each one checked out his own piece of the airplane. If a particularly tricky piece of tubing was a good fit, the engineer responsible might take it out of the mock-up, then and there, and walk off with it to make sure it was duplicated in production. If something didn't fit, then it was back to the drawing board, and a change order would have to be issued for new drawings. If it did fit, that was supposed to be sign-off time.

Quite often, it wasn't. Ken Holtby joined the celebrations at the 747 buyoff. He saw an engineer he knew and said, "What are you going to do now? You're bought off. You don't have any more job." The man grinned. "Tell you what I'm going to do. I'm going right back to start writing change orders."

It was the Boeing way. They could never leave an airplane alone. The airplane was going to be designed over again. And maybe again.

And all the time Sutter was trying to weigh it.

Boeing had notified Pan Am that the airplane was eleven thousand pounds overweight. By this time, Borger had engineers of his own based in Seattle. They were at Everett every day. They told Borger that the weight problem was worse than Boeing had admitted, and Borger flew out to make his own assessment. He quickly realized that eleven thousand pounds was an optimistic figure. He could see that Sutter was in trouble. Given the struggle that Pratt faced to squeeze more power from its engine, Pan Am, said Borger, could not accept the extra weight.

Once more, Wells sent in a team to attack the problem independently of Sutter and Webb. This time there was no talk of black parachutes. It was more like a gathering of the white togas, some with weathered crowns: all the senatorial figures were on hand—Schairer, Martin, Cook—and the team was led on a day-to-day basis by Maynard Pennell, who brought two hundred engineers from the SST program with him. Wells told Pan Am that within six weeks Pennell would present a list of changes designed to get the 747 down to the 710,000-pound gross takeoff weight that Boeing now believed was the best compromise between payload and performance.

Sutter had no personal problems with Pennell, but the weight-cutting review became a thorn in his side. The attitude of the SST engineers was that they could fix the 747 by throwing at it the new technology they were pioneering—new materials, new electronics, every flavor of the wonderworks of the future. They seemed uncaring that Sutter was beyond the point when things as radical as new substitutes for aluminum, untried materials like graphite-epoxy, could even be considered. He was behind schedule and he was being second-guessed every day by engineers who had never tailored an airplane for an airline.

As well as having to endure Pennell's team, Sutter was told to take on his own weight-saver, a veteran engineer named Charlie Brewster. In fact, Brewster had been with Boeing so long that he could tell the story of Ed Wells's arrival at Plant 1. It was Brewster who had recognized the young Wells for the brilliant engineer he was, and it was Brewster who had selflessly cleared the space ahead of Wells as he rose. Brewster was loved for his yarn-spinning about the fledgling company, but Sutter's department heads, who were supposed to spare time for him, had a technical fluency that Brewster could not match.

By now, the *esprit* of Sutter's team was such that they closed ranks around him. Thousands of suggestions poured into his office about how weight could be cut. Sutter let Brewster digest it all. Then each idea would be argued out by its originator, the department heads, Sutter, and Brewster. Each time it was a question of slimming the structures without compromising safety. About one out of every ten suggestions was acceptable, but it was an exhausting process and often the weight saving was small.

Pennell, meanwhile, had settled on a major component of Sutter's design that he thought could be changed to save significant weight: the triple-slotted flaps. By converting to double-slotted flaps they could, said Pennell, save seventeen hundred pounds in one bold stroke. Yet the triple-slotted flap underlay Sutter's whole design doctrine. It governed the 747's stalling speed, reducing it to something around 130 mph, and therefore its approach and landing speeds. More than any other single feature of the design, these flaps disarmed the criticism that the airplane would be too big to land as easily as the smaller jets. Reversion to double-slotted flaps would degrade the 747's handling in a marked way. Some of Pennell's other ideas were acceptable to Sutter, but he and Webb were appalled by the proposed change in the flaps. Nonetheless, Pennell insisted on making the change in the list he would present to Borger.

Borger turned up in Seattle with his immediate boss, Sanford Kauffman. They were impressed that Boeing's changes were so extensive. However, when Pennell came to the change of the flaps, Borger couldn't believe his ears. He waited for Kauffman to react, but Kauffman said nothing. Sutter was not present. Borger did not know whether Sutter had endorsed the change or not. Instead of directly attacking the change of flap, Borger homed in on its consequences.

"What happened to our stall speed guarantee?" he asked.

...

"We're going to have to increase that by eight knots," said Pennell, surprised by Borger's challenge.

"No way," said Borger. "I'm not the final guy at Pan Am, but I ain't gonna stand for that. You can do anything you want to the flap, as long as you meet that stall speed guarantee."

It was an empty concession, and Borger knew it: the stall speed guarantee could never be met with a double-slotted flap. Annoyed that Kauffman had not taken a stand against the change, Borger called Harold Gray, the president of Pan Am, in New York. Gray supported Borger.

Trippe, for once, was not as devious as his chief engineer. The casuistry about stall speed didn't interest him. He ruled, simply, "You've got to keep the triple-slotted flap." Pennell had to give way on what had been his single largest weight-saving idea. Borger had forced what was probably the most important defense of a basic principle of Sutter's 747, one closely related to safety, that it should be a pussycat to land. Interestingly enough, until I told him, Borger never knew that Sutter had himself adamantly refused to accept the change of flap, and would have made it an issue of his control of the design had it been imposed on him.

In the end, more than 20,000 pounds were shed from the airframe. Some of the hundreds of changes saved barely a single pound, others hundreds of pounds. At its fattest at the beginning of the year, the 747's MEW (manufacturer's empty weight) had hit 345,000 pounds. By the end of the year it was down to 328,000 pounds, and still falling. The structural integrity was never compromised.

When it came to the operating weight, Boeing staged a counterattack on Pan Am. Boullioun, Stamper, and Sutter went to New York to face Trippe. Sutter demonstrated that of 22,000 pounds they still wanted to shed, two thirds arose from Pan Am's own specifications. Trippe never spoke, but weight was cut from the food service galleys and the seats.

The degree to which Sutter consolidated his hold on the 747 did not please the engine designers at Rolls-Royce. They knew him well. While Sutter was still working on the 707, they had developed a new engine for it, the Conway. They had been in the business of jet engines longer than anyone outside of Nazi Germany, and they had a very superior attitude.

Not only did Rolls design engines. It insisted on wrapping the metal around them. The most intimate garment of the jet engine is the nacelle that houses it. The nacelle is not simply a piece of sheathing—a nacelle "flies" in the same way that any other surfaces of the airplane fly. Getting this right was, of course, part of the well-practiced Boeing geometry of nacelle, pylon, and wing. But the engine designer has vested interests in the nacelle, too—its design determines how well the engine is cooled, how easily it can be opened up for maintenance, even the integrity of the engine in flight.

When it came to fitting the Conway to the 707, Rolls's chief engineer, Adrian Lombard, realized that there were tricks to hanging a nacelle on a pylon that only Boeing knew. While insisting that Rolls would design the Conway nacelle, Lombard asked a Boeing engineer to give him Boeing's book on nacelles—the entire technical record, a portion of the same sacred texts that composed the Bible. Sutter was consulted. "Hell with that," said Sutter. "That cost Boeing a lot of money. We're not handing that over."

Lombard had been a pioneer of jet engine design in wartime Britain. He was furious at being balked by someone he regarded as a lower cog in the wheel, and complained to Wells. Lombard knew Wells and thought he knew how to work him over. A snappy Wells asked Sutter why he wasn't helping Rolls-Royce. After all, the British Overseas Airways Corporation was a big Boeing customer, and always insisted on having Rolls engines on its airplanes, so it was important to keep Rolls sweet.

Sutter explained how much of their proprietary data was involved. Wells saw the point. Boeing *sold* the data to Rolls—and Lombard never forgot that it was Sutter who had thwarted him. Sutter, in turn, was always leery of Lombard and his works, although he was as respectful as anyone of the British company's pedigree. Who could not be? There was always a touch of class about anything that Rolls-Royce turned out; the aura of that resplendently gleaming radiator on the limousine influenced feelings about the company as a whole, even though you didn't build jet engines the way you did cars. "Hand-built" was one hell of a sales pitch, and it was nice to think that the aero engines would receive the same lapidary care. But Sutter wasn't a sucker for auras. In his book, when it came to jets, the guys at Pratt & Whitney and GE were as classy as the Brits.

Now here was Lombard, again, pitching hard for the chance to hang an engine on the 747. Rolls had bet the company on its high-bypass engine, the RB. 211. (The R was for the company, based in Derby, and the B for Barnoldswick, the Yorkshire town where much of the engine work was done.) Rather than hit Sutter first, Lombard's men had been talking up the RB. 211 to Sutter's power plant team.

As ever, Rolls engineers thought they could be just that little bit more sophisticated than anyone else. Instead of the two shafts that powered the fans of the American engines, Rolls had three. Sutter didn't like that, for a start: three shafts, three spools—it was heavier and it was riskier and what was the point? But the RB. 211 had another vaunted innovation. The largest fan blades, those at the front that sucked in the air, were made of something Rolls called Hyfil. Each blade had a thin outer layer of steel and a core of carbon fiber. Rolls claimed that Hyfil made dramatic savings in weight without jeopardizing strength. Sutter looked at Hyfil and dismissed it with one word: "Oatmeal."

But Lombard kept up the pressure, and worked around Sutter. Boeing engineers went to Derby and were given the argument for the third shaft—it would make a better-balanced, smoother engine. And if you wanted the smooth, who better than Rolls? (Remember the car ad, courtesy of David Ogilvy, that the only sound you can hear at 60 mph is the ticking of the clock?) So where was the data on the Hyfil blade? Sutter wanted to know. They said Lombard wouldn't hand it over.

"Hell," said Sutter, "we're not gonna put an engine in an airplane when we don't know what's in it."

Lombard called Wells to complain about Sutter's obtuseness. Wells agreed to go to Derby himself, with the 747's engine team—but without Sutter. On that basis, said Lombard, he would be prepared to give Wells a private briefing on Hyfil.

Wells might have been far more diplomatic than Sutter—years of holding the ring inside Boeing and at the same time sweet-talking peppery airline moguls like Juan Trippe and C. R. Smith had made him indispensable as the technical ambassador—but he was more skeptical of the Rolls engine than he allowed Lombard to see. If Rolls had simply been matching the technology of GE and Pratt with a two-shaft engine and no fancy blades, it could have been a serious contender for the 747. But the RB. 211 was very ambitious, and even if it worked, Wells doubted that it would be ready in anything like the time promised. (The boss of GE, Jack Parker, warned Gerhard Neumann that if Rolls delivered everything they said they could, Neumann would be looking for a new job because "they know something we don't.")

Wells decided to vent the dispute over the RB. 211 by bringing the protagonists face to face. He sent Sutter to New York, where Lombard was waiting. Rolls-Royce personnel were living high on the hog. Lombard was in a suite at the Ritz Towers on Park Avenue (the hotel of choice for many aviation interests). Sutter turned up for breakfast to find a buffet laid out in Lombard's suite that looked large enough for twenty people. In fact, the breakfast was one-on-one.

Lombard was expansive and conciliatory. Sutter ate as much of the breakfast as he thought humanly possible. Between mouthfuls, he worked his way through the technical agenda. Finally he reached the Hyfil blades. How would they stand up to bird impact and ingested ice? Birds—sometimes flocks of them, other times just one big bird—had donated their lives involuntarily to testing the survivability of jets, sometimes stalling engines and, occasionally, bringing down an airplane. The front fan of the high-bypass engines would be like a huge, insatiable vacuum cleaner in the sky. The fan blades, if smashed by bird impact, would be sucked into the engine core and jeopardize engine and airplane.

Lombard was indignant. Hyfil, he raved, could take any kind of impact damage and keep spinning. He disappeared into his bedroom and came out brandishing a Hyfil fan blade like a samurai sword. "Watch this!" he cried, and brought the blade down in a forceful stroke. It sliced right through a coffee table. Sutter looked at the debris. It was not the kind of test he was impressed by. He politely continued to work through his check list, but on the RB. 211 his mind was unchanged.

The Rolls-Royce campaign to sell the RB. 211 in America became a heroic saga to the Brits. It was led by the company's head of sales, a voluble Irishman named David Huddie. Britain was passing through a demoralizing decline and desperately grasped any icon of its old greatness that came to hand. Rolls-

Royce enjoyed an almost supernatural status as a peerless trademark, putting it beyond rational political judgment as well as hard economic realities.

Having failed with Boeing, Huddie sold the RB. 211 to Lockheed, which designed an airplane around it, the three-engine L-1011. Rolls had to be bailed out by government funds to continue development of the engine.

John Borger had also been courted by Rolls to consider the RB. 211 for Pan Am's 747s. He went to Derby and saw the engine running on a test stand, with its Hyfil blades. All seemed to be well, but by the time Borger had reached Heathrow on his way back to New York, he heard that the test engine had failed. The problem then was in the compressor, not Hyfil.

But, as Sutter had suspected all along, the nemesis of the Hyfil blades was bird impact. The evidence that finally forced Rolls to drop Hyfil came from a gruesome rural tableau. A test engine was run up in a field and bombarded for forty hours with defrosted frozen chickens. The field became saturated with pulverized and burned bones and blood. The ultimate test was to fire *frozen* birds into the fan—thereby replicating bird impact and ice in one test. Hyfil disintegrated.

Nine years passed before a 747 flew with RB. 211 engines, and then it was due to the loyalty of British Airways, which had flown Pratt-powered 747s until the second generation of 747s and the Rolls engine caught up with each other. The design of the Lockheed L-1011, in many respects a fine airplane (and one admired by Sutter), was fatally constrained by the limitations of the RB. 211 and, for years, plagued by engine failures in service.

The relentless Huddie was knighted for selling the RB. 211 to Lockheed, and the oxygen of publicity had a tonic effect on British morale and the company's self-esteem. But behind this technological jingoism lay the flaw of hubris that, had Rolls been left to the mercies of the open market, would have proved mortal to the company.

For those who had noticed—and Lombard certainly had—there was also an instructive lesson in the RB. 211 episode about how the Boeing Airplane Company worked. It was no good trying to seduce either the senior officers of Boeing nor the foot soldiers if the chief engineer opposed you. Sutter was not even a vice president. But once he made up his mind that the Rolls engine had serious defects, he was implacable.

Sutter's brush with the visionaries of the SST over the weight of the 747 did not end his irritation with them. The concept of the 747 as a workaday stopgap until the SST went into service permeated the company's upper levels and occasionally became expressed as a matter of policy. Pennell went public in this vein with a speech delivered at, of all places, the Rolls-Royce base at Derby. He was in Europe beating the SST drum at the same time that other Boeing executives were out selling the 747. And Pennell was trashing the 747—he said it was nothing more than a cargo ship. In a few years it would be obsolete.

Pennell was shadowed by a minder from Boeing's public relations headquarters, the sagacious Pete Bush. Bush advised Pennell to strike the offending words from his script. Pennell refused. Bush pressed him, and in the end they agreed that Pennell could utter the insult, but Bush could remove it from the printed copies that were handed out. It was never reported.

Pennell's conviction that the SST was the glory machine inculcated the SST team with a bragging elitism, struggling though they were with a design that would not, by Wells's classic dicta, close. Sutter, in Washington for a particularly grueling encounter with the FAA over certification for the 747, returned to the Madison Hotel to find the bar alive with the egos of twenty of Boeing's SST engineers.

"How ya doin', Joe?" one of them asked, pulling him toward the bar. "Sure hope you're making the 747 a good cargo airplane." The embrace became one of commiseration. "You hang in there, Joe, and get the job done. Then we'll get you a job on the SST."

Of course, according to them, all the company stars *were* on the SST: Pennell, Withington, Holtby, Cook. And Wells and Schairer were looking over their shoulders. It was hard to believe that any other company could field such talent. The SST was going to take over the world.

15 ■ Strike Up the Band

It's dark. A 747 is coming in for an emergency landing. The pilots know they have only one chance to make the runway. It takes all their concentration to nurse the faltering airplane. One engine is out, a fire is indicated in another, and the warning stays on even when that engine is shut down. On the main deck, flight attendants, trying themselves to appear calm, have warned passengers that there is an emergency. Ten attendants are now strapped into rear-facing seats, one at each door. To cut down the risk of fire the pilot has killed electrical power to the cabin. The attendants can talk to each other and to the flight deck on emergency phones run on backup power, as are the emergency floor lights in the cabin.

Strong crosswinds buffet the 747 as it makes the final approach. Rainsqualls make visibility poor, and the pilot only sees the runway lights as he's almost over them. He's slightly off the centerline and tries to correct before the wheels hit, but he doesn't quite manage it and the 747 hits tarmac unevenly. The landing gear holds but with sick engines he can't use his thrust reversers to brake. With the runway slick with rain the wheel brakes are glowing red and burning up as they struggle to stop the heavily loaded airplane. After seconds that seem like minutes, she slews to a halt half on the runway and half on a taxi ramp.

The pilot signals the attendants to begin an emergency evacuation through all doors. Throughout the whole flight the doors are, by regulation, "armed"—that is, powered for rapid opening. All that the flight attendants have to do is to swing the door handles up. Within ten seconds, a power boost cylinder begins to dejam the door. At the same time an emergency evacuation slide stowed in the lower half of the door is automatically inflated, and as the door opens, the slide expands, deploys, and reaches the tarmac sixteen feet below. Gusts of wind catch it, rain splatters it, and the chute is like a writhing yellow serpent as the attendants urge the first passengers to dive down it into the night.

This is a best-case scenario. The 747 is whole and stable on all its landing gear. There is no fire, either in the engine or in the cabin. All the chutes have deployed. They can handle the wind. Nobody panics, and the worst that can happen is that you can find yourself walking around soaked to the skin in the flashing lights of the rescue wagons, dazed but offering prayers in thanks for being alive. The flight attendants have been exemplary. And the pilots think the ship is one tough bastard.

As far as the FAA is concerned, FAR 25 has been observed. The 747 has met the standard for evacuating nearly four hundred people. Maybe not in ninety seconds, the number devoutly to be desired. After all, it was night and it was wet and it was ... well, the regulations mean well, but there is such a thing as reality.

Milt Heinemann had given the 747 what everyone, including the FAA, agreed was the best "unassisted egress" system that an airplane of that size could have, short of punching so many doors into it that it would never fly. Yet the whole evacuation concept was anathema to many of the engineers. It was the device of last resort. If an airplane was thoroughly engineered it shouldn't end up getting into that kind of trouble. In truth, both views were self-deceiving: the idea that an orderly evacuation could take place in ninety seconds, no matter what the circumstances, and the idea that you could design the risk of an emergency right out of the airplane.

Nonetheless, Boeing had to go through the motions of testing Heinemann's system. This system had evolved after research into the behavior of passengers in emergencies. Getting from their seats to the doors, it turned out, was not the greatest psychological hurdle (although that required a level of decorum unlikely to be evident in scary circumstances). The real terror lay in getting from the door to the ground. People definitely preferred stairs to slides. Heinemann built lightweight stairs and tried them out. They showed very little advance over slides, and carried a weight penalty that an already overweight airframe could not tolerate.

The first evacuation tests were carried out using a rudimentary unfinished fuselage shell. Rows of crude seats were installed to reproduce the density of the 747 and volunteers were filmed as they squeezed out from between the seats and filed down the aisles to the doors. In the meantime, engineers were themselves testing the giant slides. They had to be able to unfold without being deflected in a twenty-five-knot wind blowing from any direction.

The top of a slide was attached to a gantry set at the height of the main cabin floor. A huge and powerful fan was aimed at the slide from every angle, and as the gale it generated rebounded off the steel workshop walls, engineers came sliding down, two abreast. When this scientific testing was over, it was time to try with a full load of passengers.

The first attempt was not a success. The FAA required a "representative" test sample: at least 30 percent had to be women, between 5 and 10 percent children, and about 5 percent over sixty. Most of the first test group were volunteers from the Seattle Lions Club, driven to Boeing Field in sixteen buses and given a $25 handout. They were taken into a darkened hangar, to simulate a night evacuation, and given green cloth vests with bright yellow numbers like football players. There were 560 of them. The mock-up this time more accurately represented the real cabin than the cruder version used in the early tests. An ambulance stood by.

Thirteen stewardesses waited for them all to be settled. Then, with the main lights out and only emergency floor lights remaining, the stewardesses went to their positions at the doors and, as the doors opened and the chutes were deployed, began yelling "Jump! Jump!" and out the people went into the darkness. One of the five chutes, at a rear exit, broke loose and could not be used. Instead of ninety seconds, the evacuation took two and a half minutes. There were injuries: two stretcher cases, with broken bones, a lot of elbow burns from sliding down the plastic chutes, some people hit in the head by the heels of others. Some of the stewardesses were close to tears.

In later tests, with all chutes working, the ninety second evacuation was achieved, but there were more injuries: broken ankles, legs, and arms—two or three on every test. The most dangerous and least-resolved evacuation problem was the upper deck, where there was an escape hatch for the crew on the right side behind the cockpit. Instead of a sixteen-foot drop, it was more like thirty. It had to be assumed that as well as the flight crew, flight attendants and some passengers would need to take the big jump.

Instead of a slide, there was a device the engineers called the "diaper" that strapped around the crotch and the shoulders and was played out on an inertia reel—the same principle used on car seat belts to control the rate that the belt is unspooled, in this case to keep the person in the diaper from hitting the ground too fast. As each escapee fell, he left behind a steel ribbon from the inertia reel. If the following person hit this ribbon it would cut him up. So the guinea pigs were told that as soon as they hit the ground they should run *under* the plane to retract the ribbon. Running under a crippled or burning airplane is not what you naturally *want* to do. In one test a volunteer was pushed out the hatch before the reel was in place, and was lucky to escape with only broken bones.

Word of the risks involved got around, and the eagerness to participate dwindled. One senior Boeing engineer told me, "The whole evacuation testing is ridiculous. It's scary as hell. You hurt people and you don't really solve anything."

But Boeing was, of course, obliged to persist with it, no matter how farcical. (It was still standard practice in the 1990s, and a woman taking part in a McDonnell Douglas test was paralyzed.) The FAA's own tests, carried out over the years in secrecy, were no better. Everybody—the manufacturers, the airlines, and the regulators—colluded to observe the pieties of FAR 25. In 1968, as the design of the 747's cabins was taking final shape, a few broken bones could be counted as a low price to pay for satisfying this standard. But the standard itself was shaped not by the highly variable and always fearful circumstances of in-flight emergencies, but by the entirely artificial circumstances of what was deemed to be practical as a *static test* under controlled conditions.

At work here was the chimera of scientific method. The Boeing engineers were not cynics. Safety *was* the religion that wrote their Bible. "Unassisted egress" had a scientific rationale, but only up to a point. More science should have been applied to what happened beyond that point. Several decades on, it is now conceded that in concentrating on getting people out of the airplane, too little work was done on saving them while they were still *in* the airplane. Ironically, as flying became safer and safer, it became more obvious that when crashes did occur the chances of surviving them had been underrated—by 1990 they were better than 50 percent.

Nothing showed this better than the crash of an Avianca 707 near Kennedy Airport in January 1990. This aging jet with outdated navigation equipment had trouble finding the runway in a snowstorm. It missed on its first pass, and went around again. But it was nearly out of gas. One by one, its engines died as it made its second approach, and, finally out of fuel, it crashed into a hillside. The pilots, who died in the crash, skillfully glided and virtually stalled the airplane into a "soft" crash. Eighty-five out of 158 passengers survived, because there was no fire. No fuel: no fire. With seats better anchored and designed to withstand impact, more would have survived. Fire, smoke, and impact are the real killers. Survivability is a design regime now recognized as being as productive as "unassisted egress." The regulators have been tardy in addressing it.

Al Ghery and Art Gollofon were walking from the Ritz Towers down Park Avenue to the Pan Am Building. Ghery was thinking, How can we live through this day? This is it. This is the last one I can stand.

They were from Boeing's contracts department. To use the word "contract" in its normal sense as a description of the transaction between Boeing and Pan Am would convey a misleading sense of something legally defined and tangible. In this deal, nothing held firm. The numbers were always fluid. In Pan Am's eyes, Boeing was on the verge of being delinquent. In Boeing's eyes, Pan Am was always asking for more. As Ghery contemplated the day ahead, one figure overshadowed it: Borger. He could picture Borger waiting for them, this huge, overbearing force, and he could picture Borger unleashing himself: shouting *No, no*, shaking his head, spittle flying from his mouth, jowls out of sync with his head. It was terrifying.

Gollofon kept telling himself that Borger had to be contained. Borger would say he wanted a change, some further tweak in the 747's performance. Gollofon would say it would cost Pan Am. And Borger would say he wasn't going to pay for it. Charge another airline. "We're designing the airplane," Borger would say, "and we're setting the standard. Make that basic, and don't charge for it." And Borger would act as if it were his own money.

Then, after the guy had stormed out of the room, and just as you decided you couldn't take it anymore, Borger would return and ask, like some cosseting uncle, if you'd like to join him at his cabin upstate on the lake for the weekend. Borger knew about Pavlov's dog.

("I have to explain my technique," Borger told me, enjoying the memory mightily. "In the specification stages, I would push those fellows as hard as I could, trying to get them to promise as much as I could. Once the contract was signed and everything was put in writing, then my job was to keep them honest. I learned that from my mentor, Andre Priester. He believed a good offense was the best form of defense. I wasn't as subtle as he was. Nobody ever made good all their promises. I think they did a little better than they would have done if I hadn't been on their tails. I'm proud enough to say that.")

Some of the most turbulent exchanges happened to coincide with a period of radical demonstrations against the Vietnam War. In New York, a small cadre of war opponents, the Weathermen, had been placing bombs in the toilets of any corporation thought to be on the side of the hawks. For this reason, all the toilets on the executive floors of the Pan Am Building were locked and the keys handed out only by authorized officers. No allowances were made for the Boeing men, who were spending hours with Borger on the fifty-fifth floor; each time they needed a toilet, they had to request a key.

Gollofon smuggled a toilet key back to Seattle and had copies made in chrome, to match the keys that Boeing handed over with every airplane delivered to an airline. (No airplane needs an ignition key, but the keys had become a symbolic gift.) Gollofon had a scheme in mind that centered on one of Borger's colleagues, Howard Blackwell. Courtliness was as sacred to Blackwell as belligerence was to Borger; in the negotiations, Blackwell played the straight man to Borger's blowtorch.

Opening their next negotiation, Gollofon said, assuming a pained tone, "Howard, you have had an unconscionable advantage during all the previous negotiations. We have to correct it, because it just isn't fair."

Borger was alert, Blackwell alarmed.

"We need to go to the bathroom anytime *we* want," said Gollofon. He produced the chrome keys. "We'll trade you one of these for one of yours, and then you can't hold out on us."

For the moment, all was amicable. And bladders were grateful. But two days later, Borger turned up with a new bunch of keys, much larger keys. He explained that the windows of the Pan Am Building, floor to ceiling, were pivoted at the center so that they could be spun around for cleaning from the inside. Before you could spin the window, it had to be unlocked.

Borger gave a key to each Boeing man around the table. "I've made this little gift," said Borger, "so that next time you feel like jumping out the window, you can."

His grin was all but redeeming.

The keys fitted the slot. But they didn't open the windows. Escaping Borger wasn't that easy.

While their minions were locked into these elaborate games, with many millions of dollars at stake, Allen and Trippe enjoyed intervals of leisure together with their wives. Mef Allen and Betty Trippe played golf alongside the two magnates at the Homestead in Virginia, one of the oldest golf courses in America. Trippe could be a prissy traveling companion—Lindbergh's wife, Anne Morrow, remembered him taking along his own clean sheets for his and Betty's beds each night. The big sport for Allen and Trippe remained the August fishing trips in Alaska. These were always planned months ahead with the thoroughness of a military operation. For the 1968 expedition, Allen arranged a helicopter to reach the more distant upriver waters where steelhead salmon, the sought-after prize, were more easily caught. When Allen proposed this, he was unaware that Trippe was preparing something far more momentous.

It was rarely that the two couples' sojourns together were violated by the pressures of business, but an exception was a four-day visit the Allens made in March to the Cotton Bay Club on Eleuthera in the Bahamas. Trippe had formed a syndicate with friends, including Henry Luce, to create this exclusive resort some years earlier, and it was a favorite hideaway. It had an eighteen-hole golf course designed by Robert Trent Jones and two miles of white beach. Before he left, Trippe asked for a detailed briefing on the 747 problems. Trippe took with him to the Bahamas Harold Gray, the president of Pan Am. (Trippe himself combined the title of chairman with chief executive officer.) It was unusual for Trippe to involve even his president in one of these meetings of the chiefs.

As far as it was possible for anyone to be an effective manager under Trippe, Gray had been so. He had been a pilot and a gifted amateur inventor of navigation aids. Both Pan Am's Pacific and Atlantic divisions had flourished under his command. He was respected in the company as a straight arrow, but this streak of virtue became a source of vulnerability in the devious machinations of Pan Am's political substructure. Some months before the Eleuthera retreat, Gray disclosed to Trippe that he had cancer of the lymph glands. The doctors were optimistic that it could be contained by cobalt treatments.

Gray's presence at Eleuthera did nothing to disperse the usual opacity of the conclaves of Trippe and Allen; afterward, in New York, Kuter could get no clear account of where they stood with Boeing. Once more, the roiled negotiations were left in the hands of subordinates in New York and Seattle who, comparing notes, tried to find common ground. Allen wrote a note to Trippe, thanking him for the "great time we had with you and Betty on Eleuthera," and went on to talk of the Alaskan fishing trip.

Early in May, to Allen's surprise, Trippe retired, and appointed Gray to succeed him. Allen sent Gray a note of congratulation, adding, "I had always thought of Juan as literally 'dieing [sic] with his boots on.' " Allen was half right: Trippe kept an office a few doors down from Gray, and remained a corporate incubus for years to come. At sixty-one, Gray endured painful therapy and soldiered on, but the billion-dollar company was so historically unbalanced in its upper reaches by Trippe's singular style that there was no one with the reserves of energy or instinct needed to supplant him.

Lurking in the woodwork behind the continually shredded 747 contract was the threat of legal action by Pan Am against Boeing for failing to meet its performance guarantees. This was not something that Allen and Trippe would have found comfortable to talk about—it would have ruptured the social graces of their intercourse.

But Allen foresaw the threat. As early as October 1967, he, Prince, and Yeasting had met the company's outside legal advisers from the Seattle law firm of Holman, Marion, Perkins & Stone, to try to assess what the grounds for action might be. This meeting required lawyers who were bilingual—fluent in both legal jargon and aerospeak. Faced with the deficiencies of the 747, the lawyers were unable to offer Boeing much comfort. What worried them most was the airplane's mounting weight. They calculated that every thousand pounds over the contracted weight would cost an airline $5,000 a year in sacrificed payload— passengers and cargo.

The purchase agreement signed by Pan Am had been drafted in an unreal world. When it was signed in April 1966, under the relentless pressure from Trippe, so many details of the design were unresolved that the performance guarantees were little better than moonshine. Two years later, Borger was still insisting that the fatter, 710,000-pound airplane should be capable of the same missions as the two lighter versions of the design, the 655,000-pound and 680,000-pound airplanes. Incredibly, the April 1966 contract *was the only one that Pan Am had signed!* It was left to T. Wilson, now being increasingly drawn into the 747's travails, to point out to Allen that Pan Am had not signed any change orders—in effect, Boeing was building an airplane that was not the one under contract.

As the lawyers looked for loopholes that might mitigate the slackness of the technical guarantees, they suggested three contingencies: tendering the airplane and offering compensation for damages; tendering the airplane and accepting suits for damages if the customer elected to do so; forcing the issue and hoping that if the customer refused to take delivery, the *customer* would be in breach. There was a more drastic final option, a showdown in which the airline might sue for a total breach by Boeing.

There was a pious hope offered that "if it seems probable that the company may have other performance problems or unexcused delivery delays, then it would be nice to get this problem out of the way now. . . . "

Allen decided it was better not to concede anything and to tough it out; Boeing had thirteen firm customers waiting for eighty-five airplanes, but only one airline really mattered when it came to the dangers of litigation, Pan Am. And Boeing could always involve another company that Allen felt was culpable when it came to falling short of promises, Pratt & Whitney. It was in Allen's mind that if things went legal, Boeing would have grounds to sue Pratt.

One is struck by the human architecture of what is, by the summer of 1968, a vast technical enterprise that is barely under control—a human architecture of command and execution that has had to form and reform, adapt and improvise, answer and evade. In one compartment of this Babel the steely-eyed lawyers try to quantify something as slippery as obligation. In other compartments are those men who are isolated by virtue of their arcane knowledge, like sectarians whose allegiance is narrow, fundamental, and obstinate. Their truths are finite. They cannot bend. Chief among them are Sutter and Webb. Beneath their anvils thousands toil, that the whole may be the sum of the parts.

The Everett plant, where the parts come together, is truly Babel. The first 747, N7470, is in final assembly. In mid-June the wings and fuselage are mated, the airplane a nearly consummated work, but an unbalanced one: the engines are not ready, nor the landing gear. She sits, saliently unempowered, on supporting jigs, with umbilical lines hanging open from the wings where the engines will be. Plant construction continues all around the line where seven behemoths are due to arise every month. The spasmic shriek of rivet guns cuts through the deep, distant farts of bulldozers and graders.

Beyond the apron on which N7470 will make her debut, the plant is divided from Paine Field by a highway running through a cutting. Every 747 will have to cross this highway on a bridge sixty feet wide, just wide enough to take the landing gear. On the other side is the paint shop, a modest term for a sixty-thousand-square-foot cavern with doors that weigh 250 tons.

Stamper had seen it in a worse state. Many subassemblies arrived by rail; the spur from the railroad, running at sea level below the plateau, took a sudden gradient to the plant, eight-hundred feet above—the second-steepest incline of any track in the United States. On the day they started building the spur, it rained. And it carried on raining, nonstop, for sixty-six days. It cost $5 million over the budget to shore up the mud.

The ordeal of building the plant, like the ordeal of designing the airplane, produced an obsessive dedication in the managers. Stamper would direct a man to quit and go home, even escort him to his car, only to find, five minutes later, that he had sneaked back in by another door. The coolness between Sutter and Stamper, and the reluctance of the aero establishment to embrace Stamper, was not reflected in his relationship with Allen. Stamper lived near Allen, and returned home from Everett late one night to find a plaque lying on his front step, sent by Allen. It bore a Teddy Roosevelt exhortation: "Far better to dare mighty things than to take rank with those who live in the gray twilight that knows no victory or defeat."

It was as neat a definition of Allen's own hubris as of Stamper's. But as he handed out tokens like this, Allen was visibly withdrawing above the daily torments. Like Trippe, he had reached the time to pass the torch, but unlike Trippe, Allen had prepared succession to a new generation. On April 29, 1968, T. Wilson was made president after being on the board only two years. Wilson was the first aeroman to rise so high, and he had done so by leaving that discipline long ago. He was as familiar with the aerospace division as he was with the military and commercial airplane divisions. An engineer was in charge again, but this was a very different animal from the old engineering chiefs like Claire Egtvedt. "*Real* different" to those who, like Boullioun, knew Wilson well; but it was too soon for others to understand all of what Boullioun meant.

Allen remained chairman of the board, and kept his office on the third floor of the headquarters building overlooking Boeing Field. He gave Wilson one piece of solemn advice as he handed over: "Always wear a hat when you go to New York." Wilson built himself a new presidential suite on a corner of the same floor, with bathroom and shower. Soon after this work was complete, Allen innocently asked Wilson if he could take a look at the suite. Wilson was delighted. He led Allen to his pride, the bathroom.

"Oh, hi, T sweetie," said a lissome young thing clad only in a bath towel, as Wilson opened the shower door.

The new president lost his usual steady grip and tried to back away, but Allen was transfixed, savoring the moment.

Having let Wilson squirm, Allen confessed—it was a setup, with Boullioun behind it.

One person whom nobody would have expected to indulge a joke of this kind was Ed Wells. Wells remained the unquestioned patriarch of the engineering elite. Allen's grooming of Wilson and Wilson's accession were an unvoiced wound to him. It was not that he resented Wilson, whom he knew as an able engineer and manager; such was Wells's nature that he had waited for a call that never came. Part of it was that Wells had never had the social enthusiasms that the presidency required. He and his wife, Dorothy, dined at the Allens many times, but both of them remained politely reticent and enigmatic. And part of it was that Allen had simply been there too long for Wells's own good; his time had come and gone.

Wells was by no means a spent force. He kept his disappointment largely to himself. Wilson was unaware of it. In fact, for the years Wells had left at Boeing, Wilson never made a decision on an airplane, military or commercial, until Wells had given it his seal of approval, even though that sometimes meant waiting for Wells to explore every option until his mind was settled. Wilson recalled to me a year's sabbatical that Wells had taken to teach at Stanford. On the few days that Wells spent that year at Boeing, there would be a line of senior engineers outside his office wanting advice. "It was just like taking dope for those guys," said Wilson.

Wilson's presidency was to mark the beginning of executive salaries that were more in line with the rest of the industry. On assuming the presidency, Wilson himself took a raise from $109,620 to $130,830; this put him some $6,000 ahead of Allen and nearly $50,000 ahead of Wells.

From his initial experience of the board, Wilson would have seen how Allen delegated Boeing's financial housekeeping to H.

W. Haynes, the cagey vice president of finance, as Allen also gave Prince, the company secretary, his own remit. Prince and Haynes were soul mates to Allen. Haynes stood for fiscal rectitude. He was politically, socially, and financially a conservative. He abhorred reporters and thought that Boeing's finances were no business of any newspaper. As secretive as a poker player, Haynes left the impression that he knew the cash flow down to the last cent. Wilson, however, divined that Haynes was not a "costs man"—he kept the books but, in a situation like the 747, had no control over what went out.

The 747 program, the largest drain on cash the company had ever known, obliged Haynes to see a lot of one of Boeing's nonexecutive board members, Tom Wilcox, vice chairman of the First National City Bank of New York (later Citibank). The New York bank led a syndicate that was funding the 747; in 1968 its own share was more than $34 million. Traditionally, Haynes was the man who went to the bank, but on the 747 he needed help. Most of all, he needed an airplane to show for the money.

There was great pressure on Stamper to fix rollout day, the moment when the 747 would "get out of the barn" and be anointed in a ceremony designed to get the maximum coverage across the world. Never mind that at a rollout the airplane can't fly; never mind the hoopla; rollout gave final substance to the dream, and it made bankers feel better. It was, however, something of a charade. The engineers hated it. An airplane was seldom ready when the rollout day came, and missing parts had to be faked by using cardboard patches painted silver.

"Everything was set," an engineer told me, "and so, by God, we'd roll it out if it took wooden wheels."

The 747 had no wheels at all when the date was set for Monday, September 30. N7470, as the first airplane on the line, had been part of the plant's learning curve. Not everything had mated as precisely as it should; some of the alignments as major sections came together were as much as a half inch out of true. This was not how Boeing did stuff. Remachining took time and cost money. Revisions were constantly made of the sequence in which assembly should be done. What looked right in a drawing often didn't work out on the shop floor. One of the final steps, attaching the landing gear, was nearly catastrophic.

The airplane was held up on rubber air cushions and rigid supports while the completed gear was moved into position underneath. As the cushions came out, the supports would take the weight until the gear was attached. When the final cushion was being moved out, a support gave way and another smashed right through the wing. The whole airplane now rested on only part of the cushion, which held until the gear was secure. Had the airplane been dropped on the floor from that height, it might well have broken its back, and the program would have been delayed for months. As it was, the hole was repaired and Stamper had a 747 to roll out.

Even then, all was not what it seemed. There *were* four engines hanging on the wings. But nobody had any faith that they would actually get the airplane off the ground. In a way, it was a miracle that they were there at all. Pratt had had at least a year less than would have been prudent in which to bring the JT-9 to the point of working reliably. The first engines to be run were prone to power surges and stalling. A B-52 had been converted as a flying test bed, and its appearance registered the generational jump in engine size. One JT-9 engine in its 747 nacelle replaced two of the bomber's J-57s and looked like a giant beer barrel suspended under the wing. This one engine provided more power than both the engines it supplanted. Development of the JT-9D had been sanctioned by Jack Horner, the head of United Aircraft. Horner had joined Pratt as a messenger in 1926, as Fred Rentschler took the company into the Boeing conglomerate. To get into the big fan business, Horner had taken risks similar to Allen's, building a new plant for the engine. The prototype JT-9D had been run for the first time at East Hartford in December 1966. By the late spring of 1968, Pratt had an engine ready for the B-52 tests, and these tests were still being worked through when the 747 rolled out. It was a slender margin—one engine, one airplane—on which to debug such an extensively untried machine.

The JT-9D flying on the B-52 delivered about 87,000 horsepower, around ten horsepower for every pound of its weight. The Wrights' first engine produced one horsepower for every ten pounds of weight. The most striking thing in the fan's appearance was its proportions. Compared with the old jets, the JT-9D was squat: its big forty-six-blade fan was eight feet in diameter, but only 128 inches long. More than 70 percent of its power came from the outer flow around the core, the bypass section.

As N7470 was prepared for rollout her engines were little more than decorative—but they were essential as ballast. Without the 9,600 pounds of each engine and its nacelle hanging there, the ship would have sat absurdly on its tail.

They might have played the Miss America anthem, "There She Is," but instead, the Everett High School bands assembled before the hangar that Monday struck up the Elgar march "Pomp and Circumstance." There was a thick overcast, and it was chill. Inside the plant, with the doors still closed, twenty-six stewardesses (they were not yet called flight attendants), one from each of the airlines that had ordered 747s, lined up for photographs under the airplane. The advent of the 747, icon of the future, coincided with Stanley Kubrick's *2001* and the Apollo moon missions. Courrèges made his name with skin suits that looked almost metallic. When they designed uniforms for the airlines the couture houses took their own flights of fancy. The designers treated the stewardesses as though they were intergalactic androids. Apart from one or two resolutely ethnic costumes (a kimono and a sari), the women waiting to fly the new big ship were styled in the idiom of Kubrick's space age.

Before the doors opened, there were twenty-five minutes of speeches, culminating in Allen's introduction of his old friend C. R. Smith, creator of American Airlines and now the Secretary of Commerce. Smith sang a tune that echoed back to Trippe's lobbying of Lyndon Johnson, that the 747 would be "a national asset" that would swell the billions of dollars earned by America's aerospace exports.

Although T. Wilson was the master of ceremonies, opening and closing the speeches, rollout was Stamper's day. Everett was his turf, the boggling plant his work. An impression was established then that never evaporated, that whenever the 747 caught the lights Stamper would be there in the reflection. In the ballyhoo, the Everett team—Sutter and the engineers, the plant construction team, the assembly line workers—were called "the incredibles." And at their head was Stamper. On rollout day the press office circulated an issue of the *Boeing News* with a profile of Sutter, but Sutter made no speech and was not in the limelight. He was still subsidiary in the pecking order, still not a vice president.

It was Stamper who ordered the doors opened. One of the new low-slung tractors needed to serve as an airport tug to the great ship crawled out first, with a trailing arm on the airplane's nosewheel. As the inimitable bulbous nose cleared the doors, the sun came out. None of the prodigious tide of promotion that had issued from the Boeing flacks was equal in impact to the first emergence into daylight of the 747. Only then was the scale established. Once the tail ("as big as a six-story house") was clear of the doors, she was swung alongside a stand. Boeing's corporate livery, a single maroon stripe at cabin window level and a flash on the tail, came from the same dull palette that began with the Dash-80. It was brightened at the nose, above the stripe, by the decals of the airlines that would fly the first 747s.

Stamper had orchestrated the dedication ceremony around the stewardesses. He called each of them up to the stand by name. There they were given a bottle of champagne. The idea was that on Stamper's countdown, all the bottles would break simultaneously on the 747's hull. But some of the stewardesses were not fluent in English, didn't follow the command, and began smashing bottles at random. It degenerated into a good-humored farce.

A flyby of a 707, 727, and 737, delayed by the weather, finished the party. For a brief moment, the euphoria took minds off the reality, that the 747 would go "back in the barn" for much of the winter. It was only a figurative phrase. Because the airplanes following the first in assembly would move up the line, N7470 would sit out on the concrete on the exposed plateau. All the work needed to get her ready for a first flight would have to be done in the open, in the worst weather.

Boeing's press escorts were shadowing reporters from all over the world. Among the aviation specialists brought to Everett for the rollout, one of the most respected (and feared) was Richard Cooke, of the *Wall Street Journal*. Cooke had a network of sources in Pan Am and Pratt & Whitney and other companies involved with the 747. His stories were taken as gospel on Wall Street, and stock prices followed whatever state of health he indicated. Cooke had ferreted out the discord among Boeing,

Pan Am, and Pratt. When it seemed that he might interpret this as the prelude to a complete breakdown between Pan Am and Boeing, Cooke was assured that it wasn't. Nonetheless, he stalked the story more assiduously than anyone.

In fact, what worried the Boeing press office on rollout day was not the 747's ailments, but the SST. Boeing didn't want SST stories to detract from the 747's debut. By then, the SST was in more trouble than the 747. Boeing's original swing wing concept had proved unworkable. Even using titanium, it was too heavy. Allen had to get the sponsoring FAA to agree to a delay, while Boeing reverted to the solution that Lockheed, which had lost the competition to Boeing, had pursued from the beginning: a fixed "delta" wing with separate tail.

Sutter, still beset with nightmares of his own, could reflect that the overbearing prestige of the SST team was no longer quite so apparent. Wells had been putting their work through his personal mincer, and finding it wanting. The SST was not an airplane, it was a collision of competing ideas, often individually brilliant but just as often incompatible with one another. John Borger sat on a committee of engineers from the airlines that had ordered the SST. He and the chief engineer of American Airlines, Frank Kolk, bore down with merciless ferocity on the Boeing engineers, "vying for who could shout the loudest," as Ken Holtby remembered it in painful detail.

For Sutter, the months between rollout and preparing for the taxiing trials and first flight were dominated by concerns with the JT-9D. There had been a hope that, following the example of the B-47, the 747 would be ready to fly on December 17, the anniversary of the Wright Brothers' flight. This was clearly now a pipe dream.

Early in the year, when the gap between the JT-9D's takeoff thrust and the weight of the 747 led to splenetic exchanges between Boeing and Pratt, a way had been found to squeeze, in a short burst, another fifteen hundred pounds of power out of the engine. By the end of 1969, in time for airline service, Pratt would deliver engines with water injection for takeoff. This was a trick originally used on military jets. Squirting distilled water into the turbines made the air-fuel mixture expand faster. But there was a catch: the weight of the water was more "dead" payload. It was tolerated by Pan Am only as an interim solution.

Before they reached Everett, the engines had to be flown to Chula Vista, California, where the nacelles were made and fitted by the Rohr Corporation. The first four engines, installed for the rollout, were coaxed cautiously into life for the beginning of the preflight procedures. Not until they were running reliably could any of the airplane's hydraulic and electronic systems be checked. One of the first tests was to pump fuel into the main tanks until it overflowed through the venting system, to test for leaks. Trials had already been done in a special chamber with individual fuel tanks, simulating high altitudes, with the lowest outside pressures, and subzero temperatures.

The airframe faced other critical tests that would not be completed until long after Jack Waddell made the first flight: applying stress loads beyond the limits Sutter had set for the structure until a wing snapped (this was not supposed to happen until it had endured loads nearly twice as great as any airplane would experience in service), and fatigue tests that would simulate twenty years of airline use and eventually destroy a whole airframe.

Sixty thousand pounds of test equipment went into N7470, doubling the amount of wiring. Cameras were installed to film crucial areas: one focused on the leading edge of the wing; another was on the flight crew at all times; another on the instrument panels; another under the belly to watch the landing gear and takeoff. Connie Smith, the preflight director, said it would be impossible for a crew member to cough or a rivet to pop without its being heard and seen on film.

Out on the tarmac at Paine Field, the working conditions were deteriorating. It was one of the worst winters the Pacific Northwest could remember, with driving winds and snow squalls. The engines were found to be extremely sensitive to wind effects, which could cause them to "flame out," or stall, when running at idling speed. The preflight unit could not release the airplane to flight operations until it was satisfied that the engines would provide stable power, and engineers from Pratt were literally living with the engines to nurse them into a state thought fit to fly.

Waddell did not at all like the prospect of taking an airplane off the ground with engines as fickle as these. Brooding on it, he presented Sutter with a worst-case scenario for the first flight. His concern narrowed to just a few seconds: how the engines would react as the attitude of the airplane changed as it left the ground. At lift-off there was an abrupt change of angle; the engines, like the airplane, rotated upward, and this changed what was called the angle of attack of the air entering the engines. There was actually no way of simulating this condition or its effect on the engines without committing the airplane to takeoff.

Waddell so little trusted the engines that he feared all four might stall at once—putting the airplane at risk in a situation with little margin for recovery. Without engine power, Waddell would lose all his hydraulics, and without hydraulics any ability to use the controls. The 747 would be a powerless bomb, full of gas. Sutter was persuaded to fit the test aircraft with backup electrical power to operate the hydraulics if the engines failed, and a rack of heavy-duty batteries was installed as the independent power source. Sutter thought this an alarmingly improvised solution to meet an alarming conjecture, but Waddell's writ was absolute when it came to judging the risks to the airplane.

It was not until the end of January that the airplane was passed to flight operations and Waddell could begin the first of several days of taxi tests. As his copilot, Waddell had chosen Brien Wygle, and as flight engineer Jess Wallick. For the taxi tests and the first flight the 747 would be a good deal lighter than with a full load of passengers and cargo. The main passenger cabin, stripped of fittings, was packed with rows of fifty-five-gallon aluminum beer kegs filled with water. The airplane's balance could be varied by pumping water from one group of kegs to another. More kegs were in the forward cargo hold, below the main deck, and to bring the total weight up to just over 476,000 pounds, mail bags were loaded in the aft passenger cabin.

Periods of snow interrupted the taxi tests. The runway had to be swept. When Waddell resumed the tests, stepping up the speed of his runs, there was an incident that sounded a warning about the risks of maneuvering the 747 on airport aprons. As Waddell used engine power to turn onto the main runway, a station wagon full of observers was blown into the mud, with its windows shattered, by the force of the engine exhaust. Waddell had argued for months that the 747 needed steerable landing gear to avoid making turns on high power. This episode sealed his case for the change, although it would cost $5 million in redesigning and tooling. It also began to look as though Waddell's fears about the sensitivity of the engines were well founded. An engine stall could be caused either by encountering a ten-knot crosswind or if the wind blew directly into the engine's tailpipe.

Toward the end of the first week of February, Waddell took the 747 to the brink of takeoff, at 150 mph. The nose lifted briefly. There was no blip from the engines. To lessen the risk of an engine stall from a sudden change in the angle of attack, Waddell decided that when the moment of final commitment came, he would climb out from the runway without lifting the nose too sharply. If the weather collaborated, everything would be ready for the first flight by Sunday, February 9.

While the taxi tests were carried out, the Allens had been escaping the harsh Seattle winter by taking a few days with the Trippes again at the Cotton Bay Club in the Bahamas. Told of the imminence of the flight, Allen flew back to Seattle on the Saturday evening; Trippe remained in the Bahamas. The press had been alerted that the first flight might take place the following morning, but Waddell was dubious that the weather would be good enough.

Early on Sunday, the clouds had lifted a little but the wind was gusting at between 10 and 15 mph, from the southeast. Just after 9:00 A.M., the pilot of a 707 that was being flight-tested from Boeing Field called the flight operations center at Everett and reported that a clearance was coming in from the west, toward the San Juan Islands. Waddell talked to the pilot and decided it was time to prepare to go. (This might seem a haphazard method of weather forecasting, but the Seattle area has a complex pattern of microclimates, and a firsthand report of this kind could be trusted better than any generalization.)

Allen drove up to Everett. As his station wagon turned toward the stall where the 747 was being fueled, he said to his driver, "You see all that concrete out there, Mac? If this airplane isn't a success there'll be grass growing up in those cracks on the apron." He got out of the car to walk out to the airplane with Waddell, looking as much in the dumps as he had on the day that Tex Johnston had first flown the Dash-80.

Waddell, zipping up a flying jacket over a business suit, was feeling the stress of the occasion, which had built up because of the delay. But he realized that Allen was more openly worried than he was.

"You know, Jack," said Allen, "I hope you understand that the future of the Boeing Airplane Company rides with you to-day."

"Well, Bill," said Waddell sardonically, "thanks a *lot*. I needed that!"

No matter how well prepared the team, the burden of a first flight was always the same. You had to take the airplane up and bring it down again. Only a fool would think that was easy. Case-hardened engineers would admit that however many first flights they had seen, their hearts were always in their mouths as they stood waiting to see a new airplane lift off.

16

Keeping the Jelly in the Mold

That's a big bowl of jelly up there. If those wiggles get together, why, the thing can just tear itself apart.
—Ken Holtby

The first engine was started at 11:07; all four were running within four minutes. Waddell set the stabilizer at an angle of 5 degrees, the first preparation of the controls for a takeoff. At 11:18 he called for the chase plane, an F-86 Sabre flown by Paul Bennett, to go, and the fighter took off a few minutes later. The 747 was then ready to roll, but Waddell saw buses moving on the runway. They were dropping off photographers and reporters, who were choosing their spots to get the best view, the photographers trying to guess where along the runway the 747 would lift off. Waddell waited for the buses to clear, and then called the tower to have the journalists moved farther away from the runway. He was concerned that they didn't understand how powerful the blast of the four high-bypass engines would be at takeoff, and would end up being blown into the mud like the engineers in the station wagon.

Once they were moved, the 747 taxied out from its stall, heading for the northern end of the runway. There was still thick cloud cover at fifteen hundred feet and the tower was making sure that the private planes cruising above were well out of the 747's flight path. The wind had dropped a little.

At the end of the runway, Waddell held the brakes on while the engines reached takeoff thrust and until Wallick called that he had "four stable engines." The brakes came off at 11:35 and 41 seconds. While restrained, the fans had created four hurricane-intensity vortexes ahead of the airplane as air was consumed by each of the turbines at the rate of nineteen thousand cubic feet of air a second. Now, with the thrust untethered, this indrawing of breath enveloped the airplane and moved like a great sigh through its frame as thrust was converted to velocity. Wygle called out the speeds, by the second, as the 747 accelerated. At 150 mph, Waddell felt the nose coming up. This was as far as they had gone on the taxi tests, but now he called, "Rotation," and committed to takeoff.

Only a handful of people knew about the batteries rigged up to provide backup power for the hydraulics in case the four JT-9s died as the nose came up. In these critical few seconds Waddell still had half the runway left, but if the engines stalled he would need it all, and maybe then some. Without the use of thrust reversers, and relying solely on his brakes on the slick tarmac, he would find plonking down the great plane and stopping it quite a thrill.

As the weight lifted from the sixteen wheels, relieving tire drag and friction, they passed 160 mph, and for a second, with the nose rearing up, the tail swung down toward the concrete. But lift supplanted gravity. The landing gear finally unstuck, and the tail lifted clear. Engine power remained stable.

Air immediately transformed the nature of the beast: like a beached whale released back into its natural element, the 747 was no longer ponderous but felt astonishingly nimble. She had left the ground after 4,300 feet.

Allen gripped Stamper and yelled against the blast into his ear: "She looks like the Powder River. A mile wide and a foot deep . . . too damned wet to plow and too dry to drink."

Waddell, the other Montanan, would have recognized the reference instantly, but Stamper didn't need Western roots to share the feeling. All around Allen and Stamper there were shrieks, screams, gasps. Some people were in tears. Many just could not believe anything so big could get off the ground; it seemed an awesome defiance of gravity. One young amateur movie photographer who had been too close to the backblast of the engines was blown onto his back and lay saturated in dirt-encrusted slush, his lens pointing uselessly into empty sky.

The airplane's energy and agility were communicable directly to Waddell's hands and feet—and to the seat of his pants. "Feel" was born into good pilots; Tex Johnston had it to the tips of his boots. Waddell had not flown barnstormers, but he had been a Navy pilot in World War II, and although the word "feel" conjured the lost intimacy of biplanes, where flying loads were truly felt through wires, Waddell still trusted his visceral responses to a new airplane as much as his technical intelligence. In those first few seconds, holding the 747 with his hands and feet, the seat of his pants was ahead of his head: the big ship was a natural. Surprisingly light to handle. Good response. Good feeling.

He made a shallow left turn, all the way through 270 degrees, bringing her back over Paine Field so the photographers could get some more shots.

At 11:39, in the radio room, Sutter and Webb heard copilot Wygle break away from his technical readouts and exclaim, "The airplane's flying beautifully."

Bennett in the F-86 picked them up. He called Waddell and said he was coming in close. He was Waddell's eyes where he had no eyes. The chase plane followed a delicate choreography—keeping clear of the 747's slipstream but moving gingerly all around it, over it, under it, alongside it. All the time Bennett was checking the 747's flying surfaces, the landing-gear doors (the gear and the wing flaps stayed down), the flaps, the engine nacelles. Bennett called Waddell: "The engines burn very clean. There's no smoke." Waddell did a little salute—rolling the airplane 30 degrees to the left, and then to the right. Cocky. There was a light chop in the air—the nautical term adapted well: they were nosing up toward the cloud base and they could feel the familiar instability, but it was moderated by the 747's size, as though the airframe just soaked up a lot of the chop that a smaller airplane would have been rocked by. Wygle could not contain himself. "The ole girl takes the turbulence great," he called out.

Wallick, though, had noticed a problem. The number one

engine, on the far left, was running 30 degrees hotter than the others, with no sign of the temperature dropping. They were familiar enough with the JT-9's temperament to know that they could live with the anomaly. One rogue out of four was a good score by the current standards of Pratt.

They climbed on through the clouds at four hundred feet a minute, and just after 11:42 they broke into clear, brilliant skies and smooth air, the world where the spirit rose with the sight of sun and where the peaks of Mount Rainier and Mount Baker were salient among a granite assembly anchored in layers of mist like those in a Japanese painting.

Waddell now had the visibility he needed to begin moving the airplane around, flexing its muscles, extending his sense of its feel. Airspeed was 160 knots. He tried some gentle roller coasters, moving the wheel backward and forward to see how the 747 pitched up and down. In the Sabre, Bennett was taking pictures. "Looks good," he told Waddell. It *was* good: it was uncanny how much like the simulator it was.

Many hours in the simulator had been spent fine-tuning the controls—the 747's elevators alone were as large as the *wing* of the 737. It was not just a question of finding the power to move these huge control surfaces. Waddell wanted an airline pilot to sit on top of the great ship and find her responses to be no different from those of a 707, or any smaller jet. That meant balancing the loads on each of the control surfaces through the hydraulic power system so that in the pilot's hands they were neither too light nor too heavy. To achieve this kind of sensitivity had brought penalties in weight, particularly in actuators powerful enough to move the massive elevators through 52 degrees in as little as a second.

And now, as they were still climbing west through twelve thousand feet to fifteen thousand feet over the Strait of Juan de Fuca, Waddell was ready for the first test of how good those controls would be in circumstances of serious failure. First flights were not limited to assumptions that all the systems would behave. Sutter's belt-and-suspenders fail-safe doctrine had put four independent hydraulic systems into the 747. (The Douglas DC-10, designed later, had only three and was to pay the price.) Waddell's flight test plan called for him to shut down two of them to see how he could handle the ship on the remaining backups.

Nobody could be sure how tractable such a huge airplane would be with the loss of two systems, which seriously degraded the power to the control surfaces. With the number one system gone, symmetry is gone: there is only half power to the left ailerons, the left outboard elevator, the right inboard elevator, and the upper rudder. (Sutter had split up all the main control surfaces so that surviving surfaces could compensate for lost ones.) At 11:54, Waddell told the tower he had closed down system number one.

"The handling is okay," he said. *"I can't tell the difference!"*

In less than a minute, he shut down the second system. Now he had totally lost use of the left outboard aileron, the left outboard elevator, and the right inboard elevator. He had only half power to both inboard ailerons and to both rudders. This time, there was a detectable loss of smoothness, but Waddell could still handle the 747 without becoming a muscleman: she was steady and—evidently—inherently stable. The simulator had not lied. No pilot would have trouble bringing even a fully loaded 747 home with its two primary hydraulic systems gone.

It was coming up to noon. After less than half an hour, Waddell had complete confidence in the airplane. Wygle and Wallick shared his nascent affection; the 747 had *personality*, a stateliness in motion that complemented her size, a kind of decorum. In the radio room, as terms of endearment began to flow, the euphonic calling of the names, "Waddell-Wygle-Wallick," was bringing wide grins. There was a palpable easing of tensions.

During a first flight there was always a moment when—if it went well—the preoccupation with getting the airplane off the ground and then monitoring every second of its progress became corrupted by the commercial imperatives. As Waddell flew into high noon, the Boeing bandwagon had to roll. The 747 had taken life. The journalists admitted to the airfield would never confess it, of course, but their motives were mixed. Would it crash on takeoff? Would something go wrong in the air? Such things had happened. But the new age in air travel had materialized, and the celebratory circus now began—and somewhere some bankers were waiting for news that their money had issue.

The photographers who had shot the takeoff—dispatched from newspapers and magazines all over the world—had been picked up by the buses and taken to a 727 reserved for them in which they would make an airborne rendezvous with the 747.

Vern Manion, Boeing's indefatigable air-to-air photographer, had already picked his own window and had his camera rigged; the 727 was now waiting for clearance from flight control—and for Allen, the only Boeing board member allowed on the plane.

Bennett was still trailing Waddell in the Sabre, knowing that his fighter's gas-guzzling would curtail his mission before Waddell had completed all his tests.

In the radio room, the rigorous scrutiny of the 747's life-support systems had to continue. As well as Sutter and Webb, there were a dozen flight test specialists reading out data from instruments in the airplane and keeping open lines to the three men in the cockpit. They had reached a moment when, for those like Sutter and Webb with intimate memories of the 707 test program, they would have to measure their best efforts against an old adversary, Dutch roll. Even the most rational engineer felt superstitious about this vice, and it was a high priority for a first flight to see how it would show its hand. They listened to the crosstalk.

With all four hydraulic systems restored, Waddell briefly put the 747 on autopilot to check the stability and trim, and then, just after noon, he put the outboard engine to idle to begin testing the ship's behavior with unbalanced power. They were cautious with the JT-9 throttles, because excessive movement had caused test engines to stall. There was a little buffeting in the clear air. With the gear still down and the flaps still at their takeoff angle of 25 degrees, the airplane's condition was what aeromen called "dirty," which tended to exacerbate the effects of buffeting, but the 747 soon settled down again into its natural, slightly nose-up gait.

The original flight plan had called for the landing gear to be raised and lowered at least once during the flight (flaps and gear, said the instructions, should be left down "until reaching a remote area"), but this was one of several conditions omitted from the plan finally agreed for the first flight.

At two minutes past noon, Waddell felt ready to find out whether Dutch roll could be induced. In its "dirty" mode, any tendency for the 747 to yaw, and therefore begin the cycle that led to a roll, would be heightened by the moment-effect of the dangling gear. On the 707, this had been the configuration that had rolled so badly in the hands of the trainee pilots that the airplane had fatally thrown off engines.

With the airspeed at 152 knots, Waddell switched off the yaw damper—Little Herbie's descendant. The yaw damper had what was called an "authority" in its movement of the rudder of 3.6 degrees in either direction; in other words, by moving of its own volition between these tight margins, it could sense and repress the airplane's tendency to yaw, and therefore stifle at birth the cycle that ended in a violent roll. Once he had turned off the damper, Waddell was—in principle, at least—back where the original B-47 test pilots had been when they had uncovered the vice—when, in the radio room at Moses Lake, Cook listened to Bob Robbins describe the condition and identified it, and went on to improvise the mechanical solution.

Of course, the 747, far from being the primitive beast that the B-47 had been, was the apotheosis of a regime inaugurated by the bomber and progressively refined. No one imagined that in Waddell's hands the 747 would get out of control and start gyrating about the sky. At the same time, though, Sutter and Webb knew that in some fundamental ways the 747 remained an unknown quantity: those great wings were more jelly than anyone had put into the mold before.

Waddell kicked the rudder. She snaked and wiggled, but—like some regal matriarch given a surreptitious pinch in the behind—refused to surrender her composure.

"*She doesn't want to Dutch roll!*" he called out, elated. Bennett was alongside, taking more pictures.

It went just as it had in the Iron Bird simulator, which they had never dared entirely to trust: not only was the 747 reluctant to yaw, but she positively did not want to roll. In Waddell's words, "She has good positive damping, very benign Dutch roll characteristics. We just put a good big tail on her and it worked."

Sutter had used more than just a tail that looked—and was—larger in area. Compared with the errant 707, he had thickened up the tail fin by 40 percent and given it more bite in the air. The yaw damper was still a required safety backup, but would be underworked on the 747.

At 12:08 they were ready for the next test, to lower the flaps from 25 degrees to 30 degrees. Cameras had been rigged in the belly of the airplane to record this, and they were turned on. The triple-slotted flaps were the largest control surfaces on the 747 and a *tour de force* of mechanical ingenuity. At this speed the aerodynamic forces on them were intense, and would increase with the additional 5 degrees of movement. As you look under a 747's wings with the flaps fully retracted into the wing, you see four pronounced ridges. These are felicitously called "canoes" and they conceal the tracks that guide the opening flaps into position.

Waddell felt the drag on the airplane increase as the flaps pulled down into the airstream. Then there was a jarring and alarming clunk, heard even in the radio room. It was followed by vibration.

Wygle called out calmly, "Okay. When we hit the stops on the thirty there was a sort of bump."

Bennett was underneath the 747, looking up right into the flaps. He called to Waddell, "I saw the right-hand inboard flap move a little bit, shake a little bit. What's normal?"

Waddell called out, "Sharp bump in cockpit. We're going back to twenty-five degrees."

Bennett stayed in position. "Everything still looks normal as far as I can tell, Jack. The only thing I've seen abnormal during the whole flight is just that inboard flap."

Waddell asked Wallick to leave the flight engineer's panel and go back through the monitoring machines and the water barrels into the main cabin and take a look outside at the right-hand flaps. They waited, flying on with the flaps restored to 25 degrees. Wallick came back and reported that a center segment of the inboard right-hand flap had been shaken loose and closed up a gap between the slots. It was vibrating. There was a risk it might come loose. (Afterward, it was found that bearing housings under the canoes had failed.)

At 12:10 Waddell called, "We're coming back in, because of the flap. No problem. Just being prudent."

The radio crosstalk had been on an open line relayed into Allen's 727, just preparing to take off, as well as to the radio room and tower. Allen called Waddell, reminding him that there was a party of people still hoping to fly alongside, and that Manion wanted to get air-to-air pictures. By now many of the reporters on the ground knew about Waddell's decision to terminate the flight, because they had been using shortwave radios tuned to the tower's channel. (The tower had been asked beforehand by the press office, anticipating the eavesdroppers, to switch to a secure channel, but had not honored the request.)

Waddell told Allen that there was enough time for the press plane to intercept him on his final leg into Everett, and the 727 took off, with Allen sitting on a jump seat in the cockpit. Then, to ease other minds, Waddell called Bennett. "What kind of a lookin' ship is this from out there, Paul?"

"It's very good-looking, Jack. Fantastic!"

"Rather majestic, you might say?"

"Roger. That's the word, Jack. Majestic."

Bennett had checked his fuel. He had just enough left to shadow Waddell back to Paine Field.

Waddell was flying east, back over the land and toward Lake Roesiger, where they would turn south for the final approach. By the time the 727 caught up with them, Waddell was relaxed enough to fly in formation with the Sabre off his port wing so that the photographers could get both airplanes in the shot, set against the sharp winter blue and the stubborn cloud cover below. At 12:46 the 747 was a mile north of the field's outer marker, once more reporting a light chop in the air.

From Paine Field the first sight of the 747's return was of the landing lights breaking from under cloud cover, disembodied like brilliant stars. A true sense of the airplane's size did not register until she was close to touchdown. A group in Boston had campaigned against the 747 on the basis that it would blot out the sky as it landed. This hysteria, as well as more sober doubt that the 747 would be manageable when pilots tried to place it safely in the center of the runway, evaporated in the final seconds of Waddell's approach.

Wygle was calling out airspeed and altitude. With two hundred feet to go, Waddell let her land herself: even without the full extension of the flaps that would normally have been used to help slow the landing, and coming in at a correspondingly higher speed of 150 mph, she was rock-steady. For the first time, the people watching near the runway saw the eccentric staggered landing gear, with the forward wheels tilted like the claws of a bird looking for grip.

At 12:51:55 the right-hand gear hit first, the left-hand gear hit and rebounded, and the nosewheel came down last and lightly, bearing very little load. When Waddell deployed the thrust reversers they threw up a wake of atomized slush from the melting snow alongside the runway. A light touch of the brakes, and N7470 rolled to a stop halfway down the runway. Wallick noted that the tires felt rough.

In an hour and sixteen minutes, a piece of machinery nominally costing $22 million but with a financial commitment of some forty times that behind it had, within a limited test, proved itself. What registered in Joe Sutter's mind, though, was that the 747 had gone from the original configuration drawings to its first flight in barely three years. Three years that had consumed a large slice of his life. (At one point Stamper had had to insist that Sutter take a vacation in Hawaii, he was so burned out.) He knew he could never do it again, and he doubted if anyone else would. Or would want to.

The Sabre came in to land.

Waddell was back on the ramp, shutting down his engines. The three of them on the flight deck carried out their final checks. They could not yet leave the airplane. The publicity machine required that they only come down the steps from the cabin when Allen was there waiting. They had to discard their flight jackets, don their suits, and come out looking like the straight-arrow types people expected.

They didn't mind. It was time to look happy.

A few hours after the first flight, Allen had tried to reach Trippe on the phone to tell him about it. Trippe was still in Cotton Bay, stranded there for at least two days because New York was closed down by a blizzard. The next morning, Allen sent Trippe one of Manion's pictures taken in flight from the 727 with a note: " . . . it was a beautiful sight . . . it is truly majestic and I wished for the Trippes many times."

Sixteen days later, after Waddell had flown two more tests with the flaps repaired, and successfully raised and lowered the landing gear, the 747 was ready to move to the flight test center at Boeing Field—and to give Allen his first ride. Sutter joined him. Waddell was impressed by Allen's fervor for the airplane, and by his curiosity. He wanted a running commentary on every detail. To those around him, Allen had undergone some internal catharsis after the 747's first flight. Now, watching him on the flight deck, it was as though the years had fallen away. His struggle to resolve a private contest between pride and fatigue went into abeyance. The flight acted like a spiritual remission.

He was ready for a gradual and happy abdication of power to Wilson, and was no longer interested in administration.

Seattle had so far not seen the 747. It was the first Boeing airplane not to have emerged from either Boeing Field or Renton; in flying across Puget Sound into Boeing Field, Waddell followed the coordinates called out from the tower to so many of his predecessors. Few could be blasé about such a moment. In World War II, the swarms of B-17s had tied the city's morale to the company's inventiveness. In 1955, Tex Johnston had claimed the company's dominance of the jet age with two delinquent rolls over Lake Washington. And now, to remove any doubt that Boeing lacked balls, here was the ship of ships. The big one.

Trippe had not been moved by the first-flight euphoria and its aftermath of hype. He wanted the airplane in service. By the time Waddell landed at Boeing Field, Pan Am's bodyguard of engineers in Seattle could see that Boeing was likely to miss its delivery dates. One reason, beyond Boeing's control, was that the FAA was taking a hawkish line on the 747.

This was induced partly by an almost superstitious public wariness toward an airplane that was so large. "Jumbo journalism" was becoming an industry. In fact, the term "jumbo" for the airplane had been coined by British reporters. None of the men at Boeing liked the epithet and they tried to discourage it, but they much preferred it to the alternative "airbus," which, to their relief, adhered first to the wide-bodies built by Douglas and Lockheed and was finally adopted officially by a new rival in Europe. Despite the relative success of the first flight, the reporters were looking for anything that could make the 747 seem spooky. There were stories that the 747's wake was so turbulent that other aircraft would be spun over into the earth by it. Even though the first flight had proved, if it had proved anything, that the 747 was a doll to land, fears persisted that airports would be disrupted by its approach.

The FAA had more soundly based concerns. The engines were the immediate problem; they were nowhere near reliable enough to be certified. But the airframe itself raised novel questions. The FAA had not even formed the criteria to test its endurance. Boeing had calculated that it would take around fourteen hundred hours of testing to get the 747 certified for airline operation, and 567 of those hours had been allocated for the FAA's own testing. But nobody in Seattle had expected to find more than *two hundred* FAA inspectors descending on one plane, N7470.

At Boeing Field, there was a delay while the airplane was fitted with new test equipment, including sensors on the wings for flutter testing. The F word remained the nastiest in the whole test repertoire. Nobody took it lightly, not even after thousands of hours of wind tunnel experience, not even after the Sutter twist. Flutter testing was high-risk flying.

All the known risks had been calibrated within a scientific flight plan, to be approached with care. At least, that was the hope. Waddell was a scientific pilot. But he was also, like any other pilot, still the guy with the airplane left in his hands alone. Regard the wing: 5,500 square feet of amalgamated parts with assorted duties, some independent, many collusive. An empty wing—a "dry" wing—never flew. When the 747 wing flew, it was a gas tank, a massive gas tank. Four massive gas tanks.

On his first flight, Waddell had more than thirty-one thousand pounds of fuel in each of his two inboard wing tanks, and around twenty-two thousand pounds in each of his outboard tanks. The weight of the fuel was not merely ballast in the wing, it was a calculated element of its loads and of its flexibility. As the weight of the engines, pods, and struts were an integral part of the aerodynamic balancing of the wing, so also was the weight of the fuel. The fuel could be drawn from each tank in sequences according to the influence of its weight. But before flight testing, nobody really knew *where* that weight would be needed and *when*.

As the 747's condition changed constantly—its weight fell with the burning of fuel, its speed moved upward to cruising speed, its pressurization loads increased with altitude—a single flight was, in reality, a succession of distinctly different conditions. The airframe—and *especially* the wings—had to be tuned to each of these conditions: tuned in such a way that all the dynamic forces remained in harmony.

The seditious influence in this regime, the true wrecker of harmony, the wanton invader of the airplane's structural integrity, was oscillation. The scientific intent of flutter testing was to advance by extremely cautious increments through each of the conditions of the whole envelope, knowing that at any moment an oscillation might begin. As soon as it did—and a pilot as good as Waddell would know it as the slightest of tremors picked up through the control column—you backed away, throttled back, until you figured out where the wiggle was. And what to do about it.

"This was a big limber airplane," says Joe Sutter, making it sound athletic. It was, too. "We did have to explore flutter very carefully."

Very carefully. Before Waddell took off to flirt with the F word, all the wing's nerve ends were wired through a telemetering system into recorders in the flight test center, and the recorders were hooked into the fastest computers they had. All this stuff was supposed to outpace Waddell's own reflexes. The wires would pick up a dissonance, the computers would analyze it, all while Waddell was getting alert in the seat of his pants. They had come a long way since Robbins and Osler had been unnerved by the cavorting B-47. ("Only my laundry would have known how scared I was to fly that bird," said Jack Steiner, recalling the experience.) But not so far that Waddell couldn't remember what it was like when the flutter hit. Sure, you could creep up on it by two or three knots at a time. But if you were a little too eager, or even if you were doing it ever so slowly, and it was up there waiting for you and it got you, it could feel like falling off a cliff.

And it *was* up there. And the wing sure was limber. As Waddell worked his way up through the higher speeds and altitudes, the jelly wouldn't stay in the mold. Day after day, the test center would watch the needles flicker and the computer tapes spin. It was as though the 747 were in intensive care; she needed nursing all the way. The dialogue tended to be laconic: "We have low damping, Jack."

Waddell's view of "low damping" was that the airplane would just sit there in the sky and shake.

Webb and Sutter had to take a long, slow walk around the interstices of their wing, reexamining every component of its integrity. It took six months before the 747 was cleared for flutter in all conditions—six months of laborious and meticulous test flying and six months of Sutter and Webb going back to the drawing board. Part of that time, the airplane was back in the shop for structural changes. At other times, Waddell was restricted to flying with prescribed fuel conditions, where only the juggling of the weight of the fuel between tanks kept the wing from oscillating.

The strain on the engineers was telling. Late on a Sunday evening, Webb had landed after flying on a flutter test. He went to his car preoccupied by the intransigent wing, barely hanging on to the fact that it was his birthday. As a shortcut, he drove down the runway toward East Marginal Way. Suddenly there was a spotlight on the car. Security men blocked his path. He was arrested for trespass and it took several phone calls to get released.

Underlying the disquiet over how long it was taking to deal with flutter was a question that would hardly bear thinking about: was the wing, already worked over once when the twist was devised, still susceptible to tuning without major redesign and retooling? The prospect of that in time and money was doom-laden. *"The wing is where you're going to fail."*

Sutter and Webb solved part of the problem by going against structural orthodoxy. Watching such a large mass wobble around in the sky, a structures man would have been inclined to say, "Make it stiffer, as stiff as possible." Nothing offended a stress or structures man like gelatinous metal. But—after much agony—Sutter and Webb went the other way. They *reduced* stiffness in the most errant components of the wing, the struts holding the engines. The engine nacelles had oscillated badly, and once this dance began the flutter had been appalling. Giving the struts more flexibility got things back into step—up to a point.

Then a serious tantrum broke out again at the highest speed, nine-tenths Mach, where flutter could be lethal. As before, it was in the outboard wing that the problem was acute. The twist was no cure. Here, to keep the test airplanes in the air, and to get airplanes into service, a desperate improvisation was employed. The outboard engine nacelles could be used as counter-weights against the wing's torsional misbehavior. But the nacelles were light and slender, carefully crafted aerodynamically to minimize drag. To put more weight into the actual structure of the nacelles would require elaborate redesign. What if . . . what if something densely heavy was slipped into the nacelle?

They calculated that to get the wing back into line they needed *seven hundred pounds* of ballast. One metal stood out as anomalously heavy for its mass: uranium. Yes—uranium, the ore from which the fissile material of a nuclear bomb was extracted! "Spent" uranium, despite its apocalyptic associations, was perfectly safe without shielding. And so the early model 747s (with only a handful of engineers knowing) flew with pellets of uranium molded as ballast into the outboard nacelles (it is still there).

While this engineering crisis was tormenting Sutter and Webb, Allen wanted to find a way of countering the more doleful strains of jumbo journalism. (Had they known of the 747's flutter problem, the wolves would have pounced in packs, but the flight test program was kept under tight security.) One bravura gamble suggested itself.

Allen called Wilson into his office. "T, I'm going to the Paris Air Show. I've lost my perspective. You're in charge of deciding whether the 747 goes to Paris. If you err, I recommend you err on the conservative side."

It was a typical Allen proposition: outline the gravity of a decision, delegate it, watch what happens.

Wilson, in turn, summoned Dix Loesch, the head of flight test. Better than Allen, they both knew the high risk involved. They had confidence in the airplane, but not in the engines. The power plant shop at Everett was like a field hospital, with sick engines wheeled in every day and new or repaired engines taking their place. With Waddell still progressing cautiously through the flutter testing, restrictions on the 747's airspeed and loading meant that a nonstop flight to Paris from Seattle—5,160 miles— would take more than nine hours. *Four engines for nine hours!* Could they do it?

The ignominy of failing would be a public relations fiasco; the reward of success a public relations *coup de théâtre*.

Wilson put Loesch on the line: "I want the criteria for sending this airplane to Paris."

Loesch decided that only one of the 747s in test had a chance of making it: N731PA, the fourth off the assembly line and the first of two dedicated to a program of simulating normal airline operations. Though eventually bound for Pan Am, it was still painted in the Boeing livery. (When Pan Am heard of the planned flight, it demanded that the airplane be repainted in the Pan Am colors, but Wilson refused—this was, he said, with typical belligerence, Boeing's show, and Boeing's risk, not Pan Am's). Loesch told Wilson that he wanted twenty hours' flying time with N731PA, and a full check of its systems, before he could clear it to fly the Atlantic.

Wilson accepted this. But a few days later, Loesch changed his mind. "We have ten hours on the ship," he told Wilson, "we have the engines working pretty well, and we now think that we would rather leave it where it is than put ten more hours on it."

Wilson was just where Allen wanted him: on the spot. One part of him wanted to cancel the whole thing. The other part remembered the Irish in Allen's eyes as he had proposed the flight. Wilson took the gamble.

On the surface, it looked as though Boeing already had enough confidence in the 747 to assign it like any normal airliner on a scheduled flight. Boeing announced that rather than leave from Everett or Boeing Field, the Paris flight would leave from the Seattle-Tacoma commercial airport. In truth, it was a flagrantly false display of confidence. The airport departure was chosen because it offered the longest runway, twelve-thousand feet, to give the fuel-heavy airplane a safe margin.

The flight was scheduled for early in the evening of June 2. Allen and his wife, Mef, had already gone ahead to Paris, a hint that Allen didn't want his schedule to depend on the gamble. T. Wilson delegated Mal Stamper and Tex Boullioun as the senior Boeing men on the flight, choosing to remain in Seattle himself, but going to the airport to see them off.

The fourth 747 was being flown by Don Knutson (pronounced K-newtson), known among the other Boeing pilots as a snappy dresser (he looked like a 1940s band leader, with a crisp mustache under a hawk nose and slicked-back hair) and, at Boeing generally, as an ultraconservative (Wilson placed him to the right of General Curtis LeMay, the unreconstructed adversary of the Evil Empire). Knutson's conservative instincts carried over into his piloting, and this was just what Wilson wanted. At the airport, Wilson could see that it would not be long after takeoff before the whiskey would be flowing in the passenger cabin; there were bars fore, aft, and above. (At Boeing headquarters, Wilson was one of the few people to keep drink in his office, and it was sparingly dispensed.)

Wilson cornered Knutson. "Knutson, who do you think is in charge of this airplane?"

Knutson hesitated, looking around at the assorted chiefs and very few Indians.

"You are, Knutson. Not Allen, not me, not Boullioun, not Sutter, or anybody else. *You're* in charge of this airplane."

"Yes, sir," said Knutson.

"If, for *any* reason, you have any indication that it's not good to go ahead, and you turn around and come home, or if you're over Montreal, and you want to land at Montreal, by God, you *land* at Montreal. Don't pay any attention to what anybody else says."

Wilson remembered Tex Johnston's aerobatics with the 707. Nobody could have been more removed in character from Johnston than Knutson. Keeping a straight face, he said, "And Knutson . . . when you get to Paris—*if* you get there—don't slow-roll this airplane!"

Knutson looked as though he had been compared with Karl Marx. *"Mr. Wilson!"* he said, affronted.

Wilson grinned, and felt the party was in safe hands, whatever happened.

The Twenty-eighth Paris Air Show was at Le Bourget, in the suburbs. Of all the international shows, Paris was the one most steeped in the continuing adventure of aviation. France maintained a sense of its own illustrious place in the history of flight. This spirit was resurgent in the Anglo-French Concorde—the "e" was an issue of pride and contention between the two parents of the SST—and in France's military aircraft, led by the superb Mirage series. American manufacturers accepted that Paris was the place where deals, if not done, were profitably stalked. Airlines were susceptible to the intoxicating combination of French banqueting and a joyride in the latest jet.

When Allen proposed the 747 audition, he knew that Lockheed, severely tempted to fly the C5a prototype to Paris but confronted with problems similar to those plaguing the 747, had lost its nerve and canceled.

On the morning of June 3, there was low and thick cloud cover over Le Bourget. Word had spread through the exhibitors' tents that the 747 had made it across the Atlantic and was on the last short leg between London and Paris. The public address system announced that Knutson was on final approach.

But where was the airplane?

They looked out into the clouds beyond the runway. No sound, nothing.

Then the 747 was there: still silent, floating down with flaps and landing gear fully extended, nose slightly up. Again, there was the trick of scale—at a distance she was similar in outline to a 707, and the eye could not frame her accurately against fixed objects to get a sense of proportion. Knutson kept her off the tarmac and did one slow flyby. Even pulling the drag of the flaps and gear the engines were a lot quieter than anyone expected, and they trailed no smoke.

Peering out the windows, Sutter, Boullioun, and their companions could see that the crowds were waving—it was a wonderful sight. No American airplane had landed at Le Bourget with an impact like this since Lindbergh. In the Boeing "chalet," where the heroic fliers would fall into the arms of waiting colleagues, Pan Am's brass, and selected VIPs, the champagne fusillade began even before the airplane had landed.

Knutson used little runway as he touched down, nine and a half hours after takeoff. The thrust reversers were the loudest announcement of his arrival. They taxied to a stall, where Allen was waiting at the bottom of one of the new extended stairways Pan Am had ready. Inside the airplane, Tex Boullioun led a charge to the door, but someone had forgotten to return the doors to manual from the automatic circuit that governed their use in flight. A steward attempted to open the door, but the escape chute mechanism was partially triggered and jammed it. Boullioun, steaming, had to wait while a technician was found who knew how to disarm the mechanism and get the door open.

Over the next few days, hundreds of airline chiefs, rival manufacturers, assorted VIPs, and Britain's Prince Philip climbed the stairway to get their first taste of what flying in the 1970s was going to be like. Denied its colors on the airplane, Pan Am put its own stewardesses aboard in Paris and beat its own drum.

The wide-body had arrived. Only the 747's creators knew how precariously balanced between success and embarrassment the flight had been. Number four made it back across the Atlantic to Washington, where there was more drum-beating and some overt lobbying of politicians to point out how much foreign currency the 747 would earn. Only on the last leg back to Seattle, after flying 11,495 miles, did Knutson have a problem. Over Moses Lake, the very spot where Allen had connived to seduce General Wolfe with the B-47 and thereby began the whole technical journey to the 747, one of the engines developed a surge and had to be shut down. They were only 140 miles from Boeing Field and could make it on three engines without any risk.

Once on the ground, and without pause, Knutson climbed into his car and drove back across the Cascades to attend one of his children's graduation ceremony.

17

The Ink and
Iced Water Men

"In 1966," mused one Boeing manager to T. Wilson, "everything this company touched turned to gold."

It was true. Three years earlier, Boeing had seemed the most dynamic high-tech company in the world. It had announced the 747 and was selling the idea of a complete family of jets, from the 737 through the 727 and the 707. They were producing missiles, spacecraft, rocket boosters for the Apollo program, helicopters, hydrofoils. The workforce had doubled, from 49,000 to more than 100,000.

How different it was now. Wilson had only to look at one graph, plotting the orders of commercial jets. At the beginning of 1968, they had orders for 328 aircraft, worth $2.6 billion. At the beginning of 1969, it was down to 164 aircraft, and the line on the graph was heading to zero. There had not been one sale to a U.S. trunk airline for months, and none was in sight. You didn't need a graph to portray the abyss if you went to Everett. There were seventeen 747s sitting out on the tarmac with 9,600-pound cement blocks hanging under their wings where the engines should have been. Mal Stamper saw the day coming when the value of the immobilized 747s would exceed the net worth of the company. The airplane that flew to Paris had had a charmed life; there were barely enough functioning engines for the five 747s in the test program to continue flying, and the test program was further dislocated when the third aircraft suffered serious damage in an embarrassingly public crash.

The pilot involved, Ralph Cokely, was known for an almost obsessive precision in his flying, not in itself a disability in a test pilot. Dix Loesch selected Cokely to fly the aircraft from Everett to Renton, where its cabin was to be stripped of test equipment and fitted with seats. Renton is by far the shortest of Boeing's runways, only 5,280 feet, compared with Boeing Field's 10,000 feet, and no 747 had landed there before. Cokely was anxious to use every inch of the strip. He calculated his descent over Lake Washington to the last inch. The runway ran to the edge of the water, with only an abutment of rocks between it and the lake. Cokely's approach looked characteristically on the dime, but he misjudged his final height—by just a few inches—and the landing gear was ripped off on the rocks. The 747 skidded down the strip spewing sparks from its belly.

The only gloss that the Boeing press department could put on this, the first 747 crash, was that the landing gear had been designed to shear off without jeopardizing the rest of the airplane, and particularly without puncturing a gas tank and causing a catastrophic fire, and it had done just that. T. Wilson, however, was not amused. Cokely was fired. There had been two other Cokely incidents before this one: while he was taxiing out at Boeing Field his engines had blasted away a maintenance stand on the flight line without his noticing it (he was lucky nobody was caught in the blast), and, without any reference to his flight plan, he had landed a 747 at Las Vegas. Nonetheless, he recovered his reputation at Lockheed, where he headed the flight test program for the Tristar.

Boeing's survival could be paced by a ticking clock. To get Pan Am's first airplanes delivered and into service by early 1970, the FAA would have to complete the certification process by October or November, at the latest. But Loesch was saying that there was no way of meeting that deadline: with the engine problems they had, it would slip to March 1970. A handful of people at the top of the company knew that that would be too late. By then, the company would be out of money. Tex Boullioun was among those who knew the dire truth; in fact, more than anyone else, Boullioun found himself at the center of a converging fate. He knew the daily state of the 747 program, and he knew the numbers in red ink.

Every month, Boullioun and Haynes went to First National City Bank in New York. The advance payments from Pan Am and other customers were supplemented by money from the bank syndicate, but there was never enough. To keep the 747 line moving, they had to ask the banks for more. And more. The time came when it needed more than the fiscal propriety that emanated from Haynes to strengthen the bankers' nerves. In the past, people had felt that Haynes always had money salted away somewhere that could bail out a program, but this was a crisis of a different order. Haynes needed Boullioun: he was a persuasive interpreter of the technical background. He would brief the bankers while Haynes sat alongside. "We were getting to the point," Boullioun told me, "where they were talking about—*no more*. I had to go in and do a toe-dance. They had to accept us to some degree when we talked about what it was really going to cost us. We knew more about it than they did. I had to convince them that we were going to make delivery date, and then we'd start getting paid, and that would take the pressure off."

Boullioun was messianic—had he followed his early vocation and gone into the priesthood, there is no telling where he would have stopped. He predicted that they would end up selling six hundred 747s. ("Nobody paid any attention to him," Wilson recalled, "but he was right.") But, as beguiling as he was, with his winning Arkansas drawl and his zealot's passion, Boullioun did not deceive himself: if the 747 missed its deadline by as much as a few months, the banks would shut them down. It really was that close. The company's total debt had already well exceeded its net worth of $796 million. Years later, even some of the central figures in the drama were not quite sure how the company survived. "Boeing," said one of them, with forgivable hyperbole, "will remember its three years of crisis about as long as most men will remember Pearl Harbor."

But, as with Pearl Harbor, the lingering fascination of this crisis lies not only in the measures taken to survive it, but in the question of how it happened in the first place. On this— again as with Pearl Harbor—no two accounts fall easily into step with each other. Was someone asleep on the watch? Or was it the more comprehensive failure of a system?

It is striking how recumbent Boeing's directors had been. Well down the path to ruin, in the middle of 1969, they had made no intervention. Because the 747 program was hemorrhaging so spectacularly, and because the aircraft itself so well expressed hubris, this problem obscured more fundamental deficiencies in the management of Boeing that should have been tackled much sooner than they were. The truth was that the commercial division had grown beyond the capacity of its managers to control it. The 747 program, although the greatest drain on funds, was actually as much a victim of this organic malaise as it was a cause of it. The directors' incuriosity toward the 747 reflected their blind faith in Allen and their acknowledgment of him as the airplane's begetter, as well as their sympathy for the valedictory achievement it represented for him.

Allen knew what the numbers were. He didn't seem alarmed by what they meant. When the board did ask about the program's troubles, it was easy and credible for Allen to put the blame elsewhere, principally with Pratt and partly with Pan Am and its incessant demands. Allen's confidence that the 747 would turn the corner rested, in turn, on his confidence in Stamper. Stamper never flinched in his belief that the 747 would bring such an advance in airline economics that no airline in the world with any claim to being an international carrier could afford to be without it.

Jack Steiner, who knew that all his predictions of cost overruns had come home to roost, nonetheless respected Stamper for his implacability in dealing with the board. He allowed no doubt to blemish the reports he gave to them. For his part, Steiner defended the 747 by trying to expose the underlying fallacy of the SST: its economic arguments were all based on comparisons with the costs of the 707. Steiner pointed out that if, instead, the 747's costs were used, the SST would suddenly look a lot less attractive, even when using the patently specious fuel price of ten cents a gallon, on which the SST's fuel consumption had been predicated.

The impression is very clear that Allen and the board succumbed to a mutual self-deception that, somehow, things would turn around. There was no evidence that they would; the country was in recession and airline traffic was falling far short of the growth rate Boeing had predicted when the 747 was conceived. They knew full well that they were in a cyclical business, and were in a down cycle. It was beyond Allen's energies and inclinations—beyond his will—to face what had to be done to save the company. In the depths of 1969, he ceded the role of chief executive officer to Wilson, who stared unblinking into the abyss.

Wilson called Boullioun into the empty boardroom on the third floor of the executive building.

"Boullioun," he said, "in bed last night, I got to thinking. We're going broke. The board's not smart enough to realize it, but I don't think they can avoid it for six more months. And then they're going to have to do something. And the only goddam thing they can do is fire me. Only thing they can do. If they do, they're sure as hell not going to replace me with anybody inside. So they'll go out and hire some ink and iced water type, and he's gonna come in and we're gonna stop spending any money on anything that doesn't have anything to do with a contract.

"And he'll probably screw up the research and development, and everything else."

Boullioun was always plain "Boullioun" to Wilson, but the formality was part of a long-nurtured familiarity, an inversion of the normal first-name habit that masked—to anyone who didn't know them well—how trusting a partnership they had. Now the partnership was on the line.

"Boullioun," said Wilson, "I've got a better idea. That is that you and I do what that ink and iced water type was gonna do. We can do it better. *We'll* put the screws on. And then we'll take about ten million dollars and do what we ought to be doing on research and development. We're in so much trouble ten million dollars is a drop in the bucket."

He paused.

"And Boullioun. If we don't turn this thing around, there's one guy going before me. And you know who that is."

Boullioun grinned.

Wilson told him to start by cutting $100 million out of the commercial division's operating plan.

This conversation was the beginning of a period that traumatized both Boeing and Seattle.

*   *   *

Everette Webb was on the flight deck of N7470 with Jack Waddell and some FAA inspectors. They had climbed up to 31,000 feet. Waddell was demonstrating the effect on the engines of movements of the throttle. It was unnerving. When Waddell pulled the throttles back rapidly, there was a bang loud enough to rattle the cockpit and a sheet of flame came out the engine exhausts; two, sometimes three engines would stall at a time. Waddell was not exaggerating the problem: sooner or later, any airline pilot might be tempted to use his throttles in this way, without the advantage of the height at which Waddell was flying. At this altitude they had enough sky under them to restart the engines and resume cruise speed without risk.

Quite often, the engines would stall with even relatively moderate movements of the throttle. When Boeing complained to Pratt, Art Smith, the president of the company, flew out to Seattle. In a management of uneven quality, Smith had always stood out as a brilliant engineer. He arrived at Everett as a skeptic; he suspected that to force the stalls Waddell was going beyond what was needed in normal airline operations.

This time, Wilson and Smith were in the cockpit as the airplane reached cruise altitude.

"Mr. Smith," said Waddell, "I know how to make the engine backfire. I want you to watch my hand movements. You'll notice they're very normal. I'm not banging the throttle against the dashboard."

He pulled one throttle back with a firm but steady movement. The airplane was rocked with a bang.

"Now," said Waddell, "just to show you that's not an unusual engine, I'm going to try number two."

There was another bang, another sheet of flame.

"And now . . . number three."

But before his hand could move, Smith shouted, "*Stop!* I get the point. We're going to fix that. We'll worry about how the hell it gets fixed from a business standpoint, but we're gonna fix that."

The experience had shaken Smith; Wilson, too, had not been a model of composure as the airplane shook. When it stalled, the big fan had a kick like a herd of buffalo.

The vice was not quickly eliminated. Early 747s were fitted

with what was called a throttle bar, which reminded pilots when they were throttling back to pause, until the engines stabilized, before putting them to idle speed.

Pratt's engineers were paying the price of a reckless commitment. No new commercial jet had previously flown with an engine that had no background of development in military aircraft before it was adapted to airline use. With the JT-9D, the testing that would normally have been regarded as experimental was, instead, being carried out on airplanes that were within only months of going into airline service—if the FAA would certify them, and the airplane.

In the effort to get the 747 certified, Everette Webb, who knew nothing of the grim deadlines of the balance sheet, emerged as something of a hero. He refused to accept Loesch's pessimistic forecast that certification would not be complete until March 1970. Webb recommended to Stamper that they should abandon the planned sequence of tests and, instead, improvise the flight testing around whichever equipment was available at the time. Week by week, said Webb, if the test flights were shuffled around, Webb's technical staff would adapt to what was possible.

The flight testing had, essentially, to be built around the state of the engines—literally, the state of each engine as delivered. Keeping track of the engines was like moving pieces on the Mad Hatter's chessboard. Any change to an engine changed the specification, and each specification had to be newly certified. At one point, eleven different certification procedures were being carried out, with some airplanes flying with several different versions of the engine. Eighty-seven engines were used in the testing, and sixty of them were destroyed. On N7470 alone, Waddell had thirty unscheduled engine changes. (Webb recalled wryly that Boeing developed the fastest engine-changing teams in the business—until the Rolls-Royce RB. 211 went into service on the Lockheed L-1011.) The FAA took the view that when engines of a different specification were on the same airplane, its certified performance should reflect the capacity of the least efficient engine, a policy of the lowest common denominator. This had direct repercussions for Pan Am, because it meant that the payloads of its early aircraft would be hobbled by Pratt's inability to bring all the engines up to standard in time. But by far the most serious problem with the engine, and one that was very nearly the last straw for Pan Am, emerged only after the certification tests were under way.

The nature of the problem threw unwelcome light on the way obligations were defined between Boeing and Pratt. Under certain flight conditions—including the high angle of attack that had, from the beginning, worried Waddell at takeoff—the contrasting size of the huge fan at the front of the engine and the turbines behind it induced bending stresses in the turbine casing. Pratt's engineers had not foreseen this effect (it would never have shown up in static tests). After a relatively short time in flight, the engine casings were distorted. The fit of casing and turbine blades was critical to the engine's efficiency; a high level of finesse went into ensuring that the casing was perfectly circular, with very fine tolerances for the clearance of the blades inside it. Now, with the cases bent out of true, the clearances were erratic.

Webb put it succinctly: "We had an unround situation." The unround situation became known as "ovalization," and—with shameless nerve—Pratt blamed Boeing for it. The bending happened, said Pratt, because of the way Boeing had anchored— or, to use the engineers' term, "grabbed"—the engine to the pylon. T. Wilson was dubious of this claim from the beginning, and contested it. But, as with so many of these disputes, the problem had to be fixed by the engineers while recriminations raged between the executives.

As Webb began, in his systematic way, to try to analyze the flight condition that was bending the casings, defined as deflection under loads, he realized that Pratt lacked the computing capacity to deal with it. For the first time in the whole history of the partnership between the two companies, he persuaded Pratt's engineers to show Boeing their drawings for the engine.

Webb suddenly realized that Boeing had a computer program that could be brought to bear on ovalization. It had been developed years earlier, during the design of the 727, to study the complex stresses where the tail met the fuselage. Ironically, at that time the program had been more than the computers could digest. It took an hour and a half to run the full condition, and the computers surrendered after forty-five minutes. By

1969, however, the computers were easily able to handle it. With the help of Pratt's drawings, Webb's team diagnosed how the engine casings were being stressed under high angles of attack. Until the engine casings could be modified, a temporary fix was designed with the use of a new Y-shaped yoke providing stiffness between the engine and the pylon.

Even this could not be engineered in time for Pan Am's schedule, and Webb found himself caught in the crossfire among Pan Am, Pratt, and Boeing. After a conversation with Pratt, Allen called Webb—who "was really p.o.'d," said Webb—to announce that they were suing Pratt. Boeing's lawyers descended on Webb for the ammunition to prepare litigation, while at the same time he was required to continue the struggle with the Pratt engineers to get the engine certified.

Despite these warring interests, Webb's belief that they could have the 747 certified in time for Pan Am to put it into service early in 1970 was borne out—but only by a whisker. The FAA was set to certify in November, but one vital document went missing. It had been inadvertently tossed into a wastepaper basket, which had then caught fire. Two weeks were lost while it was replaced, and finally, early in December, the 747 was cleared to carry its first paying passengers.

In Seattle, Christmas 1969 would be visited by such merciless horsemen that Ebenezer Scrooge would seem like a soft-centered philanthropist. Boullioun was determined to meet Wilson's decreed target of cutting $100 million from the operating budget of the commercial division, but Wilson had not stopped there. In October he called together all the company's top managers and said he wanted new operating plans within thirty days: "We can afford no more tolerance towards employees who do not produce or whose capabilities are marginal." The impending massacres were not just a reflection of the immediate emergency; they were the beginning of a root-and-branch change in the way Boeing functioned. It would never be the same company again. Nor would Seattle look on the company in the same way.

Boeing's share of the local economy had grown to 20 percent, and the city was bound to suffer from a corporate housecleaning on this scale. Over the next eighteen months, sixty thousand jobs were eliminated—thirty thousand of them production workers. Seattle's unemployment rate would peak at an unprecedented 17 percent. But Wilson was as ruthless at the top as he was at the bottom. The corporate headquarters staff of seventeen hundred was cut to fewer than two hundred (the carnage was more complete than the figures suggest: most of the surviving staff were replacements). Eleven vice presidents left. A generation of managers virtually disappeared overnight. Wells, probably distressed to see so many of his contemporaries emptying their desks, told Wilson he wanted to retire. Wilson persuaded him to stay.

At Pan Am, Harold Gray was losing his struggle with cancer, and he had been succeeded by Najeeb Halaby, a former head of the FAA. With typical caprice, Trippe had hired Halaby from the FAA in 1965, with the clear intention of making him his heir, and then pointedly passed him over in choosing Gray. At the FAA, Halaby had been a Kennedy appointee; he was a gilded knight of the New Frontier, a graduate of the Yale Law School and a former Navy pilot. Halaby bore a direct responsibility for Pan Am's profligate investment in the 747. Swept along by the euphoric forecasts of airline traffic growth made in 1966, he had recommended that an option for another eight 747s, bringing the total to thirty-three, be taken up.

Halaby's arrival at the top of Pan Am brought more candor and less obfuscation into the negotiations with Boeing. He couldn't wait to get his hands on the 747—literally. He held a current license for piloting commercial jets, and liked flying himself around the country in Pan Am's executive Fanjet Falcons. On November 7, he flew into Boeing Field, where the fourth 747—the airplane that Boeing had flown to Paris—was waiting. Halaby was given the very rare privilege of taking the left-hand seat in the cockpit—the captain's seat. He was talked through the engine start procedure and the preflight checks by Waddell, and then confidently turned onto the runway and took off. He turned south and did a few of the customary circuits over Mount Rainier, trying out the airplane in turbulence. Then, after reaching cruise altitude, he began throwing the 747 around: stalling out of steep climbs, whipping into tight turns, feeling the controls with two engines out. He put down at Moses Lake and did takeoffs and landings with one engine out, flying as though back in the Navy.

Halaby's panache, coming after Gray's infirmity and

Trippe's opacity, was good for Pan Am's morale. And his directness was welcome to Wilson, even though he turned out to be a tough adversary. Wilson had been running out of patience with Kuter, who ground exceeding small; he told Halaby he couldn't work with Kuter any longer, and from then on, major outstanding disputes tended to be settled directly between Halaby and Wilson, and frequently over the phone, while their aides stood by. It was quite a contrast to the Allen-Trippe calls, where much was said but nothing of material importance was ever settled.

Almost immediately, their horns locked in the most severe dispute of the three years of negotiation. Irked by the spate of engine problems, Pan Am threatened to pay only half the final payment due on the first 747s, and to withhold the rest as progress payments as the airplane was brought up to the performance guarantees. This amounted to $4 million being withheld on every airplane, and to Wilson it accelerated the prospect of Boeing's bankruptcy. When Wilson protested, in a telephone conversation with Halaby at the beginning of December, Halaby was adamant: "We want the progress and then the payments, not the payments and then the progress."

The airline was suffering from an acute decline in business. Halaby told Wilson that Pan Am would be reporting a "very substantial loss" for the year, that he feared a suit by stockholders, and that he was "letting off" fifteen hundred staff, the first cuts at Pan Am in fifteen years. Nonetheless, to his later cost, Halaby failed to decapitate Pan Am's bureaucracy, as Wilson was doing at Boeing, and it continued to function as it had under Trippe, with the diffused energy of a pool of molasses. Then, playing a card he knew would caution Boeing, Halaby said that his lawyers were arguing that they had a case against Boeing, for loss of revenues caused by delay in delivery.

With some justice, Wilson argued that all the problems were really with the engines, and that the 747's aerodynamic performance was actually better than forecast. In a call to Halaby, he pleaded that "the Boeing Company is sitting here with God only knows how much money wrapped into these airplanes, and we can't take an engine that is ten percent deficient, eight or six— whatever the number is—Pratt knows the spot we're in." Using some soapy rhetoric, Halaby left the dispute unresolved: "We know you have a strong heart and a high conscience, and we'll ponder this."

As the time neared for Boeing to tender the first 747 to Pan Am, the potentially traumatizing risk remained that Halaby would not accept the airplane. That, at least, was the threat. In fact, both Wilson and Halaby knew their companies could suffer mortal losses on the stock market if the first 747 was rejected. Jumbo journalists would get confirmation of the story they had been sniffing out for months, and the publicity would be horrendous. Halaby also had to remember another pressure: to get Pan Am's wide-body advantage established across the Atlantic before TWA received its 747s. He told Wilson, "You can't imagine the let-down feeling that exists around here by the fact that our lead time, which we bought with millions and millions of deposits, seems to be disappearing."

It took a long call between Wilson and Halaby on December 12 for each man to realize that he had pushed the other to the wall, that there was nothing more to give on each side. At 7:30 that evening Wilson told Everett to release the first 747 to Pan Am, and Halaby wrote a check for the final payment, less $2 million as a withholding—Halaby had cut his original demand in half. (It was still a stinging penalty, and it was never revealed at the time.) The rest of the money was to be paid in installments according to Halaby's "progress and then payment" principle. A prolix ten-page letter from Boeing spelled out the schedule under which this was to be done.

The next morning, a Pan Am crew which had been held waiting in San Francisco flew the 747 from Everett nonstop to Nassau, in the Bahamas, with a load of cargo, and then on to the Pan Am base at Kennedy Airport in New York.

The 747 chosen to make the first flight across the Atlantic with paying passengers was christened *Clipper Young America* at Dulles Airport, Washington, by President Nixon's wife, Patricia, on January 15. Only one of the world's airports, Orly in Paris, was actually equipped in time with a new terminal that could provide the comfort of walking directly into the airplane through movable piers, rather than by exposed stairs. On January 21, when the first passengers boarded *Clipper Young America* at Kennedy, it was a bleak, bitterly cold evening and the wind chill caught the passengers exposed on the open stairway. The 747 taxied out for takeoff at 7:29 P.M., slightly late. Then it taxied back again. It was a familiar problem: wind gusts were playing havoc with the idling engines, and they would not stabilize for takeoff. The passengers were disembarked and bused off the airport to restaurants.

Seven hours later, *Clipper Constitution* did get off the ground and headed for London, with 324 passengers—so well catered already that they passed up dinner and ate breakfast at noon, over Ireland. There were no movies, either, since the reserve airplane had not been prepared for them. It was a fast flight, only six hours and ten minutes. Despite the delay, most of the passengers were enthusiastic. The *New York Times* was moved to issue a prophecy that sounded a lot like Trippe's dream: "The 747 will make it possible for more and more people to discover what their neighbors are like on the other side of the world." From the *Christian Science Monitor* came a more spiritual hope: "As the world's physical and mental problems mount, so does the need for men to recognize the universality of their brotherhood and the oneness of their basic interests."

As the body count rose at Boeing, Wilson turned to those who flourished in adversity. Inevitably, one of these was Jack Steiner. Steiner had been loyally beating the drum for Boeing wherever it seemed likely the dwindling sales could be revived. Now Wilson gave him a large piece of Boeing to attack: he put him in charge of the Renton division, where Steiner's single greatest contribution to Boeing, the 727, looked like a rapidly declining asset, and where the 737 seemed to be dead in the water. The stretched 727, the 200, had been a cheap line extension, and looked like it: two ten-foot "plugs" in the fuselage, and little else. It was not sufficiently better than the 100 to create a new market. What was worse, the airlines already thought of it as being of a past generation, and the airplane was heartily detested by those living around airports for being noisy and dirty.

Long before he took over at Renton, Steiner had been convinced that he could give the 727 another lease on life. He reasoned that with all its development and tooling costs long since paid off, by using some "creative engineering" the capital cost of a far better airplane could be minimal. The old 727s had good economics but marginal range. Steiner needed a new engine. Despite Boeing's agonies with the JT-9D, Steiner went to Pratt and asked if its engineers could tweak the JT-8D on the 727, both to get more power and also to clean it up—reduce its noise levels to meet new FAA standards, make it smokeless, and get more fuel efficiency. Pratt said it could oblige—but only if Steiner ordered the engine blind. Late in 1969, Steiner got Wilson's approval to order thirty "new-generation" JT-8Ds in the hope that he could wrap a more seductive airplane around them.

On the face of it, it was extraordinary for Wilson to put more money and faith into the 727 at the very time when he was taking a meat cleaver to the organization. It was exactly what an "ink and iced water" man would not have done. Gambling on the 727 was like pushing an old workhorse into the paddock just as it was about to be taken over by a pack of lithe new yearlings.

Boeing would enjoy a very short monopoly of the market for the revolution it had initiated, the wide-body airplane. Immediately on the horizon were the responses of its two old rivals, Lockheed and Douglas. Both had seen Boeing's exposed flank: the 747 was too big for most domestic American trunk routes. Although some airlines, like American and United, had ordered 747s, they had done so simply to be able to offer a wide-body, not because they thought it was the *right* wide-body. Douglas was ahead of Lockheed by eighteen months. Its trijet, the DC-10, was sized for domestic carriers, as was the Lockheed L-1011 Tristar. However, more distant and unheeded as a challenge to all three American companies was an idea that had been originated in America, been rejected, and then been adopted in Europe. It was an idea as far-seeing and intuitively brilliant as the Douglas DC-3 had been.

When it came to sizing an airplane for the American domestic routes, one number transcended all others, the number of "city pair" routes. These were the most densely traveled trunk lines, routes like New York-Chicago and San Francisco-Kansas City. As soon as the chief engineer of American Airlines, Frank Kolk, set eyes on Sutter's fuselage cross section, he saw a different use for it. A wide-body that was optimum size for American need carry only 250 passengers, with a range of around 2,500 miles. And the new fans delivered so much power that you would need only *two* of them to make this package one of irresistible utility. Kolk talked to Sutter about his "wide-body twin," but Boeing had its hands full. Kolk's vision died finally at the hands of his boss, C. R. Smith, who had done so much to bring the DC-3 into being. Smith said that it was too soon in the development of the big fans to risk the safety of a large airplane on only two engines—a strangely irrational and untypically reactionary view for Smith to take, since the twin-engine DC-3 had rendered the old trimotors into dodos. In the relatively short term, Smith had something of a case, but in the time it would take to develop the wide-body twin the fans would, like all engines, get debugged and become dependable.

Kolk had very accurately described an airplane that would be of enormous appeal practically everywhere in the world. The logic of his concept was perceived and rapidly adopted by a consortium of European manufacturers for an airplane they called the Airbus, the A300B. It would be a long while before Boeing woke up one morning and realized that its most formidable international competitor had been born, transmuting Sutter's wide-body and Kolk's twin into an appealing family of airliners.

Steiner, meanwhile, realized that airlines (and passengers) that were being sold the idea of a new generation of wide-bodies saw the 727's cabin as a tired old tube. In warming over the 727, he knew that he would have to pitch against the DC-10, the Lockheed Tristar, *and* the A300B. His first trick was inexpensive, and a clever *trompe l'oeil:* to make the interior of the 727 look like a wide-body. The 727's cabin cross section was the same as the 707's. Steiner saw that the old fittings, instead of maximizing this space, actually cramped it. In fact, the 727 offered the same cabin headroom on the inside seats as the DC-10, and only a little less than on the A300B.

The "square room" look from the 747 was adapted to the 727. Of course, it was still a single-aisle cabin without cross aisles, but it looked a lot more accommodating than the old 727. Once unleashed, Steiner was convinced that his "advanced" 727 could cut away from underneath the market for the domestic wide-bodies. It could actually cruise faster than a DC-10 or the A300B, and although its operating costs per seat-mile would be higher, he could sell the new 727 for a price that would be 25 to 30 percent cheaper per seat than the new wide-bodies. The package was making sense.

But Steiner was not just a born-again aeroman. He was in Renton to shake it up, cut it down, give it a hard time for as long as it took. He put up posters to announce a savage regime, and cautioned: "When you are up to your ass in alligators it is difficult to remind yourself that your initial objective was to drain the swamp." They were hard days. Long-serving men who had lost their jobs would call Steiner at night, saying things like "What are you doing to me?"

As harrowing as these calls were, Steiner had no choice. Things were worse than most people even imagined. Airlines were defaulting on 727 orders. New customers were found for some, but the value of the sales was undercut by the cost of customizing the aircraft to each airline's whim. Steiner didn't like the overstock sitting there for all to see, so he moved as many 727s as he could out of sight behind the hangars.

The Wilson regime was engaged in a grim experiment of industrial pathology: finding the lowest actual level at which the organization could exist. Relentlessly, every nonessential expense was eliminated in the effort to find bottom. Buildings were left without new coats of paint, flower beds and lawns were left untended—and unwatered. Someone at last realized that, given Seattle's climate, rain would take care of the grass (in most cases it did, but shrubs died off). At Renton, in one instance, the cost-cutters found where bottom was in a squalid way: after they cut back on cleaning the washrooms and ended the scrubbing of lavatory floors, there was an outbreak of fungus. A janitor had to be hired.

Steiner prided himself on being a loose cannon. Wilson had told him to fix the 737—Lufthansa had been enraged by the 737's shortcomings to the point of almost losing faith in Boeing. He had also told Steiner to leave the 737 production where it was, in a plant near Boeing Field, although it came under the Renton division. In his convoluted reasoning, Steiner took this to mean the exact opposite, that it was a test of his independence. He moved the whole 737 assembly to join the 707 and 727 lines in Renton; many of the fuselage parts were common. And he began working over the 737 as he had the 727, convinced that its flaws were minor and its future underrated.

But, at the same time, he took up an extraordinary, virtually seditious idea: that the whole 737 program should be sold, lock, stock, and barrel, to the Japanese. This episode later induced collective amnesia at Boeing. Steiner certainly pursued the proposal on his own authority, without the backing of Wilson or the board. And probably without realizing the incendiary political implications of it.

The Japanese had been backing into aircraft production very cautiously, and with discouraging results. The core of their effort was a typical alliance of three major industrial groups, Kawasaki, Mitsubishi, and Fuji. When Steiner appeared in Tokyo, the Japanese consortium was about to begin testing its first swept-wing jet military transport, the Kawasaki C-1. It was like a shrunken version of the Lockheed C5a, with two engines, high wings, and T-tail. Japanese bankers were leery of this enterprise; Kawasaki's previous effort, a twin-engine turboprop, had lost money.

Steiner was familiar with the Japanese technical hierarchy, in which engineers tended to be treated reverently as professors, and knew that when it came to designing jets they looked on Boeing as the font of all knowledge. If they were serious about going into commercial jets, taking over a ready-made package like the 737 would give them a jump start—but it would also involve handing over the inner secrets Boeing most cherished. Boeing had done well with the 727 in Japan, and would do well with the 747. To win sales in some other countries, it had offered a trade-off, called "offset," in which some small parts of the aircraft had been subcontracted to that country, thereby lessening the imported cost and helping, at the same time, to create jobs.

The Japanese were much subtler. They would never appear as supplicants. Boeing sensed that as long as the Japanese were regarded as "partners," the way was open to give them pieces of an airplane, and such a deal was, in fact, negotiated in which the flaps for a long-range version of the 747 were made in Japan. This would turn out to be the beginning of a long relationship with the Kawasaki, Mitsubishi, and Fuji group.

Bruce Connelly was with Steiner and a handful of other Boeing executives in Tokyo, and it was Connelly, representing Boullioun's commercial division, not simply Steiner's Renton interests, who framed the 737 proposal: the 737 program, including tooling, was open to offer. The Japanese should write a "serious letter of proposal," and they would carry things on from there. The letter was never written, and the idea quietly died. Seattle would probably have killed it anyway, to avoid revealing too many hard-won technical secrets, not from any xenophobia—in 1970, America was not as aware of or as sensitive to Japanese technological ambitions as it is now; American roads had not been taken over by swarms of Japanese cars.

Boeing's handling of its crisis disaffected many leaders of the local community. An editorial in the weekly *Argus* caught the reproachful tone: "Boeing really did us in when it brought more than fifty thousand employees into the area to build the 747, which resulted in too much home and apartment building, too much money for schools, too many new taxes, and now too much unemployment." In Portland, the *Oregonian* said, "Seattle is paying a terrible price for allowing a single industry to so dominate its economic structure."

The real estate business withered: sales fell by at least 40 percent. A local real estate man created the epitaph for the city's hard times—he rented a billboard near the airport and put up a poster with a picture of a single light bulb and the line "Will the last person leaving Seattle please turn out the lights?"

But the Boeing massacre was not as indiscriminate as it seemed. In the first year, twenty thousand people left voluntarily. The average length of their service was six months. Wilson realized that, to this extent, Boeing had been little more than a vocational home for transients. They would stay long enough to pick up skills and save some money, and then move on. While at Boeing they had taken up the time of training staff, their productivity was low, and they turned out parts that were often rejected on the line. "We'd scraped the bottom of the barrel," said Wilson. One day, Wilson asked Haynes if he agreed with what he was doing. "I don't understand it," said Haynes, "but for Chrissakes keep doing it."

For a while, it had seemed that Boeing's long trail of lobbying failures in Washington, D.C., would be reversed by the SST program. The company had organized a block of powerful interests to support the funding for two prototypes, including the labor unions' boss of bosses, George Meany. The two Democratic Washington senators, Scoop Jackson and Warren Magnuson, were backing Boeing. On the Hill, Jackson headed the Interior Committee and Magnuson the Commerce Committee. But by 1970, Boeing was asking for a budget of up to $1.3 million for the prototypes, and few thought that that figure would be the end of it. In any event, the public mood was shifting.

For the first time, environmental groups, to whom the SST was both a violator of the stratosphere and a misapplication of resources, coalesced as an effective force. (Lindbergh felt the same way, but because of his position with Pan Am he kept his feelings private.) Interests as diverse as the Sierra Club, Friends of the Earth, and Zero Population Growth rallied against the SST, and in November 1970, the Senate voted fifty-two to forty-one against pumping another $290 million into the program. The death of the SST was sealed by a vote in both houses in the spring of 1971. The immediate cost to Seattle was another five thousand lost jobs at Boeing, to add to the 747's carnage.

For many of Boeing's engineering elite, the SST was another slice of their careers spent on a paper airplane. The $12 million SST mock-up was auctioned, and bought for $43,000 by a promoter in Florida, who made a roadside fairground around it near Disney World. Wilson thought the SST would have proved to be a debacle: "It would have been a great technical experiment, but it would have cost us $200 million at a time we didn't have $200 million." In fact, Boeing gained a significant technical fallout from the program. For the first time, the best efforts of the aerospace and commercial airplane divisions had been pooled. The next generation of Boeing's subsonic airliners, as well as later versions of the 747, had far more sophisticated cockpits and control systems as a result of pioneering work done on the SST, although a philosophical schism emerged among the engineers on how far computers should supplant pilots by using the electronic system called "fly-by-wire," favored by the European Airbus. Boeing's inclination, certainly trenchantly expressed by Joe Sutter, was to leave the pilot with the "feel" of the airplane in his hands.

With the death of the SST, it was finally clear that the 747 *was* the future for Boeing and the international carriers, as

Sutter had always believed it would be. Oddly, that conviction became the conventional wisdom at Boeing without almost anyone realizing the change in attitude. The false doctrine of the SST was set aside like some nocturnal aberration.

In this miasmal phase, when the company was, as it were, repeatedly touching itself to see if it was alive, someone finally realized that Sutter was still not a vice president. By then, in 1971, he was the general manager at Everett, a job previously occupied by a vice president. Wilson called Sutter and told him that he was, at last, to be elevated, and apologized for its having taken so long.

In his desk, Sutter had a talisman, a kind of article of faith in the airplane he had fathered. On October 29, 1968, the United States Patent Office published Patent 212,564. It had been filed on December 20, 1966, and it was valid for fourteen years. There were four drawings of the invention, separate elevations of a new machine, rendered in the anachronistic drafting style familiar from Victorian advertisements for bedwarmers or coffee grinders. The fathers of this machine claimed, on the document, "the ornamental design for an airplane, as shown and described." It was 225 feet 2 inches long, and 195 feet 8 inches wide. There were six claimants: Joe Sutter, Row Brown, Milt Heinemann, Everette Webb, and two other engineers who had helped conceive the wide-body, Don Finlay and Ken Plewis. Each received a dollar.

18 ■ Life on the Lake

It isn't democratic. Nobody gets to vote. Bill Allen votes.
— W. T. Hamilton

Ed Wells was the center of it all. Bill Allen and the board would do anything he wanted them to do.
— George Schairer

At the center of this story were two dead men, Allen and Wells. Between them, it seemed to me, they had given Boeing the qualities that they had themselves. On those qualities rested a large part of what Boeing had achieved. And yet nobody could quite agree how this personal chemistry created its singular act of fission. W. T. Hamilton recalled taking a trip with Wells and, thinking aloud as he talked to him, trying to figure out why the company seemed to get things right. "As near as I can tell," said Hamilton, "Bill Allen, who is a lawyer, doesn't know much about engineering, or manufacturing. He has a number of people he trusts in each of the critical areas, sales, engineering, manufacturing, a guy on the legal stuff. There are six or eight guys. And when these tough decisions come up, like shall we build the

Dash-80, he gets the opinion of these experts of his. . . . It isn't democratic. Nobody gets to vote. Bill Allen votes." Wells looked at him, and said, "That's exactly right. You know, the amazing thing is, he makes such good decisions on the lousy data we give him." Here you have a defining view of them both, with Wells deflating the piety of Hamilton's reasoning with that self-deprecating final thrust—thereby shifting the light away from his own role.

George Schairer gives a more intimate picture of the process: "I've been in meetings many times where we sat around, maybe fifteen of us around the table, with Bill at the end of it, and he'd just go around, whatever the subject was at hand, can we do such and such? What do you think? Nearly always he made no expression of his own viewpoint unless there was a unanimity of opinion. Hardly ever did he make a decision where a minority viewpoint was expressed. That's the kind of management that we worked these things through."

Schairer was sitting in his workshop, overlooking his dock on Lake Washington. There was a fiberglass model of the hull of his sailboat on a table. The boat itself was causing grief. It didn't back up into the dock as smoothly as he thought it should. To find out why, he had been testing the model hull in his swimming pool and using fluid dynamics to diagnose the behavior of the water.

I said, "You've spent your life looking at what air does when it passes over a surface. Do water and air behave in the same way?"

"No," he said firmly. "Very different. The mathematics of one do not apply to the other at all. The concepts are entirely different. Air is the easier of the two. Air is a terrible mess. But the water's worse."

Throughout this first interview with Schairer, I had been looking for the merciless inquisitor of legend. The physical components were intact: the formidable domed head, eyes that directly engage—and a voice still with the terse cadences of the East: "Oh, *man!*" From the beginning, he was gracious and responsive—up to a point. I sensed there was a game of a kind going on. It was a bit of a tease: he was assessing how much I knew, and keeping some kind of running equity between my knowledge and his answers. Feeding out rope, I thought, and if I failed the rope would be around my neck. Sometimes a line of questioning would lurch dangerously to a halt. In one case I offered a particularly glib piece of prompting: "What it takes is not so much the person with the theory as the person who can translate the theory into something that works?"

This brought an impassable "Hmmmmmm."

It was different when the subject of Wells was introduced. Schairer forgot the game in progress. His admiration of Wells was unequivocal: Wells was, he said, "always right."

If there was one salient decision that enabled Boeing to become the force it did, it was the commitment to build the wind tunnel. Schairer's advocacy of the wind tunnel—and, remember, he was then a newcomer to the company with no executive powers—was certainly visionary, but so was the acceptance of it. In this, the influence of the other Allen, Eddie Allen, was decisive. Allen had brought Schairer to Boeing because he recognized the company's weakness in aerodynamics. It was no use having people of Schairer's caliber if they lacked the tool that determined their effectiveness.

With manifest faith, the company left a lot of the design of the tunnel in the hands of Bill Cook, who was twenty-seven, and Bob Withington, who was twenty-two. As young as they were, they were experts in a very limited field of knowledge. The scientific value of Schairer, Cook, Withington, and their MIT connections was brought into full play when the tunnel began running in 1944. From this point on, Boeing had a far higher degree of proprietary security than it had before— higher, to significant degree, than any of its rivals, equaled only in the military research centers and in the laboratories at Caltech and NACA, all of which tended to be constrained by bureaucratic agendas and which were, in any case, not subjected to the priorities of commercial survival. It was the body of proprietary knowledge Boeing then accumulated that gave it its edge in the intensely competitive postwar environment. How Boeing eventually supplanted its formidable rival, Douglas, rested more on Boeing's work in the wind tunnel than on anything else. The suspicion endured, with good cause, that the exposure of Boeing's secrets in the tunnel at Caltech gave urgency and inspiration to Donald Douglas's riposte to the 247, the DC-1, and therefore to Boeing's loss of a market it had done much to create.

As things turned out, the decision to invest Boeing's scant funds in the wind tunnel was more farsighted than even its advocates realized. They knew nothing of the jet engine at the time. And even when the jet engine appeared, very few people in the United States understood how it required a transformation in the thinking of airplane designers. (Eastman Jacobs was one of the few, but he was too embroiled in the power games at NACA to carry through his perception.) Fortunately for Boeing, the tunnel's higher limits of power were just enough to embrace the zone of subsonic speeds that was critical in the development of the first generation of jets. Nothing less than the eventual shape of America's aerospace industry was, to a large extent, resolved by how fast each company adapted to and mastered this altered state of flight.

When Schairer finally encountered the people who did understand where the jet engine's virtuosity lay—first Robert Jones, and then the Germans—Boeing's tunnel was able to transform theory into experience in one sustained fever of empirical effort. Boeing was lucky that Schairer was able to join von Karman's mission; the institutional purists who thought that the mission might be contaminated by private commercial interests failed to keep him off it. It was true, in the long run, that Boeing did become the single greatest commercial beneficiary of von Karman's German expedition. But Schairer was scrupulous about his loyalty, first, to the national interest. He made sure that the basic data on the swept wing went to any designer who could respond. And, in any case, it was the military that acquired, in the B-47, the first fruits of Schairer's conviction that the swept wing would work on a bomber, even though it took a maverick within the military community, Pete Warden, to keep the project alive. But it was not only obscurantists at Wright Field who thought Schairer was nuts. There were skeptics at Boeing, too. It was Wells who armed Schairer. Nothing better expresses Boeing's engineering and scientific attitude than Wells's readiness to let the company slip a year behind its rivals in the contest for the jet bomber contract on the basis that without the swept wing they would be no better than anyone else. (Wells once told Allen, "We never do as well as when we realize that our best may not be good enough.") And it was Wells who added to the swept wing the element that completed the formula, that gave Boeing its unique understanding of how to make this wing fly—the podded engines on pylons.

This epochal advance was made as the leadership of Boeing was changing in style. For the first time since Bill Boeing's departure, a nonengineer took over. In effect, Wells made all the highly speculative decisions on the B-47 on his own technical authority. As Bill Allen moved in, the engineering vocabulary was becoming more recondite than it had ever been. Allen knew he could never master it. How Boeing then rose to its current primacy was decided by the way that Allen measured his own instincts against the advice he received from the small cadre of engineers he kept around him. He knew them well enough to trust them—to do more than trust them, to take awesome, open-ended risks with them. Like Bill Boeing, he turned out to be a creative conservative.

Allen's managerial lines were very short. Once an idea reached Wells, it was only one step away from Allen; there was no financial screen to pass and no budget discipline to suggest that it was a waste of time even talking to Allen about it. These were the circumstances in which the B-47 and Dash-80 were born. At the core, Boeing's fortunes were decided by a small, responsive elite. These exceptional people served the company all their lives. And, as Hamilton said, there was only one vote, Allen's. Was Allen, in truth, running Boeing in an imperial style, as Trippe undoubtedly ran Pan Am? Allen's constitutional habit was similar: he dominated his board and he took its acquiescence as a given. Inside the company, his authority was absolute. People who worked closely with him recalled his strength. "He was the strongest one," said Boullioun. Part of this strength was his unbending propriety. Part of it was the nerve he brought to those times when he knew he was betting the company. Part of it was something less tangible: the way that invested in Allen's tone and way of doing business was an unwritten code that defined how Boeing should comport itself. Sometimes he was too personally squeamish for the world that Boeing had to deal with, but was realist enough to let others handle it. A breaking point like this occurred during a particularly vitriolic exchange with Pan Am over the 747. Allen turned to Boullioun and said, "I just can't deal with this. It's all yours." He walked out. "I'd never seen him lose his temper before like that," said Boullioun.

Although he enjoyed almost proprietorial power over Boeing, Allen did not use it as did Trippe (who was, after all, virtually a proprietor—Pan Am was his creation). Unlike Trippe, Allen encouraged open dissent. He was clearly stimulated by mavericks, even if, as in the case of Schairer, he did not warm to a particular personality. Schairer's value was clear enough, and there was always Wells to handle Schairer and to explain what he meant.

One does not get the impression that Allen was entirely comfortable with Trippe. Their social junketing together was something he had to endure. Boeing owed a considerable debt to Trippe, who had persevered with a series of flawed Boeing airplanes until, with the 707-320B, the arguments of Pan Am engineers forced Boeing to improve the jet that secured Boeing's supremacy. Boeing might well have attempted to build a large commercial jet to fill the void left after it lost the C5a contest, but without Trippe the 747 would not have been the same aircraft. He was right in his belief that an airliner of that size had its place. He overcommitted his airline to it, but Boeing, in being forced to tailor it to Pan Am, had to meet the standards of the best operational regime in the business. The benchmark set by Pan Am of an operating cost a third less than the 707 was, in time, well exceeded: the 747 of 1990 had a seat-mile cost some 45 percent better than the 707's.

The influence of Charles Lindbergh through his role as Trippe's free-lance technical agent came as a surprise to me. Lindbergh was never a hero of mine. To begin with, his 1927 solo flight to Paris unjustly overshadows the first transatlantic flight, from Newfoundland to Ireland, by John Alcock and Arthur Brown in 1919. Theirs was a far more primitive craft, a twin-engine Vickers Vimy bomber, a more hazardous experience and yet a prophetic one because it demonstrated that large, multiengine aircraft were the future of long-distance flight, not custom-designed hot ships like Lindbergh's. But the atmosphere of Lindbergh's time, the deaths that preceded his flight, and Lindbergh's personal appeal all conspired to elevate him and his achievement beyond rational scale.

Lindbergh's admiration of the Nazi war machine and his collusion with those who felt Hitler should be given his run in Europe were never as guileless as his defenders later made it seem. He never really recanted, although he served out his war honorably but obscurely in the Pacific theater. However, in the light of his unpromoted and astute influence on the development of the commercial jets, from the Dash-80 to the 747, his life now seems to form a more sympathetic symmetry—in the area where he really had authority, his influence was benign. The 747 was the last aircraft that he took an interest in. He died in 1974, as its virtues were established.

Allen and Trippe did act like two potentates when they made deals without reference to any corporate checks and balances, but they were different men when they returned to their respective thrones. Trippe held court over a sprawling and deferential bureaucracy. Allen, during his most effective years, had three principal confidants: Prince, Haynes, and Wells, none of whom was required to be a cipher. That wasn't the way. Moreover, Allen prepared the company for his departure. Not only was this in great contrast to Trippe's failure to find an adequate successor, but it underlined how different Boeing was from Douglas. In 1967, Douglas was rescued by another Scot, Sanford McDonnell, and subsumed into McDonnell Douglas. The mismanagement of the DC-9 program was the final stage of the decline visible from the moment that the DC-8 was outdistanced by the reengineered 707. Douglas had been a great company, but only for as long as its founder and his veteran team of engineers were equal to the competition from Seattle. As much as anything, Boeing's superiority was one of corporate culture— free of a dependency on the caprice of one man.

T. Wilson was proud to tell me of a conversation he had at MIT when, at the age of thirty-one, he turned up from Boeing to serve his year as a Sloan Fellow. One of his professors said, "You know, the Boeing company interests me. You send somebody back here every year, and they're always good. That's not unusual. IBM sends good people every year; General Motors sends good people every year; Eastman Kodak sends good people every year. But if you've seen one IBM guy, you've seen them all. The Boeing company haven't sent two alike here yet." Wilson himself was, of course, in Boullioun's heartfelt description, *"real different."*

Of all the surviving members of the jet age elite that I met, Schairer was the most unreconstructed individualist. After my first interview with him, I discovered that he had recently published a paper that was clearly indispensable to my understanding of his work on swept wings. He had never mentioned it. I called him and asked if I could have a copy. "Of course," he said. This had, I think, been one of his tests: he was waiting for me to find out about the paper and then for me to recognize that I needed it. However, none of this chase bore any resemblance to the intellectual torments that he had devised for colleagues like Jack Steiner. I think he was mellowing.

It took a while; as late as 1975, Schairer was still sandbagging Steiner. But on this occasion, Wells led the attack. Had this been an encounter between a precocious junior engineer and his mentors, it might, at least, have been more expected. But there they were, all advanced in their careers and worthy of being thought venerable, and slugging it like old and groggy prizefighters. "Wells and Schairer," explained Steiner, "decided they had to give us a beating."

The other half of the "us" was Boullioun. Steiner and Boullioun were working on the configuration of Boeing's next jets, which, after prolonged gestation, would become the 757 and 767. It was almost constitutionally unheard of for Wells and Schairer to descend on an operating division and intervene as a pair in a process that had not yet been formally revealed to them. However, they had picked up enough of what Steiner was promoting to feel obliged to convene what amounted to a kangaroo court in a conference room at Renton.

Boullioun and Steiner arrived to find two sets of tables curiously arranged in a V, so that they faced Wells and Schairer obliquely. They had no idea of the character or extent of their sins until Wells spoke.

"We know what you're doing," he said. "You're spending your money on the trijet, and you're carrying the twin along as an also-ran."

The defendants were struck dumb. Steiner had never seen Wells as mad.

"You have it the wrong way around," Wells continued. "You put the twin in the mainstream and have the trijet as the also-ran. The way of the future is twins. You're on the wrong track."

Schairer was Schairer: "You guys screwed up. So cut it out."

They were right. By then, the Airbus had made the point. For the domestic routes that the DC-10 and Lockheed Tristar were flying, three engines involved what Sutter called "too much airplane for the job." Steiner's trijet never got beyond a desktop model.

When Steiner recounted his batterings from Schairer (this last one was the only time Wells had whipped him harder than Schairer), I got the impression that he took a kind of pride in the punishment—not masochism so much as the desire of a man simply to be seen in the same ring as the champ, even if the champ left him on the floor each time.

Wells had always been uneasy about how Boeing could protect its engineers from the inevitable growth in the bureaucracy that flowed from its emergence as an international corporate force. He fretted that only a small percentage of the engineers' time was actually "productive"—red tape and paperwork and administrative details took up the rest. He had noticed that sometimes fundamental conceptual advances were more easily made away from Seattle. He cited the first sketches suggesting podded engines, which were made while he was in Dayton, reacting to the military's aversion to buried engines. A more striking case was the creation of the B-52 in the Van Cleve Hotel.

This might be another side of the case made against Boeing's Pacific Northwest insularity. Dayton and New York were the two places where Boeing's feet got held to the fire. In each place, Boeing engineers were challenged in ways that even the internal dissent permitted at Boeing had not matched, and they were the better for having to face it. When they did, their responses were immediate.

I wondered how real the isolation of the Pacific Northwest was. Allen, with an aggressive amusement, would sometimes quote from an economics textbook in general use in colleges: "That a company may develop in a relatively unfavorable location and still succeed is illustrated by the Boeing Aircraft Company. . . . " When expressed as a mentality, as it was by John Borger and other critics, the charge of isolation was describing not so much a geographic condition as a vocational one. To that extent, it might have been explained by the company's incestuousness. Boeing men were generally that for life. The best of them enjoyed a bond to the company that had an extraordinary *esprit* about it. Quite often, this bordered on arrogance. It was frequently pointed out to me that had Boeing been in southern California, with its competing companies, the turnover of engineers would have been much higher. When valued men do leave, it is not taken well. Russell Hopps, an engineer on the 747, defected to Lockheed to help design the L-1011. When people do that at Boeing they tend to be written out of history, to turn into nonpersons.

Boeing's clannishness might well have existed had the company been located anywhere in the country where there were no other aerospace firms. The clannishness grew not because of where they were, but from a nucleus of personalities who formed a powerful collective ego. And yet they did not turn inward and become blinkered like the engineering leadership of that other regionally concentrated industry, the car manufacturers. At the very time Boeing was coming into its prime, the Detroit corporations as a whole, and General Motors in particular, were entering a sustained period of atrophy. What had once been a dynamic and quintessentially American culture of innovation and market creation, the mass production of a wide range of cars, coasted along on assumptions of its own longevity that were disastrously misplaced.

These companies were at the end of a technological cycle defined by the age of their plants and their belief in a protected market. In contrast, Boeing, despite its isolation, brilliantly adapted from one technological cycle to another, from the propeller age to the jet age, even though all the pioneering work on jets had been European. (A diverting aesthetic speculation is that the lines of the 747, drawn in 1966, remain timeless, while the lines of a 1966 Detroit sedan are offensively anachronistic.) Not only that, but Boeing was able to create a worldwide market for the jet airliner even though the Europeans had got there first. By demonstrating a production capacity far more sophisticated than the Europeans', Boeing came to dominate that market for a generation.

All this was achieved by people in the grip of what was called the "Northwest corner psychology." Seattle, however, was not Detroit. Detroit remained oblivious to significant shifts in the competitive ability of European and Japanese car companies. In Seattle, the Boeing engineers were always well informed of their international competitors' best ideas—and able to outflank them. A case in point was a British trijet, the De Havilland Trident.

This could well have been the airplane the Boeing 727 became, and could have taken a large slice of a world market for itself. (There was a precedent: a stylish British turboprop airliner called the Viscount had made great inroads into the U.S. market as a DC-3 replacement in the 1950s.)

The Trident was originally conceived for exactly the short-to-medium-range densely traveled trunk routes that the 727 was sized for—but the British designers had seen the opportunity way ahead of Boeing, or anyone else. Eastern Airlines, with many of these routes, took an early interest in the Trident. However, Eastern's boss, the legendary pilot Eddie Rickenbacker, would not buy an airplane with British engines, and Rolls-Royce was developing the engine for the Trident. De Havilland might still have got the business, by using an American engine, but for the policy of its lead customer, British European Airways.

The airplane that De Havilland first offered had a cabin roughly as wide as a Boeing 707's, with six-abreast seating. BEA said this was too big, and insisted that the airplane (and its engines) be shrunk. Ironically, Jack Steiner, who was then trying to figure out a viable configuration for the 727, went to London to give a lecture on the lessons learned from Boeing's scramble to get the body width of the 707 right. It was not a lesson that De Havilland was ready to heed: it even locked the Trident prototype in a hangar while Steiner was in London. Nonetheless, he already knew that BEA had fatally handicapped the Trident by down-sizing it.

There is a difference between being incestuous—that is, having an inbred technical elitism—and being insular. The Trident episode showed how alert to threat Boeing could be, as well as the superior productive capacity it could bring to bear once it had made up its mind which way to jump. Its early failure to foresee the significance of the wide-body twin, and therefore the threat of the European Airbus, reveals not a provincial insularity, but the arrogance of that inbred technical elitism. Wells and Schairer had to shake down Steiner to ram home that lesson before it was too late.

Steiner could reflect, though, that his reign at Renton had greatly helped to dig Boeing out of its worst crisis. In 1974 alone, $474 million of debt had been repaid, and more money was coursing in. The advanced 727 was driving the airplane's total sales toward seventeen hundred. Added to this success was the final vindication of the 737, which would go on to be a long-run bestseller in five different sizes. As for the 747, the break-even point was reached in 1978, when the orders passed four hundred. The first fifty 747s were built with a force of 27,500 workers. The four hundredth would be produced by 7,500 workers, and Everett was reaching the Boeing productivity target defined as one man-hour per pound of airplane built.

It took ten years before Sutter was satisfied with the performance of the Pratt engines. By then, competitive Rolls-Royce and General Electric engines gave the airlines more choice. The 747 had the skies to itself; by gambling on it beyond their means, and surviving the gamble, Boeing had produced an airplane that was beyond the resources of any other company to compete with. The 747 enjoys a far longer life than any of its creators could have predicted for it. Its utility has significantly shrunk the world, although that has not always been the reason why people bought 747s: every aspiring nation, liberated colony, and risen demagogue had to have an international airport and a 747 sitting on the apron in its own livery. Sometimes puzzled by the kinds of people who turned up at Seattle, Boeing nonetheless obliged.

Such an enduring monopoly is, however, bound to end. The Airbus consortium, for one, feels obliged to challenge the 747 before the end of the century. Boeing would then be forced to respond—and so the saga continues.

In 1972, Trippe and Allen were talking again about an Alaskan fishing trip—"one final fling for the old men" was the way Allen put it. He had announced that he would retire at the end of September. Early that summer, before they went to Alaska, there was a poignant reunion in New York. Boeing had donated the Dash-80 prototype to the Smithsonian Air and Space Museum, and it was flown first from Seattle to New York, where a party was being given at the 21 Club. Every veteran of American commercial aviation who could still walk was there, among them Allen, Trippe, C. R. Smith of American, Pat Patterson of

United, and Rickenbacker of Eastern. Many of them took a ride on the Dash-80. Its interior was crudely lined with acoustic padding, and it showed the wear of its years as an all-purpose test vehicle. The narrow, five-abreast cabin felt anachronistic. But the old men could remember a lot worse. They had a generational privilege: they had come all the way.

Allen died in 1985, after enduring a long struggle with Alzheimer's disease. He was eighty-five. A year later, Wells died of cancer at the age of seventy-five.

Finally, having heard many views of them (not always consistent), and trying to allow for the shortcomings of anecdotal evidence, I was left with the sense of there having been one marked difference between the two men. Allen's personality had changed in midlife; Wells's had not. But then, Allen's career had changed, and Wells's never had. Allen had said once that from the moment he took over Boeing in 1945 he'd had "a new liberal education at the expense of the Boeing company."

I think what he meant by this was that a "liberal" education would not have helped his career as a lawyer—not, at least, by his own lights—whereas he soon found that running Boeing required an openness to radical thinking, and he had surprised himself by displaying it. The dependable conservative values and fixed view of society that until then he had never really had to question were ill-matched to his new role as the first among equals. A man of lesser imagination would have stumbled; Allen grew.

To succeed at this he had to become, if not a dissembler, then something of a chameleon. In public, he was not in a line of business known for liberal sympathies. He was the baron of an aerospace conglomerate and a major producer of military machines. He enjoyed clubhouse rank with some fearsome old reactionaries in the airline business. Yet there was always about him a disdain, reinforced by experience, for cutting deals by dancing to a political measure. This lifelong Republican had a family memory, which was always in his mind, of standing up to unfettered capitalism.

The mining business has a history of fully subjugated company towns, but Montana was something even more egregious: a company state. From 1906 until well into the 1960s, the Anaconda Mining Company dictated public policy in the state and controlled much of its life, including its newspapers. This was a real blight on the conscience of progressive Republicans, and Allen's father was one of these. When he was looking for his first job, Allen knew it was out of the question for him to even think of a job with the AMC. His early romance and marriage to Dorothy Dixon cemented this attitude: his father-in-law, Joseph Dixon, was limited to one term as governor of the state because he tried to end the historic tax breaks granted to the AMC, and the company brought him down. Seattle's Republicanism was more paternalistic, and once Allen was running the company he stayed true to his father's lights. Though no union leader ever took Allen for a soft touch, the governing ethic of Boeing was light-years from that of copper mining.

I think I finally found the essence of this ethic in a speech Allen gave to his engineers in Seattle in 1950. The Cold War was casting an ever-darker shadow, but it was not the red menace that Allen targeted. It was a malaise he felt at the heart of America: "... there is a clear and consistent trend toward the impairment of the rights Americans have always enjoyed, the right to dream, to work, to achieve on our own...." The government, he said, was growing faster than citizens' ability to support it—"taking away money that should be put to work."

The speech—sometimes it sounded like a homily—was an odd mixture of managerial principles and moral exhortation. At its core, though, was an evocation of the virtues of the unregulated individual: "The release of individual energy under adequate incentives is the most creative force in the world." There was a patrician idealism driving this belief, a faith that these unbridled energies would always be devoted to benign ends. Later, as Boeing was more frequently bruised by the nation's self-serving legislators, Allen probably came to realize that his values were those of a dying age—or, at least, of the cloistered Pacific Northwest.

It seemed that Allen the elder remained comfortable with the world he had around him. At home he was more relaxed, with growing children to help the process. A certain panache even surfaced. He took to driving to the office in a 1956 Thunderbird, the classic vintage with portholes on the hood, carrying the license plate ABA 707 ("a Bill Allen 707," he explained). He liked photo opportunities where beautiful women were involved.

Wells, on whom so much of Allen's judgment rested, had no similar capacity for the public life, but he seems to have had, from a young age, a wholly satisfied inner life. I was sometimes struck by the way in which people who had never worked with Wells wondered why I was interested in him at all. To them, he had been a remote, gray figure. When I explained his almost holy status among the engineers, they were incredulous. Wells had clearly chosen this enclosed world for himself. I did, at least, get to see him in action once, on videotape. Surrounded by some of the company's best engineers, he spoke infrequently, and always cogently. It was clear, though, that he drew great satisfaction from just letting the interplay of ideas run its course. Like Allen, he was a very good listener.

Many of the engineers these men had led enjoyed a prosperous retirement. They were given stock options when the paper value was nominal, and later reaped the rewards of their own efforts. Their inclination was to stay put. The luckiest of them had bought waterfront lots on Lake Washington when they were cheap—$20,000 or $30,000—even though this had required a struggle to meet the mortgage payments. By the 1980s, these lots were often worth several million dollars. The sudden flush of money helped—to add a pool or a tennis court, or to renew the dock. More often than not, there would be a handsome sailboat tied up there, sometimes a floatplane.

They were engaging men. They still watched the company very closely, in a paternalistic way, concerned that it should never lose its tolerance of dissent. "I worry whether we still have enough of that," said T. Wilson. When Wilson ran Boeing he was conspicuous for his unaffected way of life. He drove to work in a Chevrolet Camaro. He had never moved from the house he bought as a young engineer, a heavily shaded ranch house, not on the water but near a creek in southwest Seattle. When I saw him, he was like a contented woodsman, in a plaid shirt and hunter's cap, a bottle of Jack Daniel's in the kitchen next to the coffee maker. He broke off talking to watch a bird in a tree. Others, too, were easily distracted by birds. They would ruminate that a bird's wing was as perfect a piece of engineering as they would ever see, well beyond their own powers.

A grid of freeways frames the suburbs that have spread to the north and south of Seattle, the only *Lebensraum* available because of the water to the west and mountains to the east.

These landscapes, with their franchised amenities, are monot-
onous and banal. On weekends the roads fill with campers and
ATVs and cars with skis on the roof: it is easy to escape to the
water, the islands, the valleys, and the mountains. These suburbs reflect an even-handed material progress, and Seattle is
often looked upon as a model of how a city's growth should be
managed.

Yet one can pick up a smugness in the promotion of this
life. There is a self-satisfied and sometimes patronizing xenophobia toward the much older cities of the Midwest and the
East, which have had to weather far more of America's journey
but which are, even when in a pitiful mess, often more culturally
vibrant. This xenophobia was reinforced by a wave of migration
from California. Earthquakes and other instabilities have encouraged Californians to see the Pacific Northwest rather as
envious Europeans sometimes see Swiss cantons: as a green and
fat land with some secret economic formula of its own.

Although Boeing is a small component of this perceived
alchemy, it is a very visible one. The existence of Boeing sug-
gests a worldly competence that does not emanate from, say,
lumber or fisheries. To this extent, Boeing's metamorphosis
from precocious rube to technostar has cast a glow that many
local burghers would prefer to be a little less alluring. Boeing
itself learned a permanent lesson from the crash of 1970 and,
with a far smaller share of the local economy (under 10 percent),
wants to be taken as just another good citizen in a progressive
community.

The company will never again risk itself and its stake in
Seattle's prosperity as it did with the 747. When it came to
launching the 777, its biggest project since the 747, there was
much heart-searching about a Japanese involvement to spread
the risk. The Kawasaki-Mitsubishi-Fuji alliance had worked well
as subcontractors on the 767. (There was an Italian subcontractor, too.) Boeing engineers sent to Japan realized that the plant
constructed for the 767 work could handle much more and wondered about its ultimate purpose.

As it negotiated with the Japanese on the 777, Boeing's
concern was its historical one of protecting its proprietary knowledge. As part of their taking up to a quarter of the financial
investment and having an equal hand in the design, the Japanese

proposed sending a cadre of up to three hundred engineers to work alongside Boeing's engineers as the 777 moved from the project stage into production. It was clear that the *quid pro quo* for a large Japanese cash injection would have been the lifting of at least part of the veil on the kind of information that finds its way into each aircraft's design Bible. At the last minute, Boeing backed away, and the Japanese settled for providing 15 to 20 percent of the 777's subcontracted airframe work, without carrying any of the financial risk of what was estimated to be a $4–$5 billion program.

The trade secrets were not, however, all on one side. The Japanese brought their usual assiduousness to streamlining the airplane manufacturing process, and Boeing was interested in learning from them. In fact, each side was measuring the other's capacities very carefully. Had the issue been simply one of technology, it would, at least, have been quantifiable. For example, the wing remained the single greatest concentration of Boeing's scientific mother lode, and in any deal the secrets of the wing would have been off-limits. But beyond the demarcation lines of technical authority lay an area of more subjective speculation, mixing perceived cultural dissonances with baser instincts.

It is a conventional wisdom in the aerospace industry that there is something in the Japanese hierarchical approach to running a large industrial company that ill suits the designing of airplanes. This is a version of the "blind obedience" fable: a Japanese pilot is about to fly his airplane into the ground, but the copilot cannot violate rank to challenge him and save them, so into the ground they go. It's hard to believe, for example, that it would be countenanced in a Japanese regime for the design process to remain so open to debate that the number of engineering drawings could triple from the moment when the first set was supposed to be complete. The kind of engineering heresies which were encouraged at Boeing—"management by a continuous row" was how one engineer described it—would be unthinkable in a system where the elders are called professors and are venerated. That, at least, is the contention. There is, as yet, nothing to disprove it: the Japanese have shown no taste for a risk of the kind Allen took with the 747, and their recent record with airplanes is about on a par with Brazil's, or perhaps slightly inferior.

The Japanese have demonstrated a devastating capacity to upgrade their automobile technology to match and even surpass the best European engineering, but the investment to produce a $40,000 sedan is still but a trifle compared with that to launch a program like the Boeing 777. Similarly, Sony and Matsushita have acquired large interests in Hollywood, but the global business founded on Walkmen and VHS tapes calls for an acumen able to manage a large number of individual product decisions rather than—at most—one decision every decade that can either make or break the company. One decision, and *one* machine. Bill Cook, one of the most impressive of Boeing's elders, points out: "An airplane is probably the biggest assembly of intricate parts in any independently operational unit." Phil Condit, the man who presided over the 777 decision, told me, "In this industry, you have got to make big decisions. It's very hard to make small ones."

It takes Boeing much longer to make a decision on a new program than it did. Before the 777 configuration was settled, four years had been spent, first trying to stretch the 767, and then postulating a new airplane. In that time, Airbus had designed a competitor, the A330, and won orders for two hundred of them. Some of the men who were involved in taking the 747 from its inchoate beginnings to a fixed configuration in six months shake their heads reproachfully and say that the company has grown too cautious.

But it is no longer a game that is likely to involve radical conceptual changes; the advances are now made within very well rehearsed tenets. Only airplane buffs can easily spot the difference between, say, a Boeing 767 and an Airbus A330. Subsonic flight has finite limits. The astonishing thing is that, in a very basic way, those limits were set from the moment the B-47 demonstrated how limber it was. The only two qualities of flying in this environment that are apparent to an airline passenger, speed and altitude, were fixed at the outset by the B-47 (and they were the revelation experienced when Allen took his ride in the ship). The B-47 was a crude machine, but it *was* the machine that went to the new edge and managed the condition first. Every advance since then has been one of refinement within and not beyond what the B-47 demonstrated was possible.

The refinements continue but they do not alter the condition. There has been no viable transformation of the way a jet airliner flies since the Dash-80 (the Concorde being the aberration that proves the rule). The art of designing an airliner now involves striking a fine balance of speed, fuel efficiency, range, and payload. Sometimes it seems that the criteria of success have more to do with marketing than with aerodynamics. Certainly, sizing and timing are crucial. The sameness of the competing solutions to a market opportunity simply demonstrates the sameness of the data and the reasoning drawn from them.

What few distinctions are left are as much those of attitude as of science. Inevitably, the root of the Boeing attitude is that the form is Boeing's: the reason why an A330 looks the way it does is that Boeing invented the form and no one has since found anything better. The pressure is always on Boeing to go on proving that because it fathered the genre it still executes a design with a superior understanding of the science. But Boeing's most decisive fight for the market, its final conquest of Douglas, was achieved through a series of tactical skirmishes over a relatively short period. There will be no such quick victory over Airbus; more likely, it will be a war without end. Life at Boeing can never again be as it was for the young bloods who put the unruly swept wing into the wind tunnel and persisted until it was flyable. It was one of those confluences of people, time, and place that are unrepeatable. Like Icarus, they might well have been jumping off the cliff with wax wings that would melt in the sun. Instead, they jumped off the cliff and the wings stayed whole. No one gets to jump off the cliff anymore. Those who did have a certain look about them. They are the survivors of an exclusive cult. They defied gravity, and never fell to earth.

Epilogue ■ The Distance Traveled

On January 21, 1990, the twentieth anniversary of the first scheduled airline flight by a 747, there was a modest and little-publicized party to mark the occasion in the Pan Am Building over Grand Central Station in New York. By then, Pan Am was a failing company. The causes were manifold. In the 1970s it had been crippled by its overbuying of 747s; by the first half of 1974 the airline was losing an average of $6 for each of the 5.5 million passengers it carried. Trippe's failure to prepare an effective succession did not help, but when a business is cast so indelibly in the mold of a man as mysterious as Trippe there is nothing to perpetuate except confusion. Pan Am needed to be reinvented for the vastly changed world it faced, and it never found a leader to do that in time. It finally expired, already substantially dismembered, late in 1991.

Something other than an airline died on that date. Pan Am's engineering department, built on the rigor of Andre Priester's own standards, had policed the design of many of the world's best airliners. Boeing's engineers, though badly bruised by the likes of John Borger, conceded that their work had been the better for Pan Am's surveillance, often on a daily basis, as an airplane was conceived and then took shape in metal. A few other airlines—TWA was one—had respected engineering departments, but none was as feared nor as respected as Pan Am's. In the fiscal stringency of the 1990s, little of this relationship survives. Airlines fly airplanes, they don't help to design them.

Between 6:00 and 7:00 P.M., GMT, on that twentieth anniversary in 1990 there were 342 Boeing 747s actually in the air across the world. That represented as many as 143,640 people aloft, equal to the population of a decent-size city. Including fuel, luggage, passengers, and metal, it meant that 140,220 tons was in flight, part of a steady, regular traffic of people and cargo that, day and night, circumnavigates the globe with remarkable ease.

In 1930 the Boeing Air Transport Company introduced the first flight attendants. They were trained nurses. The Boeing 80-A trimotor on which they served carried up to eighteen passengers at no more than 125 mph, and the flights were often rough. Bill Allen rode these airplanes on legal business for Boeing. He remembered one of the flight attendants, a Miss Novelli, because of an endearing thing she did with an air sickness bottle. Seeing that Allen was in distress, she drew two faces on the bottle, one with a down-turned mouth, "before," and the other with a broad smile, "after."

Allen had flown in the 80-A's predecessor, the single-engine 40-A, cruising speed at best 105 mph, carrying two passengers and mail bags. The contest between land and machine was not yet won: as a 40-A crested a ridge of the Rockies it often met a headwind greater than its airspeed and was literally blown backward, unable to continue. The pilot was in an open cockpit, helmeted, with an angora-lined leather flying suit and layers of sweaters under it, peering through goggles for bearings. Allen was huddled in a freezing box of a cabin below, ears pounded by engine noise and the wind howling like the cries of purgatory through the wires that braced the wings.

A macabre humor went with this pioneering. There was, for example, a Western Union telegram that Allen remembered, framed on the wall behind a Boeing flight manager's desk. An airplane had been leased to a Swede called Meyerhoff, and a mechanic was sent with the airplane and told to wire back about any problems, but to keep the wire brief. In due course, a simple message arrived: "Swede cranked prop—prop killed Swede—send new prop."

There was someone else with a long memory, who could still recall carrying the pungent cans of gas for the flying circus. In 1990, Robert Jones, late of Macon, Missouri, now of the Los Altos Hills, California, published a book titled *Wing Theory*. He was disappointed with the job Princeton University Press had done with some of the illustrations. One of these showed a model in the NASA supersonic tunnel at the Ames Research Center. The model was testing a new Jones passion, the oblique wing. Jones was still effervescing with ideas. "The swept wing is not the ultimate shape," he told me. "The optimum shape for supersonic speed is really a long, narrow ellipse. I'm working on a supersonic flying wing, a long, narrow oblique ellipse, big enough to contain five hundred passengers."

There was still a trace of the elf of the tunnel, and the book jacket photograph showed him in overalls ready to take up his own nifty little sport plane. The boy remained in the man, for sure. Of all those I talked to, it was Jones who struck me as the best expression of scientific insolence. It was an American quality, I thought, of equal standing to the scientific hauteur of Europeans like von Karman and Munk. Jones was very respectful of the Boeing 747—"the world's safest airplane." He had made his own calculation of its efficacy: "You know, the 747 can get better than sixty miles per gallon per passenger, good mileage for an automobile, but it goes ten times as fast."

Mostly invisible in a band of thin blue air 35,000 to 40,000 feet above the earth, the airlanes are now as densely traveled as were once the great intercontinental railroads. Everything has been done to insulate the passenger from the physical achievement of flight. In place of a pilot looking out through snow-streaked goggles for a recognizable landmark there are, in a 747-400, two technicians who leave virtually every part of navigation to a bank of computers. For most of the time, it is all routine.

Bibliography

Books

Anonymous. *From Huffman Prairie to the Moon, the History of Wright-Patterson Air Force Base*. Dayton, Ohio: USAF Logistics Command, 1987.

Bender, Marilyn, and Selig Altschul. *The Chosen Instrument, Juan Trippe and Pan Am*. New York: Simon & Schuster, 1982.

Biddle, Wayne. *Barons of the Sky, the Story of the American Aerospace Industry*. New York: Simon & Schuster, 1991.

Boyne, Walter J. *The Boeing B-52*. Washington, D.C.: The Smithsonian Institution Press, 1981.

———. *The Messerschmitt Me 262, Arrow to the Future*. Washington, D.C.: The Smithsonian Institution Press, 1980.

Cook, William H. *The Road to the 707*. Bellevue, Wash.: TYC Publishing Company, 1991.

Dorr, Robert F. *The Boeing KC-135 Stratotanker*. London: Ian Allen, 1987.

Ficken, Robert E., and Charles P. Le Warne. *Washington State, a Centennial History*. Seattle: University of Washington Press, 1989.

Golley, John. *Whittle, the True Story*. London: Airlife, 1987.

Gregory, William H. *The Defense Procurement Mess.* Lexington, Mass.: Lexington Books, 1984.

Hallion, Richard P. *Legacy of Flight, the Guggenheim Contribution to American Aviation.* Seattle: University of Washington Press, 1977.

———. *Test Pilots, the Frontiersmen of Flight.* Washington, D.C.: The Smithsonian Institution Press, 1988.

———. *Supersonic Flight, Breaking the Sound Barrier and Beyond.* New York: Macmillan, 1972.

Hansen, James R. *Engineer in Charge, a History of the Langley Aeronautical Laboratory, 1917–1958.* Washington, D.C.: NASA, 1987.

Holden, Henry M. *The Douglas DC-3.* Blue Ridge Summit, Pa.: Aero Books, 1991.

Ingells, Douglas J. *747: The Story of the Boeing Superjet.* Fallbrook, Calif.: Aero Publishers, 1970.

Johnston, A. M. "Tex," with Charles Barton. *Tex Johnston, Jet-Age Test Pilot.* Washington, D.C.: The Smithsonian Institution Press, 1991.

Jones, Robert T. *Wing Theory.* Princeton: Princeton University Press, 1990.

Kelsey, Benjamin S. *The Dragon's Teeth? The Creation of U.S. Air Power for World War II.* Washington, D.C.: The Smithsonian Institution Press, 1982.

Kuter, Laurence S. *The Great Gamble: the Boeing 747.* Tuscaloosa: University of Alabama Press, 1973.

Lloyd, Alwyn T. *The Boeing B-47 Stratojet.* Blue Ridge Summit, Pa.: Aero Books, 1986.

———. *The Boeing B-52 Stratofortress.* Blue Ridge Summit, Pa.: Aero Books, 1987.

———. *The Boeing 707 and AWACS.* Blue Ridge Summit, Pa.: Aero Books, 1987.

Mansfield, Harold. *Vision, the Story of Boeing.* New York: Madison Publishing, 1986.

Munson, Kenneth. *Airliners Between the Wars, 1919–39.* London: The Blandford Press, 1972.

Morgan, Len and Terry. *The Boeing 727.* Blue Ridge Summit, Pa.: Aero Books, 1978.

Newhouse, John. *The Sporty Game, the High-Risk Competitive*

Business of Making and Selling Airliners. New York: Knopf, 1982.

Smith, Henry Ladd. *Airways, the History of Commercial Aviation in the United States.* Washington, D.C.: The Smithsonian Institution Press, 1991.

———. *Airways Abroad, the Story of American World Air Routes.* Washington, D.C.: The Smithsonian Institution Press, 1991.

Spate, Wolfgang. *Top Secret Bird, the Luftwaffe's Me-163 Comet.* Missoula, Mont.: Pictorial Histories Publishing, 1989.

Van Der Linden, F. Robert. *The Boeing 247, the First Modern Airliner.* Seattle: University of Washington Press, 1991.

Von Karman, Theodore, with Lee Edson. *The Wind and Beyond.* Boston: Little, Brown, 1967.

Whittle, Sir Frank. *Jet, the Story of a Pioneer.* London: Pan Books, 1953.

Willmott, H. P. *The B-17 Flying Fortress.* Englewood Cliffs, N.J.: Prentice-Hall, 1983.

Yenne, Bill. *McDonnell Douglas, a Tale of Two Giants.* New York: Crescent Books, 1985.

Technical Papers

Anonymous. *First Five Years of the Air Research and Development Command, USAF.* Historical Division, USAF, Baltimore, Md., 1955.

Bateman, R. E. *Managing in a Crisis Situation.* Purdue University, Ind., Lecture Series, 1977.

Bedinger, Jon. *The Boeing 747.* Paper to the 26th annual conference of the Society of Aeronautical Weight Engineers, Boston, 1967.

Hallion, Richard P., et al. "The Emergence of the Delta Planform and the Origins of the Swept Wing in the United States," *Aerospace Historian,* March 1979.

———. *A Synopsis of Flying Wing Development 1908-1953.* History Office, Edwards AFB, California, 1986.

Heinemann, Milton. *Unassisted Egress.* Boeing Technical Report, 1968.

Jones, Robert T. *Properties of Low-Aspect-Ratio Pointed Wings at Speeds Below and Above the Speed of Sound.* NACA Report 835, Langley, Va., May 11, 1946 (NASA Archive).

———. *Wing Plan Forms for High-Speed Flight*. NACA Report 863, Langley, Va., June 23, 1945 (NASA Archive).

Munk, Max M. *General Theory of Wing Sections*. NACA Report 142, 1921 (NASA Archive).

Pennell, Maynard. "Jet Airliner Design Problems," *Boeing Magazine*, March 1950.

Schairer, George S. *The Engineering Revolution Leading to the Boeing 707*. Paper to the 7th Annual Applied Aerodynamics Conference, Seattle, 1989.

Steiner, John E. *Jet Aviation Development: One Company's Perspective*. Boeing Company, 1989.

———. *Problems and Challenges, a Path to the Future*. Royal Aeronautical Society, London, 1979.

Index

United States Patent Office

Des. 212,564   **Patented Oct. 29, 1968**

212,564

AIRPLANE

Joseph F. Sutter, Rowland E. Brown, Donald W. Finlay, Milton Heinemann, Kenneth C. Plewes, and Everette L. Webb, King County, Wash., assignors to The Boeing Company, Seattle, Wash., a corporation of Delaware

Filed Dec. 20, 1966, Ser. No. 5,128

Term of patent 14 years

(Cl. D71—1)

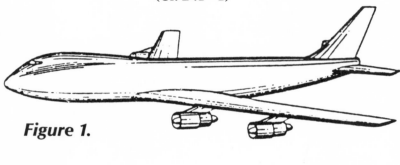

Figure 1.

Figure 2.

FIGURE 1 is a side perspective view of an airplane showing our new design;

FIGURE 2 is a side elevational view thereof;

FIGURE 3 is a top plan view; and

FIGURE 4 is a front elevational view.

We claim:

The ornamental design for an airplane, as shown and described.